Social Policy
and Sociology

QUANTITATIVE STUDIES IN SOCIAL RELATIONS

Consulting Editor: Peter H. Rossi

UNIVERSITY OF MASSACHUSETTS
AMHERST, MASSACHUSETTS

SOCIAL POLICY AND SOCIOLOGY

EDITED BY

N. J. Demerath, III
Department of Sociology
The University of Massachusetts
Amherst, Massachusetts

Otto Larsen
American Sociological Association
Washington, D.C.

Karl F. Schuessler
Department of Sociology
Indiana University
Bloomington, Indiana

ACADEMIC PRESS   New York San Francisco London

A Subsidiary of Harcourt Brace Jovanovich, Publishers

ACADEMIC PRESS, INC.
111 Fifth Avenue, New York, New York 10003

United Kingdom Edition published by
ACADEMIC PRESS, INC. (LONDON) LTD.
24/28 Oval Road, London NW1

Library of Congress Cataloging in Publication Data
Main entry under title:

Social policy and sociology.

  (Quantitative studies in social relations series)
  "Proceedings of a conference on policy research and
graduate training [held at Carmel, Calif., Dec. 1972]"
  Includes bibliographies and index.
  1.   United States–Social policy–Congresses.
2.   Sociological research–United States–Congresses.
3.   Sociology–Study and teaching (Higher)–United
States–Congresses.   4.   Evaluation research (Social
action programs)–United States–Congresses.
I.   Demerath, Nicholas Jay, ed.   II.   Larsen, Otto N.,
ed.   III.   Schuessler, Karl F., ed.
HN65.S574 1975   301'.07'2073   74-10199
ISBN 0–12–209450–6

Contents

PART I   ASSESSMENT OF POLICY RESEARCH

Section A   Social Inequities and Their Effects

62002

Commentaries

Section B Individual Stress in the Family Cycle

Commentaries

Section C   American Youth and Their Problems

Commentaries

PART II GRADUATE TRAINING AND FEDERAL FUNDING

List of Contributors

Numbers in parentheses indicate the pages on which the authors' contributions begin.

Joan Aldous (109), Department of Child and Family Development, University of Georgia, Athens, Georgia

Robert R. Alford (25), College VIII, Social Sciences Building, University of California, Santa Cruz, California

Nicholas Babchuk (149), Department of Sociology, University of Nebraska, Lincoln, Nebraska

Kurt W. Back (135), Department of Sociology, Duke University, Durham, North Carolina

Wendell Bell (251), Department of Sociology, Yale University, New Haven, Connecticut

Charles E. Bidwell (256), Department of Sociology, The University of Chicago, Chicago, Illinois

Edgar F. Borgatta (297), Department of Sociology, Queens College, Flushing, New York

Charles Bowerman (159), Department of Sociology, Washington State University, Pullman, Washington

Robert McGinnis (89), Social Systems Program, Cornell University, Ithaca, New York

David Mechanic (99), Department of Sociology, University of Wisconsin, Madison, Wisconsin

Laura Nader (267), Department of Anthropology, University of California, Berkeley, California

Albert Pepitone (273), Department of Psychology, The University of Pennsylvania, Philadelphia, Pennsylvania

Samuel H. Preston (57), Department of Sociology, University of Washington, Seattle, Washington

Albert J. Reiss, Jr. (211), Department of Sociology, Yale University, New Haven, Connecticut

Peter H. Rossi (15), Department of Sociology, University of Massachusetts, Amherst, Massachusetts

Karl F. Schuessler (1), Department of Sociology, Indiana University, Bloomington, Indiana

Howard Schuman (37), Department of Sociology, University of Michigan, Ann Arbor, Michigan

Hanan C. Selvin (279), Department of Sociology, State University of New York, Stony Brook, New York

James F. Short, Jr. (193), Social Research Center, Washington State University, Pullman, Washington

Nathaniel H. Siegel (297), Department of Sociology, Queens College, Flushing, New York

Robert Straus (123), Department of Behavioral Science, College of Medicine, University of Kentucky, Lexington, Kentucky

Sheldon Stryker (93), Department of Sociology, Indiana University, Bloomington, Indiana

Marvin B. Sussman (170), Department of Sociology, Case Western Reserve University, Cleveland, Ohio

Guy E. Swanson (182), Department of Sociology, University of California, Berkeley, California

Robert N. Wilson (186), Department of Sociology, University of North Carolina, Chapel Hill, North Carolina

Preface

This book is about an idea whose time has come. But it is also about an idea that may pass sociology by unless the discipline responds more promptly and effectively. Few items loom larger on our current agenda than the relationship between social science and social policy. But the rhetoric of relevance is not enough. It is one thing to agree with the broad premise that sociology must make a more meaningful contribution to the public interest; it is quite another to suggest how this might be done and with what consequences.

This volume represents a significant effort to confront the most vexing underlying issues. The book combines the views and analyses of some 60 sociologists in all of their heterogeneous splendor. It asks not only where we are going, but where we have been; not only what is to be gained, but what is to be lost; and not only of ultimate objectives but also of proximate steps.

Most important, the volume does not debate these issues in a vacuum. Rather the discussion emerges from a series of critical analyses of the policy implications embedded in some of the best examples of recent sociological research. These are unique essays written by and commented upon by some of the most sagacious members of the discipline. Because they assess instances of the major research directions followed during the last decade, they provide important contributions to the "sociology of sociology" and a benchmark for the future.

The Prologue provides a brief history of the events and concerns which shaped the conference from which this volume emerges. It also provides an annotated preview of the volume itself, including a description of the separate critical essays at the beginning and the more general commentaries on the state of sociology that follow. The volume's Epilogue attempts to highlight the major issues that developed not only from the written papers but from the informal give-and-take in the conference's often spirited sessions. If the term "epilogue" suggests finality, we mean it to apply only to this book. Surely the larger topic is far from resolved and is likely to linger on to haunt us all.

Acknowledgments

There are a number of persons whose contributions to this venture must be acknowledged, however inadequately in this form. The conference and volume were both funded by the National Institute of Mental Health through a grant to the American Sociological Association. As the primary funding officer, Kenneth Lutterman went far beyond the call of his duties as NIMH's Chief of Training Grants in the Behavioral Sciences; indeed, his energy and counsel reflected his own deep commitment to the larger concerns at issue. On behalf of the American Sociological Association, Alice Myers worked with characteristic skill and good cheer in arranging all of the details of the conference gathering. Norma Blohm went far beyond the role of secretary to the ASA Executive Officer in taking care of invitations, correspondence, and manuscript circulation. We are especially grateful to Lena Lo for copy-editing the final manuscripts and bringing them up to the standards of excellence which she established during her earlier 3-year term as Assistant Editor of the *American Sociological Review*. Finally we wish to acknowledge the generous help of the following persons who read parts of the manuscript and supplied suggestions for their refinement: John A. Clausen, Melvin L. Kohn, Sheldon L. Messinger, Matilda W. Riley, Karl E. Taeuber, and Harriet Zuckerman.

Prologue

KARL F. SCHUESSLER

Indiana University

OPENING REMARKS

Uppermost in the thinking of many sociologists today is the proper relationship between sociology and public policy. Should that relationship be direct and close, or indirect and remote? Should sociologists become actively engaged in social engineering, or should they be content merely to enlighten public policy at a distance. A related matter concerns better methods of training graduate students for doing policy research. This volume addresses itself to both problems.

Much of its substance was presented at a conference on policy research and graduate training, held in December 1972 at Carmel, California, under the terms of a grant from the National Institute of Mental Health (NIMH) to the American Sociological Association (ASA). However, the writings included herein are not merely a verbatim record of what happened at that conference; both papers and commentaries have been rather extensively revised to take into account pertinent discussions going on both during and after the meeting.

The relation of sociology to public policy has been expounded in a growing literature on the subject (see, for example, *The American Sociologist,* **6,** June, Supplementary Issue, 1971). This symposium adds to that literature through the endeavor of its contributors to evaluate recently published sociological findings for their bearing on public policy. Many sociologists have expressed themselves on this subject in recent times, but few have taken the trouble to specify the exact utility of particular findings for purposes of guiding policy. The papers in Part I of this volume represent such an undertaking; critical commentaries on these papers represent an extension of that undertaking. Another distinctive feature of this collection is the unusually large number of contributing authors. Because so many minds are represented in the following pages, most major themes on sociology and social policy are at least broached, although not all nuances of opinion are represented.

HISTORY OF CARMEL

The Carmel Conference was not without a history. In one view, it all started with an informal meeting of a dozen or so sociologists in Washington in the spring of 1965. The occasion for that meeting was the concern in some circles that sociologists were relatively unsophisticated in research design, as evinced in their proposals to federal funding agencies, and that possibly their graduate training was inadequate. Whatever the validity of that charge, it was decided by the group to initiate and to maintain a national dialogue among sociologists, insofar as practicable, on problems in graduate training and the quality of social research.

That effort to maintain a dialogue proceeded along two different but related paths. Under the auspices of the parent group, which came to be known as the Committee on Sociological Training (CST), conferences were held in 1967 in Bloomington, Indiana (Karl Schuessler, chairman); in 1969 at Hanover, New Hampshire (James Davis, chairman); and in 1971 at Chicago, Illinois (James Short, Jr., chairman). Shortly after the meeting at Bloomington, the Committee on Training and Professional Standards of the American Sociological Association suggested that the two groups join forces and proceed together under the aegis of the ASA. The advantages of this union were not clear to all, but no one opposed it.

The conference at Bloomington focused on the organizational aspects of graduate training and featured papers by Albert Reiss, Edgar Borgatta, and James Davis; the conference at Hanover concerned itself first with Richard Hill's projected survey of the methodological training of graduate students in sociology (see p. 285, this volume) and second with the computer as a tool in theory construction; the conference at Chicago featured papers by Dudley Duncan and Gerald Suttles on methods of training graduate students. The conferees also heard a preliminary report from Richard Hill and Robert McGinnis's report on the changing relationship between supply and demand in sociology.

In the meantime, several members of the parent group (CST) set themselves up as a "subcommittee" (Robert Hall, chairman) to consider the special problems of departments either starting doctoral programs or scrapping old programs for new ones. This group sponsored three meetings: the first was held in 1965 at Santa Barbara, California; the second, in 1967 at Chicago; the third, in 1968 at Stony Brook, New York. The conference at Santa Barbara focused on the goals of graduate training in sociology and organizational techniques for attaining them; the conference at Circle Campus in Chicago again focused on organizational devices for improving the effectiveness of graduate training; the conference at Stony Brook concerned itself with the summer institute as an interuniversity device for enriching intramural training programs.

Carmel may be regarded as the culmination of all of these activities that had their start in Washington. Many persons were involved in this movement, but of course no one was indispensable to the collective effort. Nevertheless, the editors feel obliged to mention Robert Hall and Nathaniel Siegel for having started it all by the effective use of their respective offices at the National Science Foundation and the National Institute of Mental Health, and Kenneth Lutterman for having sustained the movement in its latter phases by the same means.

CONFERENCE PLANNING AND ORGANIZATION

The prime movers of Carmel prevailed upon one of their own—James Short, Jr.—to assume primary responsibility for obtaining funds to cover the expenses of the Conference. In his proposal to NIMH, Short outlined some of the benefits that might be expected to accrue from a meeting of directors of NIMH graduate training programs in social science. Responsibility for planning the conference was assumed by Robert Alford, Jay Demerath, Howard Freeman, Kenneth Lutterman, Raymond Mack, Karl Schuessler, and Howard Schuman—all involved in one way or another in NIMH training programs. Responsibility for actually running the conference was delegated to Jay

Demerath, Raymond Mack, and Karl Schuessler, with Otto Larsen joining that group shortly after he succeeded Jay Demerath as Executive Officer of the American Sociological Association.

Initially, committee members disagreed among themselves about the main focus of the conference, with some favoring graduate training in sociology, and others favoring research and its implications for social policy. Eventually, the latter group carried the day, and it was decided that the conference should devote itself primarily to the link between sociology and public policy, with some attention to the implications of that link for graduate training.

An important factor in this decision was the feeling among some that the preceding conferences on graduate training had reached the point of diminishing returns, and that a different but related topic should be explored. Another consideration was the pressure to which sociologists were subject at the time (circa 1970) to demonstrate the relevance of their work for the public good. Still another consideration was that federal funding agencies appeared to have more interest in research with some practical value than in research with theoretical value alone. The effect of these considerations was to slant the conference away from graduate training and toward the relationship between sociology and public policy.

In keeping with the terms of the grant, invitations were extended to around 60 persons, virtually all of whom were either serving at the time, or had served as directors of an NIMH training program at their respective institutions. From this master list of threescore names, some 15 persons were invited to contribute papers on sociological research findings and public policy in a given field and lessons to be drawn from that analysis as regards graduate training. They were given the following assignment:

> Take any recent bit of sociological research in the domain as long as it (a) is not your own, (b) is worthy of high scholarly marks, and (c) contains substantial, if implicit, policy implications. In 10 pages or so, write a critique which takes the research's methods and results on faith and responds to the questions: (1) what are its policy implications, (2) what kinds of policy impact has it actually had, and (3) what changes are required in the discipline and its training if we are to produce more policy implications with greater impact in the future?

The assignment proved to be enticing: 15 of 17 persons accepted the commission—a very high acceptance rate, indeed, for such a professionally busy target group. Even more astonishing, all 15 who agreed to do a paper actually delivered on schedule prior to the conference itself. Other participants were requested to serve either as discussants of contributed papers, or as presiders over sessions. (A list of all Carmel participants is attached as an appendix.)

The opening session, held on Wednesday evening, December 6, was devoted to changing patterns of financial support for the social sciences; the closing session, held on Saturday morning, December 9, consisted of a round-up of important ideas and possible next steps that some or all at the conference might collectively take (see Epilogue). The six sessions on Thursday and Friday were devoted largely to the contributed papers and their commentaries. Readers will note that the conference program, attached as an appendix, differs somewhat from the Table of Contents of this volume. These departures were initiated partly to obtain a more natural alignment of papers by subject matter, and partly to provide discussants with a broader base on which to center their remarks.

OVERVIEW OF PAPERS AND COMMENTARIES

The papers and commentaries on recent sociological findings and implications for public policy comprise the first and longer part of this volume; the second and shorter part consists of papers on current methods of graduate training and changing patterns of federal funding for both research and training in sociology. The major issues of the conference and possible steps that sociologists might take to resolve them are given in the Epilogue to this volume.

The articles and comments in Part I have been arranged somewhat arbitrarily under three headings: (A) Social Inequities and Their Effects; (B) Individual Stress in the Family Cycle; (C) American Youth and Their Problems.

Papers by Peter Rossi, Robert Alford, Howard Schuman, John Kasarda, and Samuel Preston have a Malthusian flavor: all touch on the imbalance between people on the one side and goods and services on the other, and the social effects of that imbalance. Critical discussions of these papers are supplied by John Brandl, Franklin Edwards, Elton Jackson, Maurice Jackson, William Liu, Robert McGinnis, and Sheldon Stryker.

In the opening paper, Rossi discusses some of the factors that may nullify the impact of significant sociological findings on policy, taking Duncan's test of the notion that poverty is socially inherited as a case in point.

Alford argues that alternative conceptualizations of a given set of findings may differ in their suggestions for policy, and that one may be relatively rich and the other relatively poor in such suggestions. To illustrate his point, he offers an alternative interpretation of Turk's findings on the response of United States cities in the 1960s to the federally funded war against poverty.

Schuman discusses the import of findings based on several recent investigations into the causes of racial disorders. A major finding is that objective socioeconomic status is of negligible importance both in verbally expressed militancy and in actual riot participation. Reflecting on this finding, Schuman observes that "sociologists seem to be better, or at least more useful at disconfirming presumed important facts and relationships than at discovering new ones or even confirming old ones."

Hawley and Zimmer's study of the metropolitan community is the object of Kasarda's inquiry. The finding of considerable opposition to the merger of towns and cities carries the implication that such opposition will have to be eliminated by appropriate methods, or alternatives to governmental unification for improving services will have to be devised.

Formal models of the birth process are the specific focus of Preston's discussion of implications in research on population dynamics. Such models, according to Preston, direct attention to the importance of motivation in controlling family size. Programs designed to regulate the growth of the future population must take the human factor of motivation into account.

Papers by David Mechanic, Joan Aldous, Robert Straus, Kurt Back, and Nicholas Babchuk form the second grouping and deal largely with the problems of the sick and the aged. Commentaries are provided by Charles Bowerman, Joseph Elder, Walter Gove, August Hollingshead, Marvin Sussman, Guy Swanson, and Robert N. Wilson.

For purposes of his discussion, Mechanic considers Skipper and Leonard's experimental study of the role of communication in patient care, and Duff and Hollingshead's study of differences in patient care in private and public wards in the same hospital. Although both studies have significant policy implications, neither has had much impact, but for different reasons. The experimental findings were dismissed as trivial; the Duff–Hollingshead findings were probably rejected because of their very radical implications, according to Mechanic.

Aldous, in her contribution, takes up Holstrom's research on the two-career family and her suggestions for assuring that the career of the wife does not suffer because of the husband's, and vice versa. She particularly calls attention to Holstrom's respective suggestions that work schedules be made more flexible so that husband and wife may work at different times during the day; and that employers of women establish centers for the care of their young children during working hours.

Straus examines Cahalan's findings on problem drinking among American men, and discerns two major implications: (1) that the conception of alcoholism be broadened, and (2) that moderation be fostered and intoxication discouraged.

As his point of departure, Back takes Gove's critical analysis of societal reaction as an explanation of mental illness. He points out that the impact of such a theory on policy may depend less on its scientific validity and more on its rhetorical and ideological appeal.

Implications of Lowenthal and Haven's findings on social isolation as a factor in mental illness among persons over 60 years of age is the subject of Babchuk's critical analysis. He stresses that the major implications of these findings are limited not to older persons but hold equally for all age groups. Echoing Schuman, he notes that sociological findings often run counter to conventional wisdom and that such negative evidence may serve to rectify erroneous public policy.

The problems of American youth are the general theme of papers by James Short, Albert Reiss, Lois DeFleur, James Davis, and Doris Entwisle. Commentators include: Wendell Bell, Charles Bidwell, Herbert Costner, Troy Duster, David Heise, Laura Nader, Albert Pepitone, and Hanan Selvin.

The necessarily loose connection between theory and action, as exemplified by Mobilization for Youth, is Short's subject. In its planning stages, Mobilization for Youth (a program for preventing delinquency in New York City) was firmly grounded in Cloward and Ohlin's theory of differential opportunity; but as it took shape in the field, it had hardly more than an accidental relation to that theory.

After summarizing recent findings from surveys of self-reported delinquency, Reiss evaluates their adequacy for purposes of making public policy. His general conclusion is that "sociologists may take comfort from trying to find out why things are as they are rather than in learning how things that are can be made different, but social policy is informed more by the latter than the former."

DeFleur's topic is opiate addiction in the light of Glaser, Lander, and Abbott's comparison of addicted and nonaddicted male siblings from a slum in New York City. This investigation, according to DeFleur, points up the need to bring sociological findings to the attention of public authorities. Without such an effort, public officials will remain unacquainted with possibly important sociological findings, and consequently their policies will remain uninfluenced by them.

Why sociological research of apparently high quality, exemplified by TenHouten, Lei, Kendall, and Gordon's study of Mexican–American and Anglo high school students, is so often bare of practical import is the question Davis poses for himself. In reduced form, his answers are: (1) the concern of sociologists with the relevance but not the applicability of their findings, (2) their concern with causal rather than manipulable variables, (3) the pressure on sociologists to make do with inadequate samples, (4) their tendency to use crude statistical methods, (5) their inclination to play down ideologically repugnant findings, and (6) their perverse knack for finding low correlations.

Starting from Stinchcombe's investigation of high school students, Entwisle proceeds to the where-am-I-going crisis of American adolescents in its institutional aspects. She concludes that, since the high school is not helping all students to solve this crisis, other institutions must be called on to assist in resolving it. In particular, she regards institutionalized cooperation between the school on the one hand, and business and industry on the other, as an essential element in a solution to this problem.

The papers in Part II are something of a miscellany. Hill gives a few of his findings, in very condensed form, on the training of graduate students in methods, and speculates on the meaning of those findings. His remark that his survey would have been more revealing if he had sampled research units within the departments instead of the departments themselves has as much substantive as methodological significance. Perhaps the department is less an instrument of, and more an impediment to, sound training for research.

Trends in the participation of sociologists in NIMH training programs is the subject of Freeman, Borgatta, and Siegel's paper. The trend during the 1960s was sharply upward; the trend during the 1970s has been sharply downward. This rise and fall in participation corresponds to changes in national policy. Notwithstanding the loss of federal funding, a larger, rather than a smaller, number of persons may be expected to pursue the doctoral degree in the years ahead, according to these writers. Their argument is reminiscent of Veblen's doctrine that persons will uneconomically consume what is conspicuous when their social reputation is at stake.

Lutterman also traces the history of the social science training programs at NIMH, but in more detail and with somewhat different emphases. In his coda, he wonders why sociologists have contributed to little knowledge that might be utilized for ameliorating social conditions. The overwhelming concern of sociologists with teaching rather than research is cited as a major reason.

Although Foote was not present at the Carmel Conference, his paper very much belongs to the Proceedings. Presented to a session on the labor market for sociologists at the 1973 meeting of ASA, it is a critical reaction to some of the views expressed at Carmel. Foote keys his paper to the question, "How does training for nonacademic positions differ from training for academic positions?" After giving some answers to that question, he goes on to suggest that the greatest asset of applied sociology is the sociological perspective, and that sociologists should concern themselves principally with persons as clients of social institutions.

CONCLUDING REMARKS

There was little consensus among participants at Carmel on any specific change in graduate training, although there was agreement on the platitudinous point that graduate training is subject to improvement. The reluctance, if not unwillingness, of many sociologists to gear graduate training to policy research reflects the uncertain relationship between sociology and policy. Sociologists are seldom called upon for help in making policy, and when they are they are not always very helpful. Poincare once said that sociologists spent practically all of their time on their methods without ever applying them to anything. Today, sociologists spend much time talking about their potential for making policy without doing much about it. This is said not to discourage the dialogue among sociologists, but rather to point out that at the moment their participation in policy-making is quite limited. Perhaps the major contribution of this symposium consists in its highlighting of factors that militate against sociologists' having much influence on public policy and steps that might be taken to change that situation.

PART 1

ASSESSMENT OF
POLICY RESEARCH

Section A

Social Inequities
and Their Effects

Policy Shibboleths and the Reality-Testing of Research: Are the Poor Always with Us When We Make Sociology?

PETER H. ROSSI

University of Massachusetts

INTRODUCTION

In 1966 my colleague Zahava D. Blum and I undertook a bibliographic survey (Blum and Rossi 1968) of empirical studies of poverty, covering the period 1950–1966. The effort covered most serial publications (in which sociologists ordinarily publish) as well as monographs. Although we managed to find more than 450 factual studies of poverty, we commented then that there were only a limited few that would survive a scrutiny in which minimal quality-control standards were applied. If we had applied more stringent standard of policy relevance, perhaps only one or two of the items would have survived the further culling involved. In short, preparing the bibliographic review was a sobering and depressing experience. Up to that point in time, for over a decade and a half, sociologists and their cousins in closely related social science fields had produced little which had both probity and policy relevance. The only optimistic

15

note we could sound was to point to the considerable amount of research in support of the War on Poverty that was at that time waiting
to reach publication stage.

In preparation for this assignment I took on the task of searching
the sociological serial publications that appeared since 1966. I wish I
could state that our optimistic expectations of 1966 had been fulfilled,
but such was not the case. The 6-year run of conventional sociological
journals did change very much my dismal assessment of 1966. Indeed,
there was not a single article[1] found that I thought worthy of being
used in this paper. It might be useful for some other conference to be
concerned with why this is the case (assuming my survey is approximately accurate), but for the present I will merely assert that there are
very few, if any, articles appearing in our more prestigious sociological
journals that are both empirical and relevant to policy in the area of
the treatment of poverty.

To serve as the centerpiece of this paper, I chose Duncan's contribution, "Inheritance of Poverty or Inheritance of Race?" to a collection of papers on poverty (Moynihan 1968).[2] Duncan's paper has all of
the attributes desirable to a centerpiece: (1) It is built upon a very firm
empirical base. (2) It is addressed to a policy issue of considerable importance. And (3) The empirical data are treated with consummate skill.

The volume in which Duncan's article appeared has slipped into an
undeserved obscurity, as so many symposia proceedings have done.
So here I must admit to an ulterior motive for choosing Duncan's
work: perhaps this paper will help to rescue it from oblivion.

AN OVERVIEW OF DUNCAN'S ARTICLE

Duncan starts his article by identifying an important issue in poverty policy. He shows that many popular writers (e.g., Michael Har-
rington) and important decision makers (e.g., Lyndon Johnson, the
Council of Economic Advisors, and Wilbur Cohen) subscribe to the

---

[1] Based on reviewing *The American Sociological Review, The American Journal of
Sociology,* and *The American Sociologist.* My survey was not based on reading each
and every article in the period 1966 through the present, but only those articles
which showed some promise of addressing problems on poverty. Obviously, my estimate of zero articles is subject to both measurement and sampling error. I believe,
however, that had I broadened my survey to include journals outside our field (e.g.,
The Journal of Human Resources) or monographs, I would have found that the literature had improved. This may point to some peculiarity of our editorial policies in
sociological journals or the selective rendering of manuscripts to journals on the part
of the authors.

[2] This collection was the product of a 2-year monthly seminar held by the American Academy of Arts and Sciences attended rather faithfully by a score of social scientists, all of whom had either research or policy concerns with poverty.

view that "poverty breeds poverty," or that children born into poor families have little if any chance to escape from poverty in their lifetime.

This "inheritance of poverty" theme is the major foil against which Duncan will fence. His initial argument is that the statements supporting the notion that there are high (but how high?) correlations between the economic status of parents and their children as adults are vague. These statements also point to an intervention policy that attempts to interrupt the intergenerational transmission of this condition. In addition, Duncan observes that the "inheritance model" does not necessarily differentiate between whites and blacks, raising the question whether the poverty burden borne by blacks is a function of their inheritance of poverty or their inheritance of race.

Duncan begins his examination of this model by raising two questions: (1) "What factors, conditions, circumstances, and choices observable at one stage of the life cycle are determinative or prognostic of outcomes at later stages?" And (2) "How predictable are the outcomes at later stages from the information available at the earlier ones?" The answers to these two questions are provided in the form of path diagrams, based upon survey data collected to investigate the American occupational structure (Blau and Duncan 1967). His path diagrams trace for whites and blacks, respectively, the influence of the occupational and educational attainment of parents through the educational attainment of sons (conditioned by number of siblings in the family) to the occupation of the respondent and finally to his income.[3] Duncan's path diagrams are reproduced here as Figure 1.

The path diagrams, Duncan writes, are the best first approximation he can make to providing a model of how conditions in families of orientation affect the occupational and income attainments of sons. The path coefficients lead to two important generalizations. First, they lend little support to the idea that there is anything close to an ironbound transmission of parental conditions to the occupational and income attainments of their male children. Indeed most of the variances in occupational prestige and in income are unaccounted for by the causally prior variables used in the path model, although it can be argued without distortion that the inheritance of poverty "model" would call for at least a substantial proportion of such variance being accounted for by the parental background factors.

The second generalization concerns the striking differences between the path coefficients for whites and blacks. For whites, more of

---

[3] As in many other analyses undertaken using the OCG study, Duncan restricts his analysis to men from nonfarm backgrounds, apparently feeling that the transition from agricultural occupations to nonagricultural occupations is qualitatively different from the transitions among nonagricultural occupations.

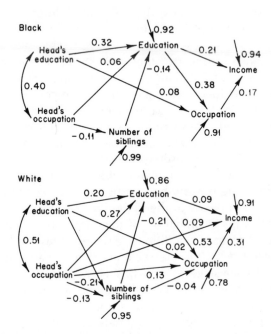

Figure 1. Path diagram for social attainment. (Figure 4–1 from Inheritance of poverty or inheritance of race? In *On understanding poverty*, edited by Daniel P. Moynihan, © 1968, 1969 by the American Academy of Arts and Sciences, Basic Books, Inc., Publishers, New York. Reprinted by permission.)

the variance in occupational and income attainment is accounted for by the earlier stages in the model. In addition, most of the path coefficients in the analysis pertaining to blacks are lower than corresponding coefficients for whites, indicating that black families are not able to transmit as much of their background advantages to their children as are whites. But even more important is the demonstration that once an advantage has been attained by a black (e.g., superior educational attainment) it is not as easily converted into other attainments (e.g., occupational prestige or income) as is the case for whites. The processes that link parental background, early attainments, and later attainments are less well structured for blacks than for whites. In other words, there is even less intergenerational transmission of socioeconomic characteristics among blacks, a group often pointed out as the prime example of the "inheritance of poverty."

Although Duncan might have rested his case upon his path models, he takes an additional step in the analysis of these data. This step is particularly important in making his findings relevant to policy. There are several reasons why the path diagrams and coefficients are not entirely patent to the legendary "intelligent layman." (1) The technique is somewhat unfamiliar even to social scientists. (2) The units of the path coefficients are in standard deviations of the variables used, a metric which has little direct substantive meaning. (3) The path diagrams (through no fault of their own) do not show one of the more important differences between blacks and whites, namely: that the means on all the socioeconomic variables for blacks are consistently below those of whites.

The critical step taken by Duncan enables one to interpret the model represented in the path diagrams in very concrete and directly understandable terms. He starts by noting that there is a considerable difference between the average annual income earned by whites and that enjoyed by blacks, $3790. Using the regression equations derived from the analysis of white socioeconomic life cycles, he substitutes black means for all the variables, deriving thereby estimates of what would be the result were blacks to attain parity with whites in each respect. Thus, making whites identical to blacks in family background would reduce the income differential between whites and blacks by $940; changing the number of siblings of whites to the average of black men would reduce racial income differences by $70. And so on, as shown in Duncan's table reproduced in this paper as Table 1.

The important end results of this analysis are: (1) The analysis indicates the relative importance of different kinds of black–white differences in producing black–white income differentials. For example, we learn that education counts less than occupation ($520 as opposed to $830). (2) Duncan shows that the processes occurring after leaving the parental home are more important in the aggregate than those that occur in the home. (3) He shows that even when whites are made to be "equal to" blacks with respect to family background, number of siblings, education, and occupation, there still remains a rather substantial income differential (37% or $1430 out of the total $3790) between blacks and whites.[4]

Duncan goes on further to add information on mental abilities. Using data from an analysis of the relationships between AFQT scores, and occupational and perhaps income attainment, he provides a more tentatively offered analysis of what would happen if one could take mental ability into account. His analysis shows that while equating blacks and whites in mental ability would reduce the income differential further, there still remains a considerable gap which is unaccounted for by any of the factors used in the model, including mental ability.

[4] Note that Duncan chooses to apply the white regression equations in these calcu-lations under the assumption that one would want to change black ability to "cash in" on their resources equal to that of whites. An alternative route would have been to use the black regression equations substituting white means which would have given an estimate of the effects of differences in means *and* differences in the strengths of the path coefficients.

TABLE 1 Differences in Means between White (W) and Negro (N) with Respect to Number of Siblings, Educational Attainment, Occupational Status, and Income, with Components of Differences Generated by Cumulative Effects in a Model of the Socioeconomic Life Cycle, for Native Men, 25–64 Years Old, with Nonfarm Background and in the Experienced Civilian Labor Force: March 1962 [a]

Number of siblings	Years of school completed	1962 occupation score	1961 income (dollars)	Component [b]
(W) 3.85	(W) 11.7	(W) 43.5	(W) 7070	
-.54	1.0	6.6	940	(A) [Family]
4.39	10.7	36.9	6130	
-.47	0.1	0.6	70	(B) [Siblings]
(N) 4.86	10.6	36.3	6060	
	1.2	4.8	520	(C) [Education]
	(N) 9.4	31.5	5540	
		11.8	830	(D) [Occupation]
		(N) 19.7	4710	
			1430	(E) [Income]
			(N) 3280	
-1.01	2.3	23.8	3790	(T) [Total]

[a] Table 4-3 from Inheritance of poverty or inheritance of race? In *On understanding poverty*, edited by Daniel P. Moynihan. © 1968, 1969 by the American Academy of Arts and Sciences, Basic Books, Inc., Publishers, New York. Reprinted by permission.

[b] Difference due to:

(A) Socioeconomic level of family of origin (head's education and occupation).
(B) Number of siblings, net of family origin level.
(C) Education, net of siblings and family origin level.
(D) Occupation, net of education, siblings, and family origin level.
(E) Income, net of occupation, education, siblings, and family origin level.
(T) Total difference, (W) minus (N) = sum of components (A) through (E).

Although Duncan carefully refrains from drawing direct implications for policy from his analysis, he does make some disparaging remarks about the slogan "Learn, baby, learn" and about the human resources analysts who have both emphasized how important it is for blacks to obtain higher educational attainment. His argument is that his analysis shows that it is even more important to work on the ability of blacks to convert their educational attainment into occupational attainment.

Duncan does not go further than these side remarks about policy. He despairs that policy-makers will not read and/or will not understand his work. He states firmly that the handicap of race is more than the handicap of family background, educational attainment, occupational position, and mental ability, and explicitly contradicts the inheritance of poverty argument. He states further that it is up to the policy analysts and policy-makers to devise the policies that would be appropriate to wiping out the racial differentials in earnings.

POLICY IMPLICATIONS OF DUNCAN'S ARTICLE

It seems to me that Duncan's article is chock-full of policy implications. First of all, it is clear that the inheritance of poverty model is clearly a dead horse.[5] Second, it is clear that policies such as the dissemination of birth control methods (to lower family size) or to increase educational attainment among blacks, while laudatory in some respects, will not have as high a pay-off as policies directed elsewhere. Third, it points up that there is a racial difference in income which persists when blacks are "made equal to whites" in most relevant respects.

It seems to me that the last policy implication is among its most important. While knowing that there are such persistent racial differences in income attainment does not tell you what to do about it, it does point out where the problem lies. It is apparently the case that more than one-third of the gross income differential between whites and blacks could be wiped out if we were able to give blacks the same ability to cash in on their personal resources as whites. Is this not an operational definition of discrimination?

[5] There are, of course, alternative interpretations of the "inheritance of poverty" model that have not been laid low by Duncan's analysis. For example, it may well be the case that present day welfare families are more likely to have children who will also go on welfare than other families are likely to have children who will remain in their respective income brackets. This is an interpretation which declares Duncan's data to be of low relevance because it refers to a historical period which lies before 1962, extending as far back as the early 1900s.

Furthermore, operating the way it does, discrimination is apparently a function of the institutional practices of employing organizations.

The job for the policy analyst is cut out for him: How to transform institutional practices so that blacks have the same ability to cash in as whites. The institutional practices of most interest are those which are most amenable to change through changes in public policy. Unfortunately, for our purposes, there are many ways in which discrimination in the sense used here could be operating, and hence there are correspondingly different ways in which policy can be changed. For example, part of the net income differential shown in Table 1 may be a function of the locational accessibility of jobs. If this is a significant factor, then one might work either through fostering residential desegregation or by devising transportation systems that would help to equalize access for blacks as compared to whites. If, on the other hand, the net income differential is a function of differentials in hiring and promotion practices, then policy-making has to be focused on ways of changing the hiring and promotion practices of employers.

What effect had Duncan's article had? None that I can discern. Moynihan, the editor of the collection in which the article appeared, was appointed President Nixon's urban affairs advisor shortly after the collection was put together. Moynihan was certainly aware of the existence of Duncan's article and most likely aware of its implications for policy. Yet, it is difficult to see in his major domestic legislation endeavor, the Family Assistance Plan, any sign that Duncan's article may have some influence. It is true that the article says very little directly about how to design a proper welfare system, but it does suggest that policy-making might be more profitably directed into other areas.

IMPLICATIONS FOR RESEARCH TRAINING

How can we train future sociologists so that they will be more sensitive to the policy issues involved in social research? It is clear to me that the answer to this question does not lie in developing additional well-trained researchers alone. I think we have been successful in doing that at least in those schools where research training is taken seriously. The more important directions lie in redirecting and developing the sociological imagination.

I am certain that a major reason why *ASR* and *AJS* over the past few years contained so few articles from which policy implications can be drawn is that such articles go relatively unrewarded in the profession. Our applied research is buried in mimeographed reports, hidden in symposia that are interred in libraries and soon forgotten, or pursued for the sake of making enough money to pay off the loan on the Volvo. For example, while there is considerable interest in evaluation research, virtually nothing of the discussions of this issue, not to mention examples of such research itself, finds its way into our professional journals. This is not to fault the ASA or its editorial cadres, rather it is to fault the entire profession. Applied research is a low prestige activity, something which will not put nails in your tenure, although it can be indulged in as a side activity or as a hobby when you have achieved prestigedom.

What this means is that our graduate departments are not fostering among our students a taste for the policy relevant and a sensibility for policy-relevant variables. We have to learn that exhausting the variance is not as important as getting a good fix on the regression coefficient for a variable that is manipulable through changes in social policy. To be more specific, it is irrelevant to know that you can account for 80% of the variance in occupational choice of college students by taking into account occupational values, family background, and self-esteem. These are not policy-relevant variables in the sense that public policy does not ordinarily concern itself with altering any of these variables. Rather, it may be far more important to note that the salaries given to persons entering occupational ladders account for 2% of the variance, or put in more prosaic terms that each $100 increase in entering salaries produces another 1000 applicants.[6]

A correlative part of graduate training should be in the translation of a policy model into empirical terms. It seems to me that this is what Duncan managed to do so well in his paper, namely to take a theme which appears constantly in policy-maker's diagnoses of the poverty problem—the inheritance of poverty—and to translate that term into an operational counterpart. It is necessary for the trained sociologist to have enough distance intellectually from our society to question each critical piece of conventional wisdom in order to be able to test that wisdom against empirical data. Many examples can be given here: the vaunted "oversupply of Ph.D.s," the notion that criminals should be "rehabilitated," etc.

Finally, it needs to be shown that policy-related research can be as technically exciting and intellectually rewarding as "basic research." There is an elegance to the design of the income maintenance experi-

---

[6] This is an entirely fictional example.

ments or to Duncan's analysis that can be as attractive as anything that is published in the *ASR.*

In short, the problem is not in the training of researchers *qua* researchers but in the training of sociologists. We have to teach our students to think in policy-relevant terms.

As to getting the results of policy-related research in the policy-makers, we are faced again with the problem Coleman had labeled as "missing institutions." The institutions that are missing are those that can occupy the gap between the groves of Academe and the halls of policy. The economists have an institution, the Council of Economic Advisors, which helps to bridge the gap in their case and provides a direct link to the executive and excellent access to the media. We need something comparable, although I would like to see stronger relationships to both houses of the Congress than those represented in the case of the Council of Economic Advisors.

The social indicators movement, if it ever gets off the ground, may also provide an institutional link. If an index of life satisfaction ever gets established as firmly as the BLS measurement of unemployment, sociologists and social psychologists will be looked upon as having something important to say. As it stands now, we often have very little of importance to talk about and often do not say it in ways that that are understood easily.

There are two messages in this last section of this paper: (1) Part of our training of sociologists and social psychologists should provide experience and practice in the identification of policy-relevant variables and problems. (2) On the institutional side, we need to build those missing institutions which can serve as a bridge between sociologists and social psychologists on the one hand and policy-makers on the other.

REFERENCES

Blau, P. M. and O. D. Duncan
  1967 *The American occupational structure.* New York: Wiley.
Blum, Z. D. and P. H. Rossi
  1968 Social class research and images of the poor: A bibliographic review. In *On understanding poverty,* edited by D. P. Moynihan. New York: Basic Books.
Moynihan, D. P. (Editor)
  1968 *On understanding poverty.* New York: Basic Books.

Ideological Filters and Bureaucratic Responses in Interpreting Research: Community Planning and Poverty[1]

ROBERT R. ALFORD[2]

University of California, Santa Cruz

Reflection on the implications for graduate training in the sociology of policy analysis in the area of community planning leads me to reinterpret Turk's (1970) findings on interorganizational networks in a way that presumably will throw my major points into sharp relief. I shall accept the methods and data of that article as given, but contrast "conflict" and "consensus" interpretations of the same data. Then I shall suggest why certain kinds of theoretical perspectives and methodological procedures are congruent with particular approaches to policy issues.

As the editor of the American Sociological Review (Schuessler 1970) pointed out in his brief summary of Turk's article, "although no implications for public policy are drawn from this finding [that the intensity of efforts in the "war on poverty" is more or less uncorrelated with the rate of poverty itself, except for cities with relatively high per

---

[1] For editors' note, please see p. 36.
[2] Affiliation at time of Conference: University of Wisconsin, Madison.

25

capita revenue] . . . such implications could be drawn, if required."
The circumstances under which unban communities can secure outside funds for improving the conditions of life of their citizens are
important aspects of the process of "community planning." Few articles in American sociological journals deal directly with planning of
any type, let alone community planning, and Turk's article seemed
close enough to meet the criteria for this conference, hence, the
selection of his article:

Turk's own abstract is as follows:

The activity levels and complexity of new interorganizational networks are observable consequents of prior degrees of social integration defined in
organizational terms. This proposition was specified and tested in terms of the
flow of poverty funds from Federal agencies to and among organizations within
the 130 largest American cities.

The city's extralocal integration was measured by the number of national associational headquarters it contained, and integration among its local units by the
incidence of communitywide civic associations as well as degree of control by
its municipal government. With some exceptions, the extralocal variable predicted the level of interorganizational activity, while local integration predicted
complexity within a portion of the interorganizational network. Expedient or normative demand, inferred from poverty rates and other forms of deprivation, only
made positive contributions to such prediction where the prior levels of integration were high.

The study provides empirical support of an interorganizational level of analysis; it outlines directions for further research in urbanized social systems; and it
demonstrates the need to employ both additive and multiplicative models of social organization.

In this article, Turk presents many imaginative cross-checks on the
data as measures of the concepts he employs within his theoretical
framework; he employs his data effectively and creatively. Thus, my
intention here is only to suggest that contrasting theoretical frameworks have different and more or less fruitful policy implications.
Consideration of such alternative frameworks in the course of research training will also improve the relevance of graduate training for
policy analysis, although there may be some contradictions between
the requirements for "scientific" practice, as now defined, and "policy" analysis.

I shall make these assumptions: (1) that conflict occurs over scarce
resources within political arenas among interest groups differing in resources (resources include legitimating symbols and myths); and (2)
that the elites of various interest groups engage in strategies to limit
conflict by (a) defining social needs as either legitimate or illegitimate
subjects of collective action, (b) responding symbolically rather than

tangibly to those needs which succeed in becoming political demands, or (c) diverting demands from political to administrative or legal arenas for decision or nondecision.

Poverty programs, it seems clear by now, were neither designed to have, nor did they have, the major consequence of truly meeting the human needs of the poor in cities. I do not have space to argue the substantive issue, since my main object is to contrast conclusions about the *content* and *consequences* of a given set of policies with conclusions about formal properties of social units. I would argue that my conclusions about policy are no less empirically based than those abstracting to formal properties. Both kinds of conclusions involve value judgments. Seemingly neutral terminology such as "interorganizational activity" contains the implicit value-assumption that the important characteristic of ameliorative programs is their relevance for the development of sociological theory rather than for significant social change.

My intent is to avoid any assumptions of either local or society-wide consensus about the functions being performed by institutions and organizations of any kind. In the absence of a theory that explains the *existing* allocation of values in a community, and the ways in which the structure of institutions reinforces that allocation of values, it is possible to start with concepts which in effect assume that institutions either are neutral with respect to the allocation of values or serve as a channeling and mediating environment within which it is possible for *any* organized social demands to evoke a meaningful elite response. It is consistent with this implicit theory about the total society to disregard the content and/or consequences of both independent and dependent variables, convert them to formal properties, and thus reduce the possibility of drawing policy implications.

EMPIRICAL INDICATORS AND THEORETICAL VARIABLES

Table 1 presents a reconceptualization of six measures according to a "conflict" rather than a "concensus" perspective on the origins and consequences of poverty programs in American cities. I do not assume that these data are the best possible measures of the theoretical variables but this consideration of research design is outside my scope.

Per capita poverty funding is used as an indicator of a *new network of federal and local organizations*—a formal property of an abstract social entity—I suggest that it also measures (and more appropriately

**TABLE 1 Two Theoretical Perspectives on the Same Empirical Indicators of
Characteristics of 130 United States Cities**

Empirical indicator [a]	Theoretical variable (Turk)	Theoretical variable (Alford)
1. Poverty dollars per capita up to June 1966	New network of interorganizational activity	Capacity for symbolic response by local elites to potential for social conflict
2. Percent of low-income families, non-whites, youths not in school	Demand	Potential for social conflict
3. Neighborhood Youth Corps project sponsored by local federation	Complex interorganizational network	Legitimating sponsorship
4. Number of headquarters of national associations of all kinds	Extralocal integration	Location of national elites in the city
5. Number of local voluntary associations which do not represent organized cleavages	Local integration	Extent of legitimation of rule of local elites
6. Existence of "reform government" institutions	Local integration	Presence of structural devices for reducing the salience of cleavages

[a] These are shorthand summaries of 6 of the 31 variables given in Turk's Table 1
(Turk 1970:6).

for policy analysis) the capacity of local elites to respond to a potential for social conflict in the community with symbolic rather than
tangible programs.

The percentage of low-income families, nonwhites, and youths not
in school can be regarded as indicating the *demand* for such programs by potential clients. The notion of demand suggests a supply–
demand market, wherein such programs constitute a valid supply of
needed commodities. I suggest that the same indicators can be used
to demonstrate the *potential* within the community for social conflict
which may generate responses by local and national elites. This interpretation avoids any presumption (implied by the term *demand*)
about the nature of the connection between the objective condition
of deprived groups and the poverty program funds available.

The existence of a Neighborhood Youth Corps (NYC) project sponsored by a local federation can indicate the presence of a *complex interorganizational network* linking federal agencies to newly created Community Action Agencies (themselves "interorganizational systems [p. 10]"). I reinterpret this measure to indicate the presence of legitimating sponsorship for symbolic responses. The broader the sponsorship among various sectors of the community, the lesser the potential opposition to the program (almost by definition), and the greater the assurance that the federal agency will not run into local trouble.

The number of national association headquarters can indicate *extralocal integration,* i.e., the external connections of a city established through associations representing a large number of national organizations. Such associations "reflected what is nationally held in common along certain specialized lines" as well as "societal rather than regional orientation [Turk 1970:5]." Another indicator of extralocal integration was the number of business establishments which "serve nonresident persons and nonlocal organizations [p. 5]." I suggest that this measure indicates equally well the presence of nationally oriented elites manning core institutions of a wide variety of types within the city who need to have no interest in common, possess no societal orientations, and serve few personal or organizational interests besides their own.

The number of local voluntary associations not representing organized cleavages (as reported by informants in the 130 cities) can indicate *local integration* by "symbolizing, serving, coordinating, influencing, or acting on behalf of the community itself [p. 7]." My alternative interpretation is that the existence of associations, which have successfully defined themselves as representatives of the community, and the absence of organized conflicting groups indicate the extent to which local elites have legitimated their rule and have isolated or made impotent potential opposition groups and movements.

The presence of "reform government" institutions (a city manager and nonpartisan or at-large elections) can measure *local integration* or "the absence of cleavage [p. 9]." They can also be regarded as structural devices for reducing the salience of existing conflicts.

I can now briefly summarize the "findings" for the same empirical data, generalized from consensus versus conflict theoretical perspectives. A major finding is that cities with relatively high percentages of nonwhites or poor families are likely to have many poverty dollars *if* they also have many national headquarters or many local voluntary associations. Interpreted from a consensus perspective: the more integrated the community is, either locally or extralocally, the more likely that demand results in new interorganizational activity. Interpreted from a conflict perspective: a potential for social conflict is more likely to be recognized, and a symbolic response generated, in cities which have national elites or local institutions which have success-fully legitimated the rule of local elites. Symbolic responses may blunt or defuse potential social conflict where elites have already been legi-timated by an appropriate social structure of rule—i.e., "community-wide" associations which have in effect monopolized the legitimate space for organizational activity.

Once again, I must remind the reader that I am not criticizing Turk's analysis (or doing justice to the complexity of either the data or the theoretical argument), but merely reinterpreting a few selected variables (6 out of 31) in a way which, I argue, illuminates some im-portant dilemmas of graduate training for policy analysis vis-à-vis so-cial science. Readers are urged to read the entire article, which deals with many questions not of concern here. Confronting such alterna-tive interpretations opens up the political and value commitments im-plied by the choice of research frameworks, and thus sensitizes the potential policy researcher to the often implicit value choices he is making.

Turk, for example, does discuss the interorganizational conse-quences of social integration and suggests that "the greater the inte-gration of a social setting, the greater is its capacity *either* to support or to resist new interorganizational activities and arrangements [1970:3]." Thus, Turk is personally hospitable to a study of conflict and resistence to social change. However, none of the variables he uses measure conflict, resistance, or the potential for change, or disin-tegration of a social system, although at several points he mentions the possibility of fragmentation and conflict. This discrepancy be-tween Turk's own theoretical openness and the potential relevance of the mode of analysis used in the article is worth emphasizing, because it shows that a mode of analysis and type of data carry consequences that may not be intended by the analyst.

The perspective of conflict is more useful than that of consensus for policy analysis because, I believe, problematic questions about the contents and consequences of federal and local programs and agen-cies for the character of community planning are more likely to be raised. That is, the consensus perspective does not make instantly visible, as does the conflict perspective, such questions as the follow-ing: Under what conditions are the poor mobilized to present de-mands? (Instead, programs are *assumed* to reflect demand.) What are the actual consequences of poverty programs for the alleviation of poverty? What are the intentions of elites in developing such pro-grams? Regardless of intentions, what are the consequences of such programs for either the maintenance or the undermining of a system of domination? I suggest that such questions as these are crucial for the assessment of particular policies.

I have saved for the last an important policy question that is not directly raised by my suggested alternative perspective since I implicitly accepted the validity of investigation of a *single* federal program. But the last two decades have seen the development of a wide variety of federal programs which overlap and even contradict each other in their funding and goals. A research design which isolates one such program and examines its correlates will entirely miss this pervasive characteristic of the impact of federal programs upon local communities. The proliferation of overlapping agencies providing funding for an enormous variety of activities in local communities is apparent to many observers of diverse policy areas, and I suggest that it is a central problem for *any* attempt at "community planning." It is this phenomenon to which I propose to devote my remaining comments, because (1) it relates most centrally to my assigned topic of community planning, and (2) it is most neglected in sociological research. I will return to the pressures upon social scientists to develop internally contradictory responses to policy questions after first sketching my own picture of what generally happens when a "social problem" becomes defined in a community.

TYPICAL POLICY RESPONSES TO "PROBLEMS"

Demands for action on a "problem"—health, poverty, crime, delinquency, decaying central cities, the environment, education, jobs—are followed by responses by political leaders and administrative agencies: new agencies are established, old agencies begin new programs, more staffs are hired, budgets are prepared, appropriations are spent. Also set up are neighborhood health centers, Head Start programs, vocational rehabilitation projects, urban renewal, public housing, and regional environmental quality boards (Rosen 1971; Ginsberg *et al.* 1971; Roemer, Frink, and Kramer 1971; Fainstein and Fainstein 1972; Alford 1972, 1974; Edelman 1972; Freeman and Haveman 1973).

But the *problem* which generated this flurry of activity is not solved. It may even get worse as more efforts are made to solve it. Nevertheless, both the public and the politicians have a sense that something has been done because of all the money that has been spent, all the offices that have been set up, all the staff hired, and all the clients handled. The programs and agencies continue; the budgets are annually appropriated.

Suddenly, the unsolved problem again becomes a crisis. Some enterprising reporter uncovers a scandal in a housing program, cockroaches in the hospitals, apathy in the classroom, no jobs awaiting graduates of the Job Corps, brutality in the mental hospitals. Or some client, taxpayer, disinterested citizen group, or aspiring politician blows the whistle. Any one of innumerable horrors awaits those who scratch the surface of almost any public institution. The result: another investigation, another set of hearings, new legislation, more administrative rulings, agencies, programs, staff, budgets. And so on and on.

These new programs are added on top of the old ones, which are hard to kill because they have gotten their own constituencies and have become embedded in the stable commitments of a government agency. The old programs may lose a trifle of their budget, become more underfunded than they were, and thus lose part of whatever capacity they may have had to solve the problem in the first place. More likely is simply the sheer expansion of the number of agencies, staff, and budgets.

Faced with a proliferation of agencies and programs, a new type of demand arises: to coordinate, plan, and integrate the manifold activities of the agencies concerned with a given problem, whether it is health, education, welfare, or law and order. A new and different type of agency or program is created: the interagency coordinating council, the planning board, the superagency. At one extreme, the functions of many subordinate agencies are merged into one giant integrated body which will supposedly allocate resources rationally on the basis of empirical and scientific cost–benefit analyses. At the other extreme, representatives of different agencies get together once a month to "communicate" about common problems.

Unfortunately, this strategy does not work. The new agency has not been given the power actually to coordinate and plan; all it can do is communicate, inform, participate in meetings, and bring together the competing agencies for exchanges of information. The new agency, far from becoming an instrument of integration and control, becomes still another part of the nonproductive administrative superstructure.

Let us assume that the process we have outlined has taken place in a large *city*. Another line of attack on the problem of coordination and planning is to go to another level of government. The *state*, not being embroiled in the petty battles of local bureaucracies, is called upon to establish some guidelines for rational allocation of resources. This does not work. The problem is turned over to the *federal* government. Surely it is sufficiently distant from the operations of particular interest groups and has enough resources so that rational definition of needs and orderly decisions about modes of organizing structures to meet those needs can take place.

Unfortunately, neither state nor federal agencies have the requisite power. they are charged with handling the *consequences* of the problem; the *causes* lie within the jurisdiction of other agencies. Health agencies establish neighborhood clinics, but the cause of ill health is poverty. Poverty agencies establish legal aid programs and local community action councils, but the cause of poverty is a lack of well-paying jobs. Job agencies establish manpower rehabilitation programs, but the cause of unemployment is not necessarily a lack of job training. Thus, the state and federal agencies are added to the array of programs and projects which consume enormous reserves of manpower and taxes, but are mainly symbolic rather than tangible responses to social needs and political demands.

If I am basically right in this sketchy description of the typical policy response, a theory and method which disaggregates programs and agencies into separate units of analysis characterized by measured variables will entirely miss an important set of policy implications for community planning. (For an expanded version of the argument see Alford 1973b.)

IMPLICATIONS FOR POLICY-RELEVANT RESEARCH TRAINING

Accepting this pessimistic picture of the policy-making process as accurate for the moment, we may ask, "Where does the social scientist fit in?" The answer is that he is typically part of the problem, not part of the solution. The reason is that research grants, consultant-ships, and contracts put pressure upon the social scientist to develop quantitative measures of available indices of independent and dependent variables. As just suggested, using *quantitative* measures (money raised, obtained, or spent, staff hired and fired, buildings built, programs established) as indicators of *qualitative* characteristics of outputs (innovation, performance, improvement, progress, welfare) may beg the question. If my previous analysis is correct, there may actually be a negative correlation between any conceivable quantitative indicator and the qualitative outputs it purports to measure. (For an extension of this argument to cover studies of the "quality of life" see Alford 1973a.) Similarly, the independent variables (characteristics of communities, programs, the "environment") are arbitrarily defined as discrete properties of a unit of analysis. If, again, my analysis is correct, this procedure may also beg the question. The *combination* of programs may well constitute the political meaning and function of elite response to a "demand" which cannot be understood if we artificially separate progams and agencies from each other for the purpose of gathering research data.

Briefly, my argument is that the dominant *research* paradigm in sociology generally and community studies in particular focuses upon consensus, integration, and differentiation. By deemphasizing the opposites—conflict, disintegration, and fragmentation—this paradigm ignores important tensions or dilemmas both in the research-making and -training processes and in the policy-making process.

I can summarize these dilemmas in terms of five polarities: (1) quantitative versus qualitative, (2) part versus whole, (3) concepts versus problems, (4) data versus theory, and (5) formal properties versus content (see Table 2). Orthodox *research* training, not oriented toward policy analysis, tends to emphasize the first half of each polarity. Quantitative data are sought which measure components of abstract concepts which are formal properties of particular social entities: organizations, communities, groups. Orthodox *professional* training tends to stress concrete problems confronting social groups or the society as a whole with qualitative causes and consequences which require a theory (sometimes poorly explicated) about the behavior of individuals and groups. Much "soft" research which accepts the second half of each polarity is done with equally partial results, because it tends to be

TABLE 2 The Relationship between Methodological Alternatives and Policy Implications

Methodological alternatives	Policy implications
1. Quality versus quantity	Shall "outputs" be regarded as qualitative or quantitative?
2. Whole versus part	Should the unit of analysis be the "program," "agency," or "decision," or the consequences for the society and all groups affected or involved?
3. Content versus formal properties	Should program characteristics be regarded as indicators of formal properties (e.g., poverty funds as interorganizational activity) or of consequences for specific groups?
4. Theory versus data	What is the "policy potential" of a given theoretical framework for the analysis of a given body of data? Or, what different data are implied by different frameworks?
5. Problems versus concepts	Is the starting point a problem (e.g., the capacity of a community or society to improve its human services) or a concept (e.g., the level of interorganizational activity)?

based on anecdotal case studies, horror stories, or global generalizations without "hard" data which attempt to separate the effects of specific independent variables.

The best research training for policy analysis will occur, I would argue, when these research and policy dilemmas are explicitly regarded as problematic in the course of graduate training, rather than seen as totally different, or even opposed, styles of research and policy analysis. Policy analysis must include the consideration of the qualitative consequences of public action for social groups, the consideration of the conditions under which intervention by government will have specified ranges of consequences, and also the conditions under which such action is possible or feasible. The level of theorizing and research might also be raised by widening the scope of questions raised and answers considered in the course of graduate training.

The dominant mode of analysis in the scientific discipline—multivariate analysis of measured properties of discrete units of analysis—may *contradict* in important respects, to my mind, the requirements for significant policy research. The conversion of content into formal properties, the whole into parts, quality into quantity, and problems into concepts may be required for a particular kind of scientific activity, but these conversions defeat the purposes of policy analysis *if* we are interested in significant, substantive social change.

On the other hand, if my earlier argument is correct, it may well be that the kind of policy analysis made possible by this type of social science is well designed to satisfy the political and administrative requirements of symbolic rather than of tangible policy research. That is, social science may become an instrument for evading rather than a means of solving problems, precisely because of its systematic neglect of the contents and consequences of public policies. Whichever answer one prefers, the underlying question remains in our training of students: What kind of social science do we want, and for whom? Knowledge for what?

REFERENCES

Alford, R. R.
　　1972　　The political economy of health care: Dynamics without change. *Politics and Society* **2** (Winter), 127–164.
　　1973a　　Quantitative indicators of the quality of life: A critique. *Comparative Urban Research* **1**, 5–8.
　　1973b　　"The limits of urban reform." Unpublished manuscript.

1974   *Health care politics: Interest group and ideological barriers to reform.* Chicago, Illinois: University of Chicago Press.

Edelman, M.

1972   *Mass arousal and quiescence.* Chicago, Illinois: Markham.

Fainstein, N. and S. S. Fainstein.

1972   Innovation in urban bureaucracies: Clients and change. *American Behavioral Scientist* **15,** (March/April), 511–531.

Freeman, A. M. III and R. H. Haveman

1973   Clean rhetoric and dirty water: The failure of federal water pollution control policy. In *The political economy of federal policy,* edited by R. H. Haveman and R. D. Hamrin. Pp. 198–208. New York: Harper.

Ginsberg, E., *et al.*

1971   *Urban Health Services.* New York: Columbia Univ. Press.

Roemer, R., J. E. Frink, and C. Kramer.

1971   Environmental health services: Multiplicity of jurisdictions and comprehensive environmental management, *Milbank Memorial Fund Quarterly* **ILIX,** No. 4, Pt. 1, 419–507.

Rosen, S. N.

1971   Change and resistance to change, *Social Policy* **1,** 3–4.

Schuessler, K.

1970   Items, *American Sociological Review* **35,** immediately preceding p. 1.

Turk, H.

1970   Interorganizational networks in urban society, *American Sociological Review* **35,** 1–19.

EDITORS' NOTE: In granting permission to reprint parts of his article, Professor Herman Turk kindly supplied us with a statement giving his reaction to Alford's analysis, and suggested at the same time that Alford's manuscript be modified in the light of these reactions. Because typesetting was quite advanced when this request reached us, we were unable to accede to it, although we did not consider it to be unreasonable. We would like here to take note of Turk's essential points, to wit:

1. that in the article in question he was primarily concerned with developing an interorganizational approach to comparative social research;
2. that he did take into account both conflict and consensus perspectives;
3. that he deliberately refrained from drawing policy implications because his concern was in developing sociology rather than policy;
4. that, while he did emphasize integration, he did not neglect organizational cleavages, fragmentation, elitism, alienation and tokenism.

Professor Turk's critical reactions were not unanticipated, since we fully expected that some authors would dissent to a greater or lesser extent from the appraisal of their work in this volume. We trust that those authors will make their views known in the sociological journals and thereby contribute to a public dialogue on social policy and sociology.

Race Relations:
Some Policy Implications,
Proximate and Remote,
of a Negative Finding

HOWARD SCHUMAN

University of Michigan

The several national commissions established during the last decade provided occasions for social scientists to become involved in re- search on broad but immediate questions of policy. Whatever one may think of the motivations that led to such commissions, or the consequences or lack of consequences flowing from them, each com- mission encouraged, supported, and published social research on major issues. In the present paper, I consider a simple but important finding reported in several independent studies carried out for the National Advisory Commission on Civil Disorders in 1968. (See both main *Re- port* and *Supplemental Studies*, 1968a and 1968b, respectively.)

When the Civil Disorders Commission was created in the wake of the 1967 urban riots, there were two different popular assumptions about the participants in the rioting, quite apart from the possibility that they represented an organized conspiracy. One assumption was that the riots were a temporary aberration of the black lumpen-proletariat: the unemployable unemployed, criminal elements, deviants, rootless gangs. As several writers have since pointed out, this "riff raff" theory reflects the classic perception of riots held by most middle-class observers, and frequently becomes the official explanation put forward by "riot commissions." The second assumption about the riots also takes account of the socioeconomic status hierarchy, but its emphasis is different. This second assumption or explanation focuses on the unemployed but not necessarily unemployable, on underemployed and low-income families generally, and more broadly on all those who live at poverty levels in inadequate housing in poor neighborhoods in central cities. Whereas the first explanation is basically a "conservative" one, which characterizes riots as an outburst by a marginal and unrepresentative portion of the black community, the second explanation is a "liberal" one, directing attention to the economic deprivations of the large black lower class in the nation's central cities. The two explanations share one basic premise: the origins and nature of the riots—and of black unrest more generally—are closely connected to the major dimensions of conventional socioeconomic status. Although the cutting points on these dimensions are placed at quite different locations by the two theories, both lead to the expectation that riot participation will occur disproportionately at low socioeconomic levels.

Perhaps the most important finding to come out of the research sponsored by the Commission was the negligible relationship between riot participation and standard measures of socioeconomic status.[1] This finding—or nonfinding—has implications for government policy, for social science research, and for informed citizens generally. Moreover, these implications extend beyond the identification of "riot participants" as such, and concern the nature of racial dissatisfaction in America more generally. Although the implications are by no means entirely clear, they deserve a more careful examination in terms of policy than they have thus far received.

In this paper, to facilitate matters, I focus on a sample survey of blacks in the riot areas of Detroit and Newark, analyzed for the Commission by Caplan and Paige (1968: 73–76, and accompanying footnotes). There were of course many problems in locating and identifying riot participants, problems which we cannot go into here, but the convergence between these survey results and other sources of data

---

[1] Actually the finding was first reported in several analyses of data from the 1965 Watts riot area, but the formal publication of these results did not occur until after the Commission's Report. See Cohen 1970.

(noted later) suggests that they are probably valid. That riot participation was by no means a random action in terms of social characteristics is indicated by relatively strong associations between that activity and both age and sex: riot participation was predominantly an activity of younger males. But the relationship between income and active involvement in the riot was essentially zero, with one important exception which we will note below. With regard to education, rioters, if anything, had slightly more years of schooling on the average than nonrioters. The evidence on unemployment and on occupational level was somewhat more in accord with popular expectation, but the relationships are too slight to make either one an important explanatory variable. In sum, objective dimensions of socioeconomic status did not prove to be crucial factors in riot involvement.

These findings from cross-section interview surveys are generally supported by other Commission reports. Fogelson and Hill's (1968) analysis of police records of those arrested during riots indicates slightly stronger relations between riot participation and both unemployment and skill level, but the associations are still surprisingly small. (Arrestee data also appear in the main volume of the Commission's Report.) For the six cities on which the authors present data, the median percentage of arrestees in white-collar and skilled jobs combined is 20%, as against an estimated median percentage of 25% for all riot area residents. Without further controls for age and other relevant variables, one will not wish to attach too much significance to this comparison; but it does appear that riot arrestees are not sharply distinctive in broad occupational level.

We may also note two other findings, cited elsewhere in the National Advisory Commission's Report, that support the aforesaid lack of relationship between riot participation and socioeconomic background. First, 1960 census data on 20 riot cities show that blacks living in "disorder areas" (defined in terms of census tracts) did not in the aggregate differ systematically in 1960 in income and education from blacks in other areas of the city (National Advisory Commission on Civil Disorders 1968a: 348–358). (It will be useful to reconstruct these tabulations using 1970 tract data as they become available.) Thus riot *areas* do not constitute particularly depressed parts of cities when only the black population is examined, although there are differences by area for whites. Second, an attitude survey, also published by the Commission (in its *Supplemental Studies*), is consistent with these results in its finding that black attitudes toward integration, separatism, and the use of violence generally are essentially unrelated to educational level and other objective socioeconomic status (SES) indicators.[2]

Summarizing these several results: the main finding is that the association between objective dimensions of socioeconomic status and riot participation is much smaller than expected in terms of *either* of the two popular theories about riot participants. And to the extent that riot behavior is an indicator of broader racial attitudes among blacks—as it seems to be from other evidence in the National Commission's Report—socioeconomic status must be viewed as a relatively unimportant determinant of black *racial* orientations. Looked at another way, racial attitudes and behavior of the kinds frequently labeled "militant" must be primarily a result of factors other than ordinary variations in socioeconomic status.

There is one important qualification to this conclusion that requires mention at this point. In their analysis, Caplan and Paige identified in Detroit a group of "counter-rioters" (persons who actively opposed the rioting), and such persons did in fact differ noticeably in income and education from the rest of the black population. Thus, although counter-rioters constituted only 16% of the Detroit sample, they made up nearly one-half of the respondents reporting incomes of over $10,000.[3] This suggests a first policy-related point: If reducing racial tension is an important goal of social and economic policies, then these policies must be aimed at much more than subsistence levels of living. There is little evidence that small increments in income or occupation are likely to have much effect on black sentiments about the justice of their position in American society. Employment as such seems to make some difference, but it is not the creation of a black working class, but of a substantial black middle class—at least in terms of income—that is needed. How this can be done rapidly in personal and political terms is a large and open question, but these studies tell us that it is the necessary direction insofar as socioeconomic status is involved. A concern with simply raising income levels along a continuous scale must be amended to include a target of substantial elevation above a rather high income level.

In any case, the traditional liberal assumption that deprivation as

[2] The present writer is one of the authors of this last report, which is mentioned in passing to round out the evidence. Later analysis of these data suggests some curvilinearity in the relationship between education and black racial attitudes, but reaffirms the basic finding that the over-all relationship is slight, especially so to income and occupation. New data gathered in 1971 also support the original analysis.

[3] Unfortunately an age control is not reported for the results, but it seems unlikely from other internal evidence that age created a spurious association here.

such, whether relative or absolute, is an important factor in black *racial* dissatisfaction must be called into serious question. This is not intended to discourage attempts to reduce unemployment or to increase levels of welfare support, for such efforts have justifications other than the prevention of racial hostility. It is rather to question the wisdom of rationalizing ordinary employment and welfare measures on racial grounds. If economic measures are to serve as supporters of social stability, they must be designed to produce something much closer to affluence for blacks—as indeed has happened of late for many previously marginal white working-class families.

The Caplan and Paige findings, and those of similar studies, also point to the crucial importance of the race-related perceptions and attitudes held by blacks, as distinct from the objective socioeconomic status of blacks. Riot participants differed from nonparticipants on a number of such variables, for example, "hatred of whites" and distrust of politicians. Such attitudinal differences are much sharper than differences in terms of socioeconomic variables (excepting age), even though the dependent variable (reported riot participation) is a quasi-behavior rather than the more usual type of attitude measure. There was and is clear evidence of rising tide of black consciousness and an increasingly open resentment against white attitudes and white dominance. This will hardly come as news to many, but to some social scientists it may seem theoretically surprising that beliefs and attitudes as such are of central importance.

Around 1960 sociology moved toward a renewed emphasis on "action" as distinct from "attitude." The desegregation of the Army during the 1950s, along with several other similar events, overimpressed sociologists with the degree to which apparent social change could be created quickly in this social sphere by forceful administrative decision and action. Attitudes came to be regarded as unimportant consequences of situations, and white racial attitudes in particular were treated as relatively insignificant epiphenomena. Although the argument contained an important truth, it ignored the long-term effects of white attitudinal resistance, as registered later in geographic movement from the central cities and in emerging voting patterns. More to the present point, it ignored the extent to which even in situations of apparent status equality, e.g., on college campuses, black perceptions of subtle racial attitudes play an important role. Although occasionally black spokesmen join white sociologists in asserting that what is important is only white action (i.e., discrimination or nondiscrimination), not white "attitudes," it is doubtful that this is actually the case. We are now speculating rather indirectly and at some distance from the Commission's empirical findings, but the absence of continuous effects by SES variables, plus the importance of the atti-tude–participation relationship and of other findings on black beliefs, suggests that black perceptions of white attitudes are fully as crucial to American race relations as are any objective status factors.

We have now reviewed two specific policy-related implications of the main Commission findings. Both challenge the assumption that economic factors *as usually viewed* are major sources of black racial dissatisfaction in America. More subtle factors having to do with self-perceived social status and social equality seem to carry more weight as determinants of black racial sentiments and actions. Beyond these specific implications—which are of course far from "proven"—the studies we have considered raise three more general questions about the relation of research to "policy" in the area of race relations, and more generally in sociology.

First, the major finding discussed here has been the *absence* of a relationship where one was expected. This seems to be typical of much social research: one fails to confirm relationships which are widely assumed on the basis of common sense or traditional belief. Coleman's findings on the impact of school quality on verbal ability provide a classic example, and the recent challenges by Rosenberg and Simmons (1972) and McCarthy and Yancey (1971) of long-held assump-tions about black self-esteem constitute an important new example. Sociologists seem to be better in, or at least more useful for, discon-firming presumed important facts and relationships than in discover-ing new ones or even confirming old ones. Perhaps this simply repre-sents the primitive state of the discipline, and once we have cleared away the underbrush we will move rapidly toward more positive policy-related findings. Better measurement of better defined and more relevant social variables may well be the key. But another possibility is that social reality is almost always much more complicated than we expect, and that whenever we focus on a simple explanation of a complex social process our results are likely to prove disappointing. By this token, sociology will usually be better at bursting balloons than at launching rockets.

Whatever the answer to the question just posed, if indeed there is any *general* answer, its consideration does emphasize the present gap between research findings and policy decisions. When one adds to the fragmentary, negative, and uncertain nature of many sociological findings the serious problems of external validity—generalizability be-yond the immediate research context—we are warned not to mistake good policy-relevant research for "social engineering." The latter assumes that research findings can be not merely relevant to, but directly translatable into, policy decisions. That assumption is certainly false, and both the sophisticated social scientist and the wise policymaker must distinguish between the genuine relevance of much research and the simplistic application of it. The danger of oversimplification is particularly great where one's research conclusions are largely "residual"—based on what is supposedly left after rejecting one or more independent variables as significant. Conversion of unexplained variance into policy-related theory and application is fraught with danger. Indeed this paper may already have gone too far out on such an imaginary limb.

Finally, the results reported here, along with some others that have or could be cited, suggest that there is still much to learn from research that is relevant to policy in the area of race relations. This point is not always appreciated. Because of the large amount of research that has been carried out in this area, and the frustrations of many who seek rapid social change, it is not uncommon to hear, "We already know the answers, what we need is action." While sympathizing with the desire for change, and aware of the vast, although uneven, literature that already falls somewhere under the rubric of "race relations," this writer believes that our ignorance and misunderstanding of racial processes, movements, and sentiments greatly exceed our knowledge and comprehension. There are very difficult practical and political problems here—not the least of which is that of sometimes having white social scientists study black citizens—but if sociology and sociologist are not willing to defend the importance of research in this area, our future policy-related conclusions will be not merely irrelevant, but wrong. And since social research requires both financial and social support, let this paper end by stressing the importance of intrepid policy decisions to the future of fruitful research on race relations.

REFERENCES

Caplan, N. and J. Paige
  1968   An analysis of a sample survey of blacks in the riot areas of Detroit and Newark. In *Report, National Advisory Commission on Civil Disorders.* Pp. 73–76. Washington, D.C.: U.S. Government Printing Office. (Reprinted by Bantam Books.)
Cohen, N. (Editor)
  1970   *The Los Angeles riots: A socio-psychological study.* New York: Praeger.

Fogelson, R. and R. Hill
   1968   Who riots? A study of participants in the 1967 riots. In *National Advisory Commission on Civil Disorders, Supplemental Studies*. Washington, D.C.: U.S. Government Printing Office.
McCarthy, J. D. and W. L. Yancey
   1971   Uncle Tom and Mr. Charlie: Metaphysical pathos in the study of racism and personal disorganization, *American Journal of Sociology* **76**, 648–672.
National Advisory Commission on Civil Disorders
   1968a   *Report of the National Advisory Commission on civil disorders*. Washington, D.C.: U.S. Government Printing Office. (Reprinted by Bantam Books.)
   1968b   *Supplemental studies*. Washington, D.C.: U.S. Government Printing Office. (Reprinted by Praeger.)
Rosenberg, M. and R. G. Simmons
   1972   *Black and white self-esteem: The urban school child*. Washington, D.C.: American Sociological Association. (M. Arnold and Caroline Rose Monograph series.)

Policy Change and Grassroots Inertia:
The Case of Metropolitan Services

JOHN D. KASARDA[1]

Florida Atlantic University

For nearly 50 years advocates of metropolitan reform have been arguing that the major dilemma facing urban America is the maze of heterogeneous and overlapping governments operating within single metropolitan areas (cf. Anderson and Weidner 1925; Advisory Commission on Intergovernmental Relations 1962; Fiser 1962; Friesema 1966; Greer 1961, 1962; Gulick 1962; Hawley 1950, 1971; McKenzie 1933; Wood 1961). The reform movement traditionally has viewed the metropolitan area as one large community that is socially and economically integrated but artificially fragmented into a plethora of separate political jurisdictions (Ostrom 1972).[2] Such balkanization is said to be the cause of public service inefficiencies, conflicts of authority, and administrative impotence in dealing with many urban problems which have become metropolitan in scope.

Metropolitan reformers further contend that urban expansion in absence of political reorganization is mainly responsible for the service–

[1] Affiliation at time of Conference: The University of Chicago.

[2] In 1967, over 20,000 local governments were operating within the 227 Standard Metropolitan Statistical Areas delimited by the Bureau of the Census (U.S. Bureau of the Census 1968).

resource crisis that many central cities are now experiencing. Their argument rests on two well-known factors: (1) The selective outmigration of wealthier individuals and commercial and industrial establishments to the suburban rings has substantially diminished the municipal tax base. (2) Municipal services, many of which serve a large number of suburban commuters who make daily use of the central city, continue to be financed by central city governments. As a result, an increasing number of public services must be provided by central cities while their fiscal ability to support these services is diminishing. The problem, according to metropolitan reformers, is not insufficient urban resources to maintain city services but the fact that ecological expansion has redistributed a large portion of the metropolitan fiscal base beyond the taxing jurisdiction of central cities.

Given this orientation to the metropolitan malady, the solution appears commonsensical: consolidate the numerous suburban jurisdictions with the central city in the form of a metropolitan-wide government. Metropolitan reformers steadfastly maintain, despite lacking clear evidence, that consolidation would not only more equitably distribute the fiscal burden for urban services throughout the metropolitan area but also create economies of scale and provide higher quality services for suburban communities.

The majority of metropolitan residents, however, seem not to be pursuaded by the arguments of the reform movement. Proposals for "metro" governments since 1945 have suffered many more voter defeats than victories. Those cases where consolidation referenda were successful have been found to owe more to unique conditions within the metropolis than to common popular sentiments or grass-roots appeal (Marando and Whitely 1972).

THE HAWLEY–ZIMMER STUDY

Convinced that metropolitan reform is a necessary condition to solving contemporary urban problems, Hawley and Zimmer carried out an extensive survey to determine the nature of people's resistance to governmental consolidation in metropolitan areas. Personal interviews were conducted with a probability sample of nearly 3000 residents and 630 public officials in central city and suburb rings of six metropolitan areas: Buffalo, New York; Rochester, New York; Dayton, Ohio; Saginaw, Michigan; Rockford, Illinois; and Milwaukee, Wisconsin. The results of the survey are presented in their research monograph (Hawley and Zimmer 1970).

The Hawley and Zimmer study began with two working assumptions: (1) Metropolitan residents are of the opinion that public services are inadequate in suburban areas. (2) Suburban residents are strongly opposed to solving metropolitan service problems by consolidating their governments with the central city. Both of these working assumptions received unequivocal support from the data. The results of the survey further showed that resistance to consolidation is not confined to suburban residents and their officials. Only 40% of the central city residents felt that either annexation or unification is the best possible solution to metropolitan service problems, compared to approximately 25% of the suburban residents who favored one of these proposals.

The roots of citizen resitance to governmental unification were found to lie in their belief that the sheer creation of large-scale administrative units will not insure effective organization, governmental responsibility, or legitimate representation. On the contrary, the majority of citizens felt that metropolitan consolidation would result in excessive centralization of political power, loss of community identity, and high taxes, without a concomitant improvement in the quality of public services. Hawley and Zimmer point out (although no statistics are provided) that most of those metropolitan residents in favor of governmental unification believe that the present fragmented structure is too costly to operate.

The adequacy of public services provided in suburban areas also was found to influence citizen opinion toward governmental unification. Respondents in smaller suburban zones with fewer public services were more ready to accept consolidation with central cities. Yet, in those suburban areas with the least adequate public services, not more than 40% of the residents approved of consolidating their political units with the central city. Another related finding was that nearly 70% of suburban residents receiving the poorest public services expressed general satisfaction with the services provided them. In suburban zones receiving slightly better public services, approximately 80% of the residents were generally satisfied with their services. Apparently, suburban residents do not expect high quality services, nor are they concerned about receiving additional public services from their jurisdictions—an assumption upon which many consolidation campaigns to date have been based.

Another finding that emerged from the survey is the lack of citizen knowledge and discussion of metropolitan-wide service problems. No more than 31% of the respondents had ever discussed these problems at public meetings, voluntary associations, or informally among friends or neighbors. Hawley and Zimmer note, however, that respondents who indicated that they had discussed metropolitan service problems were more inclined to be in favor of unification than those who had never discussed the problems.

Critique

A number of methodological and substantive shortcomings of the Hawley and Zimmer study detract from its findings and over-all contribution to public policy. First, the sample of metropolitan areas chosen for analysis was highly selective and not representative of many of the metropolitan areas in this country. Baffalo, Rochester, Milwaukee, Dayton, Saginaw, and Rockford share a common history and are located in a band of structurally similar states extending from the mid-East to the upper mid-West. All have predominantly older, industrialized central cities surrounded by numerous, well-established, incorporated suburban municipalities—conditions which inhibit widespread consolidation.

It is not fortuitous that eight of the nine successful city–county consolidations since 1945 have occurred in the South, where most metropolitan areas differ in both ecological and political organization from those included in the Hawley and Zimmer study.[3] Comparative analysis of the ecological structure, political conditions, and attitudes of residents in one or two of the successfully consolidated areas would have increased the usefulness of their study. Hawley and Zimmer evidently overlooked the fact that uncovering the social concomitants of program success is at least as beneficial to policy-makers as determining the factors associated with program failure.

Hawley and Zimmer also may be critized methodologically for their procedure of aggregating the diverse groups of suburban communities into one "suburban ring" category and computing summary percentages. Aggregation of this nature tends to obscure important relationships more than it clarifies them. It seems likely, for instance, that

[3] The nine successful city–county consolidations (and dates of voter approval) include Baton Rouge–East Baton Rouge Parish, La. (1949); Hampton–Elizabeth County, Va. (1952); Newport News–Warwick, Va. (1958); Nashville–Davidson County, Tenn. (1962); South Norfolk–Norfolk County, Va. (1962); Virginia Beach–Princess Anne County, Va. (1962); Jacksonville–Duval County, Fla. (1967); Carson City–Ormsby County, Nev. (1969); Columbus–Muscogee County, Ga. (1970). N.B.: The Miami–Dade County, Fla. reorganization (1956) resulted from a state-wide election; and the Indianapolis–Marion County, Indiana reorganization (1971), by an enactment of the Indiana state legislature.

residents of high-income dormitory suburbs would express different opinions regarding unification from those residing in blue-collar industrial suburbs, and that both groups would have different opinions from residents in the unincorporated suburban fringe. Similarly, residents of inner city ghettos may hold varying opinions from other central city residents concerning the need for metropolitan consolidation. Most of these differences are masked by the somewhat crude central city–suburban ring dichotomy utilized throughout the study.

Regarding the substantive orientation of the survey, one receives the impression that it was aimed more at superficial opinions than at deep attitudes. For example, the sensitive issues of racial attitudes among metropolitan residents and vested interests of local public officials were virtually ignored. Moreover, Hawley and Zimmer hold specific policy views which continually emerged in their analysis, and most of their findings seemed to fit their own preconceptions. In short, it is questionable if the study told planners and officials very much about citizen resistance to consolidation that they did not already know.

Policy Implications

Nevertheless, the Hawley and Zimmer study does provide information that has implications for future public policy. First, the study indicates that proposals for governmental unification are likely to continue to meet stiff resistance from metropolitan residents. Citizen antagonism toward governmental consolidation appears to be so strong at present that it is unrealistic to believe that referenda for metropolitan government will succeed in more than a few cases. Therefore, if political reorganization is to be achieved in most metropolitan areas, it will have to be brought about by federal or state intervention. Federal and state governments could exert pressure on local communities to consolidate by withholding subsidies for public services and providing financial incentives to those areas that do reorganize. Or, they can do so by fiat, as essentially was done by the Canadian government in the wholesale consolidation of metropolitan Toronto.

A second implication of the study is that if citizen antagonism toward consolidation is to be mitigated, extensive efforts will have to be made to make metropolitan residents more aware of the problems and inefficiencies engendered by their fragmented structures. To paraphrase Hawley and Zimmer, whether citizens regard their present governmental units as uneconomic or inefficient in providing public services might well be the most important factor in their receptiveness to the notion of one comprehensive jurisdictional unit. Civic and community groups interested in bringing about metropolitan reorganization should utilize heavily the mass media to inform metropolitan residents of the disadvantages of governmental fragmentation. Moreover, metropolitan service problems should be frequently and openly discussed at community meetings, in schools, and at public forums. It is important, though, that these campaigns do not place primary emphasis, as they have in the past, on possible improved service benefits to suburban residents. The Hawley and Zimmer findings imply that additional or higher quality public services are not desired by a majority of suburban residents. Perhaps the campaigns should focus more on convincing residents of tax savings they will receive while maintaining current public service levels.

Assuming that citizen acceptance of consolidation in most metropolitan areas is unlikely, a third and obvious implication is that alternative mechanisms must be developed to meet the growing metropolitan service needs. Among these could be the creation of special service and taxing district that would be metropolitan in scope.[4] A two-level governmental arrangement could be instituted in metropolitan areas with one level in charge of services that are difficult to satisfactorily provide on a local basis such as mass transit, water supply, and pollution control. The second level would consist of the present jurisdictions and provide services that are more local in nature, such as police and fire protection, garbage collection, and library facilities. With this arrangement, local identity would be preserved and decisions affecting local affairs would largely remain with the individual jurisdictions.

Another alternative mechanism which would preserve local identity and insure individual jurisdictional representation would be the formation of a metropolitan service commission in each metropolitan area. The commission would consist of elected officials and representatives of local governments and would be responsible for both regional planning and administering needed services which could not be effectively provided at the local level. In addition, the commission would serve as an agency to reconcile intergovernmental disputes

---

[4] I would like to note that the alternatives to consolidation presented herein are not original but were influenced by my reading of publications addressing metropolitan reform including, among others, Bollens and Schmandt 1970; Committee on Economic Development 1970; Fiser 1962; Greer 1962, Gulick 1957, 1962; Kirkpatrick and Morgan 1971; Marando and Whitely 1972; Ostrom 1972; Wood 1959; and Zimmerman 1970.

and foster cooperative service arrangements among local jurisdictions.

A third alternative to massive governmental reorganization would be for federal and state governments to assume greater responsibility in the provision of needed urban services. A federal or state office of metropolitan affairs would be established in each metropolitan area with the functions of aiding and coordinating efforts of local governments to meet their service requirements. These offices, financed by federal or state funds, would gather data on local resources and service needs, formulate plans and programs to meet those needs, and work closely with local jurisdictions to help them solve their service problems.

A fourth mechanism for dealing with growing urban service needs and shrinking resource bases would be the extension of federal and state grant-in-aids to local jurisdictions and revenue sharing programs. Since this laissez-faire approach would not require any changes in the structure or functioning of the local units, it may be inferred from the Hawley and Zimmer survey that metropolitan residents would find this the most acceptable of the four alternatives discussed herein. However, this approach would do little to mitigate the basic metropolitan problems of fragmented authority and responsibility, inefficient and ineffective use of tax monies, and arbitrary political barriers which block coordinated approaches to solving the growing problems of metropolitan living.

The Impact of the Hawley and Zimmer Study

In assessing the policy impact of Hawley and Zimmer's study, it may be said that this study and other converging empirical analyses of the metropolis are leading to a reassessment of planned social change in the public sector. The emphasis on advocating schemes for massive restructuring of metropolitan government or for wholesale consolidation is declining. Instead, such plans are giving way to more moderate proposals (such as those mentioned earlier) which balance the needs of the metropolitan area with the perceived interests of the local residents.[5] This is not to imply that extensive government reorganization is not required to deal adequately with metropolitan service problems, but that the social realities as evidenced in the Hawley and

---

[5] For example, much more attention is now being given to citizens' attitudes and fears of becoming alienated from their governments if centralization occurs in the metropolis (Lyons 1972).

Zimmer study preclude the successful implementation of such a policy in most urban areas.

The Hawley and Zimmer study is also having an impact on the recommendations currently being received by the Department of Housing and Urban Development (HUD) for its use in helping inner cities and surrounding towns meet their service needs. More specifically, HUD has commissioned the National Academy of Sciences–National Research Council to develop a series of working papers dealing with the viability of the local community in the metropolitan context. A number of authors of these papers are drawing on the Hawley–Zimmer findings in making their policy recommendations to HUD. No doubt other researchers and practitioners are also beginning to draw on the Hawley and Zimmer findings in formulating their own proposals for more effective metropolitan structures (cf. Marando and Whitely 1972).

MODIFICATIONS IN GRADUATE TRAINING

Having briefly discussed the metropolitan service problem and a recent bit of policy-related research, let us now address the broader question of changes required in our graduate training programs if sociological research is to have a greater influence on social policy in the future.

At present, a majority of graduate training programs in sociology appear to rest on the premise that, regardless of eventual subdisciplinary specialization, a broad theoretical perspective should be acquired by all candidates for advanced degrees. Moreover, a fundamental methodological and statistical techniques are generally emphasized so that candidates will be better able to empirically ground and evaluate sociological theory and carry out basic research. What is often lacking in training programs (and the discipline) is an emphasis on bringing about an interface of theoretical development and empirical research with social policy. Assuming that this is a desired goal, it is possible to suggest a number of specific modifications which could be made in graduate training programs that might promote a more fruitful relationship between sociological theory, research, and social policy.

First, it is suggested that along with a continuing emphasis on developing fundamental theoretical and methodological skills, during the initial year of training, a two-course sequence be offered by graduate faculty to more advanced students dealing specifically with the interface of theory, research, and social policy. The initial course would provide students with a brief overview of the contribution and possible negative impact that social research has had on public policy and discuss means by which the skills, knowledge, and technique of sociologists could be mobilized so as to produce more fruitful public policy. The first course could also provide students with an introduction to what have come to be called "social indicators" and their utility for measuring social processes and evaluating the impact of action programs.

In the second course, each student would select a practical problem of interest and present a short paper outlining a research scheme for diagnosing *and* treating the problem. The student would be expected to draw on his prior theoretical and methodological training in formulating his research strategy. Through this exercise, it is hoped that the student would obtain early and beneficial experience in relating his developing professional skills to practical problems facing society.

Next, it is recommended that sociology departments develop closer working relationships with other social science departments and co-sponsor interdisciplinary workshops on issues of social policy. Most policy issues have numerous dimenions (e.g., social, economic, political, etc.) which should be viewed conjunctively if realistic implication for social policy are to result. The interdisciplinary workshops would likely provide a forum through which graduate students and faculty of various disciplines could interact on particular issues to identify critical problems, evaluate means of social intervention, and assess the probability of achieving given objectives through specific programs of action. The problem of metropolitan services, for example, is an issue where sociologists, economists, and political scientists could more fruitfully collaborate to advance policy-relevant knowledge.

Finally, it is suggested that universities and institutes provide advanced graduate students with the opportunity to participate in a 1-year research internship with public or private institutes that deal primarily with policy-related issues. This in-service training would be underwritten by federal or foundation grants and by the institutes themselves. Active participation in policy-oriented agencies would expose graduate students to a research environment not often available in the classroom setting and would undoubtedly provide them with a greater awareness of the practical problems involved in policy formulation and program action.

REFERENCES

Advisory Commission on Intergovernmental Relations
  1962 *Alternative approaches to governmental reorganization in metropolitan areas.* Washington, D.C.: Government Printing Office.
Anderson, W. and E. W. Weidner
  1925 *American city government.* New York: Holt.
Bollens, J. C. and H. J. Schmandt
  1970 *The metropolis: Its people, politics and economic life* (2nd ed.). New York: Harper.
Committee for Economic Development
  1970 *Reshaping government in metropolitan areas.* New York: Committee for Economic Development.
Fiser, W. S.
  1962 *Mastery of the metropolis.* Englewood Cliffs, New Jersey: Prentice-Hall.
Friesema, H. P.
  1966 The metropolis and the maze of local government, *Urban Affairs Quarterly* **2,** 68–90.
Greer, S.
  1961 Dilemmas of action research on the metropolitan problem. In *Community political systems,* edited by Morris Janowitz. Glencoe, Illinois: The Free Press.
  1962 *Governing the metropolis.* New York: Wiley.
Gulick, L. H.
  1957 Metropolitan organization, *The Annals of the American Academy of Political and Social Science* **314,** 57–65.
  1962 *The metropolitan problem and American ideas.* New York: Alfred A. Knopf.
Hawley, A. H.
  1950 *Human ecology: A theory of community structure.* New York: Ronald Press.
  1971 *Urban society: An ecological approach.* New York: Ronald Press.
Hawley, A. H. and B. Zimmer
  1970 *The metropolitan community: Its people and government.* Beverly Hills, California: Sage Publications.
Kirkpatrick, S. A. and D. R. Morgan
  1971 Policy support and orientations toward metropolitan reform, *Social Science Quarterly* **52,** 659–671.
Lyons, S. R.
  1972 *Citizen attitudes and metropolitan government.* Chapel Hill, North Carolina. Univ. of North Carolina Institute for Urban Studies and Community Service.
Marando, V. L. and C. R. Whitely
  1972 City–county consolidation: An overview of voter response, *Urban Affairs Quarterly* **8,** 181–203.
McKenzie, R. D.
  1933 *The metropolitan community.* New York: McGraw-Hill.
Ostrom, E.
  1972 Metropolitan reform: Propositions derived from two traditions, *Social Science Quarterly* **53,** 474–493.
U.S. Bureau of the Census
  1968 *Governmental organization: Census of governments, 1967.* Washington, D.C.: U.S. Government Printing Office.

Wood, R. C.
   1959   *Metropolis against itself.* New York: Committee for Economic Development.
   1961   *1400 governments: The political economy of the New York metropolitan re-
          gion.* Cambridge, Massachusetts: Harvard Univ. Press.
Zimmerman, J. F.
   1970   Metropolitan reform in the U.S.: An overview, *Public Administration Review*
          30, 531–543.

Formal Models as a Guide to Social Policy: Issues in Population Dynamics

SAMUEL H. PRESTON

University of Washington, Seattle

Demography has a growing subdiscipline known as "population policy," with its own sessions at annual meetings, separate sections in compendia and bibliographies, and an increasingly specialized group of scholars. This field has grown in response to public concern about the consequences of continued American population growth, and in particular to the immediate scholarly demands of the President's Commission on Population and the American Future. Demography is undoubtedly one of the fields in sociology where policy considerations have received their most explicit treatment.

I choose not to examine a piece of work readily identified as population policy per se, in part because it makes the present task too easy, in part because the recent report of the U.S. President's Commission (1972) has already picked over the field, and in part because of a conviction that most important policy advances are dependent upon the careful preliminary work of scientists whose major concern is simply to straighten things out—to understand the nature of phenomena. I will attempt to show the policy relevance of one type of such basic research, and in the process touch upon several influential works in American population policy.

I shall focus on formal models of the birth process that were initially developed in order to identify determinants of fertility levels and variations in preindustrial populations. What started as a historical inquiry (much of its method being borrowed from mathematical statistics) has produced important implications for modern American demography. These developments have forced fertility analysis to attend more carefully to the timing of births during the life cycle of a woman. The models of interest are admirably summarized by Keyfitz (1972). It is a restatement and partial translation into layman's terms of major developments in modeling the birth process during the previous decade. The subject matter may be conveniently divided into two parts: (1) the dynamics of birth intervals once regularized sexual intercourse is initiated, which is stressed by Keyfitz; and (2) the dynamics surrounding its initiation.

DYNAMICS OF BIRTH INTERVALS

The results of birth-interval analysis may be simply stated. The interval between successive births is composed of several qualitative different subintervals: the period of pregnancy itself; the period of postpartum sterility or subfecundity, extensible to as much as 3 years by prolonged breastfeeding; and the period of exposure to the risk of additional pregnancy. The length of this latter period is appropriately viewed as the result of a stochastic process, with some specified monthly probability of conception. Because contraception affects only the length of the latter period, variations in contraceptive failure rates have much less than proportional effects on birth intervals. Since the birth rate is the reciprocal of the mean interbirth interval for women who have had their first child, the effects on the birth rate are likewise less than proportional. Depending upon the specific parameters, it may be necessary to practice birth control with five times the current effectiveness (e.g., by reducing the monthly chance of conception from .15 to .03) in order to reduce the birth rate by one-half. Likewise, an abortion preceding each live birth does not reduce the birth rate by one-half, because the abortion does not use up as much of the interbirth interval as a live birth. Both the pregnancy and the period of postpartum sterility are shorter for an abortion, particularly so if the live-born child would have been breast-fed.

What are the policy consequences of studying components of the birth interval and viewing conception as a probabilistic process? One of the contributions is clarification of some issues in the acerbic debate that has developed between advocates of family planning programs and advocates of social structural or motivational changes as methods of reducing U.S. fertility levels. By properly specifying the nature of the birth process, the models to which I referred give added force to *both* sides of the issue, while blunting many of the extreme positions that have been adopted. This dual reinforcement is possible only if the different approaches to fertility reduction are viewed as complements rather than as alternatives.

In the first place, such models focus attention on the physiological act of contraception itself. Estimates of failure rates of contraceptive techniques in contemporary American usage range from 35–38/100 woman-years of exposure for rhythm or douche to 1–3/100 for the pill or IUD's (Tietze 1964). Supposing a woman's active reproductive life to consist of 25 years with 12 cycles each year, and assuming a period of 15 cycles of sterility associated with pregnancy, a continuous and exclusive user of douche would produce, on average, approximately 6.4 births by the end of her reproductive period. A user of the IUD, on the other hand, would produce .7 births. These numbers are remarkable both for their size and their difference. The great variation in birth rates that can be produced by changes in the form of contraception fortifies arguments in favor of the development and distribution of effective, acceptable, and inexpensive methods of fertility control. Opponents have argued that family planning is not the answer to population growth (Blake 1972) since our growth rate remains unacceptably high despite the fact that virtually every married couple in America has used some form of contraception. Such reasoning overlooks the type of contraception used and the population's lack of complete accessibility to the most efficient means.

On the other hand, by demonstrating how very difficult it is to avert additional births, these models also emphasize the crucial role of motivation, both to reduce family size and to exercise the most effective contraception in this pursuit. It is well known that family-size desires in the U.S. and throughout most of the world are sufficiently high that long-run growth is inevitable even if all contraceptions were perfectly effective (Davis 1967). Bumpass and Westoff (1970) make a valuable contribution to estimating the amount of this intentional surplus by questioning American women whether each birth in a particular period was desired currently or at any future date. They increase the estimate of the proportion of births that were "unwanted" above those that had been based upon simply stated family-size "desires" or "ideals," which often involve rationalizations of previous mistakes. But even they uncover more than enough "wanted" births to produce long-run population growth.

Their calculations, which are reiterated by the President's Commission's report, indicate that the complete elimination of unwanted births in the 1960s would have removed roughly two-thirds of the fertility above the replacement level. Such calculations should be interpreted in light of models of birth intervals. They are potentially misleading because unwanted fertility is not going to be eliminated by contraception short of universal sterilization, and results for the ideal are not readily translated into predictions for the feasible. In the first place, any reduction in contraceptive failure rates to a level short of zero will produce less than proportionate reductions in unwanted births. Second, family-size desires will have to be well *below* the replacement level to produce replacement-level fertility, given the certainty of continued contracepting failures. If such desires were to evolve, the scope for unwanted fertility would increase, since women would have to practice efficient contraception for a longer period. Any absolute reduction of "unwanted" births under such circumstance would require an even greater level of contraceptive efficiency than is currently needed. What we basically require for policy decisions is knowledge of combinations of desired family size and contraceptive effectiveness that would yield some long-run growth target. By dealing only with the ideal, Bumpass and Westoff appear to minimize the importance of motivation.

We can summarize this discussion in the following way. In an experiment with up to 360 independent trials, and with a probability of success on each trial of approximately .2, radical intervention is required to keep the total number of successes down to 1 or 2. In the present case, such intervention must take the form of remarkably efficient contraception. To achieve this, couples must have access to the most effective means and be highly motivated to use them. Governmental policy must emphasize both the development and distribution of contraceptives and the modification of reproductive desires in such a way as to bring private decisions in line with social objectives.

Several specific policy corollaries follow from this type of analysis. First, in designing a fertility-reduction program, it is much more effective to induce 50% of the population to use 100% effective contraception than to induce 100% to use techniques that are 50% effective. Success in the former policy would reduce the birth rate by half (assuming the candidates to be randomly selected), whereas success in the latter would have only minor effects on the birth rate—surely altering it by less than 25%. Some concentration of governmental efforts is suggested on purely formal grounds. Second, in view of the likelihood that a considerable number of unwanted conceptions will continue in America, it is demographically desirable to have a backstop that allows these couples a second chance. Such a backstop is offered by legalized abortion. The only countries in recent decades that have achieved fertility below replacement levels for any substantial period are those where abortions are readily available. Although in the long run one abortion does not avert one live birth, Keyfitz demonstrates that the demographic effectiveness of abortion increases markedly as contraception is practiced more efficiently.

Finally, in evaluating the effects of governmental policies on fertility (especially in high-fertility populations), it is absolutely essential to recognize the nature of birth intervals. Small changes in birth rates may mask major changes in contraceptive behavior; moreover, if breast-feeding practices or subfecundity vary among sectors of a population, those sectors with larger changes in contraceptive behavior may produce smaller changes in birth rates. Conversely, alterations in birth rates may connote nothing about behavioral change but rather indicate compositional changes produced by past variations in parameters of birth intervals. For example, a major portion of the decline in fertility in Romania between 1967 and 1968 may plausibly be attributed to the legal restrictions on abortions imposed in 1966 (Sheps and Menken 1971).

Such models cannot claim credit for recent changes in American population policy, for instance, the repeal of the Comstock Act and the liberalization of abortion laws in several states. To the extent that demography played any role in these changes, its principal contribution was probably the identification of a "need" for family planning services on the part of large segments of the population. But receptivity to more technical and less obvious matters will probably increase as population policy moves beyond its initial stages.

AGE AT MARRIAGE

Thus far we have discussed only birth interval dynamics for women regularly exposed to sexual intercourse. But a second factor affecting birth rates is the proportion of women so exposed at any moment in time. In Western societies, the principal regulator of this exposure is age at marriage and proportions marrying. Although this form of control is not effective as in the past, it remains true that over two-thirds of unmarried girls aged 15 to 19 have never had intercourse, and that 90.3% of births in the United States in 1968 occurred to married couples (U.S. President's Commission 1972: 109 and U.S. Bureau of Census 1971: 44).

American marriage patterns are quite conducive to high fertility levels. Our average age at first marriage is lower than that of any other developed industrial country (U.S. President Commission 1972: 67). Delaying marriage could affect American fertility levels in several ways. (1) It might reduce the number of children born to a married couple, either by altering their desired family size or by reducing the length of the period in which effective contraception must be practiced after the desired family size is attained. (2) It would expose cohorts to attrition from death for a longer time before any particular stage of family-building is attained. This is a minor consideration, since mortality is so low during the family-building years. (3) As pointed out by Keyfitz, it would stretch out the mean length of generation. We can make this point with absolute assurance, thanks to simple mathematics. Any growth from one generation to the next will result in a lower annual rate of increase the longer the mean time between generations. Under present American conditions, a three-child family born to a woman in her early 20s would have the same growth consequences as a four-child family born to a woman in her late 20s. Merely stretching out the length of generation by 2.6 years—to the level in many European populations—would produce a 10% lower growth rate. Had our growth rate since 1800 been just 10% lower, we would now number approximately 144 million inhabitants, rather than 209 million, a reduction of 31% because of compounding (compiled from U.S. Bureau of Census, 1960:7 and U.S. Bureau of Census 1972:2).

Moreover, an important short-term bonus results from a shift toward later marriage. This bonus can be represented verbally as a "thinning-out" of births as one cohort passes a certain stage of family-building but is not immediately replaced by a succeeding cohort, which chooses instead to postpone that stage. This type of thinning-out may be largely responsible for the rapid decline in American fertility during the last decade and a half (Ryder 1970:114). Its converse, a "bunching-up" of marriages, stands out as the single most important factor in the U.S. baby boom during the immediate post-war period (Ryder 1970:112).

The policy implications of such studies, both formal and empirical, are obvious. A substantial reduction in birth rates would result if couples could be persuaded to postpone marriage. Governments have at times been convinced by such arguments and pursued measures to delay or prevent marriage. For example, various German states in the eighteenth and nineteenth centuries refused men marriage licenses until they reached age 30, and then permitted marriage only if the man could demonstrate that he had a job waiting (Langer 1963).

Such Draconian measures are unacceptable to Americans, and thus far government policy has not been motivated by arguments regarding the desirability of delaying marriage (which also extend to divorce and child health). The President's Commission's report will not prove helpful in this respect. It devotes fewer than two of its 186 pages to a discussion of the American family, and these are entirely descriptive. One reason why the demographic arguments have had so little impact is the absence of careful studies of determinants of age at marriage, upon which appropriate policies could be formulated. According to a thoughtful review by Hawthorne (1970:86), "Less is probably known about the social determinants of the age at marriage and the proportions marrying than about the determinants of any other important demographic variable." Sociological studies of these variables have been inhibited by a concentration on the relationship between an individual's characteristics and her marital status at a moment in time. We know that more highly educated women and women with higher status jobs marry later, but we cannot infer causality from these relationships because of the selection process by which these groups are formed. There is virtually a complete absence of ecological studies of marriage which attempt to relate individual behavior to environmental influences, and of longitudinal studies which identify factors in a woman's or man's life that affect subsequent marrying habits.

IMPLICATIONS FOR GRADUATE TRAINING

One point that has been made, explicitly with respect to age at marriage and implicitly for marital fertility, is the need for careful empirical studies of the role of policy-sensitive variables in demographic events. These variables can range in subtlety from divorce or abortion laws themselves to federal tax policies to sex-typing of textbooks. Unless we know how behavior responds to these variables, we cannot expect to affect demographic rates through policy changes. One way to make such matters more central in graduate training may be to ask students to prepare, at some point, research proposals suitable for submission to federal agencies. This would force students to think in

terms of problems with national scope, whose research and policy implications are to be clearly elaborated.

Such a change in emphasis will probably be discussed in other papers during these proceedings; its desirability is surely not unique to
demography. Our primary point has stressed what seems to be a more
distinct characteristic of demography: the existence of mature formal
models that permit very precise estimates of the impact of changes in
one parameter on all system variables. This paper has emphasized the
usefulness of these models not because they offer the only route to
successful policy formulations, or even the most important route, but
rather because they offer in many instances the highest rewards per
unit of effort. They can provide simple analytic solutions that would
require years of careful work to establish empirically, and then with
less than complete certainty. They help avert the error, overstatement,
and misinterpretation that sometimes result from common-sense reasoning; in addition, by providing estimates of the demographic impact
of changes in behavior, they serve to identify other types of research
required for informed policy decisions, as in the case of age at marriage. Finally, by virtue of their elegance and generality, they can attract the brightest students to the field, which is presumably not in-
consequential for long-run success in policy matters.

In my judgment, such models (which also include the stable
population, age-dependent transition processes, and multiple decre-
ment models) are relatively neglected in the demographic curricula of
many departments. They are most appropriately developed in courses
in demographic methods. But too often these are confined to basic
techniques of measuring population change and its components without consideration of the more detailed relationships that give rise to
these changes. Ideally, we would be teaching courses in demographic
methods and models, with prerequisites of calculus and linear algebra.
In many cases, we are prevented from doing this because our class-
rooms would be vacant. Most sociology graduate students do not
have this preparation, and we are competing with courses that do not
demand it. Perhaps if each major discipline within sociology required
its students to do a certain amount of relevant work in appropriate
outside departments, the competitive disadvantage would disappear
from demography. But this may be asking too much.

Special recruitment efforts by demography programs themselves
may be a more realistic goal. At a minimum, we can expect those demography programs blessed with a training grant to require the
proper preparation of their students, since its disagreeableness would
rarely offset the financial appeal. In other cases, we might accomplish

the same results by stressing the relatively favorable job market for demographers and urging a longer-run view of economic welfare. It seems clear that if exposure to this material does not come in graduate school, the sociologist–demographer will subsequently be inclined by habits of research, biases against formalism, and lack of preparation to avoid troubling himself about it. Then the study of demography within sociology would be in danger of being gradually eroded and absorbed by other disciplines more willing to make these demands of their practitioners.

REFERENCES

Blake, J.
  1972 A reply. In *Readings in population,* edited by W. Petersen. Pp. 459–469. New York: Macmillan.
Bumpass, L. and C. F. Westoff
  1970 The "perfect contraceptive" population, *Science* **169,** 1177–82.
Davis, K.
  1967 Population policy: Will current programs succeed?, *Science* **158,** 730–739.
Hawthorne, G.
  1970 *The sociology of fertility.* London: Collier-Macmillan.
Keyfitz, N.
  1972 How birth control affects births, *Social Biology* **18,** (2), 109–121.
Langer, W. L.
  1963 Europe's initial population explosion, *American Historial Review* **69,** (1), 1–17.
Ryder, N. B.
  1970 The emergence of a modern fertility pattern: United States, 1917–66. Pp. 99–123. In *Fertility and family planning: A world view,* edited by S. J. Behrman, L. Corsa, and R. Freeman. Ann Arbor, Michigan: Univ. of Michigan Press.
Sheps, M. C. and J. A. Menken
  1971 A model for studying birth rates given time dependent changes in reproductive parameters, *Biometrics* **27,** (2), 325–343.
Tietze, C.
  1964 Use and effectiveness of contraceptive methods in the United States. In *Manual of contraceptive practices,* edited by M. S. Calderone. Baltimore; Maryland: Williams & Wilkins.
U.S. Bureau of Census
  1960 *Historical statistics of the United States: Colonial time to 1957.* Washington, D.C.
  1971 Fertility indicators, 1970, *Current Population Reports.* Series P-23, No. 36.
  1972 Estimates of the population of the United States to May 1, 1972, *Current Population Reports.* Series P-25, No. 485.
U.S. President, Commission on Population Growth and the American Future
  1972 *Population and the American future.* Washington, D.C.: U.S. Government Printing Office.

Commentaries

JOHN E. BRANDL

University of Minnesota

My notions about the state of policy research and what is to be done about if flow from two premises both of which I hold strongly. First, we know less in the policy sciences as practiced in the United States than we thought we did a decade ago. Who did not assume in 1960 that, if given the opportunity to apply their techniques, macro-economists could bring the country to something better than the combination of high inflation and high unemployment that prevailed in the early 1970s? Similarly, and moving to policy areas in which I have worked during that period, applied micro-economics in the form of systems analysis for defense policy, although useful for weapons systems procurement decisions, perhaps contributed to an unfortunate and unrealistic feeling among policy-makers to the effect that defense "problems" were understandable and thus manipulable to a degree far greater than has turned out to be the case. Policy research in education has yielded mostly negative results—more resources expended in schools do not necessarily produce higher achievement scores now or higher socioeconomic status later for underprivileged children. In the days of *The Affluent Society*, was it not clear at least to some that whatever pockets of poverty existed in the U.S. could easily be dealt with? Now puzzled policy analysts studying poverty have tended to separate into two camps: some, mostly economists, arguing that whether you are rich or poor, it is always nice to have money; and others, mostly sociologists, showing that more money will not necessarily move people out of a culture of poverty.

It is fashionable these days to note that policy analysts have produced mainly negative results, have shown what does not work—in defense, education, welfare, etc. It is important to realize that the reason for this is that the models we use for measuring results are typically piecemeal, rather than global; partial, rather than general. We know that in our world, increasingly, everything depends on everything else, but our measurement techniques and calculating facilities are not up to the empirical estimation of the general systems. Thus, key influences often enter models as exogenous variables, if at all. As Alford suggests, the need of the policy-maker is for global information, but the contribution of the academic is often in the form of precise and often trivial quantitative conclusions on a small part of what is at issue. What then happens is that policy-makers, when recipients of dismaying or equivocal results of piecemeal policy research, resort to an alternative framework for decision, one which may not require any empirical investigation. "The ideas of economists and policial philosophers," Keynes wrote, modestly, ". . . are more powerful than [they are] commonly understood. Indeed the world is ruled by little else." And later, "the ideas which civil servants and politicians and even agitators apply to current events are not likely to be the newest. But soon or late, it is ideas, not vested interests, which are dangerous for good or ill [Keynes 1936:383–384]."

Rossi's paper provides an example. Rossi laments that Duncan's (1968) elegant article has had little effect on public policy. I suggest that this was not because, as Rossi (and Duncan) fear, "policy-makers will not read and/or not understand his work." Rather, policy-makers did recognize that Duncan and others had documented the difficulty blacks have in translating educational accomplishments into social and economic gains for themselves and their offspring. The Duncan analysis went far toward demolishing the "inheritance of poverty" model, but it did not so much tell what to do about the state of affairs, namely, the prejudice of whites toward blacks, as it showed what not to do even in its own framework. Frustrated at the inability of academics to produce empirical evidence as to what would be effective anti-poverty efforts, the Nixon Administration, at least for a time, espoused income redistribution by means of a negative income tax as an alternative to education and social service programs. This Family Assistance Program could be defended as good in itself on grounds of consumer sovereignty (if government does not know how to design social service programs, let people choose for themselves), and on consumption rather than investment grounds (whether you are rich or poor, and whether you and your children will gain higher status from it or not, it is always nice to have money). "The ideas of economists and polical philosophers" provided a rationale when empirical inquiry could not go far enough. The point here is not the simplicity of the rationale, but that it is not thought by its proponents to require empirical support, or to be susceptible to empirical counterargument, deriving as it does from one of several philosophical principles which are available when empirical analysis has gone as far as it can go. Whatever else has happened to ideology in recent years, it has not ended.

Somewhat similar remarks can be made about Preston's enthusiasm for mathematical demographic models. The models are not sufficient in themselves for determining policy, and some people will reject them on the grounds that mathematics is quite literally irrelevant to what are thought to be moral decisions.

Chief Justice Burger has recently provided another example, interesting for its explicitness on a variation of this point. In his majority opinion on the question of government involvement with obscenity matters in *Paris Adult Theater* versus *Slaton*, Burger (1973:42) wrote:

> From the beginning of civilized societies legislators and judges have acted on various unprovable assumptions. Such assumptions underlie much lawful state regulation of commercial and business affairs. If we accept the unprovable assumption that a complete education requires certain books, and the well-nigh universal belief that good books, plays and art lift the spirit, . . . can we then say that a state legislature may not act on the corollary assumption that commerce in obscene books or public exhibitions focused on obscene conduct have a tendency to exert a corrupting and debasing impact leading to antisocial behaviour?

Reforming the welfare system, lowering the birth rate, censoring pornography—these are examples that ideology continues to be the basis for much public policy. And that is partly because policy research in the social sciences is typically incomplete on its own terms, and partly because of the availability and even respectability of alternative political–economic systems to that of the analyst. When a sociologist decries the Supreme Court's obscenity decision and contends that Chief Justice Burger's "unprovable assumption" is potentially an empirical question, he too is resorting to an unproven assumption.

In the early and mid-1960s the sin of the policy analyst was intellectual arrogance; in the 1970s he may be subject if not to the virtue of tolerance than perhaps to the sin of despair. Now he should realize that his analysis will always be limited and conducted in the framework of some theory; and that his critics, even if accepting the empirical work on the analyst's terms, can always undermine the analysis by rejecting the tenets of the analyst's framework or theory.

My second premise is that the socialization process to which graduate students are subjected is not conducive to the production of good policy research. Alford has made this point very effectively, contrasting the prevailing research paradigm's emphasis on quantification and precision in studying narrowly defined formal properties, with policy-making needs for generality and comprehensiveness in studying situations or problems. I would suggest further that, frequently, budding academics are led to produce work that is academic in its most pejorative sense, that is, neither useful in the world of affairs, nor helpful for the advancement of science. There is a quandary here: if my first premise is true, then surely there is great need as Schuman argues, for work that explicates underlying relationships, for the development of better social theory. But, for many young social scientists, that is a trap. People with the ability to perform productive journeyman policy research labor on in Academe under the misguided impression that their work will constitute, or at any rate contribute to, a breakthrough of the sort made by Marx or Weber or Keynes.

In thinking about the training of professional policy analysts and in line with the premises set forth above, I would make the following points:

1. There is no single framework, paradigm, or discipline that encompasses public policy analysis. Policy research, formulation, and implementation have often suffered because people have been captives of a single discipline or point of view. Education for policy research should be eclectic, grounding students in several disciplines. Joint teaching of courses by two or more faculty members can be an invigorating way to prevent students from becoming true believers in one professor's discipline or paradigm (but can be time consuming for faculty).

2. There are several ways to bolster the feeble theories we do have. Two that will be of increasing importance are large scale (in contrast to laboratory) social experiments and computer sim-

ulation of large social systems. At present only rarely do graduate or professional students acquire both sets of skills.

3. Because policy analysis will rarely be definitive and comprehensive, students need grounding, not only in analytical techniques
of the quantitative social sciences, but in political philosophy
and comparative political systems as well.

4. Partly to fill the chinks in our weak social sciences, and partly
for the purpose of providing an alternative socialization process
for students, it is most valuable to have experienced public actors on faculties where applied social sciences are taught. Of
course, internships and practical exercises in cooperation with
public and private groups involved in public policy work can
also be valuable. However, setting up and maintaining productive internships, like joint teaching, are very time consuming and
expensive.

In his stimulating disquisition on the sciences of the artificial, Simon
(1969) leaves the strong impression that curricula in the applied social
sciences can be "scientized," that they can consist of utility theory,
statistical decision theory, mathematical programming, control theory,
etc. "The professional schools will reassume their professional responsibilities just to the degree that they can discover a science of design
not only is possible but is actually emerging at the present time
[p. 58]."

I suggest that recent experience has taught us that the day in which
education in the formal social sciences is sufficient, or even adequate,
training for policy-making is a long time in the future.

REFERENCES

Burger, W.
1973 Excerpts from pornographic opinions *The New York Times Magazine*, June
22, **1**, 42.
Duncan, O. D.
1968 Inheritance of poverty or inheritance of race. In *On understanding poverty*,
edited by D. P. Moynihan. New York: Basic Books.
Keynes, J. M.
1936 *The general theory of employment, interest and money*. London: Macmillan.
Simon, H. A.
1969 *The science of the artificial*. Cambridge, Massachusetts: MIT Press.

G. FRANKLIN EDWARDS

Howard University

The escalation of the concern of sociologists with social policy considerations is based upon the continuous operation of forces internal to the discipline of sociology and upon emergent external forces. From its beginnings sociology has given attention to a wide range of social problems—poverty, crime, domestic discord, slums and housing conditions, and to other aspects of personal and social disorganization. Evaluations based upon the rather unsophisticated methods of this early period almost always revealed ethical orientations and carried implications for social action and social change. It was against this background and in response to the need for improved methodological efficiency that there emerged a preoccupation with the concern for a value-free sociology which, in theory at least, would remove sociologists from any direct involvement in social action. This perspective implied that sociologists were to be concerned with the analysis of social behavior, but were to avoid specifications of the goals and ends of social action.

It should be observed, however, that even in the period in which the debate regarding the ethical neutrality of sociology flourished, sociologists became increasingly involved in government researches designed to influence planned change. This was particularly true of the New Deal Period in which increased attention was directed to problems of farm and urban communities and to the improvement of our knowledge of social trends and the demographic characteristics of the population. There were also efforts in applied sociology at the local community level as represented by the Chicago Area Project in the field of criminology. These types of involvements were broadened during the period of World War II and the subsequent two decades as sociologists participated in research sponsored or undertaken by the departments of Agriculture, Defense, Labor, and Health, Education and Welfare, and became more active participants in the work of various government commissions.

But it is fair to state that most sociologists have remained within academia and have devoted their efforts to what has been termed discipline research; they were primarily interested in analyzing phenomena of interest to them and were preoccupied with improving the methods and techniques with which they worked, all of which contributed to making sociology a more respectable discipline. Such procedures took no account of direct policy implications in the conceptualization and execution of their work, so that today, in a period of expanded interest in policy research, the capabilities and resourcefulness of sociologists to make a substantial contribution to problems of public policy are brought into question.

The interest of present and recent cohorts of graduate students in "relevant" studies, which would link sociological research more directly to the search for solutions to contemporary problems, and the decline in the level of funding by government agencies for research support and student training, together with the prospect that many sociologists must find employment in areas outside academic settings, have served as potent impulses in giving a heightened self-consciousness to the relationship of sociology to public policy. This self-consciousness and critical self-analysis are reflected in the title of the Carmel Conference: "New Directions in Graduate Training: Policy Implications of Sociological Research."

The Conference papers in the areas of "Poverty," "Race Relations," "Metropolitan Service Problems," "Population Dynamics," and "Theory and Method" provide documentation for much of what has been mentioned in the preceding paragraphs and express the discussants' views of the present limitations of sociologists, through their researches, to influence public policy. At the same time, they offer suggestions for the improvement of graduate training by which a more positive contribution to policy questions may be made in the future.

It is observed, in the first instance, that the pieces of research discussed by the several authors are essentially basic in character, and although they are directed to significant matters of policy concern, they were not initially conceived as having a direct bearing on action programs or policy solutions. Although sociologists have made substantial contributions to our knowledge base in each of the areas discussed, the authors agreed that their searches of the literature for pieces of "policy research" were not very fruitful. Moreover, the research discussions offer no suggestions regarding the manner by which the findings may be employed by policy-makers in the formulation of action programs, for the researchers did not have this as one of their objectives. However, they do, as the discussants note, provide insights into social phenomena which may be of value to decision makers. In two of the papers, for example, the tranditional assumptions of "a culture of poverty" and of the social class origins of riot participants are found to be erroneous. In another paper, the failure of demographers and population planning experts to give sufficient attention to the dynamics of the birth interval, motivation, and age at marriage in their efforts to reduce population size is revealed; and, in still another of the papers, the approach to metropolitan consolidation based upon the conception that suburbanites may be willing to support areal consolidation for the improved community services it is expected to bring is brought into question.

One agrees with the discussants that each of the papers furnished valuable insights into the areas covered, but on its own is not likely to make much of an impact on policy matters. It is, however, in the cumulative effect of numbers of studies in each of the areas that sociologists are likely to make their influence felt, for each of the papers discussed builds upon or challenges previous researches on the questions analyzed. Cumulative findings are what is useful in shaping the thinking of policy-makers on important public problems; for, in the words of one of the discussants, "Most important policy advances are dependent upon the careful preliminary work of scientists whose major concern is simply to straighten things out—to understand the nature of phenomena."

Both basic research and traditional modes of investigation in sociology have suffered from the constraints by which limited ranges of data related to complex phenomena are analyzed. Little opportunity, even in a period of expanded research support, was available for broad-scale analysis, for testing alternative formulations, or for replication of the same approaches. Some of the inherent limitation of sociology to this point, as regards its contribution to policy questions, has resulted from the scale of sociological research operations. Given the present manpower and resource constraints, it would appear that more substantial contributions of sociologists, even in the area of basic research, will come only as they are permitted to test their conceptions by applying their methodological tools to broader ranges of data in a variety of settings. This will contribute to both the improvement of techniques and to the possible outcomes of given courses of action.

It becomes increasingly clear, however, that contemporary concerns with the relationship between the social sciences, including sociology, and public policy go beyond the policy implications of research findings based upon basic research, so that, as one student has suggested recently (Coleman 1972), a new format for social science research on policy questions is required. In his judgment, the linkage of social science and policy decisions demands a closer collaboration of scientists and policy-makers in which (1) the questions for which answers are sought are framed by administrators or policy-makers; (2) the questions for research are operationalized, and the research conducted by the scientists; and (3) the results, after appropriate attention to alternatives, are given to the policy-makers for their determination of program formulation or other courses of action. One should recognize that this approach differs from conventional modes of research inasmuch as (1) the researcher may not have control over the results of his investigation after completion of his research, and (2) there are usually time limitations upon the period over which the research is conducted. But, hopefully, this type of collaboration will provide adequate resources for study of the problems for which solutions are sought, and will supply the "missing arrangements" or organizational framework which will facilitate the translation of findings based upon rational procedures into policy results. What, in essence, appears to be required is a different approach to policy research, including value considerations and methods, that has important meaning for graduate training in sociology.

Since an increasing number of graduate students are interested in research in the area of public policy and a larger number of sociologists, by necessity if not by choice, will find employment in government and private organizations, research training that will prepare them to investigate problems in these areas is required. This would suggest that, in addition to the basic training in logic and research methods, the student be given an opportunity to participate in research enterprises which focus upon policy research. It is too early to predict what this type of training will entail, but some such general direction appears clearly indicated. Hopefully, there will be an expansion of research centers devoted to research on policy issues and an increase in available internships in government agencies where policy research is undertaken. How rapidly efficiency can be developed in this most complex area would appear to be related to a willingness of social scientists to experiment and of governments and private organizations to make generous financial commitments in support of such endeavors. Whatever the developments on this frontier, it is likely that the major contribution of sociologists will continue for some time to be in the reporting of results of basic research which, however long it may take to be assimilated, will help shape our thinking about important social issues.

REFERENCE

Coleman, J. S.
  1972 *Policy research in the social sciences.* Morristown, New Jersey: General Learning Press.

ELTON F. JACKSON

Indiana University

Of the papers in this group, Rossi's argues most explicitly what I take to be the dominant view of the conference, namely, that applied work should receive considerably greater emphasis both in the activities of sociologists and in the training of their graduate students. I want to oppose this view. As I do so, I will also quarrel with Alford's call for less emphasis on multivariate quantitative analysis.

My basic premise is: what sociologists should do is make sociology, that is, develop valid theory about social behavior.

Currently, we are faced with pressing difficulties: research support is reduced; so is the number of jobs for new (and old) sociologists. Sociologists have always tended to be concerned about problems in our society. This tendency is now reinforced by concern about these two pressing economic problems of our own. Emphasizing social needs in our research and research training will, it is claimed, help us to solve our own needs by providing for a continued flow of research support and a new set of jobs in applied sociology for our Ph.D.s. But the question should be asked: Is this turn to applied work likely to threaten or hinder us in the main task of developing valid theory?

One view is that no threat is involved because there is no real distinction between basic and applied research. One cannot hinder the other because basically they are the same activity. I think this is incorrect. The distinction may be better thought of as a dimension rather than a dichotomy, but it should not be lost or blurred: the aim of sociology is to develop valid theory; the aim of applied work is to solve problems. These are not necessarily opposed activities, but their different goals will not often lead to the same kinds of research.

Another argument is that applied work has a good effect on basic work; combining the two in the same project or in the same sociologist may add energy to the research, and attention to current problems may rub the researcher's nose in crucial aspects of reality that he might otherwise ignore. Since a called-for solution to some life difficulty carries a harsher standard of success than the statistical t-test, it may spur more serious work. All this is true, I think. But in several ways applied work may also threaten the basic work in our discipline; we should accordingly temper our enthusiasm for problem-oriented research.

First, we presumably will make more basic progress by choosing research projects strictly in terms of their theoretical promise, that is, projects that will distinguish between and test alternative theories and/or that will suggest promising new theories. If any other criterion, such as the urgency of a social problem, plays an important role in the choice of research, the theoretical potential seems likely to suffer accordingly. Research aimed at social needs may even lead us to tackle problems that are intractable because of the limitation of current knowledge. The histories of physics and chemistry contain many instances of people attempting to solve problems that could only be penetrated with the aid of methods or knowledge not developed for another 50 or 100 years. If the choice of research topic turns on theoretical promise, the researcher has to estimate whether a given question can be settled and turn away from questions deemed intractable —such a consideration is less likely to weigh heavily in applied research.

This would not be such a disadvantage if our research projects could, like fruit flies, be generated and completed in a week or so at minimum expense, or if we had great stockpiles of money and talented people. However, our research absorbs prodigious quantities of time, money, and talent, and the field is poorly supplied with all three. If good people put their time on projects chosen because a social problem needs to be solved and/or because support money is available, rather than on questions chosen strictly for theoretical potential, the field has to count the cost in terms of fruitful theoretical ideas foregone.

Applied work is also less likely to be scientifically fruitful work because such research often (not always) tends to focus on a concrete situation in a search for concrete solutions. This may make it harder to think of concrete situations as instances of the working-out of general laws and to search for such laws by comparing several situations. Finally, and obviously, applied work often permits the researcher less control. He may have to negotiate the design of the study with people who are either uninterested in research or, worse, vitally concerned that the results come out "favorably." Time pressure may also force the research design or the analysis to be weakened. All of these things threaten the basic contribution of the work.

These arguments imply that we should attend mainly to sociology, that we should *not* divert any sizable amount of resources, including talent, from basic to applied research. I would argue, as Schuman intimates, that we should find ways to obtain support for continued basic research instead of adjusting our research to the new requirements of federal funding. The important thing is, to answer Alford's closing question, knowledge *for its own sake.*

What are the implications for training our graduate students? I can see several, some at variance to those urged at the conference.

1. Train graduate students to be sensitive to theoretical progress; teach them to choose research problems most likely to clarify crucial theoretical issues. They should *not* be sensitized to applied work. I find that they are quite sensitive enough already—the field is full of students who came into sociology to improve the world. The problem is to redirect that impulse toward the equally important end of improving our theory.

2. Make graduate training stronger and more intensive in both theory and methods. I would agree wih Alford that students should be encouraged to seek alternative theoretical interpretations; they should also be taught a variety of methods. Rossi argues that we are relatively successful in producing well-trained researchers. I have the opposite impression—that our research is often poorly informed by theory, badly designed, and awkwardly analyzed. Rossi's own comment, that of the approximately 450 empirical studies relevant to poverty "only a limited few . . . would survive a scrutiny in which minimal quality control standards were applied" tends to bear this out. (See p. 15, this volume.) Alford's analysis of Turk's article furnishes another example of these problems. Although it is true, as Alford says, that a fundamentally different theoretical perspective can be applied to interpret Turk's results, the major problem with the study is that the indicators are far, far removed from Turk's (or Alford's) interpretation. No choice can be made between the alternative theoretical interpretations until better measures are devised.

3. In both writing theory and interpreting results to bear on theory, students should be taught to construct explicit, rigorous models. Preston emphasizes this point, and it is echoed in Schuman's discussion of the complexity of social reality and in Rossi's praise of Duncan's translation of policy diagnosis into explicit empirical terms. It is beginning to be apparent that in many, perhaps most, areas of social behavior the number of different effects is so great that describing the structures, the relationships, and the dynamics of a situation requires an explicit and detailed model. With such a model, it becomes possible to derive (often unforeseen) theoretical expectations and join them more closely to the data. Often, constructing and working with these models will require training in mathematics, symbolic logic and statistics. That emphasis on these matters will increase seems an inescapable implication, despite the disadvantage that people in the discipline who lack these skills will be progressively isolated from some new developments.

It is obvious that I am arguing in favor of work that Alford would describe as the "dominant mode of analysis" in, sociology. I reject his suggestion that "multivariate analysis of measured properties of discrete units of analysis" leads to research that misses significant policy implications or that such a style leads to a focus on consensus and integration. Indeed, Duncan's study is an instructive counter-example. It seems to me that quantification and explicit statements of influences will usually help rather than hinder understanding. It is, for example, hard to see how a good understanding of a "whole" phenomenon can be gained without a model which combines and interrelates propositions about the variety of units and influences involved. I reject the notion that certain methodological styles are congruent with certain ideological approaches to policy issues. Accurate understanding, however gained, can be useful for either criticism or defense of the existing order.

4. The prestige of applied research should be firmly kept below that of basic research. This prestige imbalance is one of the things that keeps most of our best people doing mainly basic research.

5. Finally, we should figure out how to attract more intelligent and energetic people to sociology. Data exist to show that people entering sociology (in the sense of earning the Ph.D.) are of lower quality than those entering, for example, the natural sciences. Even if this were not true, the small number of good people doing sociological research and the demands of that research for quality performance argue that our most basic problem is that we do not have enough strong people working on research.

If our students insist on doing applied research, we should urge them to select a problem of profound human concern (not necessarily one declared relevant for the moment by a funding agency), get accurate data on the problem using whatever methods are needed, and inform the work throughout by basic theoretical perspectives so that the work will serve as well to advance our science.

MAURICE JACKSON

University of California, Riverside

Ordinarily, in sociology we focus on research findings and their relationships to other research findings, either in an anticipatory or post factum manner. In addition, at the Carmel Conference we considered the implications of sociological research findings for social policy and of social policy research for graduate training in sociology. Although the following discussion draws upon several papers given at the conference, it will concentrate on Schuman's paper as it signals a new direction and, hence, a challenge to the sociology of race relations. This paper can be viewed then, basically, as an explication of the policy and training implications that can follow from the findings of a single research study.

To begin with, Schuman's paper, like those by Alford, Kasarda, Preston, and Rossi, addresses alternatives in sociology. In this case, Schuman, in explaining riot participation, weighs a structural explanation, socioeconomic status, against a cultural explanation, attitudes. He finds attitudes but not socioeconomic status to be related to participation in riots. A somewhat similar finding is reported by Duncan (Rossi), who finds a socioeconomic explanation, "the inheritance of poverty," to be less important than "the inheritance of race," in accounting for poverty. To the extent that these findings are valid, certain implications follow for sociology, policy, and the training of graduate students. Basically, they mean a redirection of attention to explanations based on nonstructural factors, particularly in studies of a certain kind of race or minority activity such as a riot. This is not to say that structural factors can be completely disregarded.

Accordingly, the specific implications traced here will emphasize cultural explanations, a predominant way of explaining behavior in nonstructural terms. In so doing, I will discuss certain cultural features that are currently seen as important in their impact on race relations and that are most in need of elaboration.

An important cultural concept evoked recently to explain riots is "white racism." White racism can be defined as a belief in distinct races, black and white; in the intrinsic superiority of the white race; and in actions on that basis which restrict, exploit, and oppress the black race. Most simply put, policy implications follow in this way: if racism results in riot and riot-like behavior, and if it is desirable to eliminate riots effectively, then racism must be eliminated. Attention would then be directed toward finding ways to eliminate racism. But it must be briefly noted that the posited relationship between racism and riots varies under different conditions. Any number of studies can be conducted to begin to test propositions concerning the influence of theoretically specified conditions. In support of this view, Kasarda, Preston, Rossi, and Schuman all emphasize the necessity for more studies, more research, more knowledge for policy to be effective. Sociologists could conduct studies ranging from exploratory to experimental. Studies can be made of the qualities of racism, its enduring, varying, and changing aspects, the conditions under which it waxes and wanes, and its interpenetration with other factors. Studies can also be made of the transmission of racism over generations, how it is learned and how it can be unlearned. Finally, studies can be made of institutions and organizations, as well as of cultural characteristics and their relationships that seem to be most closely linked with racism. In this way, factors may be uncovered that should be modified in order to insure the modification or elimination of racism in race relations.

Graduate students can be trained in the development of the concept and subsequent theory of racism and its derivative implications and facts. They can study and explicate the various forms of racism. For example, the current emphasis on "backlash" implies the existence of a "lash." While "backlash" may refer to "lashing" blacks back into place if they start to move out, the "lash" actually refers to putting blacks in their place in the first instance. Following this kind of picture language, it may not be too far-fetched to characterize racism also as "whiplash," a situation in which blacks are lashed from the back after they have moved out of their places. At any rate, students need to be trained (1) to recognize racism, its forms, its postulated effects whether in social policy, social science, or elsewhere; (2) to develop ways of testing its relationship with other factors; and (3) to develop ways of handling it.

A second major emphasis in the area of race is learning about the culture of black people. Gaining this knowledge requires study of cultural orientations, predispositions, meanings, and understandings. There have been important breakthroughs in the study of blacks that need to be considered by policy-makers, sociologists, and graduate students. Perhaps the most significant is the change toward studying the strengths of black people, as well as the pathologies that have been of greater concern in the past. Another is to view blacks as actors as well as passive subjects. In so doing, one becomes informed about the black viewpoint and their way of looking at the world. That perspective, based upon the experience of black people, underlies behavior, and knowledge of it will enhance the understanding of behavior. It is a perspective that views white society within black society or views norms based on black experience to be important rules of behavior.

The general policy directive would be to develop policies based upon an understanding of black culture. These policies would differ in the main from those emphasizing pathologies. While the emphasis on pathologies supports racism in furnishing part of its rationale, the emphasis on strength would lead to the diminishing of racism and its effect. For example, educational and occupational changes would ameliorate the situation of black people if they relate to their characteristic needs and requirements.

Some of the points made in the papers concerning the training of graduate students are specifically relevant here. A major principle is that conducting more effective studies of social policy requires more students trained to do policy research (Kasarda, Preston, Rossi). Students need to be taught to study the contribution of the cultural orientation to social policy (Kasarda). They can be taught to consider alternatives to this approach, as well as within this approach as explicated in the paper by Alford. In addition, they need to have experience with new courses (Kasarda), which may involve policy research proposal writing (Preston) relative to the culture of black people, or internship in community agencies (Kasarda) within the black community, and other matters. They can also be taught to develop solutions for problems (Kasarda).

In conclusion, this has been a brief elaboration of some implications of the finding that socioeconomic factors are not of overriding importance in the study of race. The bearing of these implications on policy, sociology, and the training of sociology graduate students has been highlighted.

WILLIAM T. LIU
University of Notre Dame

At the Carmel conference two interrelated but distinctive issues were dealt with. The first pertains to the impact of social research on social legislations and social policies; the second deals with the specific strategies through which a policy is implemented. The former concerns itself mainly with "decisions" made between two or more compelling arguments given by people having divergent interests and moral/ideological convictions on topics involving moral or legal dilemmas. On the other hand, the latter deals with "choices" of strategies, with similar or identical goals in mind.

Sociologists have traditionally performed research activities on trend analysis and demographic indicators, going back to the works of William F. Ogburn in the thirties. These research activities have continued to play an important role in legislative and planning decisions on both federal and local levels. The works done by the Census Bureau, the National Center of Health Statistics, and other agencies which keep and analyze social indicators over time have provided information useful to collective decision-making and community actions. On the other hand, although most of the published sociological research papers have not found their ways into policy decisions, they have clarified concepts, suggested relationships of related socioeconomic phenomena, and have by and large contributed to the general understanding of the complex social environment in which social policies continue to sustain or alter the lives of many.

A different dimension of the problem of policy research deals with the *choice* of strategies. That the act of "choice" of a method subsumes the prior *decision* on a collective goal has reached general consensus. To choose a strategy, one addresses to oneself such questions as: Is the program morally justified, economically feasible, legally acceptable, or esthetically attractive? What are the short-term pay-offs and long-range consequences? Thus, the choice of strategies invariably enters into the discussion of evaluation research, and even a generic term like "policy research" has many different meainings and functions. At one level, policy research seeks to provide information about the state of affairs and enables the researcher to identify problem areas where actions are needed. At a different level the information is needed to reveal moral bases of program priorities. At a third level, policy research seeks appropriate means for the purpose of social intervention. Because of the complexity of purposes and levels of research, it is difficult to differentiate policy research from disciplinary research.

In considering the papers about which comments are made, I am left with the impression that all are relevant to policy research, though none has directly suggested one or the other course of action. On the other hand, these papers are products of a cumulative and impressive array of works typically found in the disciplinary literature, and all suggest that some fundamental *decisions* can be made with regard to social policies.

Whether scientific discoveries are integrated into the existing action system depends a great deal on the action system itself. This proposition is well accepted in the history of scientific discoveries but is seldom discussed in the social sciences. Myrdal's monumental work did not effectively deal with policy on race relations until a generation later when the climate of racial etiquette had begun to change. His second monumental work, that on Asian drama, is beginning to be noted only after violence and the rise of anti-colonial feelings had become prevalent throughout Southeast Asia. The earlier anthropoligical concepts and treatises, and perhaps some of the finest, were developed in conjunction with colonial powers' interests to understand natives and primitive people. Gerontology could not have been developed at the turn of the century when the median age of the population was in the early 20s; nor could the Hawthorne experiment be conducted if it were not for the interest of a capitalist economy—and the mysterious X was discovered not through humanitarian but through profit motive. The present behavioral science knowledge of mass communication and its effect on motivation was probably the lucky by-product of (1) psychological warfare and (2) the innovation of marketing experts. The majority of those in complex organization research in the early and formative years generated most of their powerful propositions from industrial research. And the list can go on. Without these earlier forerunners, sound policy research of the coming decade in sociology would probably have suffered from malnutrition from the very outset. One is to be reminded of the intellectual creation of Max Weber derived, by and large, from his interest in the modern bureaucracy.

Alford's paper is a good example to illustrate the relationship between sociological research and policy planning. It is ironic that Alford has done an excellent job in both praising the paper by Turk and rejecting its essence. However, the irony is easy to understand. Alford was impressed by Turk's ingenious effort to apply an interorganizational theory to community structure and behavior; at the same time, he rejects the paper he earlier praised so highly on the basis of its interpretation of the meaning of the index used, rather than on the basis of scientific methodology. For Alford, the amount of per capita dollars available in a community indicates the capacity for symbolic response by local elites to potential social conflict; whereas Turk, in his original conceptualization, preferred to relate such an *available* and concrete measure to the organizational theory, namely: the network relations among organizations in a community. Similarly, Turk believed that the percentage of low-income families, minorities, and out-of-school youths would be adequate measures of the level of demand in a community for poverty dollars. The same index to Alford means the degree to which potential social conflict is to be anticipated. Thus, the original six variables used by Turk are given additional, if not different, meaning when the researcher is committed to the belief that (1) the very nature of social processes is that of a conflict nature; (2) that the national government, in order to gain local support, had responded to local needs in a symbolic rather than a systematic way to improve the local conditions; (3) that the national ruling group basically distrusts the local communities so that resources channeled to the local communities must be legitimized through the national elites residing in the local community; and, finally, (4) that the rise of local voluntary associations would be an indication of local response to national policies. It is plausible to argue in favor of either case when the two papers are set side-by-side. As Alford points out, his own new conceptualization of variables puts more burden on policy reconsideration of the merit of poverty money thus far spent in American communities.

One might, therefore, ponder the significance of Turk's original paper, intended as it was, in Coleman's language, as a research-oriented paper, to build theories on community behavior and community planning, but a "disciplinary research" nonetheless. The same paper, if viewed from a different perspective, raises some of the fundamental questions about the poverty policy as it is implemented for fighting the losing battle on the poverty front. Alford's thesis, rightly or wrongly, gets to the guts of the power structure of the American political system and, as such, the paper will remain outside the sphere of social action, unless one might alter the basic fiber of the American political system.

Schuman's careful analysis illustrates the significance of nonfindings, or negative findings, in social research. More specifically, Schuman concludes that data failed to substantiate the assumption that typical participants of race riots are unemployed or blacks of lower socioeconomic strata. Schuman believes that many of the contributions made by sociologists are made through the process of disconfirming a point and, as the discipline matures, visible efforts will soon take a positive policy-related trend of research.

How one moves toward more positive policy-related findings is not elaborated in detail in Schuman's paper, except by stating that: ". . . better measurement of better-defined and more relevant social variables may well be the key." Here again we have trouble defining what may be the more relevant social variables.

Thus, Schuman's candid but pessimistic note reflects the state of the arts as well as the impotent role which the sociologists are playing in policy matters. One might ask, however, if the primary mission of a discipline is to be politically potent? Even if sociologists can do well in research with greater impact on policy matters, the essence of the work which is "sociological" should be carefully distinguished from that which is "nonsociological" or, at best, actions which are "derived" from sociological works. To be sure, if sociologists' negative findings have not effectively influenced policy decision, who can assure that "positive findings" would have a better chance to get into the world arena of actions?

Take, for example, Myrdal's recent volume on poverty politics in Southeast Asia; his evidence of the failure of American foreign aid programs, as well as the failure of governments' efforts to improve education and standards of living, was overwhelming. To Myrdal the problem is not so much economic ineptitudes, though that seems to be the manifest syndrome, as the total failure of a political and social system of the country. Though Myrdal never suggested that revolution is the only solution to the woes of these countries, his conclusion left the reader with no other alternatives. Would a man like Myrdal suggest revolution? It probably seems inappropriate. Thus political action based on research results would include other considerations which are beyond the scope of a scientific discipline.

Coleman's (1972) distinction between discipline research and policy research is analytically significant. However, when such distinction is viewed as a possible way to create another specialty in graduate training, the danger of having good engineering before we have a sound scientific basis is apparent. Perhaps two papers selected for conferees' comments which stand out as best illustrations of the inherent contributions made by social scientists to sound policy decisions are brought to our attention by Rossi and Preston respectively. Rossi correctly points out that, Duncan's paper, because of its sound methodology, has made an important contribution to knowledge about significant policy matters. Nevertheless, the paper "has slipped into undeserved obscurity." What went wrong? One might speculate a variety of reasons. For example, the language and presentation were too technical for action people to grasp; the implications in terms of legislative programs seemed too ambitious and therefore not feasible, given the political climate and the involved political processes of the American system. Also, one notices the omission of intervening social and human factors in the assessment, the ideological resistance, and so on. Whatever the reasons may be, one is left with the utlimate question: How would a policy researcher resolve these problems?

By contrast, Preston points out that almost all of the demographic research reports are potentially policy-relevant research. He had a different, and perhaps more pleasant, problem. He had to search the literature in demographic and population research to identify papers which are clearly *nonpolicy relevant* research. The specific paper, which Preston valued so highly, probably is more significant to discipline research than policy research. In Preston's own words:

> I shall focus on formal models of the birth process that were initially developed in order to identify determinants of fertility levels and variations in preindustrial populations. What started as a historical inquiry (much of its method being borrowed from mathematical statistics) has produced important implications for modern American demography [see p. 58, this volume].

Thus, what Preston was interested in is the impact of birth-interval assessment on the discipline of demographic science. The methods of assessment came *not* from problems of population pressure or pollution resulting from density of population (the world of action), but from historical demography and mathematical statistics (the disciplinary concerns). However, as Preston points out, the new methods of assessment, based on a sound theoretical conceptualization of the process of population increase in a society, would clearly point out where strategic problems are when, and if, one wishes to intervene directly to reduce population growth rates. As to how such intervention might be injected, Preston decided that this lies outside the jurisdiction and competence of the researcher.

The specific ways in which policy-makers use scientific research are beyond the scope of the Carmel Conference. My chief concern, after I have reviewed a number of papers, is to separate policy research from the specific outcome of such research and to deal with how such materials, once made available, are to be used. Sociologists, as professional research scholars, can improve research by building a sound theoretical framework, by refining measuring instruments, by improving the quality of data through better index construction, all of which lie within the proper scope of the disciplinary research. Problems concerning impact of such research on policy-makers would involve the analysis of quite different spheres of research undertakings. But these problems are not the exclusive properties of social scientists. Historians, for example, can use sound historical methods to assess factors and events that allow more penetration of certain arguments into policy decision processes than other arguments. When competing interests are present and conflicting values are at work, the arrangement of priorities are often beyond the weight of scientific argument, even though such scientific materials are available for sound and rational planning of programs and projects.

It seems to me that the first basic issue involved in the present discussion pertains to the differences and similarities of policy research and program evaluation research. Policy research—which concerns the impact of policy on the social and economic system—may seem to be just a variation of program evaluation research. But a real difference between the two does exist. After a carefully designed evaluation of a program, even if we are sure that the existing program is not effective, little can be done to alter the basic principles reflected in policies. For example, adding contraceptive elements into community drinking water would probably be an efficient way to reduce birth rates, or blending contraceptive additives to vitamin-rich foodstuffs would solve both nutrition and high birth rate problems in developing countries. But these measures could not be practiced because of the high value we place on individual freedom of choice.

Thus, program evaluation deals with the strategic and the tactical aspects of carrying on policies. Within the confines of general policy decision, however, experimental design on institutional strategies or structural effects with respect to the desired goals would certainly be germane to our concern. In this area, social scientists can make, and have made, some contributions. Demonstrations of the relationships between certain programs and their resultant outcomes would follow logically the usual experimental design in the tradition of the social sciences.

The second issue is to remind ourselves of the primary responsibilities of social scientists as social scientists. Theory building and methodological refinement will lead to better research, which will supply *better* and more convincing policy-pertinent information. For those who wish to make such information more useful to policy decision makers, special journals and editorial policies can be endorsed by the profession. To participate in direct policy contribution would need more information than that which is supplied by social research results alone. A complex issue deserves the attention of other experts in legal philosophy, in moral ethics, and other professional inputs. But such an ultimate task is beyond the proper scope of the discipline, or any other single discipline.

REFERENCE

Coleman, J. S.
   1972 *Policy research in the social sciences.* Morristown, New Jersey: General Learning Press.

ROBERT McGINNIS

Cornell University

The questions addressed during the course of the Carmel Conference are phrased and rephrased throughout these printed proceedings *ad nauseam*. For me to rephrase them yet once more should wreak little incremental damage. Thus: What is the nature of (sociological) policy research? Whatever its nature, should our discipline seek a deep engagement in it? If so, how should our graduate curricula be adjusted to facilitate this? In addition, I heard at least one hidden agenda question: Can a commitment by the discipline to policy research relieve the incipient imbalance between demand for and supply of highly trained sociologists?

In all of this my small pleasant assignment was to comment on the five papers, contained in Section A of this volume, by five professors from five prestigious graduate departments.[1] This task was made simpler in that all five dealt with common or at least overlapping substantive areas of application: metropolitan communities that are ill-organized to cope with burgeoning problems of population growth, poverty, and intergroup conflict. On instructions from the conference organizers, four of the five used recent research reports as points of departure. The fifth, Preston, took on an entire research area as his foil.

One prominent theme in these five papers merits our attention as much for the questions it raises as for the light that it sheds, and that theme is the failure to confirm what is generally regarded as conventional wisdom. Thus, Rossi has Duncan shooting down the "inheritance of poverty" notion. Schuman has the President's Commission on Civil Disorders shredding the popular idea that the major urban riots of recent years represented "aberration of the black lumpen-proletariat." Kasarda points to Hawley and Zimmer's falsifying the belief that metropolitan residents yearn for better public services and more efficient municipal government. Schuman puts this theme in extreme form: "Sociology *will always* be better at bursting balloons than launching rockets [italics supplied]."

No one, Schuman included, appears to deny the possible relevance to policy of such negative results, but it should be clear that such re-

---

[1] This is mentioned only to underscore the fact that these authors are highly representative of the population of participants in the conference who were, almost to a man, professors affiliated with prestigious graduate departments of sociology.

sults are remote from the constructive component that is essential to policy research. If it is correct to say that we sociologists will *always be* better gadflies than performers of applicable policy research, then perhaps we should get back to our four-fold tables and leave the social engineering research to others, who will probably turn out to be engineers and operations-research types such as Raymond Forrester and his disciples.[2] I believe that it is not necessarily correct to suggest that sociologists are and must remain altogether on the sidelines of policy research. Moreover, I believe that it would be a serious mistake for us to abandon the field to these nonsocial scientists and engineers who are increasingly laying claim to it.

In a search for integrative answers to the thematic question of this conference, I have treated these five authors as a (not so simple, not so random) sample of the population of participants. To advance this search, I have brought into play those hallmarks of sophisticated sociology, content analysis, and opinion research. By use of the former technique, I have transformed these five papers into responses to a series of trenchant, if not applicable, opinion questions. Herewith the results.

An Opinion Poll of Sociological Experts (or, Give a Man Enough Rope . . .). Several questions were constructed that pertain to sociologists' understandings of policy research. These were:

1. Do you believe that you understand what "policy research" involves?
2. Do you believe that the author of the report (or workers in the field) that you reviewed knows as much about policy research as you do?
3. Was this paper (or is this field) *relevant* to policy formation or evaluation?
4. Did it appear to have any impact on policy?
5. Should sociologists become more engaged in policy research than they are at present?

The distributions of response to these questions are in Table 1.

---

[2] Not to flaunt the sociological tradition of self-citation, I suggest that the reader refer to the review symposium in *Demography*, Vol. 10, No. 2 for opinions, including mine, about the most recent policy research produced by this group.

TABLE 1 Percentage of Response by Sociological Experts to Five Questions on Policy Research [a]

	Question number				
Response	1	2	3	4	5
Yes	100	20	80	0	20
No	0	60	20	80	20
Other [b]	0	20	0	20	60

[a] That these percentages are all multiples of 20 does not represent disdain for statistical detail. Rather, it is a subtle mathematical consequence of the fact that $N=5$.

[b] Includes no opinion, rejections of the question, or sneaky answers. Naturally, interpretations of these data are left to the reader. However, a cautionary remark is in order concerning the distribution of response to the first questions. Lest the reader make an inductive leap from this consensus to the conclusion that sociologists also have consensus about what comprises policy research, he (or she) should compare Rossi's paper with one by J. Davis that appears elsewhere in these *Proceedings*. Rossi and Davis comment on papers that are remarkably similar in both substantive problem and analytic approach. Despite these similarities, the two reach diametrically opposite conclusions about whether the papers have anything to say about policy.

The second set of distilled questions concerns implications for graduate curricula in science. Questions 6–9, but not 10, were preceded by the logical hypothesis, "If sociologists should become more involved in policy research, then . . ." The consequent questions were:

6. Should our traditional curricula be changed?
7. Should graduate work involve greater familiarization with the processes of policy formation and implementation?
8. Should the curricula give greater emphasis to modern quantitative techniques?
9. Would these changes materially reduce any future "oversupply" of sociologists?
10. Is there likely to be an oversupply of sociologists in the foreseeable future?

Response distributions are in Table 2.

One should not be surprised at the responses to the two final questions since they touch on an agenda item that surfaced only during the course of the conference. For whatever it may be worth, my own answer to the tenth question is a loud affirmative, unless the level of advanced degree production is reduced drastically in the im-

TABLE 2 Percentage of Response by Sociological Experts to Five Questions on the Graduate Curriculum [a]

	Question number				
Response	6	7	8	9	10
Yes	80	60	20	0	0
No	0	0	80	0	20
Other	20	40	0	100	80

[a] Footnotes of Table 1 apply to Table 2.

mediate future. Regarding Question 9, I am again a deviant in that I have a rather strong opinion: that a partial conversion of the field to policy-related activities probably will have little impact on demand for sociologists during the next few years in any event, and none unless we produce better evidence than I can find now that we are broadly capable of doing good, applicable policy research. This observation and the response to the eighth question lead to my final comment.

The point of policy research, it seems to me, is to provide credible assessments of the consequences of intervention in behavioral systems. Almost invariably, intervention takes the form of reallocations among scarce resources, such as funds and the working time of skilled staff. In part because these are quantitative phenomena, credible assessment becomes equated—in the minds of a growing number of policy-makers, I believe—with sophisticated quantitative analyses of solid, usually large, data bases. Quantitative research surely includes the path and stochastic models that are becoming increasingly familiar in some branches of sociology. For policy purposes, however, we must become adept at other less familiar techniques, such as Box--Jenkins (1970) types of time-series analysis, input–output techniques, or linear and nonlinear programming. Until these and similar tools become commonplace in sociology, I shall remain pessimistic about our demonstrating a capability for first-rate policy research. Nor, in light of the response to Question 8, shall I hold my breath in anticipation.

REFERENCE

Box, G. E. P. and G. M. Jenkins
    1970 Time series analysis: Forecasting and control. San Francisco, California: Holden-Day.

SHELDON STRYKER

Indiana University

The papers under review demonstrate the relevance of sociological research for social policy; they also assume the appropriateness, legitimacy, and desirability of such research. I share these assumptions, and so will not treat them as problematic beyond suggesting that a case can be made for opposing assumptions; that to hold these assumptions is not necessarily to give total or even top priority to policy research; and that it may well be that most sociologists shaping graduate training in the United States give lip service to an affirmative evaluation of policy research (and, as Rossi notes, conduct it as a "side activity" or as a "hobby") while communicating to their students their underlying scorn.

What must be treated as problematic, however, is another assumption that is made through this set of papers—namely, that *the policy ends toward which research may be conducted are to be taken as givens by the sociologists conducting the research.* Or, alternatively and bluntly put: sociology for whom?

This assumption is not, of course, explicit. Yet it may be seen in Kasarda's failure to ask why it is that the majority of citizens—*both* suburban and central city—oppose governmental unification as a solution to metropolitan service problems and so the failure to recognize the alternative values that might shape policy research. And it may be seen in his drawing (appropriately enough) from the Hawley–Zimmer research the policy implications that to effectuate metropolitan reorganization will require either federal or state intervention, as well as a campaign to make city residents more aware of the inefficiencies arising out of a fragmented structure. Thus, a "fragmented" structure which *may* maximize direct citizen control over local circumstances of life, which *may* be the answer to the distrust of extra-local authority (who could say at this point in time that such distrust is unwarranted?) that likely underlies the opposition noted earlier, is simply ruled out.

Rossi's apparently sensible point that variables are not policy relevant which, no matter how exhaustive of the variance, are not manipulable through policy changes is less sensible given a challenge to this assumption. What is or is not manipulable is not necessarily fixed in nature. To use Rossi's illustration: "family background" may be firmly fixed and not subject to manipulation (although I am not at all certain about that). Neither self-esteem nor occupational values are unchangeable, however. True, current policy-makers fail to define occupational values and self-esteem as policy relevant and *therefore* they are not manipulable. On the other hand, entering salaries are defined as policy relevant *and therefore* as manipulable. But this is precisely the point that begs to be made. Some sociologists may wish to take the currently extant definitions of policy relevance as givens, and I will not quarrel with them if they do. Surely the field of sociology cannot do so, for to do so means that the discipline must become the handmaiden of whoever holds power at a particular time, and in the long run this must mean the discreditation of the discipline itself.

One need not be (and, indeed, I am not) politically radical to make this point. Alford's sympathies are clearly not establishment oriented, yet his paper raises the same issue from another perspective. He places the policy-defining function in alternative sociological paradigms (the familiar "consensus" versus "conflict"), and his argument implies that one of these paradigms is appropriate while the other is not. This, too, turns policy relevance into a given. It takes definitional activities out of the "real" world; and while his preferred definers are nonelites rather than elites, he is no more likely than the others cited to make explicitly part of the sociological enterprise the systematic study and statement of alternative policy ends.

If policy research, whoever may define the variables, is desirable, then the questions becomes: How do we get good policy research done? Not unexpectedly and not unreasonably, the presumption is that the way we train our students is connected with the answers to this question. I do not believe that all the suggestions made in various papers will, if carried out, either make sociological research more policy relevant or improve the quality of such research as is done; on the other hand, there are implications for training not treated explicitly in the papers that would do both.

First, I believe Alford to be profoundly wrong. One need not quarrel with his argument that the specific indices used in research (his use of Turk's study is incidental and not essential) are open to alternative conceptual interpretation—although it ought to be pointed out that Alford's specific interpretations contain unexamined and hidden empirical assertions.[1] But his distinction between quantitative and qualitative characteristics of program outputs is arbitrary: innovation, performance, improvement are not inherently unmeasureable; and nothing in a quantitative attitude or approach obviates treating a com-

[1] For example, his interpretation of Turk's per capita funding variable assumes a connection between funds available and symbolic rather than real response to social conflict.

bination of programs as a unit of which measurements are taken. Conflict theorists—witness Marx—will no more find numbers uncongenial than will consensus theorists—witness Parsons. Not to train our students in the full range of available research techniques—numerical or otherwise—is to disable them. It might not be so important to refute Alford's contention were it not the case that a fair share of the field believes as he does.

Well-taken is Rossi's suggestion that the creation of a sociological organization comparable to the Council of Economic Advisors would make more meaningful the policy-relevant research that we do, in that the gap between Academe and policy-makers would be bridged at least in degree. It might even make more realistic his prior assertion that policy-related research can be as technically exciting and intellectually rewarding as basic research. The citation of the income-maintenance experiments hits home, since I have been active in the Gary experiment. Such research *is* exciting; and it *is* rewarding. But part of the excitement lies in fighting off the bureaucrat with little understanding of the requisites of technical research or the economist who assumes that he knows all that is worthwhile of relevance to income maintenance; and part of the reward lies in winning partial victories that prevent everything of concern to the sociologist (either qua theoretician or qua policy-researcher) from being scuttled. Bridging organizations, *if* they have the requisite prestige, might help. In the meantime, and before the millenium, our students must be prepared for the less than full control of their research endeavors lest their disillusionment be so profound as to drive them away from potentially worthwhile activities.

If it is true that training of graduate students is becoming increasingly more specialized, then—again assuming we wish to promote good policy research—this set of papers might well give us pause. Preston tells us that effective policy in the realm of population dynamics requires something more than knowledge about such matters as failure rates of alternative contraceptive techniques; it requires knowledge about the "crucial" variable of motivation. In short, our demographers *must* have some sensitivity to variables "in" the domain of social psychology. Similarly, Schuman tells us that the riot studies make it clear that objective black socioeconomic status explains little of that phenomenon, and he asserts the "crucial" importance of race-related perceptions and attitudes held by blacks. Thus, the policy work of those in race relations will be less relevant to the degree that social psychological variables are not taken into account. And the reverse point is made by Rossi in discussing the implications of Duncan's work: a basically social psychological model stressing the inheritance of poverty which leads—in its policy application—to an emphasis on educational aspirations and motivations must be (in terms of the evidence) radically altered to a model focusing on a social structure which prevents the conversion of educational attainment to occupational and income attainment. The moral is clear: what is policy relevant does not recognize the intellectual boundaries conventional to contemporary sociology and to its graduate programs; and we do our students a terrible disservice with respect to the potential policy usefulness of their training by insisting on these conventions and by restricting training to particular subsets of "types" or "levels" of variables.

The foregoing leads to a further questions: Do we really know what variables are and are not policy relevant (even assuming that we have overcome the limited perspectives of sponsoring agencies)? An honest answer—as Schuman makes clear—is that, in general, we do not. Since we do not, how can we train students in what is and what is not policy relevant? And if we cannot train our students in this way, does not prudence argue that we let the sociological imagination range fully over the disparate congeries of concepts currently identified with the field and encourage these students to be even more inventive than we were in extending those concepts? Should we not, in brief, pursue our task of finding out what is important, guided by sociological theory and without any a priori commitments to presumed relevance? Obviously, I think we should.

What I have been saying seems to be that, basically, we are not doing badly—from the point of view of training for policy research—with current training guidelines. If that is the case, then why is there not more and better policy research? The answer, to my mind, lies not only in what we do, but in the subtleties of attitudes conveyed. Let me make my point starkly: our students will embark on policy research and will do it well when we who guide graduate training in sociology cease to tell them—however indirectly—that policy research is less honorable, less meaningful, and less rewarding than the so-called basic research, and when we distribute rewards in a way that shows that we really mean it.

Section B

Individual Stress
in the Family Cycle

Sociological Critics versus Institutional Elites in the Politics of Research Application: Examples from Medical Care

DAVID MECHANIC

University of Wisconsin

Medical care or health services research, in contrast to biomedical research, has had little discernible impact on public policy, the behavior of health professionals, or the organization of health facilities. Although it is possible to find instances where persons with official responsibilities justify particular policies through references to specific research, there is little evidence that the initiation of policy flows directly from research findings. Research, however, may in the long run help shape the climate within which decisions are made.

Part of the difficulty in discerning the impact of research on policy reflects the vagueness of the concept of policy itself. If by policy we mean legislative and governmental administrative actions, then it is obvious that research is only one of many relevant factors that are taken into account. At this level, it is clear that the range of variables that are seen as amenable to manipulation is limited at any point in time, and political feasibility is an important consideration. If we think

99

of policy in terms of administrative actions at a variety of levels of organizational functioning, then we face a problem of diffusion of results. In a pluralistic system where there is a multitude of decision points, we would not expect that a solution demonstrated in one context would necessarily be seen as relevant or adaptable to another. Thus, solutions affecting smaller units of organization often diffuse very slowly, if at all. In considering the impact on policy, it is not apparent what criteria are reasonable to impose or what constitutes an appropriate span of time for diffusion to take place.

It may be that in the long run the most important impact of social research on policy results from the extent to which it affects the climate of thinking in the society at large. Research results and approaches diffuse in the media and have an effect on how educated persons think about problems. Policy-makers, like others, are affected by the climate of opinion in which they function, and research may have a crucial indirect role on how policy options are analyzed and how policy decisions are made and implemented.

Yet even in considering the diffusion process it is clear that some findings diffuse rapidly while others have little success. One can observe, for example, that findings in the area of biomedical technology and science have greater effectiveness than in most health services research. This is partly because the former tends to shape technology without intruding in major ways on the interests or life styles of professionals, while the latter poses greater threat to professional autonomy, work priorities, and control over work. In this paper I will examine some of the difficulties in implementing health care research by focusing on studies dealing with social and psychological factors in the treatment of hospital patients and with the failure of physicians and medical facilities to give adequate attention to such concerns.

For the purposes of this paper I will examine two studies carried out at Yale–New Haven (a Yale University teaching hospital): (1) a very specific experimental study of the role of communication in patient care; and (2) a general investigation of the quality of patient care. The first study (Skipper and Leonard 1968) rigorously performed and yielding specific results and implications for intervention, has been generally ignored. The second (Duff and Hollingshead 1968), a provocative descriptive study with both important implications but also serious methodological problems, resulted in a vigorous counterattack by elite members of the academic medical establishment (Beeson 1968; Inglefinger 1968). I wish to discuss these works as part of a larger line of inquiry, since findings documenting the failure to give adequate attention to social and psychological factors are common in

the literature (Cartwright 1964; Ley and Spelman 1967). It is my assessment that the rejection of the second study would have occurred
regardless of its methodological rigor, since similar findings have been
reported based on a variety of methodologis, and these too have been
ignored for the most part.

In the first study, reported by Skipper and Leonard, children admitted to a hospital for tonsillectomy were randomly divided into experimental and control groups. In the control group, patients received the
usual care, whereas in the experimental situation, mothers were admitted to the hospital by a specially trained nurse who tried to
facilitate communication and to maximize the mothers' opportunities
to express their anxiety and to ask questions. An attempt was made to
give the mother an accurate picture of the realities, and mothers were
told what routine events to expect and when they were likely to
occur. Mothers in the experimental group experienced less stress.
Their children experienced smaller changes in blood pressure, temper-
ature, and other physiological measures; they were less likely to suffer
from post-hospital emesis and made a better adaptation to the hospital. These children made a more rapid recovery following hospitalization, displaying less fear, less crying, and less disturbed sleep than
children in the control group. In considering this study, we note that
tonsillectomy is one of the most frequent surgical procedures performed in the United States, and the main cause of hospitalization of
children (National Center for Health Statistics 1971). Controlled studies have demonstrated tonsillectomy to be a dubious surgical procedure in the great majority of cases, and psychological problems have
been found to be a major adverse effect of the procedure, especially
in young children. Thus, the importance of alleviating the distress of
mother and child when the procedure is performed should not be
minimized.

I have discussed the study with the investigators and various other
persons associated with the hospital in which the study was carried
out. There is consensus that the study had very little impact on the
delivery of services. The innovation was not continued beyond the
study period, and it had no observable effect on the general philosophy of patient care. It is likely that the results of the study at the hospital are not widely known, and there is agreement that the medical
and surgical staffs have little interest in such studies. One of the investigators told me that a high-ranking physician on the staff asked
him why he was wasting his time with such trivial problems.

The second study, carried out by Duff and Hollingshead, describes
in some detail the general problems and complexity of a major teach-

ing hospital, but focuses on a sample of 161 patients who received care on medical and surgical services in the private and ward facilities of the hospital. The investigators extensively interviewed patients, doctors, nurses, families, and other hospital personnel, examined medical records, observed patient care, and made follow-up visits to the patients when they returned home. Many of the findings are based on Duff and Hollingshead's global appraisal of each case and, except for anecdote, it is difficult to assess specifically how they made various judgments. Yet two major findings emerge from the study which I believe are unchallengeable, despite the fragility of the methodological approach. First, it is clear that a very different style of patient care prevails on the public in contrast to the private services, and that patients on the public wards were more likely to be taken for granted. Second, this study dramatically illustrates the failure of physicians to become sufficiently aware of their patients' social and psychological circumstances and to take these into consideration in the total management of these patients. Without accepting Duff and Hollingshead's specific evaluations of the adequacy of diagnosis, the mental status or adjustments of individual patients, or on many other technical matters, it is difficult for me to see how an impartial reader can reject the more general conclusion that there was a consistent failure to give adequate attention to the life circumstances of patients in relation to thier illnesses. Nor is this observation inconsistent with observations elsewhere. The recommendations by Duff and Hollingshead are rather modest in relation to the magnitude of the issues they raise, but among them are such suggestions as "health professionals be trained to deal systematically with the personal and social factors which affect the diagnosis and treatment of patients [1968]."

Unlike many other investigators in the area, Duff and Hollingshead published their findings as a "trade" book, and it was accompanied by considerable newspaper publicity, including an article in *McCall's Magazine* (Pines 1968). Perhaps because of its public visibility it brought forth on the one hand criticism for failure to publish "results via accepted channels for scholarly communication" and on the other a public rebuttal in *Harper's Magazine* (Ingelfinger 1968).

The counterattack on Duff and Hollingshead came from two elite members of the academic establishment: Beeson (1968) of Oxford University, who had been chief of the Yale University Medical Service during the study period, and Ingelfinger (1968), editor of the *New England Journal of Medicine*. Both men, usually described as enlightened and progressive forces in medical care, offer a detailed rejoiner which at times borders on the petty. Both make an issue, for example, of the fact that Dr. Duff, an associate professor of pediatrics at Yale, described his interests in the preface of the book as "not exactly medicine and not necessarily sociology."

I do not believe that the methodological problems in the Duff--Hollingshead study were key issues in the rejection of the study since research findings on behavioral factors in disease have been generally ignored regardless of results, the type of study, or the rigors of methodology. Rigor and methodological adequacy are obviously important considerations, but it is striking how frequently weak and uncertain results are cited in support of one or another position when they support the viewpoint of the advocate. A dual standard seems to be imposed: one for studies whose findings you like, and quite another for those whose findings appear less attractive. This seems to be the case particularly when policy positions are advocated, and it supports the earlier observation that research results are used more frequently to justify policies than to suggest new approaches.

Although Duff and Hollingshead's attempt to make the issues public through the popular presentation and promotion of their book was bitterly criticized, they were at least able to elicit a hearing. Although the powers that be at Yale–New Haven were probably sufficiently angry with the results of the study to facilitate its rejection, and although the study had no apparent effect on the organization of services at the hospital, it has contributed importantly to discussions of the issues raised in the larger society and among younger health professionals. Thus, despite the study's lack of demonstrable, direct impact, it has probably generated a climate of concern. It is difficult to evaluate the effect of a "trade" book in contrast to journal articles in a particular case, but if *Science Citation Index* is any indication of the extent to which a particular project arouses interest in the scientific community, then it is clear that the Duff–Hollingshead study was considerably more successful than the Skipper–Leonard investigation. As one of the authors of the latter study wrote me in a response to an earlier draft of this paper, "accepted channels" may simply be a way of burying a study.

In considering why the Duff–Hollingshead study had little effect on the functioning of the Yale–New Haven hospital and why it would be unlikely to have effect regardless of its level of methodological elegance, I suggest that the implications of the findings are simply too radical. Such studies have little effect because, if taken seriously, they would require a fundamental reorganization of how medical services are delivered and how health personnel are trained. In this regard, Duff and Hollingshead show too little appreciation of the fundamental reorganization of medical education and practice necessary to achieve what they would like. Their limited specific recommendations, if implemented, would have very little effect in the face of the existing pattern of medical and hospital work.

It is therefore instructive to consider the larger criticisms of the Duff–Hollingshead study that are not specifically directed to their methodology or their motives. Such criticisms basically fall into two groups.

1. Both critics make the point that hospitals deal with serious organic disease and thus must establish priorities in terms of known interventions. They argue that since time and energy are limited, you do what you know how to do. As Ingelfinger puts it: " 'I rob banks,' said Willie Sutton, 'because that's where the money is.' "

2. Both critics deeply resent the unveiling if the "mystique of medicine." Both take bitter exception to what, as far as I can tell, is an accurate account of the process of obtaining autopsy permissions and of the methods used. This criticism tends to be an attack on sociology itself, since both critics imply that it was irresponsible to unmask the process. Ingelfinger describes this as "preoccupation with learning in its most ghoulish aspects," and Beeson makes the hysterical statement that "I'm sure that no lay person who has read their book will ever grant this permission after the death of a relative." I cite this because both reviews, by men of unquestionable repute, display considerable paternalism in their discussions of patient care. They imply that patients have no right to know about the more ghoulish aspects of hospital care, since the mystique of medicine is truly in their interests.

Perhaps because Ingelfinger was less personally involved, he expresses greater ambivalence in his review and is more willing to concede that Duff and Hollingshead have raised important issues, although he criticizes their one-sided presentation of them. In respect to the difficult problem of weighing the need for further diagnostic search against the possibility that psychogenic factors are the cause of the patient's difficulty, he notes that "There is no easy solution to the philosophical and moral problem, but to use this dilemma to 'prove' the narrow focus of the physician's interest or his lack of diagnostic drive verges on demagoguery [1968]."

Although Ingelfinger has probably overstated his point, he does raise a serious problem with the Duff–Hollingshead work and many other sociological studies in the "debunking" tradition. For the study is presented in terms of patient advocacy, and Duff and Hollingshead do not present the issues as seen by each of the major participants. In depicting the process of obtaining an autopsy and in its implications of disapproval of the means, it does not give attention to the high-minded ends that have produced such adaptations. And this is the crux of the issue. Both Ingelfinger and Beeson point out repeatedly the noble ends that have their associated seamy aspects, but Duff and Hollingshead chose to emphasize the seamy aspects and gave little attention to the noble ends. As Beeson notes in exasperation: "The authors' combination of smugness and naivete is hard to bear by someone who has been dealing with the realities [1968]."

I find the issue of autopsy a particularly interesting one since both Duff and Hollingshead and their critics miss or disregard what I regard as the crucial point. Clearly, autopsies are important for evalaution of work, continuing education, and improved performance; and any teaching hospital worthy of the name will attempt to obtain permissions to perform autopsies. In their zealousness, physicians sometimes commit the types of excesses described vividly in the Duff-–Hollingshead volume and may even cajole and trick persons into providing the necessary permission. While Beeson and Ingelfinger focus on the noble functions of the autopsy, Duff and Hollingshead focus on the excesses. Neither examines how to balance the needs of the teaching hospital with the rights of patients and how their families are to be treated with dignity and be given a true opportunity to consent to requests. Achieving this is, of course, a complex and time-consuming process, and teaching hospitals are busy places. But when ends come to justify contemptible methods, we pay a price irrespective of the technical gains. Physicians also come to pay a price; for we are what we do, it may be argued, and the doctor who comes to adapt functional "tricks" loses some of his humanity.

In Beeson's view, "A low-keyed, well-documented report, aimed at professionals and written for professionals, could have immense and lasting value. After all, doctors and nurses are the only people who possibly can alter the conditions of patient care [1968]." This is in sharp contrast to the Duff–Hollingshead view that *"The answer is basically a society-wide issue rather than a problem for medical professionals alone. Sickness is inextricably linked with society and society will have to look at itself for the solution [1968]."* It is within these two contrasting views that the positions on both sides can be understood.

Beeson sees the solution to problems largely in terms of the efforts and good will of individual actors. He contends that since physicians and nurses provide care, change must come through influencing them to view some forms of professional behavior as desirable in relation to others. He appears to see sociological research in medicine as ancillary to the medical function, as one more aid to assist the physician and nurse to do a better job. In this light he views the Duff-Hollingshead book as a bitter and unjustified attack on medicine itself or, as Ingelfinger puts it, opening "new veins of muck for those who make it their business to rake the medical profession [1968]." In contrast, Duff and Hollingshead are indicting the structure of medical care itself and the societal pressures and values that sustain it in its present form. Although this attack on the basic structure of medical care in America is never fully or adequately developed, it seems apparent—although not to the physicians involved—that it is not a personal indictment. This is reflected in the following way. Duff and Hollingshead frequently quoted young physicians who from time to time used expressions among colleagues that they would be unlikely to use elsewhere; this is, of course, typical in the back regions of all occupations and may even seen as a way of adapting to the stresses of work and uncertainty. Beeson, however, takes these anecdotes personally and views them as degrading:

> The criticism of the house staff extended even to attributing phrases to them which to me have a phoney ring, and perhaps merely represent what Duff and Hollingshead thought such characters ought to say! For example, I never heard the wards of the hospital referred to as "the zoo," nor do I think that the Emergency Admission Room was commonly referred to as "the pit." . . . I knew these young people well, far better than the writers of this book. I regarded them as able, likeable, dedicated and hard working—on the way to becoming outstandingly good physicians and surgeons [1968].

The basic issues of how to effectively utilize knowledge of patients' life situations in diagnosis, patient care, and rehabilitation, and how to weigh more elaborate attempts at physical diagnosis in contrast to considering other approaches to the patients' problems are difficult issues. We lack clear-cut concepts of how to appraise such difficulties or to effectively intervene, and it is natural that medical efforts should emphasize scientific medical orientations to care. However, in focusing on such problems, one risks a tendency of becoming callous and is likely to forget that medicine is a social art as well as a science. Moreover, the teaching hospital is the training ground not only for physicians who care for the desperately ill but for all physicians, and its emphases and orientations may not be well suited for much of the care physicians are called on to provide. In the care of even the seriously ill patient, social and psychological factors are of major importance; but the teaching hospitals have largely ignored these factors and thereby encouraged future generations of physicians to give them a low priority.

In conclusion, what can we learn from such controversies that may be helpful in making future efforts more effective? It is increasingly clear that if the intent of such studies is to bring about change in the contexts studied, rather than to add to knowledge or to inform the climate of general opinion, it is necessary to involve in such investigations those who have operational authority for the programs studied. In studying medical services, those concerned should be intimately involved in the design and progress of the study, and the investigation should require "informed consent" not only for the patients but also for the professionals involved. As a sociologist who works in medical contexts, I can attest to how difficult this can be. And, like the physician who fails to tell the patient everything in order to facilitate his management of the patient, the sociologist is also frequently tempted to say less than necessary in order to protect his access to the situation. I have increasingly come to believe that sociologists ought not to work on units in which the medical leadership will not accept them with a *realistic* understainding of the advantages and risks of sociological research. I emphasize the word "realistic" because it has been my experience that physicians who expect too much from behavioral science are as difficult to cooperate with as those who expect too little. It is crucial that physicians involved with behavioral science research programs in medicine have a reasonable concept of the likely product and the strengths and weaknesses of behavioral studies. It may be necessary in some contexts, such as in custodial institutions, to keep research concerns more covert, but it is unlikely to stimulate change from within. To the extent that the physicians are themselves involved in medical care research and committed to it, it is more likely that significant findings will be implemented.

It is also likely that research resulting in recommendations for fundamental restructuring of activities is unlikely to yield significant change. If Duff and Hollingshead were more analytic in their book, it would be clear that the failures of the teaching hospital cannot be resolved by simple changes here and there, but require substantial restructuring of health care financing, medical education, and medical practice. Professionals must work within the context of real constraints, and thus global recommendations for restructuring the overall approach leave helpless those who are urged to make the adaptations. In this sense Duff and Hollingshead were basically correct that the issues at stake are issues for the larger society and not just for the health professionals involved. In this sense the authors were using their observations at Yale–New Haven for a larger purpose, and their results have limited implications for reform of Yale–New Haven outside of more extensive reforms of the health care system as a whole. It is unfortunate that the study alienated some whose support will be needed in implementing the changes necessary to integrate social and psychological considerations in medical education and medical care. These differences, in part, represent conflicts of perspective that to some extent are inevitable; but they also suggest the importance of careful planning not only of the research effort, but also of the relationship of the researcher to the institutions studied.

REFERENCES

Beeson, P.
  1968 Special book review of sickness and society, *Yale Journal of Biology and Medicine* **41,** 226–240.
Cartwright, A.
  1964 *Human relations and hospital care.* Boston: Routledge and Kegan Paul.
Duff, R. S. and A. B. Hollingshead
  1968 *Sickness and society.* New York: Harper.
Ingelfinger, F. J.
  1968 The arch-hospital: An ailing monopoly, *Harper's Magazine:* 82–87.
Ley, P. and M. S. Spelman
  1967 *Communicating with the patient.* London: Trinity Press.
National Center for Health Statistics
  1971 *Surgical operations in short-stay hospitals for discharged patients: United States–1965.* PHS Series 13, No. 7, April. Washington, D.C.: U.S. Government Printing Office.
Pines, M.
  1968 Hospital, *McCall's* 79, 138–142.
Skipper, J., Jr. and R. Leonard
  1968 Children, stress, and hospitalization: A field experiment, *Journal of Health and Social Behavior* **9,** 275–287.

The Intermingling of Governmental Policy, Social Structure, and Public Values: The Case of the Changing Family

JOAN ALDOUS[1]

University of Georgia

Any discussion of the policy implications of family research necessarily entails a consideration of whether such a thing as family policy
is even possible.[2] Certainly the area suffers from numerous problems
as indicated by public concern over family failures in socialization and
social control. But, although there is a lack of agreement as to which
aspect of family interaction should be modified and toward what
goals, the real problematics of family policy in the United States do
not lie in such disagreement, but rather in the fact that influential
segments of public opinion even question whether there should be a
governmental family policy.[3]

[1] Affiliation at time of Conference: University of Minnesota.

[2] By policy, I refer to an enunciated action program which has received some sort
of legitimation through legislative approval or administration order and is designed to
influence a public problem (cf. Jones 1970:89). This definition assumes a broad
enough public consensus as to the existence of a problem to make it salient to lawmakers and officials, as well as some sort of agreement as to what should be done
to cope with the problem.

[3] A statement by a former president of the United States illustrates this attitude.
At a news conference when president, Dwight Eisenhower replied to a question concerning the federal government's possible provision of birth control information to
other countries on request, "I cannot imagine anything more emphatically a subject
that is not a proper political or governmental activity or function or responsibility
[New York Times, December 3, 1959]."

THE PROBLEMATICS OF FAMILY POLICY

The belief that government has no business intervening in family affairs stems in part from the strong emphasis on individualism in this country. Governmental policy, in this perspective, might be promulgated to advance the individual's pursuit of happiness, but families, even though they are composed of individuals and presumably dedicated to their well being, are a private venture, and, therefore, outside governmental purview.

In the past, suspicion of a national family policy was fed by the insistence of organized religion that it itself was the spokesman for family interests. Although not always speaking with one voice on these interests, religious leaders were in general agreement that church and state should remain separated when it came to policies concerning the family. Such a position enabled religious bodies to retain their special influence on the family without having to reconcile differences as to goals that government family policies would probably have made necessary. The very real diversity among families in the United States also contributed to the difficulty of enunciating a family policy by any societal institution (Schorr 1962:453–455).[4]

Although governmental social legislation has been largely directed to individuals, the ensuing programs almost inevitably affected families. Social security legislation is a good example. When the first such law took effect in 1935, the old-age provisions were limited to individuals. It quickly became apparent that individuals customarily did not live alone, and it was necessary to compensate family members of the insured worker for his death or retirement. Consequently, the old-age provisions were changed in 1939, 4 years after the passage of the first legislation. However, it took more than a quarter of a century to correct the individual bias of the original Aid to Dependent Children (ADC) provision of the Social Security Act. It was not until 1962 that benefits were finally extended to families seeking assistance where a father was present but unemployed. The legal change occurred because of a mounting belief that the ADC law by leaving out "needy father-present households" was contributing to their break-up.

Both of these examples illustrate the economic impact of governmental policies on the family, regardless of whether the policies specifically took families into account. In the case of social security legis-

---

[4] Schorr (1962) also lists the private enterprise system as another factor discouraging a governmental family policy. Since business interests have generally been hostile to all policies that would increase governmental intervention in the lives of citizens, this factor is not specific to family policy.

lation, policies directed to benefit individuals can quite clearly be modified to benefit families. But there are a number of instances where concern for individual rights runs counter to family values. The uneasy union in a democratic society between the values of social equality and personal freedom is a case in point. The family is a conservative institution not only in transmitting a significant portion of the cultural heritage to members of the next generation but also in its social placement of these individuals. Some individuals because of superior family resources have more opportunities to develop their abilities and thereby to begin their life course with unearned advantages. Attempts to equalize individual opportunities by means of governmental intervention usually involve some loss of family freedom, whether by decreasing the monetary resources parents can leave to children or by specifying merit, rather than family background, as a job requirement.

RESEARCH ON TWO-CAREER FAMILIES

The privileged opportunities an individual enjoys in the broader community due to inherited fortune or family background have been noted, and there have been a number of governmental attempts to mute these family influences. But another area in which the family operates to negate equal opportunities has until recently received little attention. This area consists of the family's internal patterns and specifically the assignment and content of family roles. The usual family structure places disproportionate constraints on the wife–mother who performs extrafamilial roles, particularly on married women who are trying to pursue a professional career.[5]

[5] The difficulties experienced by married women following professional careers cannot be dismissed as affecting too few indivduals to be of public concern. In 1972 there were 2,791,200 married women in the professions and technical positions (Manpower Report 1972:Table B-5). Highly educated professionals through financial resources, expertise, and ability to articulate their interests can exercise an influence on legislation disproportionate to their numbers, as indicated by their leadership in the attempt to pass the Equal Rights Amendment to the U.S. Constitution. In addition, the number of professional women is growing. The longitudinal study of women in the labor force that the staff of Ohio State University's Center for Human Resources is undertaking indicates a general upgrading in the occupational distribution of women. Among their representative national sample of women 30 to 44 years of age in 1967, this upgrading was reflected in an increase of professional and technical workers from 11% among the oldest age group of workers to 16% among the youngest age group of workers (Shea *et al.* 1970:Table 4.1).

The problems of this group have direct policy implications and also demonstate how policy issues may contribute to sociological theory. Married women's attempts to modify family arrangements so that they can function as professionals throw into sharp relief the interdependencies between family and occupational structures. These attempts also supply data on institutional change and its limits, as individuals try out, maintain or discard role variations and modifications in family interaction. Finally, the incipient conflict between group welfare, in this case the family, and individual development is highlighted in this issue.

For these reasons, in fulfilling the Carmel Conference assignment to abstract the policy implications of some research publication on the family, I have chosen Lynda Lytle Holmstrom's (1972) book, *The Two-Career Family*. The data of her study came from relatively unstructured interviews with 20 couples (wives and husbands interviewed separately) where both spouses pursued a career and with a comparison group of seven couples where wives had given up careers.[6] The women's occupations which fell in the humanities, social, physical, or biological sciences, all possessed high educational and training requirements (Holmstrom 1972:8). The men were primarily academicians or in the health professions, aside from a "few exceptions" who were business men (1972:202). The ages of the women were 35 or over, all old enough to face and somehow to handle the occupational and family role conflicts found in two-career families (1972:8).

Holmstrom's analysis indicates how dependent performance of professional or higher-level jobs is on a particular type of family structure. Although only one person will formally hold the position, there has to be another person to perform the family roles of entertaining, personal-effects care, and morale maintenance required by the person occupying the position. At present, career jobs (Wilensky 1961) go to men and the "career support" roles within the family go to women. The interdependencies of family and occupational structure for higher-level jobs, therefore, lie in the woman's performing the domestic activities that will serve her husband's needs so that he can devote himself single-mindedly to his career (Holmstrom 1972:6). Consequently, it goes against existing occupational and family arrangements in professional and managerial families for the wife to have a career.

Holmstrom (1972:72) details some of the specific problems flowing

[6] See Rapoport and Rapoport's (1969) article on 13 two-career families and a comparison group of three families where each woman broke off her career. The authors take pride in having presented the dual-career family concept to the academic community for systematic discussion. See also Bernard (1972) and Papanek (1973).

from the conflict between career and domestic duties for which dual career families have to develop solutions. The most serious problems center upon child rearing. Professional careers presupposes full-time study or work, yet 16 of the 20 two-career families had children. Since they lacked easy access to adult relatives, household help, and/or child-care centers, at least one member of the couple is required to remain at home to take charge of the child rearing responsibilities. Given the expectations of the occupational world, the normatively prescribed conjugal role organization, and the differential socialization of men and women, the woman became the family member who modified her career plans to meet these child nurturance requirements.

But such a solution puts the woman's whole career in jeopardy as she is never able to make a full-time commitment to it. The lack of flexible work schedules and the loss in prestige and perquisites that part-time jobs entail make it difficult for her to stay abreast with professional developments during the child rearing years. And once having lost contact with the occupational world, a professional woman seeking to reenter the job market must engage in a "catch-up" retraining period to become acquainted with current professional developments. She also must face the job competition of individuals who exceed her qualifications by reason of their full-time devotion to careers while she was performing domestic roles. If she chooses to pursue her career during the "full house" years, she experiences the frustrations, fatigue, and financial costs attendant on trying to fulfill both job and family responsibilities. Thus family role demands seriously threaten the professional woman's ability to pursue the occupational career of her choice.

STRATEGIES FOR HANDLING FAMILY PROBLEMS

The individual bias underlying governmental social policies is reflected in two contrasting views of what to do about family problems such as those just described. The first view which was reflected for many years in social work practices is to see the family as a relatively closed unit. Less attention is paid to external influences on the family than on what goes on among family members. The strategy for handling family problems is counseling with the person most directly troubled. With two-career families, theis strategy might take the form of counseling the couple, particularly the wife, as to how household affairs could be more efficiently managed. This clinical approach does not require a governmental policy rationale except in the broadest sense, since problems are defined in individual terms, with the differences between families rather than their similarities emphasized.

The second view, an environmental modification model, sees changing external circumstances as the means for mitigating the difficulties families face. The focus again may be on the individual, but there is little attempt in this model, as opposed to the counseling model, to intervene directly in the day-to-day interactions with other family members. Governmental provision of jobs, new ways of delivering health services, and various income transfer programs from one portion of the population to another are all examples of attempts to change the environment in which individuals operate.

In explicating the policy implications of the two-career family, the second model is appropriate. It should be apparent from the previous discussion that the problems experienced by such families stem from present occupational arrangements and normative gender-role assignments rather than from individual characteristics.

POLICY IMPLICATIONS: THE OCCUPATIONAL STRUCTURE

The underlying objective of policies designed to cope with the problems of two-career families is to enable the married woman to pursue a professional career and still maintain a family. The basic difficulty she faces due to existing interdependencies of occupations and family structures is the full-time demands from both. Holmstrom's suggested policy proposals, therefore, have a two-pronged approach calling for change in the job and family roles. Her first policy suggestion (1972:169), directed toward the occupational structure, is that the government should promote flexible work schedules for men and women employees within the public and private sectors. Such schedules would enable the professional woman and her husband to alternate household responsibilities. Even if the husband's traditional ideas or conventional work schedule would prevent him from taking on more family roles, a shortened work week would give professional women more time for running their household. Such a change, therefore, centering on the occupation, could modify family role arrangements or make existing ones more manageable.

In terms of feasibility, a governmental policy encouraging a flexible work week possesses the advantage of conforming to Schorr's (1962:456) "pickaback principle." According to him, "change to achieve family goals is most likely to occur when it is coincidental with other (social) developments." At the present time due to work-ers' demands for more leisure and management's concern for lesser absenteeism and greater productivity, a variety of companies and pub-lic institutions are already experimenting with a shorter work week. Although more companies and governmental agencies are trying the 4-day week, 3½-day week, 10-hour day plan, some companies are moving to a two-shift, 3½-day, 36-hour work week, with a few even trying a two-shift, 3-day, 30-hour week.[7]

Another advantage of such a policy is that no specific Congres-sional action would be needed to encourage more work schedule ex-perimentation. The Secretary of Labor would have to modify the 1938 Walsh–Healy Public Contracts Act, an act that presently requires all government contractors of $10,000 or more to conform to an 8-hour day work week. The overtime provisions for longer than this period would have to be eliminated if the large segments of the private economy doing business with the government were to be drawn into the work-week modification movement.

Such a government policy would also foster greater consideration of part-time position arrangements and might be of more benefit in the long run to professional women than changes in the work week schedule. Part-time job arrangements that do not penalize married women would ease the problems associated with women's following their professions during years of peak family demands. Employers would gain through continuity of service while women would not lose their expertise through domestic isolation from the profession.

POLICY IMPLICATIONS: THE FAMILY

The other policy proposals are directed toward the family and would modify women's roles. One of Holmstrom's (1972:173) propos-als calls for the development of child-care centers by employers of women. A government-subsidized child-care policy has already twice received legislative legitimation. The projected centers, however, are

---

[7] For semipopular reports of current work week variants, see the following: Ken-neth E. Wheeler, Small business eyes the four-day work week, *Harvard Business Re-view*, 1970, **48**, 142–147; How the four-day work week is catching on, *U.S. News and World Report*, March 8, 1971, 41–43; Why the work week pattern is changing, *Business Week*, March 13, 1971, 108–109; Paul L. Field, The three-day work week and the six-day company, *Business Management*, 1969, **36**, 25 ff.; and How is the four-day work week going?, *Dun's*, 1972, **100**, 52–54. See also Rava Poor, *4 days, 40 hours*, 1970. Cambridge, Massachusetts: Bursk and Poor.

primarily custodial and do not emphasize the intellectual training that would be needed to appeal to professional mothers. Experimentation with centers that go beyond custodial care would provide a solution to the serious problems of care of young children during the working day.

Holmstrom's work suggests three additional policy proposals. The first is a tax policy that would permit working women to deduct child-care costs as business expenses. Just as specialized personnel, office space, and equipment are necessary to the professional's performing his occupation, so too is child care for the professional woman with children. At the present time, the United States Internal Revenue Service allows child-care deductions where the working couple's joint net gross income is no more than $18,000. Beyond this figure, the allowable deductions diminish quickly. Such a restriction effectively eliminates the two-career couple from taking advantage of the deduction. Women may be discouraged from pursuing careers because of the cost of child-care services. For this reason, a policy change permitting child-care expenses to be defined as business expenses is needed.[8]

The second proposal is that the U.S. Office of Education requires states to supply home economics and shop classes to youths of both sexes. Such a policy, already being implemented on a national scale in Sweden, would operate to lessen the gender-based assignment of family roles. The superior competence and training of one sex in domestic roles would no longer necessarily exist.

A third proposal is governmental sponsorship of research on two-career families, their changing number and the consequences of these changes for family relations. Such research would focus on changes in family life as more and more married professional women become gainfully employed.

The role modifications permitting married women to pursue careers give rise to possible conflicts between individual development and the family's welfare. To this point this paper has been written from the perspective of the individual professional woman. But, because of the lack of institutionalized patterns for solving problems, two-career couples must seek their own solutions. And the marital conflicts in the role-making process may give rise to irreconcilable conjugal dif-

[8] On an itemized tax schedule, a couple where both members are employed loses $.50 of their deduction for every dollar they earn over $18,000. If their net adjusted gross income is under this amount, they can deduct $200 monthly in child care costs for one child, $300 for two, and $400 for three or more children as long as the children are under 15 years of age and qualify as dependents, according to 1972 IRS regulations.

ferences. These hazards to family solidarity should be assessed together with family patterns and community arrangements that may help to avoid them. More specific research issues concerning two-career families about which we have little knowledge include whether professional women rear their boys and girls alike in respect to the day-to-day requirements of household functioning. Another such issue is the career mother's effect on her daughter's perception of a woman's role.

THE POLICY PROPOSALS AND THE PROBLEMATICS OF FAMILY POLICY

These policy proposals possess the advantage of fitting in with existing legislative and corporate trends without requiring governmental ennunciation of family policy. They do not require governmental intervention in family affairs since they are directed ostensibly to individuals.

The proposals also have certain "spin-off" benefits that make them instrumental in reaching other governmental goals. For example, the goals of increasing black incomes to the level of white incomes have been approached only by young black families where both spouses are working, and where the head is under 35 years of age (U.S. Bureau of the Census 1971, Table 21). These proposals would promote such arrangements, since they would make it easier for all wives and not just professionals to work. In addition, these proposals would enable the federal government to reach its own goal of placing more women in advanced service levels. It is often overlooked but the Ohio State study (Shea 1970) shows that the federal government hires a greater proportion of women employees in professional and technical positions (43% of whites and 34% of blacks) than does private industry (8% of whites and 2% of blacks). And just as the federal government provided a standard for industry in interracial hiring, so can it also in work provisions for married women. Its agencies are currently experimenting with work schedules, and its employees are taking the initiative to set up child care plans.

The government, as Rivlin (1971:125) notes, is good at collecting money and writing checks but not at implementing service programs. The suggested proposals encourage other agencies or individuals to continue activities they are already undertaking or to develop programs that can serve as demonstration projects. The federal government itself, however, does not necessarily have to undertake action programs on a nation-wide scale.

FAMILY SOCIOLOGISTS AND FAMILY POLICY

The appearance of Holmstrom's *The Two-Career Family* is well timed to point up and hasten existing trends along the lines she advocates. Yet family sociologists, like sociologists in general, have rarely systematically attempted to enunciate policy. The reasons for this neglect are worth considering as they have implications for the training of graduate students.

The caliber of present family sociologists can be partly gauged from the fact that two recent presidents of the American Sociological Association, M. Komarovksy, 1972–1973, and W. J. Goode, 1971–1972, have devoted the major part of their professional careers to this specialty. But as with all specialists who study their own cultures, family sociologists as a group have been charged with taking a value-laden approach to their area of interest (cf. Kolb 1950; Heiskanen 1971). As a result, family sociologists with research pretentions, in leaning over backward to avoid value judgments, have sometimes avoided policy recommendations as well. Their recognition that the present state of our knowledge makes it difficult to specify the consequences of proposed government programs has also made them loath to give policy suggestions. In addition, the uproar over the so-called Moynihan Report (Rainwater and Yancey 1967), a report by a political scientist that plumped directly for a governmental family policy by reinforcing governmental officials' general disinterest in such endeavors, did not encourage family sociologists to make policy matters an important part of their activities.

MAKING POLICY A CENTRAL CONCERN

For their policy suggestions to have greater impact on government officials, so that the latter will encourage policy interests among sociologists, sociologists must first possess the expertise in applied matters that will increase the value of what they suggest to officials. Devising sociology training programs that will make policy development a recognized component of the sociologist's knowledge will require some fairly basic changes in the discipline. It will first of all require changes in the graduate school curriculum. The present tendency to concentrate graduate work in sociology exclusively will need to be modified so that students can become familiar with such disciplines as economics, and such applied areas as social work as well as business and industry where most people are employed. This wider range of educational experience should provide the sociologist with a better knowledge of the problems families face. Since manipulation of the family's environment usually involves economic considerations, training in economics, in conjunction with their sociological training, would provide students with the expertise to make family policy suggestions.

Education for policy-making will also require a sophisticated handling of the whole issue of values. It is all very well to call for a sociology of involvement, but the responsible professional must make explicit the assumptions and rationale that underlie the choices his policy proposals represent.[9]

A second training suggestion would be to establish internships for graduate students with public and private agencies whose operations affect families. Such agencies would include housing and urban renewal offices, state highway departments, large hospitals and clinics, family and children's agencies, administrative offices of school systems and the like. More and more, such agencies are fielding demonstration projects or experimental programs to gauge the consequences of various plans for delivering services. Student interns on such projects could gain both policy-making and policy-implementing experience. Internships with legislators would also teach sociologists the process whereby policy suggestions become translated into public law. Since such interns would presumably be serving as well as learning from the experience, bonds of reciprocity with legislators could be established. The lawmakers would be made aware of the value of the sociological perspective and so be more open to suggestions from its practitioners.

In any such training, however, one cannot overlook the academic staff at the universities. I have already described the general lack of commitment to policy matters among family sociologists. Until such an interest results in increased prestige for family sociologists, as well as other sociologists, it will be difficult to get them to devote their attention to issues of concern to government officials, particularly when the latter for one reason or another are difficult to reach. Editorial policies more open to articles dealing with public issues in profes-

---

[9] Holmstrom (1972:160–168), taking into account the research findings, presents a detailed rationale for choosing the value position from which her policy proposals derive.

sional journals, governmental funding of research projects testing policy alternatives, and departmental encouragement of seminars and courses devoted to research applications are all means for legitimating policy concerns. Conferences such as the one at Carmel and sessions at national meetings are other means for adding prestige to policy-making.

The American Sociological Association itself, as the organizational representative of sociology, can play a part in increasing the policy impact of its members. Establishing a policy development division of the ASA with foundation support would be one means for publicizing to sociologists and policy-makers alike the relevance of the discipline. Such a division could be the means for initiating seminars and conferences on potential and present public issues. By bringing together government officials and sociologists whose work is relevant to the officials' concern, both parties will become better acquainted with the relevance of sociology to critical issues. The ASA can also alert its members to issues before the Congress and the Executive Branch where sociological expertise could make a contribution. Again, the sociological perspective would be made salient to policy-makers.

As far as family sociologists are concerned, it is doubtful that the climate of public opinion will permit the enunciation of a government family policy in the near future. However, policies in limited areas such as the provision of family planning services or income maintenance programs for the poor will have direct consequences for the family. Sociologists interested in the family should be prepared to make suggestions on these matters and, with more policy-oriented training and more open channels of communication, more policy-makers may be listening. Certainly, the closeness of family sociologists to the issues of central governmental concern suggests that they might exercise leadership in policy relevant activities.

But before concluding on this fairly optimistic note, I would like to issue a *caveat*. I began this article by asking whether a family policy was possible in this country. My policy suggestions did not presuppose any such government pronouncement. Now I would like to raise the larger question of the extent to which sociologists as a whole should be involved in policy formulation. For unless we are willing to put aside our commitment to the discipline and enter the political arena as partisans, we will have little to say about whether our proposals become public policy. Officials and lawmakers make policy, and the reasons for their choice of programs do not customarily derive from social science knowledge. However, if we were to become partisans for our proposals, we would have lost the claim to intellectual expertise that constituted our argument for being listened to by policy-makers in the first place. Thus, the commitment of a major part of the discipline's resources to a public issue orientation could lead to frustration among sociologists because policy-makers pay little attention to them, or to the loss of their status as social scientists if sociologists take an active part in policy-making. Perhaps, in addition to considering the policy implications of sociological research, we need to examine in greater detail the implications for sociology of a concern with policy.

REFERENCES

Bernard, J.
    1972 *The future of marriage.* New York: World.
Heiskanen, V. S.
    1971 The myth of the middle-class family in American family sociology, *The American Sociologist* **6,** 14–22.
Holmstrom, L. L.
    1972 *The two-career family.* Cambridge, Massachusetts: Schenkman.
Jones, C. O.
    1970 *An introduction to the study of public policy.* Belmont, California: Wadsworth.
Kolb, W. L.
    1950 Family sociology, marriage education, and the romantic complex: A critique, *Social Forces* **29,** 65–72.
Manpower Report of the President
    1972 U.S. Government Printing Office.
Papanek, H.
    1973 Men, women and work: Reflections on the two-person career, *American Journal of Sociology* **78,** 852–872.
Rainwater, L. and W. L. Yancey
    1967 *The Moynihan report and the politics of controversy.* Cambridge, Massachusetts: M.I.T. Press.
Rapoport, R. N. and R. V. Rapoport
    1969 The dual-career family: A variant family and social change, *Human Relations* **22, 3–30.**
Rivlin, A. M.
    1971 *Systematic thinking for social action.* Washington, D.C.: Brookings Institute.
Schorr, A. L.
    1962 Family policy in the United States, *International Social Science Journal* **14,** 452–467.
Shea, J. R., *et. al.*
    1970 Dual Careers, Manpower Research Monograph No. 21, U.S. Department of Labor, Superintendent of Documents. Washington, D.C.: U.S. Government Printing Office.

U.S. Bureau of the Census
   1971   *The social and economic status of the black population in the United States.*
          Current Population Reports, Series P-23, No. 42. Washington, D.C.: U.S.
          Government Printing Office.
Wilensky, H. L.
   1961   Orderly careers and social participation, *American Sociological Review* **26,**
          521–539.

Reconceptualizing Social Problems in Light of Scholarly Advances: Problem Drinking and Alcoholism

ROBERT STRAUS

University of Kentucky

This essay on the social-policy implications of recent research on alcoholism is based on Cahalan's (1972) investigation of problem drinking among American men. In this paper, Cahalan reports selected findings from a longitudinal research program initiated in the early 1960s and designed to offer some new perspectives on the nature and distribution of drinking practices and problem drinking through survey research based on national probability sampling of households. (For earlier published reports from this research, see Cahalan, Cisin, and Crossley 1969; Cahalan 1970.)

The findings have to do in particular with the drinking problems and their correlates of one group of men initially surveyed in 1964–1965 and restudied in 1967, and a second group of men, ages 21 to 59, sampled nationally in 1969. It must be stressed that these findings are based on men living in households, and exclude homeless men and those living in institutions. This is of particular significance because sociological studies of alcoholism from the 1940s were based almost exclusively on data obtained from institutionalized or skid row populations; and studies of the 1950s and 1960s have been limited primarily to these groups plus alcoholics who were undergoing treatment or were members of Alcoholics Anonymous. Thus, prior to the work of Cahalan and his colleagues, most of our data on the social correlates of problem drinking have been based on persons whose drinking was associated with incarceration, isolation, treatment, or some form of formal help-seeking. In general, these earlier studies have depicted alcoholism as a condition most commonly found among men in middle life and most often developing after a fairly long progression toward dependency on alcohol, and/or their loss of control over drinking. Prior to the research under consideration here, estimates of around five million alcoholics in the United States had been commonplace.

For his analysis, Cahalan employed 13 categories of problem drinking: (1) "heavy intake" (based on quantity and frequency); (2) "binge drinking" (intoxicated for more than a day at a time); (3) "psychological dependence" (reliance on alcohol to change moods); (4) "loss of control" (inability to stop drinking once started or to refrain from drinking at inappropriate times); (5) "symptomatic drinking" (including sneaking drinks, anticipatory drinking, blackouts after drinking, drinking to alleviate hangovers); (6) "belligerence"; (7) problems with wife; (8) with other relatives; (9) with job; (10) with friends or neighbors; (11) or difficulties involving the police; (12) or finances; (13) or personal health. Specific problems were classified according to two levels of severity and whether they had been experienced "ever" or within the last 3 years ("currently"). In addition, an index of social consequences of drinking was employed.

Five of Cahalan's key findings have been selected for brief presentation and comment, preliminary to a consideration of their implications for social policy.

(1) A majority (72%) of American men interviewed in their homes recalled and reported some experience with at least one type of problem associated with drinking. Fifty per cent of the men had experienced one or more problems within the last 3 years; 55% reported one or more problems at a "high" level of severity, including 36% of the total sample who had experienced a high severity level problem within the last 3 years. Problems most commonly reported, according to the percentages reporting these problems both "currently" and at "high levels" of severity," included: heavy intake (13%), trouble with wives (14%), psychological dependence (9%), belligerence (9%), and symptomatic drinking (8%).

Comment. The high prevalence of drinking problems reported by this sample of American men indicates that previous estimates of the number of persons suffering from problem drinking have been both too low and based on an unrealistically narrow conception of the dimensions of alcohol-related pathology.

Although definitions of alcoholism have been subject to much variation, there has been a tendency in recent years, among those studying these problems, toward defining alcoholics as persons who *repeatedly* drink in ways which *for them* threaten personal or psychological health, or interfere with meaningful interpersonal relationships, or prevent or reduce effective fulfillment of responsibilities to family, job, or community. The criteria of problem drinking employed by Cahalan are all consistent with this definition. However, the lay public's conception of alcoholism is still primarily derived from institutionalized persons and those undergoing rehabilitation, and is more that of a progressive, irreversible phenomenon which invariably involves a vicious spiral-type acceleration toward greater and greater complications.

Cahalan's sampling of the household population study suggests that many persons who have once manifested symptoms of alcoholism have been able to alter their drinking to avoid problems. In fact, only about one-half the men who reported ever having had these particular problems reported experiencing them within the last 3 years. This clear indication of a *remission* in problem drinking points to a need to identify and study in depth the sizeable population of problem drinkers who do not become caught in irreversible progression. It is quite possible that this previously unidentified and unheralded population can provide important clues regarding experiences and motivations which contribute to changes in destructive drinking patterns in young problem drinkers. This line of inquiry could lead to a major breakthrough in the development of effective preventive intervention.

(2) Drinking problems were more prevalent among men ages 21–24 than among men in any other age group. Forty per cent of these young men living in households were reported as having a "high current over-all problems score." These included 26%, symptomatic drinking; 19%, problems with wife; 15%, problems with friends or neighbors; 15%, belligerence; 12%, loss of control; 11%, financial problems; 10%, problems on job; 10%, binge drinking; and 10%, problems with police. These prevalence figures for young men were roughly twice that for any other age group.

Comment. Cahalan's findings indicate that in the late 1960s problem drinking was a very significant phenomenon for young adult males. Although data for all men, comparing rates of problems "ever" experienced with those of "current" problems, would support the optimistic view of an apparent, rapid decline in drinking problems after the age of 25, only future study will tell us whether these findings also indicate the more alarming phenomenon of prevalence rates which are particularly high for this generation. Such a finding would have distressing future implications because Cahalan's data clearly support his conclusion that "the seeds of longer-term serious problems with alcohol are usually sown by one's drinking habits in one's early twenties and not so much by habits not acquired until one's forties [Cahalan and Room 1972:1475]."

Missing from the Cahalan study are data on drinking practices and problems among young men prior to age 21. Numerous studies of high school and college-age populations indicate that drinking in American society begins during the teen years for most persons and that the nature of drinking practices and problems is closely related to such varied factors as parental example (role model), peer group pressures (conformity), and perceived restrictions (rebellion, assertion, or alienation). One, therefore, must be cautious about interpretations based on drinking by persons in their early 20s without considering also that the "seeds" of such drinking occurred at even earlier ages.

(3) A comparison of the "wetter" (with few local option prohibitions, minimum legal restrictions on availability of alcohol, or absence of temperance-oriented religious and social groups) and "dryer" (with more local option prohibitions and other legal restrictions, greater concentration of temperance orientation) regions of the country revealed that dry regions had three times as many abstaining men as wet regions (21% vs. 7%) but that more drinkers in dry areas than in wet areas tended to have problems and get into trouble associated with their drinking. In addition to residents of dry areas, men belonging to conservative Protestant religions, irrespective of area of residence, tended to have a high prevalence of social consequences if they were drinkers. High social consequences included health, injury, or financial problems, together with specific interpersonal or social problems, all associated with high intake and/or binge drinking.

Comment. Numerous studies have suggested that temperance orientations and legal prohibitions of alcohol use, although they reduce the number of drinkers in a population, may actually contribute to more problem drinking; that in such situations persons who drink in defiance of restrictions tend to drink heavily, frequently, and in socially inappropriate situations. The significance of Cahalan's finding lies in the fact that data from men living in households add support to other indications of the paradoxical impact of both legal prohibition and a temperance orientation on problem drinking. The finding suggests the presence of subcultures in most "dry" regions which impose pressures to drink heavily.

(4) Drinking problems of high consequences are reported *most* frequently by men from the lowest social class (using Hollingshead's Index of Social Position) and *more* frequently by men from the lower-middle than from the upper-middle or highest social position. The greatest prevalence of high consequences (33%) is found among men ages 21–24 in the lowest and lower-middle social positions.

Comment. Early sociological studies of problem drinking, based on institutionalized populatons, revealed a heavy lower-class weighting. Studies based on alcoholics seen in special alcoholism treatment programs and members of Alcoholics Anonymous show a heavier weighting of alcoholics in the middle and even in the upper social strata. This finding reflects, in part, factors of social selection in these particular samples. The weighting of problem drinkers in the lower social strata in Cahalan's sample is especially significant because the sampling procedure excluded the institutionalized and the homeless which would weight the distribution even more heavily toward the lowest class. These findings show that high-consequence drinking is three times more prevalent in the lowest than in the upper-middle and highest social classes. They compel a modification of recently common beliefs which held that problem drinking was relatively evenly distributed throughout all social classes.

(5) In addition to age, socioeconomic status, and religion, other significant correlates of problem drinking are large city residence, childhood deprivations, and race. Among the various correlates of problem drinking, environmental factors predominated for the most part, although specific personality characteristics such as impulsivity, and lack of ego resiliency were found to be significant.

Comment. The overwhelming significance to problem drinking of such social factors as age, socioeconomic status, urban residence, and race, as identified by Cahalan's study, makes it incumbent upon students of social behavior to concern themselves with the formulation of social policy aimed at effective intervention, as well as with policies concerned with responding to the more usually identified consequences of problem drinking.

SOCIAL POLICY IMPLICATIONS

Reconceptualization of Alcoholism

In this paper the terms "alcoholism" and "problem drinking" have both been used. Cahalan, noting the general tendency in society to think of all alcoholics as having progressive dependency on drinking and loss of control over drinking, adopted the term "problem drinker" as more inclusive of the varied phenomena falling within the scope of his study. Irrespective of which of the terms—"alcoholic" or "problem drinker"—is used, it seems clear that social policy should be directed toward altering and broadening the public's concept to include all people whose use of alcohol repeatedly leads to problems. The definition of "alcoholism" (cited earlier) is consistent with this goal, but prevailing popular conceptions are more restrictive.

Ironically, one factor which restricts the conceptualization of alcoholism is the medical model which defines alcoholism as a "disease." The medical model was initially promoted in the 1940s and has been advocated since then by many persons especially interested in alcohol problems, including the fellowships of Alcoholics Anonymous. Its promotion was a form of deliberate social policy aimed at reducing the public stigma and altering moralistic connotations of alcoholism. It was also hoped that the medical model would stimulate (1) a greater sense of responsibility for, and greater involvement in, rehabilitation of alcoholics by the medical profession, and (2) a greater sense of public responsibility, reflected through governmental programs of research, treatment, and prevention. In varying degrees all of these goals have been achieved, although there has been more change in public attitudes and governmental involvement than in the attitudes and activities of the health professions.

Despite the obvious social usefulness of the disease concept, it is clear from Cahalan's findings that the medical model has outlived its usefulness as a unitary form of conceptualizing alcoholism. That model is far too restrictive. By defining alcoholism in terms of progression, physical damage, withdrawal syndrome, loss of control, and dependence, it encourages society to exclude and to excuse problem drinkers who do not fit these criteria. Thus, the medical model, by permitting exclusion of several million problem drinkers from the concept of alcoholism, has indirectly supported social norms that encourage the very patterns of alcohol consumption that generate problems. Furthermore, it encourages young people and others who do not manifest disabling physical or psychiatric symptoms to deny their problem drinking, despite the complications in their personal lives caused by problem drinking.

Recommendation. Cahalan's study demonstrates the compelling need for a major reconceptualization of the nature of alcoholism, the identification of problem drinking, and the distribution of these alcohol-related problems in contemporary society. In particular, it is suggested that an effort be made to achieve, at both the public level and among the helping professions, a perception of varied types of alcoholism and problems related to drinking, and to introduce a *social environment model* of alcoholism and problem drinking to complement the medical model. This is essential both as a focus for needed further research and as a basis for delineating realistic modes of intervention. For a recent effort in this direction, see Straus 1973.

The Youthful Problem Drinker

Most studies of drinking behavior in American society have focused on either the onset or the long term consequences of drinking. There have been numerous reports on the drinking practices of high school and college youth (although not on college-age youth who do not attend college) and some retrospective studies of the drinking careers of persons identified as alcoholics. But we know very little about the early drinking careers of individuals in the work–family–community (as contrasted to school–college) setting. Cahalan's findings make it obvious that this critical gap in sociological knowledge about drinking must be filled. Furthermore, Cahalan's own effort at longitudinal research serves to emphasize the virtual void we have in any kind of research which has followed drinking behavior prospectively over time.

Recommendation. Cahalan's suggestion of a remission phenomenon can only be studied and confirmed by longitudinal projects. The importance of studying the remission process in problem drinking is dramatized by the impossibility of mobilizing resources to "treat" all of our problem drinkers even assuming that the skills and techniques for effective treatment were availabe. Basic longitudinal research should be supported involving an early identification of problem drinkers and the detailed case study of life experiences associated with both remission and progression. Such research must be considered basic to the development of a program of preventive intervention designed to shift problem drinkers from a progression course to a remission course. In this endeavor it is hoped that survey research will be supplemented by case study methods to permit micro- as well as macro-analysis of this critical social process.

Changing Drinking Behavior

Repeated efforts to control alcoholism and problem drinking by prohibiting or restricting the legal availability of alcohol have failed to produce the desired goals. Historically, and in our contemporary society, there is evidence that "dry" compared with "wet" areas do have fewer users of alcohol, but that those who do drink in violation of restrictions generate such a disproportionate number of problems that the net impact on society is negative. Cahalan's comparisons of the prevalence of problems in "wet" and "dry" regions should serve to forestall any move toward further restricting the legal availability of alcohol as a means of controlling alcoholism. On the other hand, his data do validate previously indentified differences in the prevalence of alcohol pathology among different segments of society, and they suggest that several factors of social environment are significant correlates of problem drinking. There is in these findings the implied force of social sanction influencing whether drinking is moderate and functional or leads to intoxication and problems. There are clearly some groups in society in which most people use alcohol but few people experience problems, and in which drinking in moderation is sanctioned but intoxication is effectively controlled. (The Orthodox Jewish example is often cited, but one might also include the family-centered drinking that was apparently commonplace in seventeenth century Puritan New England.) Not since the early temperance movement for "moderation" was superseded in the 1850s by the prohibition movement has there been in American society an exerted effort aimed at controlling intoxication *without* threatening man's preciously held "right" to drink.

Recommendation. In view of the magnitude of problem drinking in American society, and especially the concentration of problems in the young adult age groups identified by Cahalan, a national policy of fostering moderation and discouraging intoxication is suggested. This would involve replacing an "anti-drinking" approach in alcohol education at all levels with emphasis on "how-to-drink" safely and responsibly. At the same time, the images of drinking behavior promulgated by the mass media should be modified (as a matter of social responsibility) to eliminate the current emphasis on uncomplicated intoxication, the uses of alcohol for coping, and the association of heavy drinking with status, prestige, popularity, wealth, and success. Instead, the media should be encouraged to associate socially desirable goals with abstention and moderation, to encourage nonchemical coping, and to portray more realistically the consequences of intoxication. Policy decisions in this direction should be guided by studies of the norms and sanctions of societies which have effectively controlled intoxication.

In light of the magnitude of problem drinking in the United States, the elimination of advertising of alcohol beverages seems tentatively a reasonable social policy. Ideally, such a decision would be based on research designed to test the relationship between advertising and patterns of drinking behavior, and to test the assumption of the alcohol and advertising industries that advertising merely influences "brand" choice. In the absence of such research, the elimination of advertising of alcohol beverages would seem to pose few undesirable social consequences and might reduce the exposure of the entire society to repeated association of drinking with such images as gusto, success, distinction, virility, and seductivity.

Preventive Intervention

Even prior to the expanded conceptualization of the magnitude and variety of alcohol problems which emerges from Cahalan's study, it has been apparent that the effective control of alcoholism lies in prevention. All of the helping profession resources in the country would hardly be capable of "treating" all of our alcoholics even if our treatment technology were more reliable than it is.

Although the high prevalence of problem drinking in young people was rather unanticipated, it probably represents, as Cahalan suggests, a relabeling of behavior that has previously been ascribed to "sowing wild oats." From the viewpoint of prevention, the possibility of a remission phenomenon is encouraging, but even a 50% spontaneous remission rate would leave roughly 20% of the male population involved in problem drinking during roughly the second third of their lives. The questions still remain as to whether and how effective preventive intervention can reach this group. Before further considering prevention, we must remember that alcoholism comes in many varieties, each with multiple probable causes, and personalized courses. There can be, therefore, no magic prevention formula but at best numerous strategies, some of which hopefully may prove appropriate to some kinds of problems.

Cahalan's "seed" theory suggests looking at the young adult drinker. For the most part he is married, employed, and living in a household. For the most part his problems with drinking involve his family, job, and community. A social environment model for problem drinking suggests the need for research designed to identify the uses and meanings of alcohol in relation to basic roles and round-the-clock activities of users. Cahalan's study provides only general cues. At this point we can only translate cues into the identification of areas to be explored further. Three logical areas for further study include the relationships between alcohol consumption and the performance and satisfactions achieved in sexual behavior, employment, and leisure time. All of these areas provide great potentialities for satisfaction and fulfillment; all can incite anxieties and impose disappointment and frustration; all are areas in which the norms of society and the expectations of individuals often far exceed experienced rewards; all are areas in which the chemical actions of alcohol on the central nervous system can alleviate anxiety, dull disappointment, and provide illusionary satisfactions while impairing performance.

There is evidence that the significance of alcohol consumption in relation to work and leisure varies greatly according to types of employment and socioeconomic status. Cahalan's finding of a heavy weighting of drinking problems in the lower socioeconomic strata, especially in younger men, suggests that these strata should be a special target for further study. To what extent is drinking related to unemployment or apparent unemployability? How does it relate to the monotony of totally impersonal assembly-line type jobs? How does it relate to the length of the working day, week, or year? To what extent is drinking correlated with absence of opportunities for active participant involvement in recreational or other so-called leisure time pursuits? Some factories are experimenting with "humanizing" their production lines and trying to give their workers more identification with the product of their efforts, and are measuring "results" in terms of quality and quantity of production. Drinking behavior might be introduced as an added variable to such studies. In a similar way studies might be designed to measure the use of alcohol among persons engaging in participant as compared with passive recreation. Other studies should focus on the use of alcohol by indivduals whose jobs demand unusual concentration or who are employed beyond their levels of ability. It must also be remembered that drinking has become ritualized in many work and recreational situations. A special target for study perhaps should be those responsible for high level decision making in business, industry, government, and the military establishments, although how such groups could be brought to sponsor research on the role of alcohol in their own decision making defies imagination.

Although Cahalan's study and, therefore, this paper have considered only drinking practices of men, and although the epidemiology of problem drinking among American women is known to vary considerably from that of men, it should be obvious that many of the policy implications considered here are relevant to both sexes.

IMPLICATIONS FOR THE PROFESSION

Of the questions posed for the Carmel Conference, this paper has dealt primarily with the first: the policy implications of Cahalan's study. The study is too recent to have had significant impact on policy, although Cahalan's earlier reports are reflected in the December 1971 Report to Congress on *Alcohol and Health* from the Secretary of Health, Education, and Welfare.

Finally, there is the question of implications for the discipline and its training, if in the future we are to produce more social policy recommendations with greater impact. In this regard I would first like to suggest that we must have greater variety in the methodological techniques sociologists are prepared to apply and better training in the building blocks of survey research. Too often, our students learn to master the most sophisticated techniques and rigorous methods of data analysis but do not learn how to generate fruitful and relevant data. They ask questions before they learn to identify what the appropriate questions are, how the questions can be phrased so that they are consistently understood, and how to elicit responses so that interpretation is consistent with the intended meaning. We, therefore, must be sure that our students have had experience in interviewing and developing survey instruments before we send them out to direct inteviewers and administer surveys. These comments are based on general observations and are not, of course, related to Cahalan's paper.

My second recommendation concerns longitudinal research. Although Cahalan's paper is based on a longitudinal project, its fruitfulness serves simply to identify the paucity of, and great need for, more longitudinal research in our field, and the special need for such studies with respect to the study of drinking behavior. Students should be encouraged to think of problems which they can project into the future and in which they can make substantial career investments. This implies the desirability of much more support for longitudinal research than is now available from granting agencies.

Finally, the meaningful application of sociological research to social policy rests only in part with the ability of the sociologist to ask questions, rigorously pursue data analyses, or critically evaluate the validity and reliability of findings. We must build into the sociological way of thinking some anticipation of the Social significance of our efforts. As Sumner so aptly insisted, we must consistently ask: "What of it?"

REFERENCES

Cahalan, D.
   1970   *Problem drinkers.* San Francisco: Jossey-Bass.
   1972   Problem drinking among American men aged 21–59. A paper presented at the 30th International Congress on Alcoholism and Drug Dependence in Amsterdam, September, 1972. (See Cahalan and Room 1972, below.)
Cahalan, D., I. H. Cisin, and H. M. Crossley
   1969   *American drinking practices: A national study of drinking behavior and attitudes.* New Brunswick, New Jersey: Rutgers Center of Alcohol Studies.
Cahalan, D. and R. Room
   1972   Problem drinking among American men aged 21-59, *American Journal of Public Health* **62,** 11:1473–1482.
   1974   *Problem drinking among American men: A monograph.* New Brunswick, New Jersey: Rutgers Center of Alcohol Studies.
Straus, R.
   1973   Alcohol and society, *Psychiatric Annals* **3,** entire issue.

Policy Enthusiasms for Untested Theories and the Role of Quantitative Evidence: Labeling and Mental Illness

KURT W. BACK

Duke University

In the sociology of mental health a fundamental division in theory and method has developed in recent years. This is but a part of a larger debate, encompassing questions of social reality, of the nature of man and of the appropriate method in sociology. In discussions of mental health the issue has been clearly joined; it has direct implications for practice. Gove's (1970) article assesses some of the evidence on this issue and is a good anchoring point for a discussion of fundamental problems on the sociology of mental health.

Policy-related research frequently takes the goals of a particular policy for granted and tries to find methods to reach these goals most efficiently or evaluate the effectiveness of this particular policy. Discussions of basic theoretical problems, however, may lead to a new look at the goals of a policy, a redefinition of goals, and an implementation of these very different goals. These implications of a new theoretical approach are often not worked out by the theorist himself; the application to policy occurs typically through a gradual absorption of the new ideas into cultural presuppositions, and this process can be analyzed only in retrospect. Such analysis has been done in the field of mental health by Foucault (1965) in *Madness and Civilization* and Rothman (1971) in *The Discovery of the Asylum;* both show that special institutions for the insane developed in the eighteenth and early nineteenth centuries in response to new views on human nature and prevailing social conditions.

The current theoretical controversy between the psychiatric and societal reaction theories which Gove discusses reflects a similar basic choice in outlook as well as in implied policy. Here, we can observe the process by which the new theory emerges and by which it may be accepted as a base for policy. The logical relevance of research findings to possible policies is not the only factor that determines their impact on policy. The way in which the results are presented, the appeal of the reasoning, and the relationship to current ideology are some of the factors which affect the relationship between sociological research and actual policy. The debate on theories of mental health permits us to see this process as it occurs, not to be reconstituted from historical records. We can study it and still influence it in its relation to current policy.

In discussing the policy implications of Gove's paper, we shall proceed in three steps. (1) We shall present (a) the theoretical problem and Gove's contribution to the discussion, and (b) the implication of this theory for public policy. This will be followed by a discussion on the probability of the importance of the debate and of the specific article for public policy. (2) The reasons for the accepting of evidence, namely, the general logic of evidence, and the appeal of different methodological approaches are discussed. This then leads to the question of acceptability of styles of research and presentation, and those social conditions which will determine the receptive atmosphere. (3) We shall discuss strategies for usefulness of theoretical discussions in general and of Gove's paper in particular from both the point of view of scientific methodology and the relation to the social policy.

SOCIETAL REACTION AND PSYCHIATRIC THEORY

Gove addresses himself to a theory which has become very popular in the last decade, under the names of "Societal Reaction" or "Labeling Theory," through the work of Erikson, Becker, Scheff, Lemert, and others. This theory is proposed as a general theory of deviance; its main conceptual advance lies in its distinction between two types of deviance—primary and secondary. Primary deviance is defined as commission of certain acts which may be considered as deviant according to prevailing social norms. However, the theory attaches little importance to this stage in a sociological sense. Secondary deviance arises when the person who may have committed the deviant act has to confront his being labeled as deviant; the labeling, not the act, leads to the development of a deviant role, the sociologically important aspect of deviance.

The theory encompasses a broad variety of deviant acts. Gove concerns himself with only one type of deviance, namely, mental illness, and we shall do the same here. In his discussion, he follows Scheff (1966) who has done the main work on labeling theory in mental illness. It is sufficient for our purposes here to look at Scheff's formulation.

Scheff calls the particular phenomenon "residual deviance," which societal reaction defines as mental illness. Behaviors so labeled are not defined by any particular institution, as legal transgressions or moral transgressions are, but they are recognized as transgressions against those customs which are followed implicitly in society. An example of such a custom might be facing a person when speaking to him and not laughing when saying, "I am sad." Transgressions against these are the primary deviances which form the raw material of the societal definition of mental illness. Secondary deviance is induced when a person's residual deviant behavior is labeled as mental disease. Given this definition of mental illness, Scheff's theory of societal reaction proceeds in several steps as expounded by him and summarized by Gove. (1) Everybody is likely to exhibit some residual deviant behavior; (2) some people are caught by the institutions dealing with mental illness and labeled as mentally sick; and (3) this process is practically irreversible; labeling brands a person indelibly as mentally sick. Thus, it is the institutions themselves which lead to mental disease and nothing in the persons themselves. As Gove points out, this theory relieves the scientist of worrying about the causes of the primary deviance and points his attention to secondary deviance and the processes leading to it. The theory can be opposed to the "psychiatric" traditional theory which defines mental illness as an aspect of an individual's personality or behavior.

THE EMPIRICAL TEST

The problem that Gove sets for himself is to find empirical tests for the societal reaction theory of mental illness. In the article he does not provide any original data, although he uses some data which he has collected himself and presented elsewhere. In a later paper (Gove and Howell 1972) Gove compares psychiatric and societal reaction theory using only original research.

Presumably, in order to test a theory empirically we have to be able to negate the statements made by it. One would have to say, for example, that residual deviant behavior is not widely distributed in the population, that there is no arbitrary pull toward labeling specific peoples as deviant, or that just labeling is irrelevant, that labeling is not a one-way process, and that the labeling does not adhere to people for a long time. However, in actual practice we cannot test the statements in this way. In most of the writings of these labeling theorists, the theory is not quite stated as an all-or-none affair; rather, it is implied that secondary deviance or societal reaction is important and primary deviance is not. In fact, the theory is presented as a description of a process. However, in testing the question, Gove chooses to follow a quantitative procedure. We shall return later to the questions which this testing procedure raises.

Gove goes on to examine three logical derivations of societal reaction theory. (1) If labeling is a purely social process, independent of actual behavior, then admission processes to mental hospitals should be extremely perfunctory. (2) If labeling is a one-way street and changes the person completely into the deviant role, the stay in the hospital should be extremely long and any pretense of cure should be nonexistent. (3) Again, if labeling is a one-way street, there should be no effective processes through which people change back from a deviant to a nondeviant role.

Very little research data are available to test these propositions exactly as stated. Gove has surveyed the literature and presumably has located the bulk of the data that are relevant to the hypotheses. This procedure is open to the charge of selectivity, but Gove claims, and there is no reason to doubt him, that he has used all the relevant data which have been collected in a usable form.

Gove first examines data on admission to hospitals. He begins with voluntary admissions. According to societal reaction theory, voluntary admission should not be an important event since in this case, patients look for the label themselves. However, a great proportion of today's hospital admissions are voluntary (self commitment), and further, only a minority of people who try to get committed on their own are accepted. It seems that labeling is not a random process but is related to some difinite criteria. Data from involuntary commitment point in the same direction. It is true that many commitment procedures are quite cursory; in some places commitment rates of over 90% show that no real decision based on evidence is made at these hearings. However, the hearings themselves are preceded by a detailed screening by a psychiatrist. If there is no psychiatric prescreening, commitment rates are much lower. Thus, a definite attempt is made to find some objective standards of health. For instance, in Clausen and Yarrow's (1955) pioneer study on paths to the mental hospitals, the behaviors described are not common residual deviances but a series of extremely bizarre and dangerous acts, such as threatening to kill one's spouse. Only after acts of this kind occur and other people connected with the person cannot cope with the behavior at all, commitment procedures are instituted. Even then, people try to avoid labeling the patient for a long time, avoiding ascribing insanity to a person close to them.

The second derivation, that labeling is an irreversible process and that entrance into hospitals is a pathway to an almost permanent status, is refuted by data on length of stay at the hospital. It seems that this argument of the societal reaction theorists was based on hospital conditions prevailed in the past, where care was mainly custodial. Since the advent of drug therapy and other rapid treatment methods, a stay in the hospital is relatively short, as Gove shows.

Finally, there is the question of role reversibility outside the hospital, which in psychiatric parlance is a question of rehabilitation. Gove cites some data showing that, controlled for status variables, ex-mental patients show as much adjustment to society in role interactions and other conventional measures as nonmental patients.

The data presented in the paper do not lead to any particular issues of policies which would be implemented quickly. The facts collected for this discussion would be insufficient guidelines for improving admission or commitment procedures in mental hospitals. However, the issue to which the research is addressed has deep implications for policy which go beyond procedural improvement.

If taken to its logical conclusion, labeling theory would lead to radical change in mental health policy. Instead of providing more facilities, especially for in-patients, policy would have to be directed toward protecting "residual deviates" from being caught in a bureaucratic network in which they may be stigmatized and changed but from which they rarely benefit. Thus acceptance of this theory would imply a radical change in policy, including the closing, or at least reorganization, of mental hospitals, and either an educational program to improve tolerance of deviance, or designing institutions to protect helpless labeled-individuals from the nefarious influences of the mental health establishment. Merely improving existing institutions —or using additional funds to provide more mental health facilities— would only compound current mistakes.

Thus, the potential implications of the theoretical conflict are far-reaching and its resolution could change the course of legislation and administration of mental problems. However, we may also safely predict that a few journal articles such as Gove's will not determine future legislation and executive action. There are several steps between the kind of reasoning present in the article and its acceptance or rejection as a base for public policy. The understanding of these steps is in itself a problem of sociology, namely of persuasion and influence. As the issue of labeling theory against psychiatric theory has been discussed so much, at least within the professional group, we can trace here some problems of application of sociological research, especially when it seems to lead to a radically new theory.

In analyzing the potential influence of labeling theory, as well as of Gove's critique, we can look at two steps—one is methodological, namely the nature of evidence which is relevant, and the other is the use of the language in which the findings are expressed: reasoning and persuasion. In both fields we shall have to take into consideration the influence on different audiences: professionals, students, policy-makers and the general public.

THE METHODOLOGICAL ARGUMENT

Scientific evidence follows a set of rules; this is what we call methodology. Within this set of rules the researcher can make a choice, depending on his training and preference, and will still stay within the accepted rules. Some of the differences have become so large, however, that one course of argument may seem quite irrelevant to another. The influence of the argument or of the resulting strength of one side or another on policies will then not be based on some logical necessity deriving from the method itself. What this might be we shall discuss later under the heading of style and influence.

What Is Evidence?

Gove's data are carefully analyzed and comprehensive; they do not give support to the hypotheses he derived from societal reaction theory, and hence cast doubt on the degree of validity of the theory.

It is not clear, however, whether this procedure can disprove or confirm the theory. Societal reaction theorists describe the process of labeling and secondary deviance, but they do not say that it occurs all the time or that all the steps need to occur. They do describe other counteracting processes: Lemert (1967), for instance, devotes considerable space to the subject of denial of deviance; he declares that it is because denial is so difficult that deviants readily accept the label and that secondary deviance becomes an efficient way of maintaining deviant behavior.

It might be objected, therefore, that Gove's analysis misses the point and is not relevant to the theorizing of the societal reaction theorists. There may easily be different modes of thought, even among sociologists, and one type of reasoning would be inapplicable to another type. We can discern some issues where contrasts between different modes can have especially important consequences for methodology.

Quantification

One of the points at issue is the meaning of quantification. Gove's argument is primarily numerical, using frequency statements as evidence. He cites percentages to show that it is likely that societal reaction has little to do with admission, length of stay in hospitals, and reintegration into the community. However, the postulates of the societal reaction theorists are not quantitative. The statements on which this theory is based are either descriptions of actual events or typical sequences abstracted from observations. The actual claim is only that these processes do happen; however, the language of the writing might lead the reader to believe that they are almost the exclusive processes.

Gove is in a difficult position in testing this theory with purely quantitative methods. Percentages may seem picayune beside the bold sweep of the writings of the societal reaction theorists. Moreover, what kinds of statements could negate the theory? If the theory points only to the existence of secondary deviance, then a negation would have to assert that it never happens. But if a certain degree of importance is implied, then data can lead to a definition of degree of importance. The reaction theorist may retort that this is not a relevant definition, but he is left with the challenge of providing an alternative one.

Data Selection

Gove's approach and that of the societal reaction theorists also differ in the kind of data they use and the way they analyze them. Intuitively two points are clear. There are some very extreme behaviors and attitudes which can be called mental illness and which may become dangerous or unmanageable within society. In this context we can say with some confidence that mental illness exists. On the other hand, there are some borderline cases which cannot be so easily classified. Here societal reaction might become important. Gove's data and the general practice of psychiatry would convince one that for the most part it is possible to determine, with high confidence and reliability, who is well and who is not. This would mean that mental illness is an objective fact, as far as objective facts can be said to exist in the world at all (the "psychiatric model"). However, in borderline cases assignment is very difficult. It is here that arbitrary assignments may be made: the arguments of the societal reaction theorists address themselves to this area. The ways in which borderline cases are treated make very impressive reading; these cases also give insights into elusive social mechanisms. However, the relative scarcity of these borderline cases is important; to stress their importance might obscure the real social situation. The methodological dilemma is, therefore, that quantitative techniques may describe over-all conditions of society but qualitative emphasis on the borderline conditions might be at least as interesting and valuable.

This may be part of a general contrast in type of data. Quantitative techniques describe the general features of society. Those who use these methods describe their procedure in such great detail that errors can be detected very easily, and are open to criticism in those instances where personal judgments are given as "hard data." Societal reaction theorists have concentrated on those ambiguous conditions where social processes can be shown to work clearly. Many of these theorists are also good critics of methodology. However, by showing the weaknesses of quantitative techniques using such vivid language, they may distort social reality in their own way.

Logic of Inference

We may now return to the question of whether all of Gove's excellent reasoning and analysis is beside the point. Are the two theories —societal reaction and psychiatric—really on the same level, and can a meaningful choice between them be made? For instance, Gove's data leave some patients unaccounted for by the psychiatric theory, and it would be reasonable here to postulate the workings of societal reaction theory. Even when only a few cases are involved, the societal reaction theory would be justified. For humanitarian reasons alone, a point of view which directs attention to grave abuses is important. We might remember that in a legal framework, the unjustified deprivation of a freedom of even one person is a grave question of civil rights. While societal reaction theory alerts us to abuses, it may not be a firm base for dealing with the general problem of mental health and illness.

Even these mild statements may not make societal reaction theorists feel the impact of Gove's approach. It may be that they are working on entirely different systems of logic. Theories can make statements in three quantitiative forms: A exists at all, A occurs always, A occurs to a more or less definable degree. Testing a theory involves possible negation of the appropriate statement. In the first case this would mean showing that an event never exists; in the second case a counterexample would be sufficient; and in the last case demonstrating a statistical or meaningful difference would counteract the original statement.

The issue here seems to be a contrast between the first and the third type of logic. Societal reaction theorists assert more or less emphatically that labeling and secondary deviance do exist and should be taken into account. Tables such as Gove's would necessarily include cells showing individuals who conform or do not conform to societal reaction theory. It may be safely predicted that the procedure of the societal reaction theorists will continue to be dependent on finding situations in which societal reaction can be demonstrated and they in turn will describe these cases in vivid terms. Questions of frequency of these situations are not of interest to them, and in this sense Gove and the societal reaction theorists are talking past each other.

SOCIAL INFLUENCE

Style and Audience

From the point of view of pure science, it may perhaps be irrelevant which kind of logic is used. However, to reach policy-makers and influence their actions, certain techniques may be more efficient. This is then not a question of scientific method but communication.

recourse to societal pressure, and that the sociologists's task is to see how these pathological conditions in individuals interact with social mechanisms. After the first shock of showing that the social mechanisms do exist, Gove's approach then shows how to integrate this finding into general sociological theory.

Another view of the effects of the societal reaction theory would be to consider it as an addition of several variables into the framework of population theory. To predict symptoms and outcome, one should include not only the etiology of the patient but also the characteristics of the situation and the committing personnel. By considering all these variables, we can measure the relative importance of all conditions and the weight of both theories.

Ideological Basis

As indicated before, one of the reasons for the success of societal reaction theory is to be found within the social and political climate. A theory which blames society for any restriction of deviant behavior can be applied to an argument that mentally ill persons are a type of persecuted people in our society, and this argument will appeal to people of some political orientations who see many current institutions as illegitimate agencies of control. One may wonder, however, whether the same people would feel that the deviance of the "Watergate group," for example, is purely a question of societal definition. Again, as in the pure methodological argument, the theory might have the beneficial effect of forcing society to take a closer look at the processes of definition and rehabilitation of the mentally ill. It might also have the adverse effect of leading laymen to attack all institutions dealing with the mentally ill on general principles, to view the mental health movement as a brainwashing ogre, and to deny any social value to mental health. In a quickly changing and communicating society like ours, ideas like this can easily take hold. It is hard to see what kind of boundaries to set to some probably valid criticism.

Here a quantitative evaluation like Gove's can be of great help. There may be logical difficulties in evaluating a theory like the societal reaction theory in quantitative terms. However, by setting the two approaches side by side, showing new facets of them, and evaluating them quantitatively, one can set limits on their social importance. One can make estimates of what proportion of the people in mental hospitals today are there because of such extremely deviating behavior that they are dangerous to themselves and others, how far the label and the stigma can be made reversible and have been made so, and what the difference is between the hospitalized and nonhospitalized cases. One can show that a person's being hospitalized is not a purely chance occurrence. Careful data analysis of this kind might add the sociologist's contributions to mental health to that of the psychiatrist.

CONCLUSION

Perhaps this is again a question of language. The novelty and the vivid examples of societal reaction theorists will impress some social reformers and also probably evoke strongly defensive reactions from officials working within the present systems. Quantitative language is less impressive and hard to understand for people who have no similar training. It may not make an immediate impression on the policy-makers, but in the long run it will be fruitful for sociologists who want to give definite meaning to limited statements. Resolution of the theoretical argument will provide a better basis for deciding on the direction of policy.

REFERENCES

Clausen, J. and M. R. Yarrow
   1955   The impact of mental illness on the family, *Journal of Social Issues* **IX,** 4.
Foucault, M.
   1965   *Madness and civilization.* New York: Pantheon Books.
Gove, W. R.
   1970   Societal reaction as an explanation of mental illness: An evaluation, *American Sociological Review* **35,** 873–884.
Gove, W. R. and P. Howell
   1972   The reasons for mental hospitalization: A comparison and evaluation of the societal reaction and psychiatric perspectives. An unpublished manuscript presented at the 67th Annual Meeting of the American Sociological Association, August 28–31.
Lemert, E.
   1967   *Human deviance, social problems, and social control.* Englewood Cliffs, New Jersey: Prentice-Hall.
Rothman, D.
   1971   *The discovery of the asylum.* Boston, Massachusetts: Little Brown.
Scheff, T.
   1966   *Being mentally ill.* Chicago, Illinois: Aldine.

Applying General Variables to Specific Problems: Aging and the Life Cycle

NICHOLAS BABCHUK

University of Nebraska, Lincoln

Articles by Lowenthal (1964) and Lowenthal and Haven (1968) will serve as a point of departure for these remarks on aging and social policy. In the research reported, the authors focus on subjects who are 60 and older. The practice of equating research on aging with the aged or retired is common though subjects in such inquiries often fall within an age range commencing at 45 or 50. While aging studies are concerned mainly with individuals who, chronologically, are middle-aged or aged, most students of this subject (cf. Riley and Fonner 1968; Riley, Johnson and Foner 1972; Rose and Peterson 1965) agree that many of the variables central to their interests are salient for every age cohort. By way of example, the quality of social relations available to an individual may be as important to the well being of an infant as to a person in his 70s or 80s or persons of any other age group.

Initially, Lowenthal, and, later, Lowenthal and Haven focus on the relationship of social deprivation, particularly various forms of social alienation or isolation, to the development of mental illness in old age (drawing, among others, on the work of Faris and Dunham 1960; Hollingshead and Redlich 1958; Meyer and Roberts 1959; Kohn and Clausen 1955; Townsend 1957; and Pagani 1962). The complementary notion that social isolation might be a crucial aspect of the aging process itself (cf. Cumming and Henry 1961; Blau 1961; Phillips 1957) is also considered. Taking into account such variables as sex, socioeconomic status, and age, Lowenthal and Haven seek to determine what effect age-related traumas such as the death of a spouse, onset of serious illness, or retirement status might have had on the psychological well-being of the aged they studied.

Both a cross-sectional and longitudinal design are utilized. In the cross-sectional design, individuals drawn on a stratified basis from 18 census tracts in San Francisco are matched and compared with a population admitted to a psychiatric screening ward of a hospital in that city. In the longitudinal study, information is gathered from a panel of 280 sample-survivors of those persons who were drawn from the community and interviewed on three different occasions at approximately annual intervals.

The two inquiries are closely linked to each other. Indeed, several additional reports by Lowenthal have appeared which explore other aspects of the larger project from which these two articles stem.

These studies suggested a number of conclusions which were unexpected. Lifelong extreme isolation (or alienation), for example, did not necessarily result in the kinds of mental disorders that brought persons to psychiatric wards. In fact, lifelong isolates tended to have average or better morale than others in the sample. However, those who tried to establish relations with others and failed proved particularly vulnerable. Stated differently, persons who attempted to develop primary ties but who did not succeed were more prone to serious maladies when they became older than those who had not made an attempt to cultivate ties within others.

Physical illness (determined by asking respondents about major changes that appeared after the age of 50) was often antecedent to both isolation and mental illness; it loomed as very important in measures of the feeling state or morale of the individual. Age-linked trauma such as widowhood or retirement did not, with certain exceptions, bring about mental illness. To be sure, such traumas were often coupled with poor morale for a period of time, but apparently the deleterious effects of such events were not lasting. Individuals who fared best when beset by trauma proved to be those who had primary ties with others. The authors found that the presence of an intimate served not only as a buffer against gradual social losses of role obligations (for example, retirement) but also against more traumatic losses as well. In sum, primary ties were critical to good mental health and high morale. Intimates or primary friends were unable to play a mediating role in the psychic adjustment of the respondents only in those cases where the latter had developed a serious physical illness. Serious physical illness was directly related to poor morale.

A distinction was noted between isolation and loneliness. Being along was not necessarily connected with loneliness though many who lived alone were lonely. Predictably, isolates were most likely to have low socioeconomic status. The frequently imputed relation between isolation and low socioeconomic status was fully borne out.

In this brief summary, it is impossible to do justice to the problems, concepts, discussion, suggestions, and conclusions embodied in the two articles. The statement does, however, provide a point of departure for a number of observations.

One fact which becomes striking is the centrality of isolation, contact, and intimacy as these relate to mental well being and the ability of the individual to be effective at every stage of the aging process. Most of us are aware of this. We recognize that the ability of people to cope with their environment is predicated on the nature of their link to others. The need to interact with others, to be stimulated, and the quality of ties between individuals are important at every age; but in the discussion which follows, we will focus on these needs and several policies which have been adopted or which might be considered for adoption in fulfilling these needs at the two extremes of the life cycle.

Spitz's (1945) inquiries into hospitalism and Davis' (1947) explorations into the effects of extreme forms of isolation provide special insight on the import of interpersonal relations and the quality of interaction in the early stages of life as these bear on the willingness to live, susceptibility to disease, and the development of self. Infants apparently require continuous human response. When denied the opportunity to interact frequently and intimately with others, infants often become highly susceptible to disease regardless of the high standard of hygenic conditions which surround them and, on occasion, apparently show little will to live. When infants are provided with sufficient care for survival, lack of contact and stimulation can interfere with abilities to relate to others, to learn, and to behave effectively in their environment. Neglect in the early years can result in permanent impairment. The longer the period of time that the child is neglected, the more difficult it becomes for him to adjust later on.

The significance of a stimulating environment for infants and children has been recognized for some time. At the same time, researchers have noted that the absence of a stimulating environment is correlated with social class. Although ties which bind individuals to each other are not necessarily lacking among those born into the lower and working class, there is evidence that individuals who come from higher rather than lower socioeconomic backgrounds have more extensive and richer ties with others. This evidence is substantial in the field of social participation (Axelrod 1956; Babchuk 1965; Freeman, Novak, and Reeder 1957; Kaufman 1944; Litwak 1961; Scott 1957). It is not surprising that greater participation and closer ties are directly related to social class considering the importance which is given to socializing the young to cultivate interpersonal skills, to relate to others, to operate effectively with symbols, and to develop autonomy and independence in middle-class families. Such skills can be acquired regardless of socioeconomic background, but they are more likely to be stressed and more easily acquired among those born into families representing higher socioeconomic status.

To compensate for both physical and social deprivation, a number of social policies have been developed and adopted with regard to the needs of the young. Head Start and day-care programs are cases in point. Aslo, television programs such as *Sesame Street* and, more recently, the *Electric Company* have been designed to motivate children to learn and to develop verbal skills. These programs appeal to young children irrespective of whether they come from an advantaged or disadvantaged environemnt. It is too early to assess the effectiveness of such programs measured over time.

Although it is hazardous, given our state of knowledge, to conclude that individuals who are neglected, as young children and adolescents are, will be prone to become isolates or less able to relate to others as adults, this may well be the case. Lowenthal and Haven's data indicate that many of those who were in their sample were "loners" and isolates in early adulthood.

Isolation, or lack or contact, may be most devastating in its consequences to the mental health of the very young, but its consequences are important for young and old alike, for the favored as well as those who are not. Numerous studies emphasize this point, especially in linking isolation and alienation to stress and effectiveness. Ellis and Lane (1967) show that upwardly mobile or "favored" youth, youth who have been screened for their "middle-class" characteristics and academic achievement and social promise in high school, disproportionately experience isolation and personal strain when enrolled in a high-status university setting where they are disassociated from those to whom they have been attached in high school. Though this experience may be traumatic during the college years, and even for a time after graduation, undoubtedly some of these individuals have positive associational ties to fall back on which facilitate their transition through this marginal period (Litwak 1960). Isolation may also characterize those who are downwardly mobile. Blau (1956) and Wilensky and Edwards (1959) suggest that individuals who are downwardly mobile or "skidders" often find themselves with fewer interpersonal resources as they become older. The decrease in contact with intimates experienced by "skidders" probably contributes to the alienation and disaffection expressed by such persons. Other literature could be cited in which isolation, stress, and alienation are related.

These findings can be juxtaposed to those reported by Lowenthal. She found that lifelong "extreme" isolates manifested considerable geographic mobility, were nonconformist, and totally disassociated from others. Although they appeared always to have been alienated and "loners," few of them mentioned loneliness as a problem. It was clear that such individuals had been ineffectual in many ways dating back to early adulthood and probably earlier. Most were unskilled or semiskilled and had itinerant job histories, came from the lowest socioeconomic levels, and were predominantly male, single, and in poor physical condition. This description applied to the hospitalized as well as nonhospitalized respondents. In contrast, respondents who had histories of lifelong "marginal" social adjustment came more often from more favorable backgrounds. They had more education and some held white-collar positions. A number had married but were divorced or widowed at an early age. This group, as young adults, had made an attempt at conventional social adjustment and failed, whereas the "extreme" isolates had never tried. The "marginal" isolates were subclassified into a "defeated" and a "blamer" category; they were more prone to be lonely than the "extreme" isolates.

Probably a substantial number of young adults are isolated, and alienated, and ineffectual, but their proportion is difficult to ascertain. More attention in terms of research and social policy decisions have been directed toward the young and old than those in between. Perhaps it is assumed that those in their twenties and thirties are more able to fend for themselves and cope with isolation and deprivation.

As with the very young, a number of policies and programs have been introduced to deal with problems which confront the aged and to insure that they maintain their vitality and do not become isolated from society. Many of these programs are designed to cater to the special dietary needs of the elderly, to make sure that they have medical care and remain healthy, to have counselors available to them when the need arises, and, in general, to maximize the opportunities for the aged to associate, to maintain contacts with each other, and to cultivate new relationships. Apart from Medicare, which is helpful for the aged and their families in the medical sphere, other programs provide facilities such as home handyman services, reduced bus fares, "senior-handi" bus services which transport on a "portal to portal" basis, home counseling, and home health care. Special recreational centers in increasing numbers are also being provided. Such services are good vehicles for keeping the aged out of institutions and for insuring that they lead a more normal existence. These programs are tailored to meet problems which confront the participants without regard to financial need, and this policy should encourage participation.

Although these programs are designed to deal with specific problems, they have the consequence of helping older people to maintain their network of associations and remain active in society. Indeed, these programs can serve as catalysts to increase the number and perhaps enhance the quality of ties between individuals. If the evidence on the relation between physical and psychic well-being and close interpersonal ties is correct, then such programs should not only be strongly supported but expanded.

A number of difficulties remain, however, despite the impressive array of programs which have emerged. These problems become apparent from research of sociologists, such as Lowenthal and Haven, and have implications for social policy.

In policy terms, the above investigators indicate that the aged, especially those requiring special attention. are likely to be poor, isolated (going back over a long span of time or due to the loss of spouse in a more immediate time period), men more often than women, single rather than married, without relatives, and in particular difficulty if they have recently incurred any serious illness. Locating such individuals and involving them in various programs would probably be a formidable task.

In this respect, those employed by the Social Security Administrations, or their counterparts at the city and county level, might be enlisted to identify the isolated and aged who have problems. They would be supported in this task by others such as social workers, visiting nurses, trained volunteers, and the aged themselves. This cadre, with training, could serve as resource persons expert in the programs that exist. They would encourage the aged to seek professional counsel and to take advantage of the available services and would be oriented toward all of the aged whether in good health or not. Apart from being "activists" alert to identifying the isolated and those with problems, they would personally see to it that the aged homeowners contact carpenters or electricians should these be needed for home repair; they would contact those in charge of "senior-handi" bus services when necessary, make certain that meals would be provided under emergency conditions, arrange for nursing care, provide counsel or be referral agents when needed, and the like. This effort would require considerable cooperation and coordination among various agencies and their personnel but would be manageable. Identifying those who required help could be expedited by utilizing readily accessible information from records of those who, for the first time, were seeking Social Security benefits; from admission records of hospitals and clinics; and from material dealing with the issuance of survivor insurance benefits. Such records and the events which precipitated them could serve as starting points to locate the aged who might be faced with difficulties at fixed points. Should help or advice be required, it could be administered at that time. Contact with the aged would then be established so that social services might be proffered at a future time when necessary. Periodic checks, no doubt, would be required to ascertain whether an individual's circumstances had changed, but this matter could be handled with a minimum of intrusion on the privacy of the aged if proper safeguards were employed on the part of the professionals.

In policy terms, insuring that the aged will be viable and well adjusted, at both the individual and societal level, is desirable. But it is difficult to ascertain whether inquiries similar to the one by Lowenthal, and Lowenthal and Haven have resulted in initiating programs which seek to accommodate problems confronting the aged. Sociologists have not been particularly good publicists in presenting or disseminating their findings. Relatively few of them have been involved in policy programs even though they often have expertise.

Throughout this report, it has been suggested that a more holistic orientation be adopted toward studying problems of the aged and that the starting points in such studies be "pushed back" to an earlier chronological age. Research is already geared in that direction.

Also evidence throughout this report is the applicability and salience of general and widely used sociological concepts and theory irrespective of the population specifically under study. Alienation and isolation, for instance, have significance for behavior of the very young, those in adolescence, young adults, those in middle age, and the elderly. Similarly, the ability to enter into primary ties and to be on intimate terms with others is important for the individual irrespective of age; those with social skills have clear advantages over those who do not; physical health is related to social well being. If the student has a sound grasp of concepts and theories, he ought to see their relevance in widely divergent arenas of behavior. Stated differently, basic knowledge and technical skills in the discipline, lend themselves to understanding regardless of the substantive focus. The latter can be acquired more readily than the former whether such information is put to use in policy terms or not.

With respect to training programs, the Lowenthal and Haven study has the virtue that it entailed the examination of an area which is preeminently policy oriented. Not only could their work be viewed in the light of previous policy which incorporated a substantial population and significant problem, but their findings could be translated into policy decisions which might have a greater likelihood of being effective and meaningful. Both researchers had great familiarity with environments in which their subjects functioned, and this familiarity lent itself to formulating the problem they explored, in gathering the data, and in interpreting them. It would be profitable, in theoretical and applied terms, if students at both the pre- and post-doctoral level could be introduced to research problems and experiences under similar circumstances.

REFERENCES

Axelrod, M.
> 1956 Urban structure and social participation, *American Sociological Review* **21,** 13–18.

Babchuk, N.
> 1965 Primary friends and kin: A study of the associations of middle-class couples, *Social Forces* **43,** 483–493.

Blau, P. M.
> 1956 Social mobility and interpersonal relations, *American Sociological Review* **21,** 290–295.

Blau, Z. S.
> 1961 Structural constraints on friendship in old age. *American Sociological Review* **26,** 429–439.

Cumming, E. and W. E. Henry
> 1961 *Growing old.* New York: Basic Books.

Davis, K.
> 1947 Final note on a case of extreme isolation, *American Journal of Sociology* **52,** 432–437.

Ellis, R. A. and W. C. Lane
  1967 Social mobility and social isolation: A test of Sorokin's dissociative hypothesis, *American Sociological Review* **32**, 237–253.
Faris, R. E. L. and H. W. Dunham
  1960 *Mental disorders in urban areas.* New York: Hafner.
Freeman, H., E. Novak, and L. G. Reeder
  1957 Correlates of membership in voluntary associations, *American Sociological Review* **22**, 529–533.
Hollingshead, A. B. and F. C. Redlich
  1958 *Social class and mental illness.* New York: Wiley.
Kaufman, H. F.
  1944 *Prestige classes in a New York rural community.* Memoir 260. Ithaca, New York: Cornell Univ. Press.
Kohn, M. L. and J. A. Clausen
  1955 Social isolation and schizophrenia, *American Sociological Review* **20**, 265–273.
Litwak, E.
  1960 Occupational mobility and extended family cohesion, *American Sociological Review* **25**, 9–21.
  1961 Voluntary associations and neighborhood cohesion, *American Sociological Review* **26**, 258–271.
Lowenthal, M. F.
  1964 Social isolation and mental illness in old age, *American Sociological Review* **29**, 54–70.
Lowenthal, M. F. and C. Haven
  1968 Interaction and adaptation: Intimacy as a critical variable, *American Sociological Review* **33**, 20–30.
Meyer, J. K. and B. H. Roberts
  1959 *Family and class dynamics in mental illness.* New York: Wiley.
Pagani, A.
  1962 Social isolation in destitution. In *Social and psychological aspects of aging,* edited by C. Tibbitts and W. Donahue. Pp. 518–525. New York: Columbia Univ. Press.
Phillips, B. S.
  1957 A role theory approach to adjustment in old age. *American Sociological Review* **22**, 212–217.
Riley, M. and A. Foner
  1968 *Aging and society: Volume one. An inventory of research findings.* New York: Russell Sage Foundation.
Riley, M., M. Johnson, and A. Foner
  1972 *A sociology of age stratification.* New York: Russell Sage Foundation.
Rose, A. M. and W. A. Peterson
  1965 *Older people and the social world.* Philadelphia, Pennsylvania: F. A. Davis Co.
Scott, J. C.
  1957 Membership and participation in voluntary associations, *American Sociological Review* **22**, 315–326.

Spitz, R. A.
   1945   Hospitalism. In *The psychoanalytic study of the child.* Pp. 53–72. New
          York: International Univ. Press.
Townsend, P.
   1957   *The family life of old people.* London: Penguin Books.
Wilensky, H. L. and H. Edwards
   1959   The skidder: Ideological adjustments of downward mobile workers, *American Sociological Review* **24,** 215–231.

Commentaries

CHARLES E. BOWERMAN

Washington State University

Prevalent in the Carmel Conference is the feeling that sociology should contribute to public policy formation and testing, discussion of some of the difficulties of our role, and a search for ways to become more effective. Three major themes deal with methodological problems in policy-oriented research, providing a theoretical and empirical base for policy decisions and effective communication of our knowledge. These themes are well illustrated in the papers by Aldous, Back, Mechanic, and Straus. Back best emphasizes some of the methodological problems of subjecting policy-relevant theory to empirical test. Straus gives an excellent example of a study which leads to conceptual clarification and presents data for outlining the nature of a problem area. Mechanic discusses problems of communication of research results and difficulties of gaining acceptance. Aldous brings out some of the social contexts that may affect problems at the personal and family level.

In searching for some kind of unity among these four papers, it appeared that the variety of policy-related difficulties with which they deal may stem from the fact that they are primarily discussing single studies with limited scope. Consequently, I would like to raise the question of the effectiveness of a single study, or an aggregation of single studies, for policy considerations. The "single study report," as found in the typical journal article, describes the design, findings, and conclusions of one study. By custom, research reporting is preceded by a "theoretical justification" in which the author attempts to place his study within the literature, show how it follows from and fits into some body of theory, and cites a few other studies relating in some way to his own research. The "conclusion" section may contain suggestions for action if the research relates to social problems or policy. The theoretical justification is necessarily limited by space and is highly selected because of research scope and intent. The methods of design, data collection, and analysis are not normally subjected to self-criticism and validity evaluation because of personal perspective and problem limitation; and suggestions for action are limited by the scope of research problem. Although such studies are the building-blocks of sociological knowledge, one can question whether singly, or in aggregate, they are adequate as a basis for recommending public policy or testing consequences of policy decisions.

As an alternative strategy for making ourselves useful, I am suggesting comprehensive and systematic reviews of sociological knowledge bearing on one issue. The objective would be to make use of the best "state of the art" reports that sociologists can provide, right now, to map the extent and nature of the problem; identify relevant concepts; critically report, evaluate, compare, and integrate research bearing on the problem; and provide a broad theoretical framework for understanding the problem and its origin. It would outline various alternatives for action, and anticipate consequences of various courses of action for different segments of the population under various conditions, and point out areas of ignorance and doubt. In general, such reviews would attempt to provide the best possible sociological base for accurate and useful thinking about the problem. They should be up-dated, periodically, with new research, revised theory, and the results of reality testing. Space precludes an elaboration of the advantages of such reviews, but it should be obvious that implications of sociological research for public policy and action can be drawn with greater confidence, and be more widely accepted, if based on a larger mass of evidence and a comprehensive overview of all elements of the problem.

It is implied above that interpretation of policy-oriented research is most usefully based on a mass of evidence rather than on single studies. However, communication of what we think we know must be accompanied by an assessment of possible error in research conclusions. Error statements, probabalistic or verbal, are standard in research reporting, but may need to be handled somewhat differently for policy research because of differing consequences of error. For example, when we are testing a theory, we usually want to minimize the probability of making a Type I error, whereas in policy research it may be a Type II error that we cannot afford. For example, we might prefer to eliminate TV shows with violence, even if they really have no effect on viewers' inclinations to violence, rather than continue to show them if there is a slight indication that they might have an effect. In my opinion, formal significance testing should not be applied in policy research unless we are very certain of our assumptions, but the same kind of thinking should be applied informally in interpretations made from any research.

Only passing comment has been made of another type of sociological influence on public policy. Mechanic says there is little evidence that our research findings have had direct influence on public policy, but he goes on to state that research may "help shape the climate within which decisions are made," and "in the long run the most important impact of social research on policy results from the extent to which it affects the climate of thinking in the society at large [pp. 99–100, this volume]." Influence through impact on public attitudes is also implied in the suggestion by Straus that effective control over alcoholic problems lies more in prevention than in rehabilitation. Though we cannot demonstrate the degree of influence, few would doubt that sociology has had a considerable effect on public opinion in the last few decades. As Back points out, the language we use for communicating within the profession is often not appropriate for public communication, and meanings may be significantly altered in the translation. It is clear that any concerted effort by the profession to make its knowledge more available for public consumption will require more effective strategies than are presently being used. If our research and theory is to get into the mainstream of public thought, we have a sobering responsibility to see that we are fully, honestly, and fairly represented. Communication to a broader public should be viewed as an important and respectable professional activity, and not be left to the journalists.

Our most effective influence on public thinking may be through the classroom. Generations of students become a fairly large segment of the voting public. Many will be in positions where they can directly influence policy-making, or will be teachers and community leaders with influence on the opinions of others. In addition to continually improving the knowledge base made available to students, we should seek better procedures for aiding students to incorporate sociological wisdom into their methods of dealing with the problems of society.

Although one of the main tasks of the conference was to explore new directions for graduate training in sociology, relatively little was said about training, except by inference. It is clear that the sociologist of the future who is to make a research contribution to policy matters must develop an arsenal of technical and methodological skills. Theoretical training and knowledge of the substantive literature must be broad, rather than narrowly specialized, since applied problems have numerous facets that cannot be adequately approached from one narrow point of view or specialization. The dissertation customarily provides experience in exploring a narrow problem in depth. This type of training for policy-oriented research might be more fully developed. Aldous has suggested that an extensive practicum, or problem-case experience, be incorporated as a part of graduate training. The nature of the practicum would of course have to vary with the problem, but would (1) probably come late in the graduate career, (2) include some field experience to find out first-hand about the "practical" aspects of the problem, (3) involve an effort to bring to bear whatever sociology can offer to understand the problem and suggest a course of action, and (4) possibly include some applied research to test out the fit between theory and reality. In addition to providing training in working on applied problems, such experience could help the student integrate his previous knowledge and further develop research skills.

JOSEPH ELDER

University of Wisconsin, Madison

In his paper on Lowenthal's articles, Babchuk makes a point frequently repeated in these sessions: it is difficult to tell in advance what content area of sociology will generate the most salient findings for whatever specific content area that is currently under examination. Let us assume one is interested in "aging." There is no guarantee that the best way to understand the "aging" process is to study those who are aging. In fact, Babchuk argues: to understand "aging," one may want to study infants. To support his own argument, he cites Lowenthal's observation that a key variable associated with good mental health during age-linked trauma (e.g., widowhood, retirement) is the presence or absence of primary ties. Those with primary ties generally survive the trauma better than those without. Babchuk relates this finding to infant studies, citing evidence that infants are able to learn more quickly when they have frequent, intimate contact with others. Drawing a parallel, Babchuk suggests that the aged must learn to cope with widowhood and retirement just as infants must learn to cope with new stimuli in their environment. Both for the aged and for the infants, primary ties are critical for maintaining "good mental health and high morale" during the learning experience. Babchuk's indentification of a common process within divergent fields of data corresponds to what Georg Simmel called "pure," or "formal," sociology, or what we today might call "basic" sociology. If Babchuk is correct, "basic" research on learning processes may have as much to say regarding the problems of aging as some other research specifically dealing with the aged.

Babchuk's paper, however, looks at the other side of the coin as well. For some aspects of a given content area, *only research in that content area* may shed light, since some aspect of that phenomenon occurs only in that content area. For example, Lowenthal indentifies some "life-long isolates." These are aged persons who, from their late adolescence, have lived as social isolates, without benefit of primary groups. Babchuk notes many lifelong isolates "often tended to have average or better morale than others in the sample [p. 150, this volume]." In short, here are a subset of the aged who behave differently from the majority. And they could not have been identified unless one was working with the aged. (It is hard to conceive of the parallel of a "lifelong isolate" in an infant-learning study!)

Who are these lifelong isolates, and why do they differ from the majority? Lowenthal identifies them as predominantly male, from the lowest socioeconomic groups, of unskilled or semiskilled occupations, single, and nonconformist. Why do they differ from the majority? From a fairly early age they seem to know how to learn without the assistance of primary groups. Beyond that, Lowenthal's article explains little. But it does point out a group worthy of further study. And it implies that if there is one way young people can be "immunized" against the traumas of growing old (as was the case with these lifelong isolates), there may be other ways as well. What might these ways be? Clues may come from any of a number of content areas of sociology: stratification, mental health, the sociology of occupations, social psychology, the sociology of religion, the sociology of knowledge, etc. Insights may be acquired by looking at the process of aging in other cultures. Are the traumas of widowhood or retirement as great in other societies as they are in ours? Or do other world religions or other family patterns "immunize" the young against the traumas of aging? The next "breakthrough" in the sociology of aging may come from a content area that on the surface appears to have little to do with aging.

What are some policy implications? Taking Lowenthal's major finding regarding the importance of primary groups for the mental health and optimism of the aging, one can ask: "Do the institutions we have set up for the elderly actually maintain or expand their networks of primary ties?" What occurs to primary ties in nursing homes, retirement villages, self-maintained homes in old neighborhoods, or arrangements where aging parents live with their grown children? Knowing that the shared debilitation of the elderly does not mean they share much else in terms of perspective, aspirations, etc., one might predict that for certain types of elderly, a particular institutional arrangement *will* maintain and expand primary contacts, and for other types of elderly, the arrangement will *not*. How can one identify the different types? Here one has a good research question, even if one does not have good answers.

What are the training implications? I see four: (1) Our graduate students need to receive good *general* training in sociology and related fields. To go back to the beginning: it is difficult to tell in advance what content areas of sociology will generate the most salient findings for whatever specific content area that is currently under examination. Insights may come from small-group experiments, learning theory, stratification propositions, or diffusion studies. In addition to courses in theory, statistics, and methodology, our graduate students need courses in a rich variety of content areas. (2) Our graduate students need to acquire a cross-cultural perspective. Out of a range of possible patterns, values, and structures, the West exhibits only a limited set. Even brief cross-cultural comparisons may dispense with certain variables and higlight certain others. (3) Our graduate students can begin almost immediately, gathering some of the hard, factual data that are still not available in many content areas. Regarding the aging, we need to know such simple facts as: How many elderly maintain their own residences? What are their special problems? How many elderly live with their children? What are *their* special problems? How many elderly live in institutions? What are *their* problems? Are there differences either of residence patterns or of problems with such categories as race, socioeconomic status, ethnic group, region of the country? Do the needs, aspirations, or anxieties of these categories differ? etc. These types of hard data are needed by those planning for the aged. Furthermore, they may help the aged themselves decide more rationally what course they prefer to follow. (4) We as the trainers of graduate students in sociology need to expand our occupational-network ties. Those professionally engaged in the field of aging can help us identify what areas need hard, factual data. They can give access to their own data. They can help provide the internships and apprenticeships that could be so useful for our students. And it is possible that, as they discover what sociologists have to offer them by way of theory and data, they will recognize the need for sociologists to be attached to their staffs on a permanent basis; so in the long run students with graduate degrees in sociology may find themselves with professions in the field of the aging. Then indeed the expansion of our occupational network ties will have been worth it.

WALTER R. GOVE

Vanderbilt University

Many scientific disciplines contain both a theoretical and an applied component, with the consequence that research developments in that discipline have an obvious and generally sympathetic audience. This is not the case with sociology. For example, sociology, applied or otherwise, does not have responsibility for either setting policy with respect to, or overseeing the care of, the sick and the aged. Furthermore, there is undoubtedly a consensus in society, and probably also among sociologists themselves, that sociologists should not have such responsibilities. This view has obvious implications for the extent to which sociology will have an impact on public policy. In areas such as medicine, where another dicipline has prime responsibility for both research and care, the prescribed role for sociology is likely, as Mechanic suggests, to be merely ancillary. However, even if sociologists accept this role, they often will have little direct impact on policy because (1) they are not the professionals with prime responsibility in that particular field, e.g., medicine, and (2) their research will usually bear on issues (however important) that are of only tangential interest to the professionals who have prime responsibility. Sociologists not accepting an ancillary role may be cast into the role of the "debunker." In this case, the ensuing debate will be primarily ideological; it will ignore specific insights and recommendations, and revolve instead around the issue of expertise and professional competence. Sociologists who use a debunking strategy may expect to have little direct impact on policy although they may, as Mechanic suggests, have an effect on the general intellectual climate within which the policy-makers operate. In areas such as the family, where there is no discipline responsible for setting and implementing policy, and in fact no over-all policy, the sociologist is immediately thrust into the political arena where ideological considerations are of paramount importance.

In the area of public policy, solutions to problems to a large degree reflect the factors of power, ideology and practicality. As intimated above, sociologists lack power. Now let us move to the arena of ideology. Mechanic, in his paper, notes that there seem to be two different standards for evaluating studies: one for studies whose results you like, and the other for studies whose results you dislike. I think this is an accurate reading of the history of science. However, in the area of public policy, because there is no tradition requiring the judicious weighing of evidence, we can expect evaluations to be even more greatly affected by ideology. Furthermore, policy-makers generally dislike the conclusions and recommendations of most sociologists because (1) sociology as a scientific discipline does not have a built-in bias that favors the institutions of a particular society; and (2) there is a conflict in ideology between most sociologists and most persons in power, and because the ideology of sociologists shapes their investigations, the conclusions and recommendations of sociologists often will not interest, and may even antagonize, policy-makers.

Let us now turn to the issue of practicality. Most sociology is concerned with developing and understanding social processes, with a particular emphasis often being placed on understanding the "underlying cause" of a given phenomenon. However, as Gouldner (1957) has noted, a policy science has requirements that are quite different from those of a discipline such as sociology. As he indicates, a policy science will be concerned with locating independent variables which not only have a major impact on the dependent variable in question but which also are amenable to control. Thus, many independent variables that are of interest to the theoretical scientist will be of little interest to the applied scientist because (1) There is no technology for manipulating the independent variable, (2) the values of society prohibit its manipulation, and/or (3) the cost of manipulating the independent variable far outweighs the potential gain. Thus, the policy scientist will be concerned with locating variables which he has the technology to manipulate, will be permitted to manipulate, and can economically manipulate. A brief perusal of the sociology journals will show that most sociology research simply does not focus on such variables and thus is not relevant to those who make policy. This means that if sociology is to increase its relevance to policy, it must shift its emphasis toward variables that can be manipulated.

In the above analysis I have sought to account for the negligible direct impact of sociolgy on public policy. Given the characteristics of both sociology and public policy, there is little reason to assume that this pattern will drastically change in the near future. As most sociologists are concerned about the human condition and want to do something to improve it, this lack of impact is apt to be a source of continuing frustration. One possible solution is for the discipline to enter the political arena as a partisan. However, as Aldous has noted in her paper, if we do this we will "have lost the claim to intellectual expertise that constituted our argument for being listened to by policy-makers in the first place [pp. 120–121, this volume]." Furthermore, as I have argued elsewhere (Gove 1970), there are a number of reasons for believing that a partisan posture would have a detrimental impact on the discipline itself.

Another approach to the involvement of the discipline in public policy, one which I would recommend, is for the descipline to develop a forum where policy issues can be presented, analyzed and debated in the same manner as we deal with traditional sociological topics. The most effective format for accomplishing this would be, in my opinion, a sociology journal, preferably sponsored by the American Sociological Association, which is concerned specifically with social policy. Sociologists are demonstrably concerned with policy issues; if they will be given professional recognition for doing sociological work in this area, it seems reasonable to assume that they will do it. Furthermore, if policy research became an integral part of the discipline, most graduate programs would expand to include training in this area. It should not be anticipated that these developments would produce an immediate increase in the impact sociology has on public policy. However, if sociologists in the future increasingly come up with viable solutions to the problems that concern policy-makers, I predict that in the long run their expertise will be utilized. The makers of public policy both need and desire help in solving their problems. The neglect of sociologists by policy-makers is correlated with the paucity of sociological solutions to policy questions.

REFERENCES

Gouldner, A.
   1957   Theoretical requirements of the applied social sciences, *American Sociological Review* **22**, 52–102.
Gove, W.
   1970   Should the sociology profession take moral stands on political issues?, *The American Sociologist* **5**, 221–223.

AUGUST B. HOLLINGSHEAD

Yale University

My remarks are focused on the themes developed by the five essayists found in Section B of this volume rather than on the researches they drew upon for their statements. These comments, then, are reactions to reactions: the reaction of the author of these comments to the reaction of the author of each essay to the research he chose to discuss.

The general theme of the conference was policy implications of sociological research and graduate training. As Aldous and Mechanic point out in their opening remarks, the key issue within the context of the conference is the question of what policy is. They briefly develop the theme of the kind of policy involved in a particular situation. Are we discussing public policy formalized by law and applicable to pertinent segments of an entire society? Are we considering organizational and institutional policy pertinent only to a small segment of a society such as members of a religious sect or a fraternal organization? Or are we confronted by informal policy that inheres in the folkways of a society? While Aldous and Mechanic do not answer the questions they raise about policy, the fact that they see the importance of the issue is worthy of comment.

As social scientists, we may argue that social policy should be based upon research. This position, however, raises other questions: What kind of research? By whom? For what purpose? Closely related to this problem is one that the American Sociological Association has wrestled with for years, and inconclusively: Should the Association attempt to influence social policy by formal actions? This is a moot question, and sociologists as individuals differ sharply on issues relevant to it. I suspect that the position of a particular sociologist on policy issues in his community, his state, or the society at large, is dervied more from his value orientation and status in the society than from the research findings of his fellow sociologists.

The publication of research findings is an essential element in the communication process. However, publication is not enough. Even if printed in a professional journal, research findings may not have any discernible impact. To influence social policy, they must be read or heard about. This point, illustrated by Mechanic's discussion of the research done by Skipper and Leonard, was ignored by the medical profession. On the other hand, Duff and Hollingshead's research attracted so much attention that it stimulated a counterattack by physicians high in the hierarchy of medical research and education in the United States and England.

The implications of research findings for training are found in each of the five essays under review. Babchuk makes the point that aging is a lifelong process and to understand it the whole process from conception to death should be studied; focusing upon one or two phases of the life cycle in research or training should be avoided. Aldous correctly points out that in research on the family we should take into consideration different types of families and the circumstances under which they live. Straus commends Cahalan for broadening research on alcoholism to males in the community, not merely in skid rows, custodial institutions, and Alcoholics Anonymous. Straus goes on to stress that we should expand our studies of the use and abuse of alcohol to females of all ages and males under 21 years of age.

In his discussion of Gove's paper, Back develops the theme that students should be aware that the appeal of social reaction theory may be traceable to the biases of sociologists for a socioenvironmental model to explain mental illness and the rejection of the psychiatric model, which is essentially the medical model of disease. Mechanic also develops this point of view in his discussion of the research reported by Duff and Hollingshead on medical and surgical patients. Finally, the suggestion is made that internships might be considered as a way to acquaint sociologists with the points of view held by the helping professions and the kinds of problems they deal with daily.

In sum, more communication of theoretical positions, methodological procedures, and training is needed. Internships, in which sociologists work with other relevant disciplines, should result in a better understanding of the problems each discipline faces than is now prevalent.

MARVIN B. SUSSMAN

Case Western Reserve University

The major purpose of this critique is to explore how policy-relevant research may be incorporated into old and propsed models of research training. The task is to formulate and implement a training program which is cognizant of the funding options provided by donor agencies in the 1970s, and which harmonizes academic ideologies and practices centered on quality basic research training in the behavioral sciences, with the cry for the study of (and hopefully answers to) significant societal issues and problems. Is it possible to provide to novitiates entering the behavioral sciences, sociology in particular, a type of training experience that is in the best traditions of practice in the field; that does not compromise on thoroughness and in-depth study of theory, methodology and statistics; that creates enthusiastic financial support from donors; and that is congenial to the faculty. The answers to this rhetorical question is a qualified yes.

Initially examined is the area of social policy research: its meaning, problems, caveats, and uses in relation to research training. In doing this, I shall use some of the Carmel Conference papers for illustrations, explanations, or as points of departure for further elaboration. The main objective, therefore, is to provide a rationale for "social policy" research in the training of sociologists and some guidelines for such activity based upon a pilot endeavor in this area.

FEDERAL POLICIES/PROGRAMS AND CONSEQUENCES FOR FAMILIES

This discussion of policy and potentialities for research is limited to the consequences of policies for families with varied structural properites. Varied family structures or forms refer to all types of families which differ from the nuclear family of procreation of husband and wife and offspring, most often found in neolocal residence with male heads in roles of providers and female heads in homemaking roles.

Since policy is defined variously by researchers, policy-makers, and users, and is open to wide interpretations and usages according to one's posture and position in a social system, it is critical to define policy in the context of the present discussion. One way to approach a definition of policy is to view it as a model of what should be. The very statement of principles of what ought to be automatically fixes a policy as a static concept. Its components are bench marks against which to measure behavior and thus, being a set of ideals, make it inflexible. It is essentially a conservative document even though it may have liberal intentions. From the very beginning of its statement, a policy becomes increasingly traditional because the changes, which occur in a society or a group, automatically move any policy along a course where it ends at the traditional pole of the radical–conservative continuum.

Policy is, however, more than a statement of principles. It usually has an "action" component designed to implement the policy. It does something to and for people through programs. Programs such as housing for the elderly, aid to dependent children, revenue sharing, rehabilitation for the disabled and disadvantaged, loans to veterans, family planning services, and myriad others, have legislative bases. Organizational bureaucracies are formed to implement the law which purports to reflect the policy; services are "professionalized" over time. Program activities may be in consonance with the intent of the policy. If not, a policy may be modified to "fit" the developing experience. Political salience and social conditions influence such actions. In sum, policy is more than a value position; it has legal and organizational instrumentalities to act on behalf of clients as well as their caretakers.

If one reviews pieces of legislation derived from policies developed in this society, it is obvious that very few of these are directed toward the "welfare" of the family. In their formulation few consider the family as a unit engaged in interaction in relation to its own set of values, norms, and standard of behavior. However, most policy-based legislation with its programs of categorical aid for individuals has consequences for the person's family.

The old age provisions of the initial social security legislation, enacted during the Roosevelt period, did not recognize that the individual recipient lived in a family, and that some financial benefits should be given to families to handle emergencies and extensive periods of aged dependency. Monies for funeral expenses, medicines, and other services during illness were required by families in order to meet home-care responsibilities. A series of changes in social security legislation commenced soon after the 1939 enactment, and has continued to date with each new piece of legislation, reflecting a reduction in the financial burden of the family for aged persons and transferring this responsibility to the society through society-wide economic transfers (Kreps 1965; Sussman 1965).

Congress recognized that children may need economic support when parents are unable to provide for them. It enacted Aid to Dependent Children (ADC) legislation and stipulated in cases where the child was abandoned by the father, the recognized breadwinner in the family, that the child would qualify for such assistance. At the time, the legislators did not recognize that they could not treat the child outside the context of the whole family. Some fathers who were highly motivated to support their families were unable to find jobs. Those fathers who chose to stay with their families, even though out of work, were penalizing their children because the latter became disqualified to receive financial aid. In not abandoning their families, unemployed fathers maintained the erroneous common belief that laziness and desire to live off the public dole were the major reasons for not working.

The consequences of this policy to help poor children was to encourage the abandonment of the family by the unemployed father so that the child could qualify for ADC. Many children and their parents suffered under this kind of legislation. As Aldous notes, it took almost 25 years after the initial enactment of ADC to change the law allowing unemployed fathers to remain with their families without disqualifying the child for financial help under the ADC program.

Well-intended policies, aimed to correct some individual deficit, often can have unanticipated or negative effects upon family structure and relationships. Other illustrations are programs providing rehabilitation to the individual who may be handicapped as a consequence of extended illness or disability. Such isolated concentration may jeopardize internal family relationships and identification. It is not uncommon for "normal" children to develop behavioral problems and perform poorly in school when parental and human-service-agency energies and support are focused on the ill or disabled child. Sibling relationships may also deteriorate with the nondisabled child experiencing parental deprivation (Sussman, Weil, and Crain 1966).

A Theoretical Perspective and Rationale for Policy/Family Research

In a period of new federalism in which the government's thrust is to consolidate and cut back the federal involvement in the lives of its citizens, it is important to assess the resources and abilities of the family to cope with the education, health, and welfare of its members. Also it is necessary to understand to what extent families at all income levels do or could provide for their members services which were previously provided by outside groups. What policies facilitate or constrain development of independence of dependence of families in their relationships with bureaucratized organizations and institutions? To what extent can the family either alone or in cooperation with agencies provide these services for itself?

In recent years government officials such as HEW secretaries, program heads, and members of Congress have become sensitized to the shortcomings of American society, such as the inability of existing policies and institutions to provide adequate housing, education, jobs, and social services to all citizens, and to reduce discriminatory practices against minority groups. Issues of this order are now considered national problems. They exemplify "failures" of the society to "do right" by its members. Unemployment, poverty, alcoholism, disability, drug addiction, mental illness, and the elderly are among a few national concerns. To tackle these and to help those beset and afflicted with these problems, new policies have been formulated and programs have been developed. Each of these is a costly investment and further adds to the growing organizational and institutional structure of human service system with major foci on treatment over prevention.

This costly and extensive development has resulted in the posture that there now is urgently needed review and evaluation as to whether these service systems are responding adequately to each national problem. Unfortunately, in focusing on whether institutions are meeting the needs of individuals with problems, we have ignored a fundamental organizational and behavioral feature of all human societies; primary groups like families, family networks, or peer groups are critical interactional systems for the individual and have great influence on receptivity, responsiveness, and cooperation with any human service program. The conceptual fallacy is that institutions and organizations believe that when they care for, educate, or "handle" individuals and their problems—such as drug addiction, alcoholism and the like—they are dealing primarily or soley with individuals rather than groups, those in which the individual has primary relationships. No doubt the low success rate of many programs has been because agencies have used an institution/individual model rather than an institutional/primary group approach in providing services. Using the institutional/individual service model ignores the group influences upon the individual who is the target for treatment or care.

Family/Policy Foci

There is an urgent need to research the implications of government policies upon the capabilities and competencies of the family to "make it" in the society, as well as the well-being and quality of life for the whole family. For example, programs aimed to overcome "deficits" (because of disability) with concentrated efforts on afflicted individuals rather than considering family structure and the matrix of relationships (treating the family as a social unit) may seriously jeopardize the life styles, ambitions, and motivations of other family members. Policies and programs aimed at treating or providing services to the family as a whole over current patterns of individual service should be given the highest research priority (Melville 1973).

Sociologists have almost totally ignored legal institutions, laws and legal practice, and their relationship to family structure and functioning. The February 1967 issue of *Journal of Marriage and the Family* raises a large number of questions for research. One basic approach is to determine the reciprocal influence between law and the family. What influence does success or failure of the family have on the creation of new laws or the modification of old ones? What are the current implications that laws pertaining to abortion, age of marriage, welfare, housing, economic security, etc. have for structure, functions, mobility, and utilization of talent of family members? Previously mentioned is the need for research on divorce. Considering the variability of divorce laws and concomitant variations in property settlement, child support, and alimony, one could posit the question as to the impact of divorce upon the reorganization of the family's role structure.

Problematics of Policy Research

It is with some hesitation that I, along with others (Mechanic 1972; Weiss 1972) raise the issue: Will research have any impact on policy formation and program development? Yet it must be voiced even at some discomfort to one's image, work roles, and life style.

Mechanic's Conference paper examines this issue by presenting two case studies. The first is concerned with "treating" the mother and child while the child is undergoing a tonsilectomy (Skipper and Leonard 1968). Clearly demonstrated in the research is the fact that if the dyad is given comfort, explanation, and time to be together in the pre- and post-operative period, the anxiety of both the mother and the child, as well as the time for the child's post-operative recovery, is reduced. There is less psychological scarring among children of the experimental group than the control group. The study was done under controlled conditions.

Yet the impact of these findings upon hospital, policy and procedure was nil. In fact, physicians in the hospital who heard about the study asked the investigators why they were wasting their time studying such an insignificant problem. This is a fascinating and yet disturbing finding because tonsilectomy is one of the most frequent surgical procedures in the United States and, as an elective procedure, I believe it is the main cause for hospitalizing a nonill child. While there is a serious question over the need for tonsilectomies, there is no question about the psychological problems associated with this surgical procedure, especially in very young children. The child is separated from parents for perhaps the first time in his life. It is difficult to understand why there would be opposition to changing practices, i.e., treating the dyad, perhaps the whole family, when the evidence is so clear-cut. The surgical procedure itself is insignificant compared to those related to malignancies; outcomes are almost 100% successful in contrast to other surgeries. Is it reasoned that since "good" outcomes are almost 100% assured, why fuss with the interpersonal problem inasmuch as the reduction in anxiety that may result is not worth the effort or investment? These are unanswered questions. The failure, in this instance, of research data to bring about the desired changes in procedures by mere communication of such knowledge substantiates the perspective that policy-makers must be committed to the undertaking (regardless of techniques used to obtain involvement) if rseearch findings are to have any impact on policy formation and program implementation, as Mechanic points out.

Research findings perceived as being too "radical" will not be taken seriously and, if at all possible, those who oppose them—such as institutional policy-makers, practitioners, and professionals—will attack the research as being "methodologically unsound" or "theoretically irrelevant." If the methodology is above reproach, other grounds for attack would be charges of "exposing" the organization in an unfriendly manner with an open invitation for outsiders to rip it. The investigators can also be charged with not knowing what the "real" issues are, because what they are asking in the way of reform is impossible to do without a major "traditionectomy" in current practices.

Attacks such as those just described were made on Hollingshead and Duff by Beeson (1968) and Ingelfinger (1968). Mechanic, after analyzing the Hollingshead/Duff experience, says

It is increasingly clear that if the intent of such studies is to bring about change in the context studied, rather than to add to knowledge or to inform the climate of general opinion, it is necessary to involve in such investigations those who have operational authority for the program studied. In studying medical services, those concerned should be intimately involved in the design and progress of the study, and the investigation should require "informed consent" not only for the patients but also for the professionals involved [p. 107, this volume].

It is my view that a program of policy research involving the family would best begin with looking at current policies and programs and their effects upon families, rather than starting out with "basic" research and then seeing how one might effect new policies. Even this approach is no solution to the problems of acceptance and implementation. The study of Skipper and Leonard examined existing medical care practices involving children and parents, but the impact of this research had no effect in changing current hospital policies. These are some of the caveats of family/policy research undertakings.

Training in Relation to Policy Issues

One of the major developments in the 1960s and 1970s has been the emergence and increased visibility of various forms of family (Sussman 1971; Sussman et al. 1971). One apparent outcome of such visibility is that these different forms of family have different issues and problems to solve, both within and outside the family. They differ contextually in their role structure; consequently, where husband and wife are living together with children, and with or without relatives, there is quite a different marital role structure than the type that exists in the more traditional family. This would be the case in the dual-work family compared to the traditional family of procreation of husband working with wife at home as the homemaker. Problems involved in handling the normative demands of nonfamily groups and bureaucracies are obviously varied according to the type of family the person is residing in at a given point in time over the life cycle.

For our discussion, perhaps most important are the relationships of such family systems with outside agencies and institutions, especially in areas clearly delineated as human services. One essential question is the extent to which supportive human service systems have actually been supportive of different forms of family. If human service systems are supportive under a traditional ideology, it becomes quickly obvious that what they do can often hurt, inhibit, or retard the full development and expression of members of variant family forms, rather than actually be supportive.

The following, adapted from Sussman's paper entitled "Family Systems in the 1970s," is a description of variant family forms as well as our estimate of their prevalence in American society today (Sussman 1971: 40–56).

Family Type	Estimated Percent Distribution	
1. Nuclear family—husband, wife and offspring living in a common househould ("intact," first marriage)	45	
a. Single career		30
b. Dual career		15
1) Wife's career continuous		no estimate
2) Wife's career interrupted		no estimate
2. Nuclear family—husband, wife and offspring living in a common household ("intact," *remarried*) No estimate of career patterns	10	
4. Nuclear dyad—husband and wife alone: childless, or no children living at home	15	
a. Single career		4
b. Dual Career		11
1) Wife's career continuous		no estimate
2) Wife's career interrupted		no estimate
4. Nuclear dyad—husband and wife alone: childless, or no children living at home (*remarried*) No estimate of career patterns	5	
5. Single-parent family—one head, as a consequence of divorce, abandonment, or separation (with financial aid rarely coming from the second parent), and usually including pre-school and/or school-age children	15	
a. Career		11
b. Noncareer		4
6. Three-generation family—may characterize any variant of family forms 1, 2, or 3 living in a common household	2	
7. Kin network—nuclear households or unmarried members living in close geographical proximity and operating within a reciprocal system of exchange of goods and services	2	
Emerging Experimental Forms	6	
1. Commune family		
a. Household of more than one monogamous couple with children, sharing common facilities, resources and experiences; socialization of the child is a group activity.		

(continued on page 178)

Family Type	Estimated Percent Distribution
b. Household of adults and offsering—a "group mar-riage" known as one family—where all individuals are "married" to each other and all are "parents" to the children. Usually develops a status system with leaders believed to have charisma.	
2. Unmarried parent and child family—usually mother and child, where marriage is not desired or possible.	
3. Unmarried couple and child family—usually a com-mon-law type of marriage with the child their biolog-ical issue or informally adopted.	
	100%

The "single-parent" family, largely a consequence of separation and divorce, has become a target of policy research and program action by such government agencies as the Office of Child Development. The essential policy questions are: What are the necessary support systems now required so that the single-parent family can function as a continuing concern? What minimal social and environmental conditions are required so that children can be optimally socialized?

For some "family watchers," a policy should go beyond providing supports for nontraditional families; additionally, it should promote the value of desirability of variant family forms—such as the single-parent—for those who choose it, and foster nondiscriminatory behavior against those "forced" into it. Variant forms of family should be "legitimized" and provided the same legal rights and services accorded the "standard" family.

A related question is: What current practices should be discarded because they denigrate, in this instance, the single-parent status and precipitate punitive behaviors? A perplexing research question is whether the single-parent family household can provide the appropriate living environment for the effective socialization of children into new roles and identities. This query is exacerbated by the actions of court judges in divorce cases who in recent years are increasingly awarding the custody of children to fathers. This is a basic shift from the old pattern of 95% child custody awards going to women; therefore, the question is: more specifically, What "new" kinds of supports are now required if a father with single-parent status is to maintain an effective and creative environment for parental roles?

Policy is intertwined with legal statutes and judicial decisions. In the case of the single parent, the question is constantly raised as to what necessary moral qualities a parent must have in order to gain and hold custody of children. The grounds for divorce in most states are still based on fault, the culpability of one and the innocence of the other marriage partner. The adversary process used in divorce proceedings requires that one party be proved guilty on any of the "grounds" for divorce, while the other marriage partner is judged innocent of any wrongdoing. It follows that the award of custody of children would be given to the innocent party with the expectation that the rights of custody are related to the continued innocence of the parent. Innocence may be an inappropriate term, and a more accurate description is a healthful environment for children. What is judged healthful is usually related to traditional values of sexual morality. Jurists today are faced with cases involving critical decisions for which there are few precedents. The "classic" type is where a divorced woman who has custody of her children has in her home a male to whom she is not married. This is a form of "trail remarriage" with the male involved in "parenting." Some judges are ruling that this bonding is immoral behavior and is reason for taking children away from the divorcée. Children are then institutionalized, given up for adoption, or awarded to the father if he will have them. This ruling seems to prevail even though the evidence suggests that some of the men in these "trial remarriages" turn out to be better fathers than the biological ones were. And the participants in such arrangements do not look upon themselves as living in "sin" but perhaps providing bases for a marriage—or at least a living arrangement, i.e., a personal marriage contract—comfortable to all parties involved. These are a few of the policy questions involving the status of the single parent. There is a paucity of research regarding these issues; the opportunity exists for empirical research on the single-parent family as part of the training process.

Single-Parent Family: A Pilot Project in Graduate Research Training. The family mental health training program at Case Western Reserve University has adopted a training format which, in addition to seminars concerned with theory, research, and statistics, also provides a "learning by doing" experience with the graduate students taking full responsibility for developing their own projects. The process involves the formulation of the significant problem; conducting the field study; data analysis; and preparation of the findings for publication. In the past 2 years the program has moved away from a parity model —in which faculty and students participate on an equal basis—to one of complete student participation and control of the research process with faculty and staff functioning in consultant roles. The project is a study of adaptive behavior of single-parent families as a consequence of divorce.

This training "experiment" has been enhanced by the availability of some funds which permitted students to obtain a stratified sample of over 400 cases using both free-form and fixed-form questions. The theoretical perspective is that of a family as a social system which is continually influenced by the environment through the relationships its members maintain with other social systems. When a major change occurs in the family, such as divorce, the remaining members must adápt. The bases for this approach of family response to change is derived from systems theory (Buckley 1967, 1968). Some research questions are: Does reliance on human service systems or on family and friendship groups produce the more successful patterns of adjustment? How have children reacted to the separation/divorce? What are role reallocations—children's and spousal relationships with separated/divorce members—and the possible sources of kin and organization support to manage a one-parent household?[1]

Implications for Graduate Training

This pilot project has both policy and nonpolicy implications for the following publics: students, mentors, community human service organizations, and national policy-makers.

Students

1. Exposure to policy issues with examination of consequences of policy implementation for members of a "variant" family form, the single-parent family.
2. Contact with policy implementing social control and human service organizations during various stages of the research process: from the initial period of problem formation to discussions on the meaning of findings.
3. Exposure to a milieu which encourages assuming responsibilities and rights for the project.
4. Experience in all phases of the research process from problem formulation to article writing.

[1] Copies of the research proposal and instruments can be obtained by writing to NIMH Training Project, Institute on the Family and the Bureaucratic Society, Case Western Reserve University, Cleveland, Ohio 44106.

5. Awareness of the problems of single-parent families, and the community and the national organizations which serve them, with the potential to function in disseminating mediating roles.
6. Involvement in and commitment to spin-off research and theory development.

Mentors
1. Experience in the consultant role within the context of the training process.
2. Experience with quick testing of abstract (sometimes far out) ideas with opportunities for hypothesis testing and formulation.

Community Human Service Organizations
1. Exposure of staff and administrators to discrepancies between their perceptions of the "problems" and those of their clients.
2. Consciousness of the efficacy of the organization's policy, of covert staff-administration hostility, staff-client tensions, etc, and of possible changes in the organization.

National Policy-Makers
1. Consciousness of the "needs and desires" of a target population and policies by which those needs might be met.
2. Awareness of the consequences of a policy through program implementation.

REFERENCES

Beeson, P. B.
 1968 Special book review of sickness and society, *Yale Journal of Biology and Medicine* **41,** 226–240.
Buckley, W.
 1967 *Sociology and modern systems theory.* Englewood Cliffs, New Jersey: Prentice Hall.
 1968 Society as a complex adaptive system. In *Modern systems research for the behavioral scientist,* edited by W. Buckley. Chicago, Illinois: Aldine.
Duff, R. S. and A. B. Hollingshead
 1968 *Sickness and society.* New York: Harper.
Ingelfinger, F. J.
 1968 The arch-hospital: An ailing monopoly, *Harper's Magazine* **237,** 82–87.
Kreps, J. M.
 1965 The economics of intergenerational relationships. In *Family intergenerational relationships and social structure,* edited by E. Shanas and G. Streib. Pp. 267–288. Englewood Cliffs, New Jersey: Prentice Hall.

Mechanic, D.
    1972 *Public expectations and health care.* New York: Wiley.
Melville, K.
    1973 Changing the family game: Treat the system, not the individual, *The Sciences* **13**, 17–19.
Skipper, J., Jr. and R. Leonard
    1968 Children, stress, and hospitalization: A field experiment, *Journal of Health and Social Behavior* **9**, 275–287.
Sussman, M. B.
    1965 Relationships of adult children with their parents in the United States. In *Family intergenerational relationships and social structure,* edited by E. Stans and G. Streib. Pp. 62–92. Englewood Cliffs, New Jersey: Prentice Hall.
    1971 Family systems in the 1970's: Analysis, policies and programs, *Annals of the American Academy of Political and Social Science* **396,** 40–56.
Sussman, M. B., W. B. Weil, and A. J. Crain
    1966 Family interaction, diabetes and sibling relationships, *International Journal of Social Psychiatry* **12,** 35–43.
Sussman, M. B. et al.
    1971 Changing families in a changing society. In *Report to the President: White House Conference on Children, 1970.* Pp. 227–238. Washington, D.C.: U.S. Government Printing Office.
Weiss, C. H.
    1972 *Evaluation action programs: Reading in social action and evaluation.* Boston, Massachusetts: Allyn and Bacon.

GUY E. SWANSON

University of California, Berkeley

Each of these papers embodies a scientific concern and a concern for the common life, and each shows us again that research can enlarge and correct the vision with which we act. But none of them leads us to anticipate the principal decision on policy that I observed at this conference. That decision was made on the afternoon of the first full day when the conference divided into two smaller groups, each discussing the relations between policy research and a graduate education in sociology. In each group, one question, although never mentioned, was both asked and answered: Are you willing to forego large federal grants if, in order to get them, your department has to reshape its graduate curriculum and provide a considerably greater emphasis upon policy research? The answer—almost unanimous—was "Yes." I agree with that answer. It provides the basis for my comments.

The question is not whether to educate for research that has social implications. All research has social implications, direct or indirect, important or trivial. Most sociologists enter our profession because they value research that has direct and important social implications, and most of the research described in the papers before us meets these standards. What is more, implications of the studies under review are known outside our profession. The labeling theory of mental disorder is now a commonplace among psychiatric social workers and mental health "activists." A great many medical administrators take it as fact that the quality of medical care received by the poor is inadequate and too often is administered with large doses of disrespect. Large numbers of policy-makers are sensitive to the role conflicts of educated women and to the threat posed by social isolation to the personal integrity of the aged.

The mass media and special interest groups have taken these ideas to still wider publics. Tens of thousands of students have encountered them in our courses. Conceptions and findings from these and related studies have, as Mechanic says, become a part of the framework of ideas and opinions through which a potent sector of the public interprets our social order. They join many other conceptions in that framework that were taken over from sociology: such conceptions as anomie and alienation, bureaucratization, class struggle, collective excitement, urban ecology, the lonely crowd, and crises of identity—to name but a few of those that have been important.

The immediate question is whether to educate for research that has a more specific and immediate bearing upon policy. For practical purposes, policy research is research conducted on behalf of someone who, in his official capacity, is going to make a choice that depends upon the findings. He is going to allocate resources and facilities in one way rather than another. Unless this research makes an appreciable difference in eliminating, reinforcing, or otherwise guiding the allocations that are within his powers, he finds it of little use.

To conduct effective policy research, one must work closely with the policy-maker. Likert, Lazarsfeld, Whyte, Gardner, and many others have described what this entails. It means extensive consultations with the policy-maker to insure that the design of the research is responsive to the problem as he currently understands it. It means getting together with him over the results of pretests to see whether the kind of information actually being obtained will enable the policy-maker to make one choice rather than another. It means consultation at all stages to make certain that the policy-maker's chief lieutenants are willing and able to implement the choices that may be indicated by the kind of findings that the research can actually provide. If the research has an "R and D"—research and development—component, it means conducting a similar collaboration in translating policy into the specific operations of specific programs and in participating in the evaluation of at the least the early results. It means a clear understanding by everyone, including the researcher, that the findings from research never lead directly to policy, that policies are not self-implementing, and that the resources of method, fact, and theory that one draws upon from one's science will usually require painstaking elaboration and specification before they are of much use in application.

If the research reviewed by Aldous, Babchuk, Back, Mechanic, and Straus really had met the criteria for policy research, there would be no need for a conference like this one. A large fraction of studies conducted by sociologists are of the type summarized in their papers. This research is published, cited, and respected, and it is built upon the kind of graduate education that we presently provide. It seems clear to me that these studies are not examples of what normally is meant by policy research. They were occasioned by social concerns, and most of them have implications for policy; but they were conceived and conducted under imperatives other than those of collaboration with a policy-maker in his selection of a course of action.

One sign of these other imperatives is the discrepancy between the findings they report and the actions they advocate. Aldous seems to say that we should have a national policy with regard to families. Straus recommends a ban on television advertising by breweries and distilleries. Skipper and Leonard and Duff and Hollingshead propose specific changes in medical practice. Babchuk wants more training in verbal skills for children of the poor so that they will be less likely to be socially isolated when they are old; he wants more seeking-out of older people by social workers and public health nurses in order to promote involvement in community programs for those who are isolated. I happen to sympathize with the intent behind each of these proposals, but none of them follows directly from the research. Instead, each of the other writers and myself tacitly supply a set of assumptions about the programs that are feasible, desirable, and adequate. We come as citizens and advocates. We do not, in these proposals, come to policy-makers as professionals to clients, or as one co-worker to another, in a joint effort to develop a new program. We throw our weight on the side of changing the directives under which policy-makers operate, to force one particular choice rather than another.

This role is valuable, just as policy research is valuable, even indispensable. And I appreciate that research of great scientific value has been done with policy in mind. Indeed, many scientists get access to information they need as scientists, *only* by serving as policy researchers in complex organizations, the mass media, certain professions, and so on. For people with scientific interest in these subjects, competence in policy research is often a necessary methodological skill. It is equally necessary for sociologists to serve as policy researchers, with methodological competence, if they want their research to be intimately connected to the formulation of policies.

In most large universities there are opportunities to acquire competence in policy research: opportunities through courses and internships in programs on public adminstration or urban and regional planning, and opportunities in schools of education, business, public health, natural resources, law, and social welfare. At some universities one can become prepared in a science and in policy research through doctoral programs that link one or more academic departments and one or more professional schools: for example, the Doctoral Program in Social Science and Social Work of the University of Michigan, the Committee on Human Development of the University of Chicago, and the Graduate School of Public Policy on the Berkeley campus of the University of California. It seems a waste of resources to duplicate within departments of sociology the programs on policy and planning already offered elsewhere on our campuses.

It seems a mistake on other grounds as well. A science is supported for its usefulness, but it can be available for use only if it is cultivated. The essence of any science is a body of empirically validated and logically coherent theory. The aim of doctoral education in a science is to provide students with the capability of evaluating and extending that theory. Assuming that a science of sociology has a particularly worth while contribution to make, it will be made by people trained specifically as sociologists. A graduate program in sociology with a different emphasis will misrepresent what is presumably its special competence and will fail to meet the distinctive obligations that justify its existence.

Nonetheless, I think we can and should strengthen our contribution to policy research. Programs combining scientific and policy concerns provide models for what is needed: systematic training, genuine competence in a science and in the design and conduct of research relevant for policy, social support for students, help in financing their education, and in placing them in jobs that will enable them to use their special talents. As the directors of these programs have commented: the traffic moves in both directions. It is not just a matter of gaining experience in the formulation of policy available to social scientists, but a matter of making some truly relevant preparation in social science available to prospective practitioners. The latter seems at least as difficult as the first. Both require our initiatives and our collaboration with colleagues in professional schools—and as policy researchers!

ROBERT N. WILSON

University of North Carolina, Chapel Hill

Gloom was the prevailing tone of the Carmel Conference. Sociologists in humility assembled and confessed that they had left undone those things which they ought to have done, and done those things which they ought not to have done. But I think it would be wrong to assume from this orgy of self-deprecation that there is no health in the sociological enterprise. I should like to comment on the two questions embedded in the conference title: how social science research has influenced and can influence policy decisions; and how graduate education might be shaped toward more efficacious participation of sociologists in policy processes.

Much of the discussion and many of the prepared papers set forth how feeble have been the consequences of sociological research for social action. In the policy area I know best, the sociology of health and illness, I should be inclined to adopt a more sanguine view. My theme is consonant with Mechanic's assertion that "—there is little evidence that the initiation of policy flows directly from research findings. Research, however, may in the long run help shape the climate within which decisions are made [p. 99, this volume]." This shaping of the climate, I believe, is precisely the way in which our work is significant for policy. What effect we have is not in the form of a specific item of evidence that leads to a specific decision. Rather, it occurs as a cumulation of data and thought that builds toward a general argument favoring this course of action rather than that—much as a legal argument develops from many and varied strands of evidence. Three prominent examples of this process may be cited in health matters.

During the last two decades there has been a gradual shift in the philosophy and organization of mental hospitals, conveniently labeling the change from custodial to therapeutic care. Sociological research among hospital staff and patients was a significant force in this by no means completed change. In the more recent past, the National Institute of Mental Health has embarked on a master strategy to promote the community mental health center movement. This concept of a community-based linkage of comprehensive services to the mentally distressed stems in part from two types of sociological activity. The first was the body of studies in social epidemiology that demonstrated the pervasiveness and uneven distribution of psychological distress, the second was the labors of the Joint Commission on Mental Illness and Health, whose reports directly preceded legislative and adminstrative action. Finally, and still more recently, we have seen the adoption of a section on the behavioral sciences as a standard portion of the National Board's examinations for medical students. Here, sociologists were among those pressing for this innovation, and they have helped to frame questions for it. This directly affects medical education, and eventually may be expected to alter health policy. It is very important to note that in all three instances sociologists worked in collaboration with other social scientists and with health professionals. The sense of problem and the deployment of investigatory strategies in policy research are inherently interdisciplinary.

Several illustrations from other social problem areas might also be mentioned. The work of Myrdal and his collaborators in *An American Dilemma* was unquestionably a factor in changing race relations in this country. Elton Mayo and his colleagues, in their research and writing on the "human relations" approach to industrial organization, had an effect not limited to the education of successive management cadres in the Harvard Business School. I choose these instances not only because they support the observation that social research has in fact influenced policy, but because of the *kind* of research they exemplify. They tend to be scientifically modest descriptive/analytic studies, in which the investigators patiently observed, interviewed, and amassed a case from evidence of all sorts; probably Myrdal, Mayo, and others like them never "proved" anything, strictly speaking. I think we are currently guilty of *hubris* in our efforts to apply sociological knowledge to policy formulation, expecting too much of ourselves in the way of tight demonstrations of cause-and-effect, and too little in the way of accurate description, empathic understanding, and clear writing.

One of the ways in which social scientists are likely to affect decisions is through their increasing involvement in evaluative research on social programs. Such inquiry is very difficult, subject to all sorts of extrascientific pressures, and methodologically messy. It is not an immaculate procedure, being inevitably spotted all over by incursions from the real world. But it is the only game in town, so we might as well play. Here, in what some have termed "action research," the investigator may be simultaneously assessing a program and promoting its objectives. However, there is nothing wrong with this as long as he knows what he is doing. In program evaluation there is a special need for good natural history accounts, for interpersonal competence, and for straightforward English prose. Program evaluation is perhaps intrinsically "reactive." By studying the phenomena, one is decidedly going to change them. Yet it might well be argued that the sociologist in this arena should not be anxiously trying to minimize the "Hawthorne Effect," but rather be busily promoting and exploiting it.

I should like to underline the remarks of several conference authors about graduate education in the social sciences, and its relation to more and better research having policy implications. Babchuk notes that, if students are to be equipped for effective policy research, they need in their advanced training program to gain some thorough exposure to the world in which policy is in fact made and pursued. Babchuk proposes something on the model of internships. Surely we need a device for intensive field work for the student's immersion in a milieu. Only if such an experience or series of experiences is a central component of graduate education can the student gain that intimate knowledge-of-acquaintance, and that familiarity with social action "on the nerve," required for effective policy research. Further, only in this fashion can he cultivate the interpersonal skills essential for sustained interaction with policy-makers in operating organizations.

In connection with Babchuk's suggestions, and also in keeping with Straus's call for more varied types of graduate education for research, I should like to stress the importance of field work as a portion of the doctoral dissertation. Clearly, not every dissertation need be based on the student's firsthand field experience. But for students contemplating policy research, this set of learnings seems critical. Here I should deplore what appears to be an increasing tendency for students to undertake so-called secondary analysis for the doctoral thesis. Certain of our most able candidates go through graduate school acquiring batches of theoretical and methodological elegances, but scarcely ever meeting any people. Straus asserts that one thing our students need to learn is the art of asking the right questions. An investigator's sociological imagination is stimulated, and his ability to frame generative question is enhanced, by absorption in the human enterprise.

Finally, Aldous maintains that if sociologists are to work on policy issues they require interdisciplinary training during their graduate education. I noted earlier that the examples of influential research in the health field all entailed the sociologists' collaboration with a variety of other professionals, within and without the social sciences. Here I just wish to reemphasize that there is probably no such thing as "pure" sociology in policy research. Graduate training, then, must encourage fairly deep familiarity with neighboring disciplines, perhaps especially psychology and anthropology. It must, too, begin to introduce the student to a few of the many other worlds in which his policy research will surely entangle him: the worlds of the practicing professionals, the administrators, the politicians, the full ferment of communities and organizations in process.

Section C

American Youth
and Their Problems

The Natural History of an Applied Theory: Differential Opportunity and "Mobilization for Youth"

JAMES F. SHORT, JR.

Washington State University

THE LEGACY

Crime and juvenile delinquency are "naturals" for the analysis of sociological influence on social policy, so varied have been the research efforts and theoretical formulations of our colleagues in this area of human behavior and so "applied" the contexts within which most of these efforts have taken place. One need only reflect on a few classic examples: (1) Thrasher's (1927) work with Boys' Clubs of America delinquency prevention efforts in New York City; (2) The founding of the Chicago Area Project by Shaw and McKay (1942) and their colleagues, and their long-time association with the Illinois Institute for Juvenile Research; (3) Burgess' (1928) pioneer studies of "Factors Determining Success or Failure on Parole," undertaken at the request of the Illinois Parole Board and subsequently adopted for use by that board in determining parole policies and practices.

Note that although these efforts began in the middle and late 1920s, their impact, particularly that of the latter two, is considerable even today; and the Boys' Club has had recent contact with social scientists in conducting experimental action-research programs (Mattick and Caplan 1964). Also, during this earlier period sociologists were involved with representatives of the International Association of Chiefs of Police and others in development of the Uniform Crime Reporting System adopted by the Federal Bureau of Investigation. This system, despite its weaknesses and abuses, brought new standards of uniformity and objectivity in the reporting of particular types of crime, including the *Index Offense,* a composite measure based on accurately reported serious crimes. On the negative side, the Uniform Crime Reporting system became the basis for the official and public definition of "the crime problem"; and despite the pioneering work of Sutherland on white-collar and professional crime, Landesco and others on organized crime, that conception for many years was the dominant sociological conception because data concerning it were available. That we have allowed it to dominate the public conception of crime even to this day is to our discredit, although imaginative and persistent sociological efforts to change this conception have been made since at least the 1920s.[1]

Following these relatively promising beginnings, direct sociological participation in efforts to cope with crime and delinquency waned somewhat, although empirical and theoretical work in the discipline continued, including, for example, Sutherland's contribution to the monumental *Recent Social Trends* (1934) and the evolution of his theory of differential association; Sellin's (1938) articulation of the importance of culture conflict in crime; and the ecological studies and criminal histories which came out of the Illinois Institute for Juvenile Research (Shaw and McKay 1942). Prison reform also continued during this period, prodded by Harry Elmer Barnes, Thomas Mott Osborne, James E. Bennett, and others of sociological persuasion, if not formal training.

Three other sociological "events" of special importance for sociological involvement with respect to crime and delinquency policy occurred in the late 1930s and early 1940s: the first was Merton's (1938) "Social Structure and Anomie"; the second, the papers and later the book, *Street Corner Society,* by Whyte (1943); the third was Tannenbaum's (1938) *Crime and the Community.* The first was important be-

---

[1] I refer to the many attempts to secure other measures of crime, as in self-report and victim surveys, and to more recent studies of white-collar and organized crime.

cause it brought conforming and deviant behavior together into the same paragiam and provided an important basis for the theoretical flowering which occured thereafter with respect to crime and delinquency. Merton's paradigm also had important implications for crime and delinquency control, for it challenged all programs predicated upon what has come to be known as the "evil causes evil fallacy." However, these implications were neither spelled out nor acted upon immediately. Two decades passed before the "action implications" of the paradigm and its embellishment by Cloward and Ohlin became the primary intellectual thrust behind the largest federally funded delinquency program in history.

Street Corner Society was a landmark because it described in detail important types and processes of *organization* in areas of the city which had been characterized as *disorganized,* following the Chicago School (but not as contrary to it as some have imagined, since earlier work by Chicagoans Thrasher, Shaw et al., Landesco, and Sutherland had described gangs, professional and organized crime, and underworld relations with legitimate institutions). Whyte's contribution was to document more systematically and at a microlevel, organizational forms and processes which others had described in macrosociological terms, or from the perspective of individual rather than group "natural histories." And it provided a significant critique of traditional settlement house approaches to community service and to the directions then dominating professional social work.

Tannenbaum's *Crime and the Community* was important because, together with the symbolic interaction perspective, it provided the basis for later development of the most recent sociological perspective to be "applied" to juvenile delinquency control, the "labeling" perspective. More about this later.

OPPORTUNITY STRUCTURE THEORY

Prior to *Delinquency and Opportunity* (Cloward and Ohlin, 1960), Cloward had published in 1959 an article based on his Ph.D. dissertation (written under Merton's direction) in which he modified Merton's paradigm. The nature of the modification is reflected in the article entitled: "Illegitimate Means, Anomie, and Deviant Behavior." To Merton's basic independent variables, the culturally prescribed goals of success and the availability of legitimate means to attain these goals, Cloward added the intervening variable, availability of illegitimate means. This development has been anticipated, but not articulated, by Shaw and McKay, at least as early as 1942, and by Kobrin in a 1951 paper, as Cloward noted in his article. I reiterate this point not to detract from Cloward's contribution, but because it illustrates a principle of great importance for the relation of sociological theory to social policy. The principle is that sociological theory typically is crescive, developing by slow and often uncertain increments suggested by either an empirical discovery or a conceptual modification (such as that suggested by Cloward). One implication, I believe, is that those who would leap to specific concrete social engineering proposals on the basis of new developments in sociological theory are likely to find themselves on shaky grounds. There is a scarcity of both social-policy oriented theory and replicated studies demonstrating valid and reliable knowledge (see Reiss 1970). We do have increasingly reliable techniques of investigation and measurement and growing bodies of knowledge in many areas; and the general cry for relevance leads inevitably to increasing concern with relevance for policy.

The Cloward modification of the Merton paradigm—together with its further development with Ohlin, hypothesizing two types of delinquent subcultures—is set forth in Table 1. A third delinquent subculture, the retreatist, is hypothesized to result from "double failure," i.e., failure to achieve in *both* legitimate and illegitimate (conflict or criminal) terms.

Essentially this paradigm became the basis for Mobilization for Youth (MFY), a large-scale delinquency prevention program on New York City's Lower Eastside (Mobilization for Youth, Inc. 1961; Piven and Cloward 1971; Weissman 1969 a, b, c, and d). But this succinct formulation distorts the processes of theoretical development and of policy formation, and neglects entirely the nature of the policies actually implemented. To begin at the beginning, "the idea which . . . developed into this proposal [MFY] originated at a meeting of the Board of Directors of the Henry Street Settlement in June of 1957 [Mobilization for Youth 1961:iv]." "The idea" was that a comprehensive program should be undertaken, "commensurate in size and scope with the dimensions of the problem" (from "the alarming growth of delinquency on New York's Lower Eastside) [pp. iv–v]." The effort to secure funds for a large-scale action program, the report continues, took 4½ years to complete, including a 2-year planning phase financed by the National Institute of Mental Health.

In the first stage of this process a "many-faceted action program" was formulated by institutional representatives on the Lower Eastside, involving "settlement houses, other social agencies, religious institutions, and civil organizations"; and a quite separate research design

TABLE 1 Social Context and Modes of Delinquent Behavior: A Paradigm

STRUCTURAL FEATURES		
I. *Independent Variable*	(Integrated Areas)	(Unintegrated Areas)
A. Culturally prescribed success goals	Internalized	Internalized
B. Availability of legitimate means to success goals	Limited; hence intense pressures toward deviant behavior	Limited; hence intense pressures toward deviant behavior
II. *Intervening Variables*		
A. Institutional norms	Incomplete internalization	Incomplete internalization
B. Availability of illegal means to success goals	Available	Unavailable
1. Relations between adult carriers of conventional and criminal values	Accommodative; each participates in value system of other	Conflict; neither group well organized; value systems implicit, and opposed to one another
2. Criminal learning structure	Available; offenders at different age levels integrated	Unavailable; attenuated relations between offenders at different age levels
3. Criminal opportunity structure	Stable sets of criminal roles graded for different ages and levels of competence; continuous income; protection from detection and prosecution	Unarticulated opportunity structure; individual rather than organized crime; sporadic income; little protection from detection and prosecution
4. Social control	Strong controls originate in *both* legitimate and illegal structures	Diminished social control; "weak" relations between adults and adolescents
III. *Dependent Variable*		
A. Expected type of collective response among deliquents	Pressures toward deviance originate in limited accessibility to success goals by legitimate means but are ameliorated by opportunities for access by illegal means. Hence deliquent behavior is rational, disciplined, and crime-oriented	Pressures toward deviance originate in blocked opportunity by *any* institutionalized system of means. Hence deliquent behavior displays expressive conflict patterns

was developed by "faculty members of the Research Center of the New York School of Social Work of Columbia University . . . [p. v]." NIMH's review found this proposal "to lack a sufficiently unifying principle . . . to make it the researchable laboratory experiment that its sponsors intended it to be," but in late 1959 NIMH funded a proposal for a planning grant which took "as the unifying principle the hypothesis developed by Cloward and Ohlin in their recent book, *Delinquency and Opportunity* [p. v]." Thus, the book, which figured only remotely in the original action proposal by the Henry Street Settlement, became the "unifying principle" of the final Mobilization for Youth/action-research plan.

The MFY document, published at the end of the planning period, is explicit concerning the relationship between the theory and the action program even in its title: "A Proposal for the Prevention and Control of Delinquency by Expanding Opportunities." The introduction to the proposal is explicit, also, concerning another matter:

> Two types of theory are required to underpin a demonstration program. One body of theory should provide a framework for understanding the sources of the social condition which is to be changed; the other should consist of a framework for altering or modifying that condition. During the planning period, intensive work has been devoted to these theoretical tasks.

> An appropriate program of action is not necessarily self-evident once a theory of causation has been evolved; it cannot simply be assumed that once we know what the trouble is we will have little difficulty remedying it. The task of developing a theory of action which is consistent with the theory of causation is, of course, immense. This is a primary reason why two years have been devoted to the planning and preparation of this proposal. During this period, action and research personnel have attempted to fashion a general theory of action and a set of specific programs which are consistent with the theory of causation with which the project begins [pp. viii–ix].

The "Guidelines to Action" in the proposal explicitly relate to the Cloward and Ohlin (1960) theory:

> In summary, it is our belief that much delinquent behavior is engendered because opportunities for conformity are limited. Delinquency therefore represents not a lack of motivation to conform but quite the opposite: the desire to meet social expectations itself becomes the source of delinquent behavior if the possibility of doing so is limited or nonexistent.

> The importance of these assumptions in framing the large-scale program which is proposed here cannot be overemphasized. The essence of our approach to prevention, rehabilitation, and social control in the field of juvenile delinquency may be stated as follows: in order to reduce the incidence of delinquent behav-

ior or to rehabilitate persons who are already enmeshed in delinquent patterns, we must provide the social and psychological resources that make conformity possible. . . . Our program is designed to enlarge opportunities for conformity and so to combat a major source of delinquent behavior among young people [pp. 44–45].

The task of developing "a general theory of action and a set of specific programs which are consistent with the theory of causation" was formidable, but the effort was made and a huge (by comparison with most such efforts) program was mounted, with a far clearer and closer relationship between the two sets of theory than is customary, and with a much more ambitious research program built into the effort. Cloward, as Director of Research, was given "equal billing" with the Directors of Action and Administration in the MFY Organization Chart (MFY, 1961:231).

Despite this effort, the connection between the theories of causation and action appears tenuous and uncertain in later developments. The emphasis of the "action theory" was solely on changing legitimate opportunities. Illegitimate opportunities, posited as an intervening variable by Cloward and Ohlin, were to be made less attractive by making legitimate opportunities more available, and by better equipping youngsters to take advantage of such opportunities. And the focus of action programs was less on specific delinquent subcultures than on youth and community problems in general.[2] Again, the program document is explicit:

In our earlier discussion of illegitimate opportunity systems, we described the system of interests in some slum areas which supports the development and continuity of criminal careers. We have no expectation that our program can materially influence this system, and thus we doubt that we can appreciably reduce the rates of entry into professional and organized crime [p. 88].

The belief is expressed, however, that petty crime, such as "shoplifting, amateurish robbery and burglary, and other types of simple theft," can be reduced by "expanding the availability of conventional opportunities."

[2] Joseph Helfgot, currently studying MFY, reports that most Lower Eastside gangs "ignored MFY and at times were openly hostile to the organization through vandalism." He notes that the primary organizational method utilized by MFY was to rely upon traditional voluntary organizations. Thus, for example, "in the social protest phase of the organizations, local recreation clubs were approached, not street gangs" (personal correspondence). I am grateful to Mr. Helfgot and to others with whom I have corresponded or talked in the course of preparing this paper.

Cloward, in personal correspondence, defends the effort to manipulate legitimate opportunities rather than illegitimate means on grounds that they pertained, in theories of deviance, to the larger question of choices among alternative types of deviant adaptations. "Why delinquency rather than suicide, for example; or one type of delinquency rather than another?" Since MFY "was oriented toward *preventing* delinquency, not toward converting one form of delinquency into another . . . it focused on the legitimate opportunity variables, as it should have." He also notes that "the legitimate opportunity features of the theory directed attention to social structure as the main variable to be manipulated—as distinct from personality, which has been the emphasis in social work since World War II. We decried clinical approaches, and called for programs to open legitimate opportunities—i.e., youth employment training, new educational programs, etc. In this respect, opportunity theory was the over-riding perspective, not alone in MFY but later in the poverty program." Among those with whom I have corresponded in connection with this paper, there appears to be consensus that MFY drew its intellectual support and legitimation from this broadly sociological perspective rather than from the more distinctive element in *Delinquency and Opportunity*, the role of illegitimate opportunities. It appears also to have been the case, however, that social structural variables proved extremely difficult to operationalize and to manipulate in the program effort, and that most MFY funding was directed toward changing individual characteristics, e.g. job training and education (Helfgot 1972).

The level of theoretical variables upon which the program was based is more than a mere quibble for academics. From the standpoint of the practitioners, the relationship of the theoretical orientation and social practice was even more important. Harold Weissman, official chronicler of the "Mobilization for Youth Experience," writes (personal correspondence):

> . . . the people at the top of MFY quickly lost interest in Opportunity Theory per se, in their desire to engage in a variety of social protest. Second, the issue should not be posed as social theory and social policy, but social theory and social practice. It is in the translation of theory into practice that tremendous gaps appear. Social workers need operable variables, and theory that is operationalized. This is what Opportunity Theory was not.

Bertram Beck, who became Director of MFY in 1965, at a particularly turbulent time in the organization's history, notes that "the heart of the crisis . . . had nothing to do with fiscal management but was obviously related to the social-protest activities which had been con-

ducted in a fashion that left Mobilization [MFY] without any substantial source of ready protection [Beck 1969:147]." The emphasis in
these statements on social protests is not reflected in the level of
funding for such activity (which was quite low), nor, acording to a
current student of MFY, does it reflect the actual level of such activity
(Helfgot, 1972). It seems likely, however, that the statements reflect
real concerns of the organization with public image and with threats
to fundings.

Returning to the relationship between theory and policy, a current
student of MFY notes that MFY changed its primary emphasis from
concern with juvenile delinquency to concern with poverty, as funds
became available through the "war on poverty" (Helfgot 1972). Cloward defends the shift as consistent with opportunity theory. Com-
menting on an earlier version of this paper in which that theory was
characterized as obtuse, he notes:

> What action people found, rather, was that a general orientation toward "oppor-
> tunity structure" did not very clearly specify exactly what they should do—how
> were youth employment programs to be effective, for example, when you
> couldn't get minority youth into construction trades? Or how were educational
> opportunities to be created when you had the entrenched bureaucracy of the
> schools to deal with? They thus (and rightly) found *Delinquency and Opportu-
> nity* too vague when it came to the pragmatic questions of putting a meaningful
> opportunity program together. The problem was not obtuseness, but vagueness
> at the level of action implications. The theory was general; it did not translate
> automatically into a specific set of program prescriptions.

And in respect to my point that the "crisis theory" of organizing
low-income people for political action was more important to action
efforts both in MFY and in subsequent programs than were the ab-
stractions of opportunity theory, he states: "One was a general
perspective guiding the program; the other was a very specific theory
of how low-income people could be (and subsequently were) organized for political action."

But this view begs important questions. What is the relationship of
the "specific theory" to the "general perspective"? The lack of specificity of opportunity theory led mobilization "to attack pragmatically
the problems of the neighborhood, leaning on the theory when it
was helpful, ignoring it at other times, and expanding it on others
[Weissman 1969d:195]." In this epilogue to the four-volume series
describing the MFY "experience," Weissman chides the research department for not producing "a comprehensive critique of opportunity
theory based on the Mobilization for Youth Experience [194]."

In the mid-1960s, Piven and Cloward made their case for mobilizing the poor, and the argument was more fully developed in their book *Regulating the Poor* (1971). This book takes as its basic thesis the notion that relief-giving, historically and to this day, has been the most effective way to deal with the political pressures of the poor when these have been activated. The "crisis theory" of the welfare rights movement is perhaps best summarized in the words of Piven and Cloward: "a placid poor get nothing, but a turbulent poor sometimes get something [1971:338]." The similarity of this "theory" to that of the late Saul Alinsky is striking, as are other features of the MFY and poverty programs to other sociological "action theorists," e.g., the use of indigenous community organizers and establishing contact with institutionalized youngsters as a prelude to their social reintegration upon release, as urged by Clifford Shaw 30 years earlier.

This is not the place to analyze the success of these efforts either in "curbing delinquency" or "solving poverty," though considerable effort continues toward such assessment (Helfgot 1972). It is sufficient at this point to note that MFY probably is the single most comprehensive delinquency control program ever undertaken. Opportunity structure theory, shortened simply to "opportunity theory," subsequently became the fundamental paradigm for this nation's largest scale delinquency control effort. More than this, it became a sort of prototype for the Communtiy Action Programs of the "War on Poverty." It was, as Piven and Cloward note, "the Great Society's first community action program"; indeed "the first Great Society agency [Piven and Cloward 1971:277,290]." As MFY developed, that larger battle was joined by both the intellectual and the action leadership and their followers. In the process, delinquency prevention became a secondary, though still important, objective.

The relationship of opportunity theory to the national effort was even more complex than that between Mobilization and the theory. MFY was the first and largest of several programs for delinquency control mounted by the federal government in major American cities. But the decisions to mount a large-scale effort to control delinquency and subsequently large-scale programs to provide mental health and other services to inner city areas throughout the country were political decisions, "a response to new political imperatives" (following Piven 1968; Piven and Cloward 1971). Once those decisions were made, opportunity theory became an important organizing principle, particularly after Ohlin was brought to Washington, D.C. to administer the new federal delinquency program. As Special Assistant to H.E.W. Secretary Abraham Ribicoff, Ohlin—and therefore the theory—

were important intellectual influences in the program. The President's Committee on Juvenile Delinquency and Youth Crime, appointed to provide leadership for the program, was chaired by Attorney General Robert F. Kennedy, with Ribicoff and Secretary of Labor Arthur Goldberg as members. The Special Assistants to Kennedy and Goldberg were not social scientists; they were persons with political connections and journalistic experience.

SUMMARY AND APPRAISAL

The common, and perhaps the prevailing view of sociologists, I suspect, is that "Opportunity Theory clearly suggests specific, relatively modest social policy innovations to control juvenile delinquency [Gallaher and McCartney 1972]." That was my impression, too, prior to undertaking this project.[3] Apparently the persons responsible for policy-making and implementation at MFY did not find it so. What did happen, it appears, is that sociologists—primarily Cloward and Ohlin, and many others, too, as the President's Committee on Juvenile Delinquency and Youth Crime and the "War on Poverty" were established and programs expanded—were able to influence the course of juvenile delinquency research and action, and research and action related to poverty, welfare, and other problems (Piven and Cloward 1971; see also Marris and Rein 1967; Donovan 1967; Moynihan 1969). They did so and they continue to do so, most often by participating in review of funding proposals for both action and research programs, by carrying out research (often related directly to action programs, and by consulting in other ways with these programs, and occasionally by entering more directly into the design and implementation of action programs. All except the last of these are in the "enlightenment" mode of relating sociological knowledge to social action. The latter clearly falls within the "engineering" mode (Janowitz 1972).[4]

There is ample historical precedent for both of these modes. I have already referred to one of the better known cases of sociological en-

[3] Indeed, I wrote in 1965: "Not since the advent of psychoanalysis has a theory had such impact on institutionalized delinquency control as the theory, explicit or implied in Delinquency and Opportunity [Short, Rivera, and Tennyson 1965:56]." I still believe this is true, though the influence of opportunity theory appears to have waned in recent years, and its relation to action programs probably was not as direct as I had thought.

[4] For discussion of these conceptions of sociological knowledge and a vigorous defense of the enlightenment conception, see Janowitz (1972).

gineering, the Chicago Area Project (Kobrin 1959; Shaw and McKay 1942), conceived and engineered during its early history by Clifford Shaw and other sociologists. It should be pointed out, however, that even in the early years Shaw and his colleagues functioned as much in the enlightenment mode as in direct involvement in the operations of Community Committees (consistent with Shaw's insistence upon indigenous leadership and community self-determination). More recently the Highfields project (McCorkle, Elias, and Bixby 1958), modeled after McCorkle's conception of "guided group interaction," has received much attention, as have "The Provo Experiment," and other experiments designed, directed, and evaluated by Empey and his associates (Empey and Rabow 1961; Empey and Erickson 1972).

Integration of theory, policy, and practice certainly has been closer in the latter of these projects than in most attempts to "apply" sociological theory. Yet problems similar to those alluded to in the MFY experience occur. In a particularly thoughtful response to this paper, Empey reports on his own experience (personal correspondence):

> I found staff members responding to emergent problems on ad hoc and individual bases, rather than turning to the theoretical guidelines of the project for solutions. There are always pressures to do this because . . . the problems of individuals often conflict with the problems of the organization and with what the theory says should be done. Therefore, faced with an ideological conflict, staff members reject the theory and do what they think is best for the individual. Consequently, I found myself continually having to say to staff that they should turn to the theoretical guidelines for answers as to what they should do when a problem emerged rather than responding on an ad hoc basis. Had I not been there, had I not been adamant in my stand, I believe our programs would have moved further and further away from their theoretical bases. It is often not the theory that is at fault, but emergent problems which cause people who run programs to discard the theory. The result is that the theory often does not get a test.

Thus we return to the continuing tensions between theoretical specificity and problems of ongoing activity; betweeen theoretical guidelines and ad hoc solutions pragmatically selected. Problems of this genre clearly need to be added to the agenda of applied sociological concern.

Two even more recent large-scale programs in the delinquency field may be taken as illustrative of the enlightenment mode. They may be described briefly:

(1) Under the auspices of the Youth Development and Delinquency Prevention Administration, the federal government has launched a

large-scale effort to divert young people from the juvenile justice system.

> The broad outlines of the strategy were developed at a meeting called by the Youth Development and Delinquency Prevention Administration in early 1970. Those who attended were representative of the professions most concerned about youth problems and included law enforcement officials, educators, sociologists, and practitioners and researchers in the fields of juvenile delinquency and youth development. *The strategy calls for the establishment, nationwide, of youth services systems which will divert youth, insofar as possible, from the juvenile justice system by providing comprehensive, integrated, community-based programs designed to meet the needs of all youth, regardless of who they are or what their individual problems may be* [emphasis in original] [Gemignani 1972: 8].[5]

This program includes among its "measurable objectives" provision of "more socially acceptable and meaningful roles for youth and reduction of 'negative labelling.' [Gemignani 1972:1]" Let us hope that plans and funds for research are sufficient for sociological evaluation of the pilot programs currently under way in 23 communities throughout the nation.[6]

(2) At the University of Michigan, the National Assessment of Juvenile Corrections is conducting a "comprehensive national study of correctional programs for juvenile offenders" (Sarri and Vinter 1972). Here the goal is "to expand knowledge about juvenile corrections by rigorous use of social science theory and methods; and to yield useful directions for policy change [p. vii]." The research panel for this program consists largely of prominent sociologists. Other sociologists serve on the "correctional programs" and "law and policies" panels.

Frankly, I am not certain how to classify MFY in terms of the engineering vs. enlightenment distinction. During its turbulent history it appears to have included elements of both. Perhaps that is one of the problems with the distinction; in many cases it surely is a matter of relative emphases. Janowitz (1972) points out that the distinction between basic and applied sociology is sharply drawn in the engineering model and quite blurred in the enlightenment model. In any case, I admit to serious reservations concerning the role of sociologists in recent poverty programs, whether the role is currently interpreted by Piven and Cloward or by others. Piven and Cloward credit the "large role played by various professionals, especially social workers and so-

[5] The program is not without its critics. See Kobrin (1972).
[6] Theoretical and empirical assessments of this program are under way, e.g., those by Kobrin (1972), Klein (1973), and Cressey and McDermott (1973).

cial scientists, who provided the rationales for the Great Society" with obscuring the political interests at stake in these programs and therefore allowing them to proceed.

> Each measure was presented at the outset as a politically neutral "scientific cure" for a disturbing social malady. Each concrete program that evolved was couched in the murkey, esoteric terminology customarily used by professionals, a terminology that obscured the class and racial interests at stake, so that few groups could be certain who would gain or lose. Finally, the professionals and social scientists lent an aura of scientific authority to what might otherwise have been perceived as political rhetoric. By thus observing the fact that the federal government was about to give something to the blacks, opposition by white groups was deflected [Piven and Cloward 1971:277–278].[7]

This analysis coincides, as Piven and Cloward note, to Raab's characterization of the rationales of poverty programs as "a kind of sociological surprise ball."

> Every few unwindings some new thesis is exposed which changes the character of the whole package. But the package is so tricky that legislators, politicians, social workers, and various segments of the public tend to stop at the thesis which suits them best [Raab 1966:47, quoted in Piven and Cloward 1971:277].

Piven and Cloward note that this view differs sharply from other analyses of the origins and the fate of the Great Society programs. In a lengthy footnote (1971:279) they explain these differences:

> Donovan, like several other political scientists who are cited below, approaches his analysis from the perspective of accepted interest-group theory, and is left concluding that the initiation of the programs is something of a puzzle, for no significant pressure groups were at work. He then, however, invokes the lack of active group support to account for the political troubles that subsequently beset the programs. Moynihan, on the other hand, ascribes the genesis of the programs to the ideas of professionals, mainly social scientists, who counseled federal officials—"those liberal, policy-oriented intellectuals who gathered in Washington and in a significant sense came to power, in the early 1960's." He attributes the travails of the programs to the fact that these ideas were foolish, as were the politicians who were "taken in" by them. Marris and Rein have a similar view, though they are more sympathetic to the professionals. They trace the programs to a blossoming of reform idealism, mainly among professions in the foundations, the universities, and the federal government. Once implemented, however, the Great Society programs were said to have floundered on the resistance of the local politicians and bureaucrats.
>
> We ourselves do not believe that the stupidity or cupidity of particular political leaders or their "idea men" have much to do with the origin or fate of programs of such scale and duration. Nor do we believe that the initiation of these

---

[7] This and the subsequent quotations credited to Piven and Cloward 1971 are from Frances Fox Piven and Richard Cloward, *Regulating the Poor*, © 1971 by Pantheon Books, a division of Random House, Inc. By permission.

legislative measures can be ascribed to special-interest groups. Instead, we think that the Great Society programs were promulgated by federal leaders in order to deal with the political problems created by a new and unstable electoral constituency, namely blacks—and to deal with this new constituency not simply by responding to its expressed interests, but by shaping and directing its political future. The Great Society programs, in short, reflected a distinctively managerial kind of politics.

In none of these views are the roles of social scientists—their intelligence or their disciplines—wholly admirable, to make the most charitable construction. We may well question how long social science, and social scientists, will be supported and granted credibility if we not only obfuscate but are used to obfuscate, rather than enlighten. Perhaps the most important lesson from this chapter in intellectual and political history is, as Piven suggests:

> the lesson of how much the social science of an era was the creature of political circumstance . . . . First, certain theorists gained ascendancy because they became linked with federal programs and federal support, influencing . . . the kind of sociology that was done in the 1960's; and, of course, the political climate of the time supported these tendencies. But the social scientists who fancied themselves social engineers were not in fact performing an engineering role [personal correspondence].

CONCLUSION

I must apologize for encroaching on the province of those at this conference who are discussing poverty and problems of the cities. But that—quite properly, I believe—is where an important sociological perspective on delinquency has led. Sociological evaluation of the programs discussed in this paper—as distinct from evaluation of their success in delinquency control or in making progress toward the elimination of poverty—is difficult. Perhaps a beginning has been made, though I find it difficult to be optimistic.

I have argued elsewhere that sociological evaluation—monitoring social policies and their implementation according to sociological principles and theories—results in greater contributions both to ameliorative social action and to sociology as a discipline than traditional designs which focus on "before" or "after" states of whatever phenomenon we may be studying (Short 1968).[8] My personal preference

---

[8] My use of the term "ameliorative" may seem either bland or too status quo in its implications. I do not intend it to be so. With Becker and Horowitz (1972) I believe "good sociology is often radical. A sociology which is not good, however, cannot be radical in any larger sense." My argument thus refers to what I feel is necessary to "good sociology."

is for a professional sociology in the enlightenment mode, whether with respect to evaluation, institution building, or simply "doing sociology" and so contributing to knowledge. I believe it is in this mode that we can make the greatest advances in knowledge toward the creation and the maintenance of a better society. I am skeptical of the likelihood of success of the engineering model, but equally skeptical of "enlightenment" efforts which are, by design or inadvertance, confusing, misleading, or both. There is, after all, no substitute for good research, design, methods and data, and for good theory and responsible interpretation.

Whatever new training programs or organizational efforts we may design—and I believe these are called for—must be constrained by these familiar, but sometimes forgotten, principles.

REFERENCES

Beck, B. M.
   1969   Mobilization for youth: Reflections about its administration. In *Justice and the law,* edited by H. H. Weissman. New York: Association Press.
Becker, H. S. and I. L. Horowitz
   1972   Radical politics and sociological research: Observations on methodology and ideology, *American Journal of Sociology* **78,** 1, 48–65.
Burgess, E. W.
   1928   Factors determining success or failure on parole. In *The workings of the*
   [1968]   *indeterminate sentence, law and the parole system in Illinois,* edited by A. A. Bruce, A. J. Harris, E. W. Burgess, J. Landesco. Pp. 205–249. Montclair, New Jersey: Patterson Smith. The first date is the date of publication by the State of Illinois.
Cloward, R. A.
   1959   Illegitimate means, anomie, and deviant behavior, *American Sociological Review* **24,** 164–176.
Cloward, R. A. and L. E. Ohlin
   1960   *Delinquency and opportunity: A theory of delinquent gangs.* Glencoe, Illinois: Free Press
Cloward, R. A. and F. F. Piven
   1966   A Strategy to end poverty, *The Nation* **2,** 202, 510–517.
Cressey, D. R. and R. A. McDermott
   1973   Diversion from juvenile justice system. National Assessment of Juvenile Corrections' project. Ann Arbor, Michigan.
Donovan, J. C.
   1967   *The politics of poverty.* New York: Pegasus. The quote cited in this paper is from a footnote on p. 248 in F. F. Piven and R. A. Cloward's *Regulating the poor.* New York Pantheon Books.
Empey, L. and M. L. Erickson
   1972   *The Provo experiment, evaluating community control of delinquency.* New York: Heath.

?, The Public Interest **3**,

-294.

h design statement. **The**

e Research Council.

nois: Univ. of Chicago

iation, Pacific Sociologi-

inquency, American So-

he United States. **Report**
Trends. Pp. 1114–1167.

inn.

ss.

for youth experience.

youth experience. **New**

ation for youth experi-

experience. New York:

igo Press.

ition, American Sociological

le delinquency research. A

the juvenile justice system,

: representation of the poor.

ial of Sociology **78**, 105–135.

positions of juvenile offend-
California.

merican Sociological Review

nt, Annals of the American
-29.
ems and limits. Paper deliv-
lies in honor of Henry D.

nunity action in the United

escriptive account of its ac-
Michigan: Institute for Social

igical Review **3**, 677–682.

f delinquency by expanding
h.

ity action in the war on pov-

, Social Service Review **42**,

rban programs as a political
l problems, edited by E. A.

s.

Raab, E.
   1966   A tale of three wars: What war and which pover
           47.
Reiss, A. J.
   1970   Putting sociology into policy. *Social Problems* **18,** 28
Sarri, R. C. and R. D. Vinter
   1972   *National assessment of juvenile corrections: Resea*
           Univ. of Michigan.
Sellin, T.
   1938   *Culture, conflict and crime.* New York: Social Scien
Shaw, C. A. and H. D. McKay
   1942   *Juvenile delinquency in urban areas.* Chicago, I
           Press.
Short, J. F., Jr.
   1968   Action-research collaboration and sociological eva
           cal Review **10,** 47–53.
Short, J. F., Jr., R. A. Tennyson, and R. Rivera
   1965   Perceived opportunities, gang membership, and d
           ciological Review **30,** 56–67.
Sutherland, E. H. and C. G. Gehlke
   1934   Crime and punishment. In *Recent social trends in*
           of the President's Research Committee on Socia
           New York: McGraw-Hill.
Tannenbaum, F.
   1938   *Crime and the community.* Boston, Massachusetts:
Thrasher, F. M.
   1927   *The gang.* Chicago, Illinois: The Univ. of Chicago P
Weissman, H. H. (Editor)
   1969a   *Individual and group services in the mobilizatio*
           New York: Association Press.
   1969b   *Community development in the mobilization fo*
           York: Association Press.
   1969c   *Employment and education services in the mobi*
           ence. New York: Association Press.
   1969d   *Justice and the law in the mobilization for yout*
           Association Press.
Whyte, W. F.
   1943   *Street corner society.* Chicago, Illinois: Univ. of Ch

Inappropriate Theories and Inadequate Methods as Policy Plagues: Self-Reported Delinquency and the Law

ALBERT J. REISS, JR.

Yale University

Surveys of self-reported delinquency have become fairly commonplace, although the number of surveyors probably exceeds the number of surveys. A major goal of these surveys is to detect *all* offenders in a population and then to estimate their prevalence for race, sex, age, and social class strata. The estimates presuppose that a prevalence rate based on self-reports of delinquency is a reliable estimate of the true rate in a population. These estimates of prevalence rates and comparisons of offenders with nonoffenders are commonly used to test competing theories about the causation of delinquency, to assess existing social policies and practices for officially defining and processing delinquents, and to make recommendations for dealing with the "problem of delinquency." My particular concern in this paper is to summarize briefly major studies on self-reported delinquency that reach essentially the same conclusions and then to examine their methodological and technical foundations, paying particular attention to their adequacy for social policy on law enforcement. Implications of this critique for sociological training concludes the discussion.

DESIGN OF SELF-REPORTED SURVEYS OF DELINQUENCY

A few words must be said about the archetypal design of surveys of self-reported delinquency before summarizing the findings and their implications for social policy. In that design, the study population comprises all or a probability sample of adolescent school students in selected school districts. Anonymity is assured the students who complete a self-administered questionnaire that includes items defining an unweighted index of delinquency. Most indexes are based on items from the Nye and Short (1957) seven-item delinquency scale or the Dentler and Monroe scales (Dentler, Monroe. Zamoff, and Zamoff 1966). Six of these items used by Hirschi (1969) in the Richmond, California Youth Study are given below as typical items in an index or "scale" of delinquency:

1. Have you ever taken things (worth less than $2) that did not belong to you?
2. Have you ever taken things of some value (between $2 and $50) that did not belong to you?
3. Have you ever taken things of large value (worth over $50) that did not belong to you?
4. Have you ever taken a car for a ride without the owner's permission?
5. Have you ever banged up something that did not belong to you on purpose?
6. Not counting fights you may have had with a brother or sister, have you ever beaten up anyone or hurt anyone on purpose?

Responses are either yes or no; intervals of frequency of the behavior: never, more than a year ago, during the last year; and occasionally whether or not any official action by the police or others resulted when detected. A youth is usually classified as delinquent when admitting to behavior for *any* item in the index. Only a few studies use some criterion to differentiate among offenders based on frequency of offending.

Only one U.S. study reports the reliability of response to index items (Clark and Tifft 1966, for a college class in sociology). Four studies report a validation of the index items (Reiss and Rhodes 1959; Erickson and Empey 1963; Gold 1966; Clark and Tifft 1966); and Hirschi (1969) used court records of delinquency to validate the delinquency score. Only two U.S. studies—based on interviews rather than an anonymous questionnaire—gathered information on the specific nature of the delict to test the validity of self-reports (Reiss and Rhodes 1959; Gold 1966).

SUMMARY OF FINDINGS

Reviews of these studies have sought to resolve conflicting evidence (National Council on Crime and Delinquency 1970). The following findings are reported most frequently:

1. Except for acts of personal violence, blacks are no more likely than whites to violate the law.
2. There are no significant differences in delinquency by social class whether measured by father's occupation or parental education.
3. Between the ages of 12 and 17, there are only small differences in rates of delinquency, with age 15 the age of maximum delinquent activity.
4. Sex differences in delinquency are small and decreasing.
5. Delinquency involvement varies little by size of place.

Those same findings emerged in the 1972 statewide survey in Illinois conducted by the Institute of Juvenile Research (1972:9–11).

IMPLICATIONS FOR SOCIAL POLICY

Several inferences often are drawn from these findings that have relevance for social policy. Some studies state them explicitly; in others they are implicit in the discussion.

(1) Official statistics of delinquency underestimate the true rate of delinquency in a population. A majority of adolescents who have violated the law at least once are not detected by the police; and of those detected, an official record is not made in a substantial proportion of cases. The policy implications for police detection and discretion are far from clear in discussions of these findings, whether, for example, there should be changes in the level of enforcement or the exercise of police discretion to officially process delinquents. At issue, of course, are questions of fact, such as whether increased levels of policing increase rates of detection of offenders and the means by which control can be exercised over discretion.

(2) Official statistics of delinquency are said to give a biased description of differences in prevalence rates by race, socioeconomic status, age, sex, and size or type of community. Official statistics are considered mere indicators of differential behavior of official agents of the criminal justice system in detecting and labeling members of social categories rather than indicators of true differences in delin-

quency for social categories in the population. Some studies conclude that official agents of the police and courts discriminate against the poor, blacks, males, and residents of the inner city out of prejudice and practice. Again, the policy implications are vaguely stated, skirting such issues as whether the police should show equal vigor in enforcing the law against middle-class or white youth, thereby eliminating discrimination on these grounds, or whether law enforcement should be changed in other ways.

(3) Law enforcement leads to secondary deviation; official processing of delinquents increases their rate of delinquency (Gold 1970). Changes in law enforcement and criminal justice policy so as to reduce official labeling and processing of offenders, therefore, will reduce rates of recidivism.

METHODOLOGICAL FOUNDATIONS

How firm are the methodological foundations of these findings and the inferences drawn from them? The methodological and technical foundations of these studies do not invite confidence in the conclusions.

(1) The studies usually confuse prevalence and incidence rates. What is commonly reported as an incidence rate is actually a simple prevalence rate of offenders in a population. The index of delinquency is made up of an arbitrarily selected list of delicts and any person qualifies for inclusion if committing any offense at least once is acknowledged. The same criterion usually holds for offense-specific comparisons. Prevalence statistics mask enormous differences in rates of offending among adolescents in a population and in the incidence of offenses. For the few cases where estimates of the rate of offending are calculated in self-report studies of delinquency, officially defined delinquents account for substantially more of the offending in a population and for the commission of serious offenses. Rates of offending in self-report studies, moreover, confirm the substantial differences by race and social class observed in official statistics (Gold 1970; Reiss and Rhodes 1959). It seems highly questionable to develop social policies from findings on simple prevalence rates, ignoring substantial differences in incidence rates.

(2) The most carefully designed study in delinquency is that of Wolfgang and his collaborators (1972). In selecting a 1945 birth cohort that resided in Philadelphia between their 10th and 18th years, they obtained all police records of offenses for the cohort. Among the

major findings of this study, two are of special significance of our discussion. First, there was a sharp differentiation among males who committed five or more offenses and those with fewer offenses; the former were defined as chronic recidivists. Chronic recidivists accounted for 18% of the offenders but more than half of all offenses known to the police, and they were disproportionally concentrated among blacks and lower socioeconomic status groups (Wolfgang, Figlio, and Sellin 1972:245–48). Second, probabilities of desistance from delinquency drop sharply after first and second offenses, but beyond the third offense, the desistance probabilities level off (1972:245). These findings, among others in Wolfgang's investigation, call into question any simplistic explanation of the effects of labeling and official processing.

(3) The detection of crimes depends upon mobilization systems. Data on self-reported delicts should be reasonbly consistent with findings on detection and mobilization systems. There is ample evidence that the police are primarily reactive to citizen mobilizations for offenses involving juveniles rather than proactive (Black and Reiss 1970; Reiss 1972). Self-reports of victimization from crime disclose that blacks, lower socioeconomic status groups, and residents of the inner city are disproportionally victimized by common crimes (Biderman 1967). Data on place of residence of victim and offender, moreover, show marked propinquity patterns in offending (White 1932; Reiss 1967; Smith 1972). These data offer strong evidence that, in the aggregate, offenses, offenders, and victims are disproportionally concentrated among groups disproportionally represented in official statistics of crime and delinquency. Although such findings do not necessarily question findings on simple prevalence rates, they are at odds with similar conclusions about incidence rates. If small differences exist in simple prevalence rates, substantial differences exist in incidence rates.

(4) Although the findings from studies of informally and officially processed juveniles by the police are not altogether consistent, altogether they raise questions about the suppositions concerning police discretion implicit both in the design and findings from self-reported studies of delinquency, and in the inferences about official processing and labeling of delinquents. Sudnow (1965) provides evidence that criminal justice agents do not operate with concepts of statutory violation (implicit in the design of self-report studies) but with models of "normal crimes." Piliavin and Briar (1964) found that deference and demeanor were major factors in police discretion to arrest juveniles; and Black and Reiss (1970) report that most police–juvenile contacts

are initiated by citizens, that police arrest of juveniles depends on the manifest preferences of citizen complaints rather than police preferences, and that situational evidence is an important factor in police discretion to arrest juveniles. Monahan (1972) found that a detailed examination of police discretion for 21,000 cases contacted by the Philadelphia police in 1960 provides little evidence for widespread discrimination in police practices.

PROBLEMS OF INFERENCE AND SOCIAL POLICY

Considerations of brevity for the assigned task limit further examination of studies of self-reported delinquency and their consistency with findings from other investigations. We turn now to summarize briefly some of the problems in design and inference presented by studies of self-reported delinquency that make it difficult to develop social policy with respect to law enforcement.

First, it should be noted that self-reported studies of criminal violations of the law focus almost exclusively on youth rather than on adult populations. Studies of adult delicts that constitute the exceptions are of interest since they appear to have arisen from questions of social policy about consensual or "victimless" crimes. There are self-report studies of adults on drug use, sex offenses, gambling, and minor delicts such as drinking and traffic violations. Focusing on juvenile rather than adult violations also scants questions of comparative analyses of white-collar as compared with common criminal offenses. From a social-policy perspective the relationship of juvenile delicts to patterns of adult criminality (white collar vs. common criminality) requires investigation.

There is reason to presume that the focus on self-reported delinquency, rather than self-reported adult criminality, follows from considerations of expediency rather than from theoretical or policy considerations. Youth in schools are captive populations and historically presented fewer problems of cooperation and informed consent.

A second problem presented by these studies is the absence of measures of reliability and validity for the self-reported delicts. Of particular concern for any policy implications is the dependence for validation on officially recorded delinquency. The procedure of validation tends to assume that, if it were not for the vagaries of law enforcement, all other self-reported delicts would pass the test of "true" or "official delinquency." This is a questionable assumption at law as it might be for sociology.

Third, law enforcement policy is less dependent upon prevalence rates for offenders within a population than on their rate of offending, or on an incidence rate. Patterns of offending and victimization are likewise of more importance to law enforcement strategies than are simple prevalence rates. Surveys can be designed to answer questions of this kind, although many of the problems of measurement such as telescoping events are not easily solved. The confusion of prevalence and incidence rates in the literature leads to erroneous policy inferences.

Fourth, prevalence estimates for a population depend upon the criteria selected for determining delinquency. In the absence of a standardized instrument, who is defined as a delinquent depends upon which norms are selected and how many delicts comprise the index of delinquency. The literature shows variation from 5 to 40 items defining a delinquency scale. The more items there are in a set, the less serious the behavior covered by most items in the set, and the more likely one is to find no differences by race, sex, age, or social class. Even when there are a small number of items for self reporting, correlation among any 2 items is generally .3 or less, and the correlation between official record and self-reported record is not much greater (Hirschi 1969).

Fifth, there is a marked tendency for sociological investigators to take the role of law enforcement of court officer in defining delinquency by formulating questions. To give but one example, an item "During the last year, did you ever stay away from school just because you had other things you wanted to do?" becomes a measure of "truancy," which in turn is treated as a measure of delinquency. The police are usually not concerned with truancy. Apart from the fact that under the law truancy is usually regarded in terms of a concept of "habitual truancy," the police are not normally mobilized for truancy unless it be at the initiative of school officials. Moreover, data from schools on the prevalence and incidence of truancy or absenteeism contradict the findings from self-reported studies of delicts.

Sixth, the sampling frame in self-report studies rarely gives all adolescents an equal probability of being drawn, and among those drawn the loss rate due to absences or noncompliance often is one-fourth or more of the adolescent cohorts. Where one is attempting to measure prevalence or rates of offending in a population, such losses are serious, since they occur disproportionally among dropouts from school or/and lower status youth.

These observations may suffice to indicate that almost all studies have serious design deficiencies that make valid and reliable inference problematic. At the same time, it should be stressed that the problems of design are not insoluble. For almost every deficiency in design, one can point to a sociological investigation that has made a reasonably successful effort to surmount the problem. Yet subsequent studies fail to take account of this success. A good question is, Why?

IMPLICATIONS FOR TRAINING SOCIOLOGISTS

What are the implications of the foregoing comments for training sociologists, the open agenda of this conference? Some of the implications may be apparent from what has been said, but a few brief observations may serve to focus discussion of changes in sociological training.

First, investigators are ordinarily not trained to formulate research that is closely integrated with matters of social policy. As Biderman observes, the roles of academicians as producers of new knowledge are poorly integrated with those of imparters of knowledge through educational institutions. Their knowledge-producing activities consist mainly of production for science building, to support advocacy of specific or general political or social policies, and to meet the requirements of organizations supporting research (Biderman 1970:225). Whether the formulation of policy research problems should be left to policy-makers as Coleman (1973) argues is moot. Much depends on how intellectuals are trained in universities and integrated into policy-making bodies, as may be apparent from a comparison of the roles of English and American intellectuals in public life and bureaucracies. The organization of social science training in American universities has been oriented to the like interests of professionals and the common interests of science building rather than to the common interests represented in collective regulation.

Clearly, the major theoretical and empirical work on delinquency has been oriented toward the science building activities of understanding the causes of individual or group delinquent behavior. Such theories of causation probably are less relevant to matters of social policy than theories of how one may change behavior, situations, organizations, and systems. Theories of social intervention and of social control that produce change are generally poorly developed in sociology and poorly taught in graduate training. The current focus on evaluation research tends to be not only atheoretical but fundamentally does not address itself to matters of social policy and social change. There are a few models of research on delinquency that begin to address these questions, the most noteworthy studies being those by Short and Strodtbeck (1965) on the role of detached social workers in delinquency control programs, and by Wolfgang *et al.* (1972) on disposition contingencies in processing delinquents in the criminal justice system.

Much of the investigation on self-reported delinquency that bears on policy questions of law enforcement, however, emerges from ideological positions that are formulated as theoretical positions (Hirschi 1969). Studies of delinquency are more likely to carry implications about the *intent* of law enforcement officials than about the nature of social control systems of detection and enforcement. Law enforcement is seen as discriminatory, for example, rather than as an operating system of detection.

Another striking fact about the theoretical formulations that lie behind most studies of self-reported delinquency is an almost exclusive attention upon characterizing persons in terms of a deviant status on the assumption that any event of violating characterizes the person in a violator status. The behavioral event becomes a status attribute. This is the sociological investigator's form of labeling that bears a striking resemblance to the sociologist's characterization of law enforcement and other officials as labelers. What sociologists try to explain then is the status label they have attached on the basis of behavior that may occur only once (and that of a particular kind). Absent in such formulations is attention to the behavioral act in social situations, the victims, and the consequences of having violated a specific law. Even though, on occasion, the respondent is asked whether he was picked up by the police, this fact is rarely related to specific behavioral acts, so that one might learn more about the relationship of law enforcement to social situations of violating that are detected and not detected. Are the theft delicts of middle-class youth, for example, substantially different from those of lower-class youth, causing both detection and law enforcent to be different? Certainly there are substantial differences in the detection and enforcement systems for white-collar crime as contrasted with that for many common crimes that are the major object of sociological inquiry.

Second, let me state some conclusions about how training in survey research may affect investigation. I have noted that surveys of self-reported delinquency pay little attention to the formulation of indicators and indexes, to problems of their validity and reliability, and a general inattention to the standardization of instruments. Is not much of this inherent in the current training and practice in survey research? The typical survey and the typical training in survey research is treated as a *de novo* enterprise. The students and the investigator ideally start with a problem and some theory and then go to work. They develop questions and, ideally, pre-test them. The criteria for an adequate pre-test of a survey instrument are vague. Usually there is an examination of variation in response to items as a measure of the potential discriminative utility of the items and concern for the ease and length of administration. There is vague talk about examining the internal consistency of responses to items, and occasionally items are included to test consistency in response or response sets.

This pattern of questionnaire construction and training is in sharp contrast to that commonly practiced in test construction in psychology, where students are trained in the development of valid and reliable standardized instruments. There is, of course, nothing inherent in survey research that precludes attention to these matters. The excellent studies of the U.S. National Center for Health Statistics (1965a, 1965b, 1966, 1967) on self-reported health status and care and the Bureau of the Census victimization surveys "pioneered" by sociologists attest that this need not be the case. The U.S. Bureau of the Census (1970a, 1970b) and the Law Enforcement Assistance Administration (1972), for example, have undertaken an elaborate series of studies on the validity and reliability of measures of victimization before proceeding to a national survey.

Perhaps it is not beside the point to say that standards of sociological research should be at least those of research agencies in government if we expect to affect social policy. Much more is required than new entrepreneurship for each survey.

A conclusory statement may be in order. Sociologists may take comfort from trying to find out why things are as they are, rather than in learning how things that are can be made different. But social policy, in my opinion, is informed more by the latter than by the former.

REFERENCES

Biderman, A.
   1967   Surveys of population samples for estimating crime incidence, *The Annals
           of the American Academy of Political and Social Sciences* **374**, 16–33.
   1970   Information, intelligence, enlightened public policy: Functions and organi-
           zation of social feedback, *Policy Sciences* **1**, 217–230.
Black, D. J. and A. J. Reiss, Jr.
   1970   Police control of juveniles, *American Sociological Review* **35**, 63–77.
Clark, J. P. and L. L. Tifft
   1966   Polygraph and interview validation of self-reported deviant behavior, *Amer-
           ican Sociological Review* **31**, 516–523.

Coleman, J.
1973　Ten principles governing policy research. Reported in *Footnotes* 1 (March): 1, American Sociological Association.

Dentler, R., J. L. Monroe, B. Zamoff, and R. Zamoff
1966　*Five scales of juvenile misconduct.* New York: Columbia Univ. Press.

Erickson, M. L. and L. T. Empey
1963　Court records, undetected delinquency and decision making, *Journal of Criminal Law, Criminology, and Police Science* **54**, 456–469.

Gold, M.
1966　Undetected delinquent behavior, *Journal of Research in Crime and Delinquency* **3**, 27–46.

1970　*Delinquent behavior in an American city.* Belmont, California: Brooks/Cole.

Hirschi, T.
1969　*Causes of delinquency.* Berkeley, California: Univ. of California Press.

Institute for Juvenile Research (IJR)
1972　*Juvenile delinquency in Illinois: Highlights of the 1972 adolescent survey.* Chicago, Illinois: Institute for Juvenile Research, Department of Mental Health.

Law Enforcement Assistance Administration
1972　*San Jose methods test of known crimes.* National Institute of Law Enforcement and Criminal Justice, Statistics Division, Washington, D.C.

Monahan, T. P.
1972　The disposition of juvenile offenders by race and sex in relation to the race and sex of police officers, *The International Review of Modern Sociology* **2**, 91–101.

National Council on Crime and Delinquency (NCCD)
1970　Hidden crime, *Crime and Delinquency Literature* **2**, 546–572.

Nye, F. I. and J. F. Short, Jr.
1957　Scaling delinquent behavior, *American Sociological Review* **22**, 326–331.

Piliavin, I. and S. Briar
1964　Police encounters with juveniles, *American Journal of Sociology* **70**, 206–214.

Reiss, A. J., Jr.
1967　Place of residence of arrested persons compared with place where the offense charged in arrest occurred for Part I and II offenses. *Report to the President's Commission on Law Enforcement and the Administration of Justice* #5. Univ. of Michigan: Center for Research on Social Organization.

1972　*The police and the public.* New Haven, Connecticut: Yale Univ. Press.

Reiss, A. J., Jr., and A. L. Rhodes
1959　*A socio-psychological study of adolescent conformity and deviation.* U.S. Office of Education.

Short, J. F., Jr., and F. L. Strodtbeck
1965　*Group process and gang delinquency.* Chicago, Illinois: Univ. of Chicago Press.

Smith, M. W.
1972　An economic analysis of the intracity dispersion of criminal activity. Unpublished Ph.D. dissertation, North Carolina State Univ.

Sudnow, D.
1965　Normal crimes: Sociological features of the criminal code, *Social Problems* **12**, 255–276.

U.S. Bureau of the Census
   1970a   *Victim recall pretest: Washington, D.C.* Demographic Surveys Division.
   1970b   *Household survey of crimes, second pretest: Baltimore, Maryland.* Demographic Surveys Division.
U.S. National Center for Health Statistics
   1965a   *Reporting of hospitalization in the health interview survey.* U.S. Department of Health, Education and Welfare, Washington, D.C., Series 2, No. 6.
   1965b   *Health interview responses compared with medical records.* U.S. Department of Health, Education and Welfare, Washington, D.C., Series 2, No. 7.
   1966   *Interview responses on insurance compared with insurance records.* U.S. Department of Health, Education and Welfare, Washington, D.C.: Series 2, No. 18.
   1967   *Interview data on chronic conditions compared with information derived from medical records.* U.S. Department of Health, Education and Welfare, Washington, D.C., Series 2, No. 23.
White, R. C.
   1932   The relation of felonies to environmental factors in Indianapolis, *Social Forces* **10**, 498–509.
Wolfgang, M., R. M. Figlio, and T. Sellin
   1972   *Delinquency in a birth cohort.* Chicago, Illinois: Univ. of Chicago Press.

Problems of Research in Response to "National Emergencies": Drugs and Addiction

LOIS B. DEFLEUR

Washington State University

In recent years considerable attention has been devoted to the issue of drugs in our society. The mass media have offerd vivid accounts of drug use and drug problems. Politicians and interested citizens have pressed for programs of control, prevention, and treatment. Large amonts of money have been allocated to such purposes. In 1973, for example, the federal government alone provided over $700 million for various drug-related programs.

Sociologists have been involved in these developments. They have been called upon as consultants. Research projects have been commissioned, and numerous opportunities for employment have become available in a growing "drug abuse industry." In spite of this involvement, very little sociological research in the area of drugs has been published in the major sociological journals. The sociological literature that has accumulated on drugs has usually appeared in journals of more specialized nature, such as *Social Problems, Journal of Health and Social Behavior, New Society,* and *Criminology.* For the most part, such works have concentrated on descriptions of types of populations involved in drugs and their patterns of usage. Some have generated and tested specific hypotheses concerning such usage. (For some typical examples, see Davis and Munoz 1968; Klein and Phillips 1968.) In general, however, sociological studies of drugs have neither developed from a sophisticated base of sociological theory nor contributed to the development of such a theory. Furthermore, most drug research has not been particularly sophisticated methodologically. This results, at least in part, from the inherent difficulties of studying phenomena that are publicly stigmatized and must be concealed from official agencies. Because of such limitations, most contemporary drug research that has been published could be rather severely criticized on both theoretical and methodological grounds.

These shortcomings restrict the number of available studies from which to choose for the purposes of the present paper. Nevertheless, in examining recent research articles, I have selected one that seems fairly typical: Glaser, Lander, and Abbott's (1971) investigation of addicted and nonaddicted siblings in a slum area in New York City. Although this particular research suffers from the theoretical and methodological limitations characteristic of investigations in this area, it does seem to contain certain policy implications and can be summarized briefly in the following terms.

According to the authors, this study was designed to test their "relative deprivation—differential anticipation" theory of opiate addiction. They hypothesized that this theory applies to recent opiate usage in slum areas of large United States communities. In their initial discussion of this theory, they fail to define systematically either the variables or the relationships between them. Instead, the authors state: "We shall first set forth and justify the 'relative deprivation–differential anticipation theory' in terms of a few gross dimensions and ethnographic impressions [p. 511]." They summarize some of these dimensions and impressions from the sociological literature. The authors' summary statement of their theory indicates that several factors are to be investigated: ". . . the 'relative deprivation–differential anticipation' theory explains today's slum drug usage primarily by the fact that this usage gives addicts a sense of belonging and achievement, even many periods of hope, in sharp contrast to the 'atonie' or 'tonelessness' for them of the 'square scene' [p. 512]."

From their theoretical discussion, the two crucial variables appear to be *sense of belonging* and *achievement*. However, when we examine the data, we find that they are only indirectly linked to the theory. No rationale is provided for the content of the interview schedule or subsequent testing of the theory. We find immediately, then, the usual theoretical and methodological limitations of this type of research; the variables are not well defined, and it is not possible to determine (from the discussion) what types of quantitative indices would adequately test the theory.

The research procedure compared 37 pairs of addicted and nonaddicted siblings of the same sex from a small area in a slum of New York City. The respondents were interviewed by trained interviewers who were long-time residents of the area. Data were gathered on the following kinds of variables: (1) home background, (2) education, (3) history of drug use, (4) delinquent and criminal experiences, (5) occupational histories, (6) anomie and alienation, and (7) several additional miscellaneous factors. Comparisons of the siblings on these variables are outlined in a large table and discussed in the text of the article. In light of the small number of subjects studied and the fact that they constituted a nonprobability sample, it would be inappropriate for the authors to employ sophisticated statistics. Thus, the data are presented in a very simple form—utilizing numerical totals and percentages. No attempts are made to assess in probability terms the extent and the magnitude of the differences between the addicted and nonaddicted siblings. As is obvious, it is not possible with this type of data to provide an adequate test of the theory under investigation. The authors do exercise considerable caution in attempting to draw conclusions from their research, but they finally assert that: "We interpret these data as supporting the 'relative deprivation–differential anticipation' theory [p. 519.]"

GENERAL POLICY IMPLICATIONS

Given the methodological flaws and inadequacies in theoretical conceptualization, there are consequent limitations on the strength of policy inferences which should be made from this research. What can be accomplished from a study such as this is to pinpoint some of the most salient differences between siblings who have developed very different life styles, and suggest some of the implications that follow from these differences.

In comparing data from the addicted and nonaddicted siblings, the researchers maintained that one of the most important differences was the greater extent of the addict's early involvement in delinquency and other deviant activities. In addition, the addicts appeared to have had more arrests and incarcerations than their nonaddicted siblings. These activities had resulted in many interruptions of their educational and occupational careers. There were few differences in home situations and relationships with parents for the two types of siblings. The addict siblings scored higher on anomie and alienation scales than nonaddicts. But, as the researchers point out, their study cannot unravel whether this is more consequence than cause of the different life styles of these siblings. Over-all, there was a progressive differentiation of the addict deviant and the nonaddicted, nondeviant careers of these young people. As the authors indicate, it appears that the nonaddict was insulated from drug use through an early commitment to conventional and conforming institutions, but the causal sequence of these processes are not unraveled in this study.

As was pointed out, one of the clearest differences between addicted and nonaddicted siblings was involvement of the addicts in illegitimate activities of the street at a very early age. As a result of this involvement, addicted siblings had earlier deviance, arrests, incarcerations, etc. The social consequences of this early deviance made later efforts at conformity difficult, and undoubtedly resulted in barriers to legitimate careers.

The policy implication which can be tentatively drawn here is the desirability of early detection of these youthful deviants coupled with affirmative or divertive action for such individuals (presumably before the onset of opiate addiction). It would appear to be difficult, if not impossible, to attempt reorientation of drug users after they have progressed through a long history of deviance and drugs with all of the accompanying social consequences. At this point, the possibility of rehabilitation in a treatment program, primarily aimed at alleviating drug dependence, is quite limited. Particularly among urban slum users, it is clear that this drug use often followed other types of deviant activities, and that it occurred at later stages of their lives. Thus, the whole cycle becomes reinforcing. While it is true that most urban drug programs are quite cognizant of this fact, they have been able to do very little to break the cycle when addicts come to them at later stages in this process.

Another general policy implication from this article stems from the finding that more addicts had unrealistic career aspirations than did their nonaddicted siblings. Drug use seemed to provide a form of status gratification for these individuals. Through the use of drugs and associated behaviors, such youth could feel like "big shots." or as Feldman (1968:133) labels it, "stand-up cats." Of course, immediate status rewards of this type impede later, legitimate career opportunities. The sequence of delinquency, school retardation, occupational problems, and drugs tends to reduce opportunities for individuals, regardless of their abilities. An obvious implication of such findings is that opportunities should be made available to slum youth which would provide possibilities of achieving some type of immediate status and success early in their lives. Such youngsters need to have either legitimate achievement avenues open to them at an early age, or efforts need to be made to lessen the status rewards currently associated with deviant activities such as drug use. While this is not a new idea, its importance is reiterated in the Glaser *et al.* (1971) research.

An even broader policy implication emerging from this research is the recognition of the highly varied and contrasting nature of life in slum areas of United States communities. Again, this is hardly news to sociologists. The researchers point to differentiations found between youth of similar age in a given neighborhood as additional evidence of the diversities and sharp contrast of slum life. These contrasts occur even within single households. Thus, programs aimed at drug abuse, prevention, or treatment in urban areas should attempt to take into account these variations. If such programs are predicated upon assumptions of a homogeneous population, they contain a built-in failure factor. While this is a rather general and obvious fact, in the past it has been difficult to develop drug programs which adequately provide for sharply contrasting personal conditions.

POLICY IMPLICATIONS FOR WHOM?

Most sociologists who do not specialize in drug problems would respond to the results and implications of the research by Glaser and his associates as offering nothing new. It simply reinforces ideas and findings available in other contexts in the sociological literature. However, we need to interpret such research within the perspective of the kinds of people who are actually involved in drug policy-making. In the main, these are not theoretically sophisticated sociologists but politicians, organizational leaders, and various members of the public.

During the last decade, "the drug problem" has been a significant social issue. Public concern has been high, and all levels of government have responded with various programs and policies. But what are some of the behavioral assumptions that have been used as bases for policy formation in this myriad of social programming? The Second Report of the National Commission on Marihuana and Drug Abuse (1973) has tried systematically to examine this important question. They characterize the current public conception of and response to the drug problem as being confused about both assumptions and objectives. For the most part, public views have been more reflexive than rational and proposed solutions more situation-oriented than strategic. As they state:

> The *ad hoc* responses to use of specific psychoactive drugs have interfered with examination of the fundamental questions relating to behavior patterns and the appropriate means of social control. . . . Patterns of drug-using behavior have been ignored except as an afterthought of intervention. When increases in prohibited drug use continue to escalate, policy-makers respond, not by reassessing the problem from different perspectives, but rather by pressing for evermore costly mechanisms of control; costly both in terms of resources and important social values. [1973:24–25].

Thus, what the Commission criticizes rather vigorously are policies emanating from primarily emotional convictions rather than the foundation of research knowledge which has accumulated. They recognize that many fundamental questions about the causes of drug use remain unanswered, but also they emphasize the vital need for increasing *public* knowledge that could change many erroneous conceptions.

While findings such as those from Glaser and his associates may simply reaffirm common sociological principles, many of these ideas contradict popular imagery about the origins, patterns, and consequences of drug use. Thus, one important kind of policy implication of such research lies in the need for dissemination and utilization of such information by politicians, organizational leaders, and the public who currently lack sociological perspectives. Reiss discussed this same point several years ago in his presidential address to the Society for the Study of Social Problems. He states that:

> The inadequacy of sociology for social engineering need not necessarily preclude its having utility for policy matters . . . sociological knowledge serves intelligence and enlightenment as well as engineering functions in public knowledge . . . and it can be used to influence the views of broad publics on social issues, contributing to their enlightenment [1970:292–293].

This kind of consequence of research knowledge in the area of drug use, therefore, is adequate justification for imputing policy impact even to studies that do not break new ground in basic sociological theory, but which do reaffirm sociological principles in drug-related activities.

Certainly, it would be premature to imply that research knowledge, such as that from the Glaser *et al.* study, has had much impact on the attitudes or views of broad publics. Nevertheless, there is some evidence of emergent attitude changes among a few decision makers and politicians. In particular, the two reports (1972, 1973) of the National Commission on Marihuana and Drug Abuse have incorporated recommendations which indicate an awareness of findings from sociological research.[1] While the extent to which there will be utilization of these recommendations is still a question, it does indicate some degree of "enlightenment."

THE SOCIOLOGICAL PROFESSION AND EMERGENT SOCIAL ISSUES

In an attempt to address the question of what kinds of changes would be required in the discipline and training of sociologists in order to produce *more* policy impact in the area of drugs, it is necessary to return to a few points that were brought out in earlier paragraphs. For example, our limited literature indicates that drug use, as a research topic, does not hold the interest of a large number of sociologists. Recent research that has accumulated in this area does not seem to be particularly significant theoretically, or methodologically, which limits its significance in a policy sense. Furthermore, most of the policy interest in the area of drugs stems more from public concern and pressure on politicians to "do something" than from sociological interest in the problem. There is little doubt in the *salience* of public concern. In fact, the current administration has designated drug abuse as "a national emergency." The more general issue, then, is one of delineating the role and response of sociologists when public opinion focuses on some condition in the social order and defines it as a particularly important social problem. Perhaps a more appropriate way of examining this issue would be to ask: What are the *limitations* in the ability of the discipline to respond to social issues that arise rapidly as

[1] For example, the Second Report of the National Commission on Marihuana and Drug Abuse argues for drug prevention programs that provide alternative solutions to problems of youthful populations. ". . . there is no reason why these prevention programs should emphasize drugs at all. Their focus should be on alternative methods for meeting individual needs and on other ways for a person to cope with his particular set of problems. . . . Among teenage youth, particularly in high-risk socioeconomic settings, the types of opportunity needed most desperately are improved education and meaningful, long-term employment [1973:403]."

"national emergencies"?[2] Given these limitations, how can they be circumvented?

The heart of this issue appears to lie in the dual phenomena of disciplinary specialization and prevailing career patterns in academic sociology—factors which are common to other professionals whose primary employment is in academic institutions. Such specializations and career patterns tend to result in *inflexibility* on the part of individual researchers and the discipline as a whole. Colleges and universities are characterized by a general inability to shift pools of scientific personnel to emerging problems in our society. Typically what happens when a particular area becomes defined as "a national emergency" is that those sociologists who happen to be specialized in the area find their services in extremely high demand. However, there are simply never enough qualified people to go around, and we are not well organized to mobilize those who are both qualified and willing. New graduate-training programs and research policies are often implemented quickly to fill the gap. However, these are really not very satisfactory for a number of reasons.

The main disadvantage to programs designed to train *new* specialists is that attention to the original problem suffers a very serious time lag; it takes years to train new Ph.D.s and to get them actively involved in productive research. By that time public concern may have shifted to a different social problem. In short, this system for training results in poor and inefficient use of personnel. Its "pay-off" is too little and too late. Furthermore, such training policies do nothing concerning the underlying problem of inflexibility. Those who could contribute the most, namely, proven scholars and established researchers who happen to be committed to other specializations, are often ignored simply because it is difficult to attract them to new research areas.

RETOOLING FOR "NATIONAL EMERGENCIES"

The problem thus concerns both professional organization and training. One possible solution to the training problem would be to design shorter, more intensive retooling programs for scholars who have already completed their doctoral degree and who are currently

[2] The implicit assumption here is that sociologists want to respond to emergent social issues. To discuss the related question of whether sociologists *should* respond is an additional, complex issue.

working successfully in other areas of specialization. Given the high level of interest in social issues among sociologists, it seems likely that considerable numbers might be attracted to new areas which promise policy impact and, of course, research and publication possibilities. These scholars could be brought together in contracted programs at specific institutions for the purpose of acquiring a new specialization and focus of interest. The challenge is not only one of creating such training facilities but also one of affecting changes in the academic system itself in order to motivate participation. There would have to be a shift in career incentives, safeguards, and rewards for individuals undergoing this modification of career direction. Once the training was accomplished, however, it would be possible to utilize intensely the "retreaded" specialists for the time necessary to help meet the "national emergency." The cost should be considerably less than starting from scratch with new Ph.D.s. The time factor would probably be 1 year rather than 5 to 10. The individuals involved would also be proven performers rather than unknowns. Furthermore, since "national emergencies" typically became established social problems, the investment of both the individual and the government is not likely to be wasted in the long run.[3]

The idea of shifting personnel is hardly new. Numerous existing programs (fellowships, institutes, post-doctorals, etc.) attempt to provide time and freedom for scholars who want to acquire new specializations. However, these individually oriented and rather unstructured efforts do not provide for large enough numbers of sociologists or clear enough research foci to move quickly into "emergency" problem areas. Thus, we need to consider new ways of both structuring training and organizing the profession, so that the needs of individual research scholars are met and the ability of our discipline to contribute to the shifting priorities of our society is enhanced.

REFERENCES

Davis, F. and L. Munoz
  1968   Heads and freaks: Patterns and meanings of drug use among hippies, *Journal of Health and Social Behavior* **9,** 156–164.
Feldman, H. W.
  1968   Idealogical supports to becoming and remaining a heroin addict, *Journal of Health and Social Behavior* **9,** 131–138.

---

[3] This is not meant to imply that it is desirable for each "emergency" to become institutionalized as a never ending problem.

Glaser, D., B. Lander, and W. Abbott
   1971   Opiate addicted and non-addicted siblings, in a slum area, *Social Problems*
           18, 510–521.
Klein, J. and D. L. Phillips
   1968   From hard to soft drugs: Temporal and substantive changes in drug usage
           among gangs in a working-class community, *Journal of Health and Social
           Behavior* **9,** 139–145.
National Commission on Marihuana and Drug Abuse
   1972   *Marijuana: A signal of misunderstanding.* First Report. Washington, D.C.:
           U.S. Government Printing Office.
   1973   *Drug use in America: Problems in perspective.* Second Report. Washington,
           D.C.: U.S. Government Printing Office.
Reiss, A. J., Jr.
   1970   Putting sociology into policy, *Social Problems* **17,** 289–294.

On the Remarkable Absence of Nonacademic Implications in Academic Research: An Example from Ethnic Studies

JAMES A. DAVIS

National Opinion Research Center

I have been requested to report on a journal article that (1) is worthy of high scholarly marks, (2) contains substantial, if implicit, policy implications, (3) is about public schools, and (4) is not my own. To lighten the burden, those who made the request did not ask me to also design a perpetual motion machine, improve the cultural level of prime time TV, or find an article that was intentionally whimsical and lucidly written.

As a good soldier I tried to follow orders, and as a sober scientist I begin by reporting my field procedures. First, I went back through the last 2 years of the *American Sociological Review,* but could not find any articles about public schools at all. Second, I proceeded backward through the Avis of sociological journals, the *American Journal of So-*

ciology, until I came to an article about schools. After glancing at it to see that it was not absolutely wretched, I vowed to report on it, regardless of what it said. Which I will do now.

The article in the American Journal of Sociology (July, 1971:89–107) is "School Ethnic Composition, Social Contexts, and Educational Plans of Mexican-American and Anglo High School Students," authored by Warren D. TenHouten, Tzuen-jen Lei, Francoise Kendall, and C. Wayne Gordon. Quite the opposite of being wretched, I judge it to be a good job.

Let me summarize it briefly.

The authors are concerned with a six-variable path model à la Sewell and Turner.

In English, the dependent variable is a high school student's expectation of attending college, and the authors wish to explore the direct effects of parental socioeconomic status, ethnic composition of the high school, IQ, parental encouragement, and peer encouragement.

The data come from questionnaires (read out loud) and test scores for reasonably probabilistic samples of 12th graders in five Los Angeles public high schools. N's are as follows: 315 Mexican-American boys, 309 Mexican-American girls, 226 Anglo boys, and 229 Anglo girls.

Analysis centers on running path coefficients for the model within the four sex-by-ethnicity subgroups and comparing the magnitudes of the various effects, direct and indirect. Things turn out to be just about what you would expect from previous research: the coefficients are positive (with one exception), and the magnitudes are all small. The authors also note that in almost every case the coefficients are smaller in the Mexican-American samples.

From this, the authors draw three conclusions: (1) Each of the variables in the model is important; (2) "ethnic comparisons are important to research on the educational plans and achievements of youth"; and (3) "it is easier to explain variance in groups educated to have high verbal skills than in groups with low verbal skills."

And I draw the following conclusion: the article has virtually nothing to say with policy implications, direct or indirect. By which I mean this: If I were a person with enormous authority or influence in public schools, there is nothing in the article that would persuade me to favor one course of action over another.

Since a good bit of what I will write from here on may appear harsh, let me emphasize two points before I become too grouchy. (1) The authors nowhere *claim* any specific applications of their results.

These are requested by the organizers of our conference. (2) I believe that the article is of good quality and as representative of contemporary research in refereed journals as a sample of one (N = 1) can be.

Other than the massive fact that the article was not intended to be applied, why is this piece—and I would claim there are dozens like it in the literature—so barren of practical import? I came up with six reasons, two each to be filed under the headings, "conceptual," "statistical," and just plain "bad luck in the findings."

Conceptually, we have "relevance vs. application" and "nonmanipulable variables."

I think that sociologists too often fail to distinguish between "relevance" and "applicability." This paper is certainly relevant—if by relevance we mean being addressed to a matter of general social concern. Indeed the first sentence is as follows: "The low level of educational achievement among Mexican-American youth in American society represents a continuing social and political problem." Anyone who is collecting data on the aspirations of minority youth can hardly be accused of ivory tower irrelevance. But the sheer fact of studying content that is in the public policy spotlight does not guarantee that the results will be of any use to anyone. I suspect that the next few years will see a tremendous increase in the number of articles about minority group members: women, poor people, homosexuals, or, more precisely, population groups to which the writer does not belong. Fine. But we should not kid ourselves that a focus on topical content means that the results will ipso facto be useful in solving problems.

Indeed, it might even go the other way. When one is studying topical content, it is awfully easy to assume that the results must be socially useful regardless of what they are, but when one is doing research on, say, group dynamics among Episcopal bishops, there is some pressure to come up with practical implications. To be utterly cynical, I will hazard the guess that if this article had been about the difference in path coefficients between students at Andover and Exeter, it might not have been printed. The referees would have (justifiably) said, "So what?" Strangely enough, relevance may be self-defeating in terms of application, if we assume that any article about a topical group has high priority, regardless of the "So what?" question.

The second conceptual problem is that the authors happened to choose a set of variables that defy manipulation (with one exception, discussed later). There is nothing much anyone can do about parental

SES, measured intelligence, parental aspirations, and peer aspirations. Given variables immune to manipulation, findings—no matter how smashing—will have little import for those making social policy. I suppose one might argue that the paper implies that if the SES of Mexican-Americans could be raised, their young people's college aspirations would increase, but that sounds more like the original problem than its answer.

I do not know why sociologists lust for nonmanipulable variables, but we do. I supsect that no more than 5% of the data reported in our journals treat variables that a policy-maker could even dream of changing. I further suspect, without a shred of evidence, that if the authors had used manipulable variables, they would have jeopardized their chances of publication. If their paper had been on "The effects of an information campaaign on the aspirations of Mexican-American youth" or "Role playing as a means of changing youths' college aspirations," I think it quite likely that a journal referee might say, "While this is an excellent article, I really think it belongs in an educational or psychological journal." At least I can hear myself typing such doom-shaped phrases.

In sum, I think the intellectual folkways of our discipline lead us to favor relevant content but to be somewhat prejudiced against pragmatic content.

Next, we consider two statistical barriers to application.

First, the sample is so small (five high schools) and the take rate so low (60%) that results would hardly be compelling even if policy recommendations had been spelled out in capital letters. I am not saying that it is easy to obtain massive and representative data on Mexican-American youths; but I am saying that sampling is not given high priority as a criterion for publication in top flight sociology journals. We pay careful attention to statistical analysis, to theoretical import, and to coverage of literature, but I suspect that no article in the history of the discipline has ever been rejected solely because of inadequate sampling. When one considers the nit picking industry that emerged subsequent to even such a massive study as the Coleman–Campbell–Mood report, it would appear that sociological research that suggests policy applications requires much more in the way of technical credentials than the publication standards of even leading journals.

As a twist on the same point, we note that the authors made no attempt to shore up their central conclusion by reference to other research. It would have been easy to compare the magnitude of regression coefficients for blacks and whites in a wide variety of published studies to shore up the claim that regression coefficients are lower in groups with lesser academic achievement. An even simpler test would be to find data comparing similar regressions for samples from different years in school. That the authors did not take this step is probably due to the "relevance halo," the belief that the salience of the sampled group is sufficient to justify the research. But the consequence is similar to that for sampling per se—there is no very strong argument with the reader who wishes to "tune out" the findings.

The actual statistical analysis, while carefully executed and reported, has two aspects that minimize policy implications.

First, the authors chose to report standardized partial regression coefficients, not raw partial regression coefficients. The choice has been widely debated among methodologists, and I am not qualified to understand that argument, much less enter it. Nevertheless, it remains that raw regressions are the natural language of applied social science. When one finds a raw coefficient of, say, 3.14, one can hardly avoid saying, "and this means that if we could raise mean scores on the independent variable, by one unit, scores on the dependent variable will increase by an average of 3.14." Such statements may be discouraging or impractical in the context of a particular problem, but they are put in a form that leads directly to policy consideration. Perhaps such a simple matter as requiring the publication of raw as well as standardized regression coefficients could change the policy-making potential of our research considerably.

A second statistical matter is the authors' decision to run four separate regression analyses, rather than sticking ethnicity and sex into the model. If ethnicity had been a variable within the model, it would be hard to avoid policy-relevant conclusions such as, "This much of the achievement difference between Mexican-Americans and Anglos comes from SES, that much from peer influence, etc., etc." Why wasn't this done? I really do not know. Sometimes workers in this area take this approach to avoid having to state the sometimes embarrassing ethnic differences that could turn up. (What would feminists say if it turned out that all the sex differences were due to the lower IQ's of women?) Perhaps the investigators felt uncomfortable with the "dummy variable" techniques that would be necessary to incorporate two qualitative variables in the analysis.

Whatever the reasons, two key statistical decisions—both quite justifiable by the standards of rigorous methodology, but neither required by them—led to a form of analysis that minimized the policy implications of the study.

Having considered two conceptual matters and two statistical matters, we turn to a final pair which can be called "just plain bad luck in the findings."

The first unfortunate result is the outcome for the one manipulable variable, ethnic density. The authors find some evidence that Mexican-American students have higher college aspirations in schools where they are in a majority. This finding, if valid, has a clear cut policy implication: If you want to raise the level of aspiration of Mexican-American students, resegregate the students. I happen to oppose this policy strongly, and I am not persuaded that the evidence is very compelling here. But if there is any policy implication that follows from the article, it is a pro-segregation one. Consider, as a hypothetical experiment, what would have happened if the results had gone the other way. Despite the fact that the magnitudes are very small, I am certain that the policy implications would have been discussed at length if their import had matched our value positions.

The second piece of bad luck is that almost all of the coefficients are very low. The average R for the four endogenous variables across the four populations' subgroups is .337. The point is granted by the authors, and it is perhaps unfair to call it luck since it seems to happen to all of us all the time. But one is quite unlikely to pound the pulpit and demand immediate action when one's system can account for about 11% of the variance in the items. The point is too sad to labor here.

CONCLUSIONS

Assuming that the various matters mentioned here—a focus on relevance versus application, opting for nonmanipulable variables, nonpersuasive samples, preference for statistics that mute policy implications, findings that present value tensions, and low correlations—are general in our field and not specific to this one article (I am willing to make that assumption), what general conclusions can be drawn?

I think it depends on how much emphasis should be given to the last two matters.

If one gives heavy stress to the "bad luck in the findings," it is easy to become pessimistic about the possibilities for applied sociology.

Stepping back from the victim article per se, it is possible to draw some rather gloomy conclusions. It is no secret that social scientists working in the area of education are in a period of intellectual crisis. The burden of the findings in massive educational research over decades has been the elimination of variables rather than their discovery. In terms of academic performance, we are pretty sure that expenditures, buildings, teacher characteristics, classroom size, television, etc., etc., etc. do not have any impact on academic achievement. At the college level, extensive research has led to the negative conclusion that once student-input characteristics are controlled, college characteristics do not make any appreciable difference in anything very important. A few years ago, I had the opportunity to work on the problem of why people resist positive mental health programs. A review of the literature persuaded me that the problem is false: people seek mental health programs, but the mental health movement has nothing useful to tell them. Add to all this the negative results on the evaluations of psychotherapy, the dozens of evaluation research projects that fail to find a single example where positive results are reported, and perhaps the ultimate irony—the inability of social research to show that people are even affected much by hard core pornography —and we find little to support optimism for applications. Indeed, I think it fair to say that with the single exception of the Skinnerian behavior modificationists, there is no area in the behavioral sciences today where the research workers (as opposed to the ideologues and essayists) are confident that they can name any manipulable variables pertinent to social policy.

But in contrast to such pessimism, there is an optimistic position and a middle-of-the-road position.

The optimistic position is based on the remaining conclusions. Each boils down to a conceptual or methodological folkway that seems to inhibit applied foci in our research. There is no reason why we are locked into the tradition that relevance is better than application, that real sociological variables are the ones that can not be changed, that good sampling is not an important criterion, and that we should stress statistical procedures that blur applied implications. Folkways are not easily changed, but taking the Skinnerians at their word, I am certain that reinforcement works on social scientists as well as for social scientists. I am unwilling to write us off until we have tried the route of rewarding professional work that has concrete applied pay-off.

The middle-of-the-road position is rather different from the other two. It is simply that we have a false model of the whole business. It can be called the Los Alamos model. We tend to assume that social policy should work like the development of atomic weapons: the pure scientist tells the decision maker, "Hey, we have some pure research findings that suggest we can build an atomic bomb," and the decision maker says, "Well, I can't understand all this fancy stuff, but here's some money to try to make a bomb." I think this model fails on the following counts.

First, except for economists, social scientists have no entree to the places in society where real decisions are made. A lot of us spend a lot of time in Washington—but it is heavily concentrated in the lower levels of government—and with people who themselves have an academic style, not a policy-making one.

Second, I fear that in most policy areas, the policy-makers know more about the topic than we do. President Roosevelt knew nothing about atomic physics, but political and social decision makers have to know a heck of a lot about society, if only to get to where they can make decisions.

Third, social decisions are not made as simply as decisions to produce military hardware. One can let a contract to produce a military weapon. Even if we knew for sure that school desegregation was good, or bad, how in the world could we arrange to desegregate or resegregate America's schools?

Are there alternative models? I can think of one, although perhaps not a glamorous one. If there is any area of applied social science that is a success, it is the commercial political pollster. We tend to consider their results as technically unsophisticated but, in terms of our beloved functional theories, they must be doing something for somebody, because they are surviving and making money at it. Why?

First, because they work for people at the top of the decision-making hierarchy. Second, because they provide narrow but useful help to the decision makers. As a regular Washington visitor, I am struck by the following proposition: the higher you go in the federal government the more they desperately need simple facts, and the less they need theories, models, schemes, and programs. What is more, they need them a great deal faster than the glacial rate of information flow provided through the academic process of books and journal articles. If sociology is to play a truly applied role in this country (and I am making this assumption only because it is the topic of this conference, not because I myself am fully persuaded), I suspect that it will be through the unglamorous route of providing the top-level decision makers with fast, reliable, isolated pieces of information about our large, heterogeneous, and changing society, not through finding social equivalents of the atom bomb through access of the ASR and AJS.

Sociological Understanding versus Policy Design and Intervention: The Adolescent Crisis

DORIS R. ENTWISLE

The Johns Hopkins University

The "adolescent crisis" embraces two rather different questions: (1) "Who am I?"—an identity crisis (in Erikson's sense) focused on sex and family roles, on the integration of the total personality, and on the internalization of personal standards of morals and values. (2) "Where am I going?"—a search for a purpose in life focused on "growing up," on the adolescent's future role in the larger society, and particularly on his occupational role. In this short paper I will be concerned mainly with the second question, in part because crises over the future seem to be less easily resolved, or resolvable, for some youths than for others.

I wish to start from Stinchcombe's (1964) study of alienation among high school students. His interest centers about the "articulation hypothesis" (p. 49): for students who see high school articulating with future job and future status, the school is a profitable, or at least meaningful, holding pattern. The articulating students are not likely to rebel. For other students, those who will eventually make up the manual working class in the next labor-market cohort, there is a high degree of expressive alienation. The high school, then, helps resolve (or perhaps does not exacerbate) the where-am-I-going identity crisis for those students who are not entering the labor market upon graduation. For others the high school does not resolve the identity crisis.

Stinchcombe's data concern a mostly blue-collar high school of a decade ago. They show alienation to be concentrated among those who are not being paid in the "realistic coin of future adult advantages," thus confirming his notions about disarticulation as a cause of rebellion. Stinchcombe sees rebellious behavior as largely a reaction to the school itself and to its promises, and not as a failure of the family or community (p. 179). (This could imply that a change in school policy will deal with the problem. More of this later.)

It is almost superfluous to point out that much of the rebelliousness of both high school and college students seen in the latter 1960s may be interpreted at least partly in terms of Stinchcombe's disarticulation notion. The disarticulation for college students came first from questions like "What has this training got to do with going to war?" and later from questions like "What use is a college degree when Ph.D.s and many engineers are out of work?"

Before drawing some policy implications from Stinchcombe's study, let me first point out that as high school attendance became universal the intrinsic value of a high school diploma shrank. Forty years ago possession of a high school diploma was a definite mark of prestige. Now the diploma per se, apart from its value as a passport to the next institution, is valueless because of its virtual universality.

Second, articulation requires some fostering from both sides—from the school as it prepares students, and from business firms and employers who will receive these students. Articulation may be difficult for firms to foster because no one has yet specified what the school does that the firm later draws upon, if indeed the school does anything in that category. Even in technical settings, where firms such as Westinghouse and General Electric hire engineers, there are no data (to my knowledge) showing that performance on the job is correlated with college grade-point average. Generally such scholastic barometers are not good predictors of "life performance." Indeed, I would wager that engineers after 2 years of college would perform just as well as 4-year graduates, if they were hired "blind."

Now, from the other side, could the school foster articulation? Could the school provide more meaningful activities for those who will enter the job market soon? I am not very optimistic about this possibility. Most school personnel are not only unacquainted with the world of affairs but often have consciously withdrawn from it. Almost by definition those vocations which could provide meaningful and profitable employment for working-class youth are outside the purview of secondary school teachers and/or require capital. The service trades, for example, plumbing, electrical contracting, and the like, are entered mostly via social connections leading to apprenticeships or direct on-the-job training. Small owner-operated businesses—laundries, surveying businesses, cleaning establishments, service stations, restaurants, farm—are the same. People who own these businesses decide whom they will employ and then train their employees directly. The high school can offer very little in the way of useful socialization for such jobs. For these areas where meaningful and remunerative blue-collar jobs exist, then, the high school offers little guidance.

Stinchcombe's research implies that unless articulation between the school and the occupational structure is fostered, unless youngsters see the school as instrumental in solving their occupational identity crisis, rebellion and alienation will follow. I have already suggested why such articulation is not likely to be increased by employers, on the one hand, or by schools on the other.

A policy implication that can be drawn from Stinchcombe's research—one he does not draw—is that since the school as an institution is not helping to solve the identity crisis for all of its students, other institutions must help in the task. A recent suggestion by Coleman (1972) is that economic institutions must join in the education of the young, open their doors, and be learning places for young persons. He has called for "a breaking open of the economic institutions of society, from factories to hospitals [p.14]." To manage this, he suggests providing the young with entitlements that could be redeemed by businesses and other enterprises. The young, starting about age 12, would be integrated into the economic activities of society, while continuing to receive academic instructions in school. He visualizes radical change in economic organizations to incorporate the young, for then economic organizations would be work-places designed for learning efficiency as well as productive efficiency. Coleman's proposal calls for the integration of young people very early with the occupational system and, if carried out, would provide young people with much more control and support than they now receive to help resolve the identity crisis of "where-am-I-going vocationally."

In passing, I should note that the progressive exclusion of the young from the labor market—as school-leaving ages and minimum-working ages have been raised over the past century—can be seen as attempts to limit the labor supply analogous to immigration restrictions (see Bakan 1971). Surface humanitarian concerns may obscure the fact that these arrangements are highly functional for older members of the labor force; therefore, the kinds of changes Coleman looks for may tap sources of resistance that run deep.

However these issues are seen, and whatever implications are drawn, Stinchcombe's research points to a set of problems extant in one institution, without suggesting what changes are desirable or feasible or what other institutions might do. In attending to the second item of my assigned task, then—to indicate what impact this particular research has had—I must sadly note that it has had little or none. Schools and firms have not been prodded into improving articulation, and indeed disarticulation is becoming endemic. In the latter 1960s, student rebellions increased and affected other groups—college students—who were newly in a position of disarticulation. Perhaps Stinchcombe's research has caused us to understand better the college rebellions, but the research has had no direct policy effects that I can see. It has not caused colleges, for example, to offer more vocationally oriented programs. Such vocational emphasis, if anything, seems less now than a decade ago. About 60% of high school graduates now enter colleges of one kind or another. For many of these students, attendance at community colleges is more an extension of high school than a beginning of college, and it is not at all clear how, or if, entry into the labor market is eased by attendance at a 2-year college.

Stinchcombe's research has broad policy implications, namely high school as an institution must be changed if it is to serve some of its clients in solving their identity crises. However, his research does not suggest which of many changes should be made. It does not, in other words, offer research on the viability or feasibility of various policy changes, or even enumerate a set of policy changes which should be considered. Like most research, it attempts to analyze and understand some social phenomenon. Whatever suggestions emerge for altering the phenomenon are rather incidental.

An analogy will point up the distinction between research aimed at understanding social phenomena and research aimed at social policy development. If an engineer has a circuit which exists but which does not work well, he can analyze the circuit's behavior, measuring currents and voltages between nodes, and arrive at a precise analysis of how that particular device works. However, this analysis is a long way from designing a circuit that will meet certain output specifications at a given cost with a given degree of reliability. It is the old dichotomy between analysis and synthesis. Given a device, or an institution, one may analyze it, but this analysis may help little in *designing* a different device or institution, or in suggesting a systematic set of possible alternatives that will make the device or institution more effective. "Design" implies the use of inventiveness and intuition, creative problem solving, and is an elusive, not to say scarce, ingredient in any kind of human activity.

I have just indirectly made a rather pessimistic statement. Let me be more direct. I fail to see how graduate training in policy research can do much about explicit training in the areas of policy formulation per se. Before decisions can be made about *evaluating* a particular policy or set of policies, presumably a set of policy alternatives must be enumerated. Training in methodology of policy evaluation is possible and some schools already have some such training. But more generally the invention of policy, the recognition and listing of the policy alternatives, must recognize problems and cast those problems in some form where a set of solutions can be proposed. It is an especially difficult instance of "design."

This leads to the third part of my assignment. How can the discipline and its training be altered if we are to produce more policy-oriented research? Design in its broadest meaning, as I have just tried to indicate, seems to be the most difficult of human activities, and a most difficult activity to teach, if indeed it can be taught. Yet it seems that what I call design, in the long run, is the primary ingredient of successful policy research. It is the specification or enumeration of policy alternatives that are "good" in some sense, with recognition of the many facets of a policy linked to its over-all impact. In current discussions on policy research, we find much more emphasis upon the methodology of evaluation research than upon "design," perhaps for the same reason we find emphasis on methodology in our better graduate schools. At least methodology can be dealt with in some fashion. It *can* be taught. The processes by which good policy alternatives surface are not teachable, any more than other kinds of invention are teachable.

I turn now from considering general issues to more specific ones. If the discipline is to produce research with more policy implications, such research must be rewarding. Even if we cannot figure out how people invent good policies or what to do to or for students to help them become inventors, we can reward policy-inventing behavior when it occurs. The federal government, so far at least, has supported extramural policy research mainly in the area of education. First, then, resources have to be provided directly to sociologists for carrying out extramural policy-oriented research, or institutions outside the academy whose major concerns include policy research must be made into hospitable work places for sociologists. Second, not much, if any,

of this previous research has directly involved choosing alternatives—
what to do next, what policies to try—the really interesting questions.
For example, the question has not been whether one should either
improve cognitive skills of mothers *or* direct language enrichment
programs at children, but rather, given children as targets, how to
evaluate various kinds of ad hoc language enrichment programs. Policy research, therefore, has been peripheral to sociology's reward system or to academic reward systems generally, where research is defined in terms of contributions to basic knowledge. One language
program may show up a little better than another but, if it does, there
is usually little purchase on why it is better, and even less on
whether this route is the best. After all, if mothers were targets, several children might benefit, and the exposure of children to mothers
in the first five years of life far exceeds in time the exposure to a pre-
school. Prestige in the discipline is tied more to achievement in basic
research than to the application of research findings to policy problems. Policy-related research differs primarily from "pure" research in
that consequences other than "truth" become relevant. The execution
of good policy research, then, may have little relevance to prestige in
the discipline.

Fennessey (1972) suggests a general analysis for policy problems, focused on a pay-off cube where the pay-off parameters are explicitly
conceptualized along three demensions: (1) alternative program com-
positions, (2) alternative vectors of nonmanipulative parameter values,
and (3) outcome variables. A particular pay-off cube classified certain
parameters as manipulative and nonmanipulative, and so implicitly
suggests a certain range of effort to be invested in a policy. He considers pay-offs mainly in terms of positive results of a policy.

Consider an analogue of Fennessey's policy-research cube: a pay-off
cube for researchers in social policy. Perhaps the discipline should explicitly formalize such a cube and consider its implications. Right now
the researcher may have low pay-offs from policy-oriented research
for several reasons. One reason, mentioned already, is simply a lack of
available funds outside educational research. Another reason is that
the researcher must share control of the research with others outside
the academic community. In fact, if, as Fennessey suggests, task forces
are set up to formulate pay-off cubes for policy research, and if persons who execute the policy research are outside these task forces, researchers may have little intellectual investment or ego involvement in
the research. One kind of pay-off treasured by academicians, in addition to prestige in the discipline, is the freedom to formulate their
own problems and to set their own work style and work pace. Maybe

one of the nonmanipulative parameter values in the researchers' pay-off cube has to signify their (justified in my opinion) intellectual vanity and independence.

As far as graduate training is concerned, it seems to me that policy research, like other research, will be learned by doing. To teach graduate students how to conduct research requires them to become involved as active participants in an ongoing research enterprise. If pay-offs can be arranged to persuade more sociologists to become involved in policy research, there will be considerable spin-off for students. The pay-off cubess for researchers should incorporate some provision for students. One way for work places outside the university to be made attractive for sociologists is to break open those work places to sociology students, in an analogous manner to the way Coleman suggests for work places to open up for students of all types. The only thing I can add is that the work places are unlikely to become hospitable spontaneously.

REFERENCES

Bakan, D.
    1971   Adolescence in America: From idea to social fact, *Daedalus* **100,** 979–996.
Coleman, J. S.
    1972   How do the young become adults?, *Center for Social Organization of Schools, Report No. 130,* May. Johns Hopkins Univ.
Fennessey, J.
    1972   Some problems and possibilities in policy-related social research, *Social Science Research* **1,** 359–383.
Stinchcombe, A.
    1964   *Rebellion in a high school.* Chicago, Illinois: Quadrangle Books.

Commentaries

WENDELL BELL

Yale University

Reading the papers prepared for the Carmel Conference and listening to the discussions of them, I came to three major conclusions concerning policy research and graduate training—or, perhaps more honestly, I should say: My three current prejudices were reinforced by my selective reading and listening. The three are : (1) continuation and elaboration of training in sound methodological skills, especially in the collection of data, (2) a shift in theoretical perspective toward variables that are subject to manipulation by human beings; and (3) a shift in general orientation from one that is largely limited to the past and present to one that prominently includes the future.

SOUND METHODOLOGY

Davis speaks of the policy-maker's need for simple facts. Reiss finds weaknesses in the methodological and technical foundations of the studies he evaluates "that make it difficult to develop social policy with respect to law enforcement." And after considerable personal involvement in policy-related activities himself and a review of what probably is the "single most comprehensive delinquency control program ever undertaken," Short concludes with these familiar, but sometimes forgotten, words: "There is, after all, no substitute for

251

good research, design, methods and data, and for good theory and responsible interpretation."

This point needs to be stressed. For me, it means that we should continue our present emphasis on methodology in graduate training. And I include in the term "methodology" everything from the use of equipment and elementary statistical skills through advanced quantitative skills and qualitative skills, such as interviewing, to such activities that begin to overlap with theoretical skills, such as the specification of variables, the selection and clarification of concepts, and logical analysis. If we speak nonsense instead of knowledge, as we sometimes demonstrably do, then we have very little of worth to say to anyone, including social policy decision makers. Thus, we need to do better than we did so that we can raise the general standards of methodological competence.

Beyond this, however, there is something neglected in current methodological training. We do not give sufficient attention to the techniques and requirements of collecting good data, which are, after all, the foundation of all sociological work. Inadequate samples, poor questions, response-distorting sequences of questions, stilted interview situations, unthinking labeling of variables, uncritical acceptance of the meaning of responses, ethnocentric interpretations of other cultures, among many other vices, characterize much of the sociological literature, even in the most respected professional journals (as long as the data, such as they may be, are wrapped in the garb of what is currently considered to be sophisticated statistical analysis).

This is, perhaps, too harsh a judgment, because it is a matter of emphasis rather than an all-of-one-none-of-the-other situation. And ideally both data *and* analysis should pass muster. Yet there may be a tension and some contradiction between the concern for mathematizing sociology and the concern for good data, that is, for data that accurately represent the real, ongoing social situation and the behavior of persons in that situation. There is the current need to feed the waiting computers, to crank something in and to crank something out. Perhaps the greatest vice of all is the mindless use of available categories with no thought given to alternative categories more likely to give some presumptive evidence of sociological structure. A regression analysis can be done, perhaps with as many as 30 or more independent variables, each contributing a bit to a total explained variance of the dependent variable of (if we are lucky) 30% or so.

To give a partial illustration of what I mean, Cressey (1953) found that the legal definition of embezzlement was inadequate for his sociological work because it did not define a homogeneous class of criminal behavior. Thus, he redefined embezzlement, his dependent variable, eliminating such behavior as forgery and limiting it to criminal violation of financial trust, the position of financial trust having been taken in good faith. This was not a trivial research decision on Cressey's part. No amount of pounding and running of the data through computers could have resulted in his neat findings without such a redefinition, since the behavior sequences and causes are quite different for forgers on the one hand, and, on the other, for persons who violate financial trust without intending to do so when they take the position.

Another thing that Cressey did that illustrates my point is that he grouped a number of variables into a more general one, at a higher level of abstraction. For example, earlier research had shown small correlations between embezzlement and such things as gambling, drinking to excess, going with women other than one's wife, etc. Cressey formulated the concept of the nonshareable financial problem—a financial problem that a person feels he or she can reveal to no one—as one of the common causes of the criminal violation of financial trust. People who gamble, drink too much, and "womanize" are more likely than those who do not to find themselves with a nonshareable financial problem. How much more powerful it is to have a single principle than to have a large number of lower-order variables in a regression equation. Furthermore, one now has the kind of knowledge that can be used to deduce other specific activities that may lead to a nonshareable financial problem. This is especially important because in different times and places what is considered nonshareable may change, yet the general principle may apply nonetheless.

On the surface this particular principle may be more difficult to apply in policy situations than others, since, presumably, if a financial problem is truly nonshareable, it would be concealed even if direct questioning were used. However, any number of indicators can be deduced, including the three already mentioned, about which data may be obtained in order to identify people who are likely to have nonshareable financial problems.

MANIPULATIVE VARIABLES

The selection of categories for sociological research and theorizing has other neglected aspects as well. One is, as Davis notes, that sociologists seem to lust for nonmanipulative variables. In the paper that he reviews, for example, "the authors happened to choose a set of variables that defy manipulation, with one exception . . . ." Assuming that there is more than one way to organize information about a given situation, why can we not sensitize our students to the need for using variables that are subject to manipulation, that give people handles they can use to intervene? Remote, impersonal, natural, or inevitable forces that cannot be manipulated may have to give way to variables that can be manipulated if sociological knowledge is to become more useful in social policy.

Since Durkheim, the chief sociological focus has been on how society shapes people. We have neglected the questions of how people shape society and each other. Few social organizations and institutions in the modern world just happen. Rather, they are made to happen by people who are more or less consciously pursuing certain goals and values and who are more or less using their knowledge of social causation, such as it is, in the actions they take. The fact that things so often turn out differently than expected shows how limited and inadequate such knowledge is.

FUTURISTICS

Clearly, manipulative variables are useful to the policy-maker in that they permit intervention to control the situation rather than action limited to adaptation or no effective action at all. A related point concerns time perspectives. A decision maker is concerned not only with past facts and present options, but also with future possibilities. He is concerned, as Entwisle says, with social design and with a "systematic set of possible alternatives." As I have said elsewhere (Bell and Mau 1971), there appears to be a new science of futurism emerging. (Different labels for it are now used, but "futuristics" may win out.) Although a few (but growing number of) sociologists are participating in its development (Eldredge 1972), social futuristics is at the moment dominated by economists, engineers, systems developers, chemists, physicists, mathematicians, management scientists, computer specialists, and the like. One reason may be that such professionals are more comfortable than are sociologists when dealing with a time frame that includes future thinking, prediction, and forecasting.

Sociology would be of greater use to polciy-makers and policy-implementers if it were conducted in an expanded time frame with explicit concern for the alternative possibilities for the future. And techniques such as trend extrapolation, systems analysis, the Delphi technique, cross-impact analysis, surveys of intentions, relevance tree analysis, scenario writing, technology assessment, monitoring, dynamic modeling, simulation, and gaming can be taught. Yet our failure to deal with the future is notorious, with a few notable exceptions; and our resistance to altering our disciplinary ways and graduate training to remedy the situation is ironic. In making claims for scientific status, sociologists claimed that, like other scientists, prediction was one of their aims. It is, after all, a criterion of verified theories. Such a view is now generally accepted. For example, Schuessler (1968:418–419) says that "sociologists now take prediction of the forms and processes of social life as one of their principal tasks." Moreover, he is not talking about relationships among variables that occur simultaneously; he is referring to future events. Yet, as Schuessler (p. 418) says further, "The social purpose of prediction, whether of physical or social events, is to secure a measure of control over what otherwise would be less manageable circumstances . . . . Practically all predictions are potential instruments of social action, enabling the group either to facilitate a favorable outcome or to impede an unfavorable one."

If this is so, and I believe that it is, then one linkage between the science of sociology and social policy is to be found in futuristics, that is, in taking the aim of prediction seriously as a major task of sociologists. This, of course, is not a simple matter, because there are no future facts. Predictions are not simply made for us to stand back and watch them unfold. They are made in a context of evaluation and power, with the possibility of expanded and enlightened consciousness. Knowing predictions can inform action to accelerate or prevent their occurrence. Thus, taking social prediction seriously means to get involved in a complex web of feedback between forecasts—social scientific images of the future—and actions, not to mention being involved with the knotty problems of social differentiation and subgroup interests. But, as I see it, despite the rather stressful tensions between trying to study society and simultaneously trying to help redesign and recreate it (Oxaal 1971), there is a legitimate merging of the science role and the policy role in the sociologist's concern for prediction.

REFERENCES

Bell, W. and J. A. Mau (Editors)
    1971   *The sociology of the future.* New York: Russell Sage Foundation.
Cressey, D. R.
    1953   *Other people's money.* Glencoe, Illinois: The Free Press.

Eldredge, W.
1972 Teaching the sociology of the future. In *1972 American Sociological Association seminar on the sociology of the future,* edited by A. M. Harkins.
Minneapolis, Minnesota: Univ. of Minnesota, Office for Applied Social
Science and the Future.
Oxaal, I.
1971 Methodology and the quest for utopia: A case study from El Dorado. In *The
sociology of the future,* edited by W. Bell and J. A. Mau. Pp. 294–323. New
York: Russell Sage Foundation.
Schuessler, K. F.
1968 Prediction. *International encyclopedia of the social sciences, Vol. 12,* edited
by D. L. Sills. Pp. 418–425. New York: Macmillan & Free Press.

CHARLES E. BIDWELL

The University of Chicago

These papers will remind the reader of something well known to
sociologists but often forgotten, namely, that their discipline is not
"pure" but "applied"; it is a discipline that lacks a distinctive conceptual and methodological purview. Nevertheless, in both its early and
more recent forms, sociology is unique among the social sciences in
the *breadth of its curiosity* about society. Theory-building in current
sociology is likely to be a sterile exercise. Fruitful sociological knowledge more often comes as sociologists try to answer questions that
flow from their perceptions of what their society is like now, or their
conceptions of what it might become. These are Reiss's two kinds of
questions: why things are as they are, and how things that are can be
made different.

Sociology is distinctive in another way. As Janowitz (1973) reminds
us, sociology was born out of a concern to create knowledge that
could guide modern societies, and, despite its vicissitudes, that concern remains lively in present-day sociology. So sociology is applied in
two senses. (1) It necessarily involves the application of "borrowed"
ideas and methods to questions substantially generated by sociologists'
experiences of their own societies, their affinities and affiliations, and
their beliefs and values. (2) At least for many sociologists, it is an attempt to gain knowledge that is useful. But here usefulness means
knowledge that is public and broadly and generally applicable to
some range of social problems and social decisions, not knowledge for
private and particular interests or of narrow and trivial applicability.

To me, creating such knowledge is the main business of sociology, appropriately so even if sociology should come to have more generative theory of its own than it presently possesses. Also, creating such knowledge is the proper bearing of sociology on social policy—an issue vexed by much confusion and vagueness of terms.

From these two statements, it follows that the task of sociologists is the old-fashioned but enduring one of creating cumulative, reliable, and general knowledge. It also follows that sociologists have an old-fashioned but enduring moral commitment: to serve the general interest rather than particular interests, and to contribute to the fund of public knowledge.

The five papers in Section C of this volume speak in a variety of ways to these matters. Short shows how fine the line is between sociological theory theory and ideology, and how easy it is to cross this line when the sociologist becomes directly involved in programs of social action and when his theory is somehow to "orient" action—especially if it lacks a substantial base of evidence. Short's cases may remind us that knowledge, rather than theory per se, is the firmer guide to action; no one should be surprised at the fragility of sociological notions in a political arena. His cases also suggest to me that the sociologist will serve social policy more truly and more effectively if he resists the strong temptation to be *engagé.*

Davis and Reiss both show how direct the link is between the technical quality of sociological research and the utility of its findings. For example, inattention to sample design, mindless *de novo* instrumentation, or failure to assess the reliability and validity of one's instruments, each reduces the reliability of findings and their contribution to cumulative knowledge. Reiss, moreover, describes a case in which persons who sought to draw together sociological findings for policy purposes, through their inattention to technical criteria, created the appearance of a knowledge base that does not in fact exist. Seriousness of scholarship is as paramount for the sociologist who would synthesize as it is for the sociologist who conducts research.

Davis and Reiss also point up the centrality for truly useful findings of the ability to ask good questions (which I would take to be the ability to sense the key components of social situations and to translate them into powerful variables and powerful research designs) and to think systematically (e.g., attention to the difference between prevalence and incidence). One can scarcely quarrel with their strictures, yet how little attention in sociological training is given to the development of effective ways of fostering either generative or systematic thinking. And if these abilities, indeed, cannot be taught very well, how little attention is given to identifying their early signs and attracting to sociology persons who show them.

Davis and Reiss also place heavy emphasis on research that centers on the means of social change: on "manipulable variables" and on "learning how things that are can be made different." Again, it is hard to quarrel, but Davis himself suggests that emphasis on manipulable variables may mean stress on problems that are less than interesting, less than general, and less than central to main lines of sociological inquiry. But research of a more broadly reformist, even utopian, cast may have profound implications for society and sociology—witness, to pick a recent example, Titmuss' (1971) *The Gift Relationship.*

At the same time, I believe that knowledge of what is ineluctable and constraining in societies is important and useful. Witness Stinchcombe's (1964) *Rebellion in a High School,* an excellent example that Entwisle reviews. To know something about discontinuities between the high school experience and students' conceptions of their destinations in adult society may indeed inform social policy. But if one were to ignore the social organization of the economy and of life histories in American society—on their face less manipulable than high school curricula—and work to reduce discontinuity only through school reform, what would result? Probably little. Indeed, the prime question may be how to alter the seemingly unchangeable—in point of fact a very realistic and very pressing task of sociological thought and research.

But before one sets out to solve a social problem, one must know not only its structure and etiology but also its points and intensities of occurrence. Stinchcombe's case study does not document such things among American high schools or high school students, nor was that its objective. But without such documentation, how can one array priorities for either analysis or action? So from a somewhat different perspective we come again to the need for reliable knowledge, not only in the analysis but also in the documentation of social events. Davis, with some misgivings, stresses the importance of information to senior policy-makers. I would stress its fundamental importance for sociology.

In these remarks I have said very little about the obligation of sociologists to make their findings and ideas public, to serve general rather than particular interests. The authors of the five papers have said little on this point, but it is of great significance. A good deal recently has been said about the peculiarities of "policy research" in the social sciences in contrast to its "purer" forms (e.g., Coleman 1973). Certain of these peculiarities center on nonreplicability. From what I already have said, it should be clear that I do not believe that inattention to replicability will serve either sociology or society well. Others of these peculiarities center on the private character of much "policy research"—the right of the client to keep secrets, justification of restrictions on publication, and the like. I believe that to engage in research of such private character is a failure of commitment to scholarship, and that means a failure also of social responsibility. It is wrong-headed, I think, to view any client, even a government, as a surrogate for the general social interest.

In sociology to make one's work public means to subject it to the review of one's peers not only on technical grounds but also for honesty and objectivity of reporting, inference, and interpretation. Such review, given the fine line between ideas and ideology in sociology, is imperative. Moreover, public knowledge is at least potentially available to all who want or need it, although we may have to build mechanisms for making this potential actual.

In sum, I believe that there is less of a difference than some of the papers suggest between doing sociology—in either its activities or its rewards—and serving society. I believe that time, effort, and resources spent on improving the quality of sociological research (not worrying much about such distinctions as "pure" vs. "applied") will bring a greater return to useful knowledge than a comparable investment in building new institutions intended to link sociology and social policy. The link already is there.

Finally, I believe that less noise about the ideological alignments of sociologists—demands that we affirm whose side we are on—and more serious effort toward building and testing the "theories of social control and of social intervention" that Reiss (and now Janowitz 1973) advocates would be eminently healthy. If sociology and sociologists are indeed to contribute to the rational control of social change, there is no task of higher priority for sociological scholarship.

REFERENCES

Coleman, J.
   1973   Ten principles governing policy research. Footnotes 1 (March).
Janowitz, M.
   1973   Sociological theory and social control. A mimeographed paper.
Stinchcombe, A.
   1964   Rebellion in a high school. Chicago, Illinois: Quadrangle Books.
Titmuss, R. M.
   1971   The gift relationship. New York: Pantheon.

HERBERT L. COSTNER

University of Washington, Seattle

The basic premise of this brief commentary is that worthwhile social policy research imposes more demanding requirements—methodologically, substantively, and administratively—than those commonly met in most other kinds of sociological research. From this premise, I draw the conclusion that if policy research is to become a major sociological enterprise, graduate students trained to do policy research should be selected, not simply for their interest in such matters or their low prospects for obtaining an academic position, but because of their high potential for meeting these demanding requirements. They should, in short, be among the "cream of the crop." Furthermore, the demands of worthwhile social policy research suggest that graduate training for this role should be more thorough and more rigorous than the training currently typical of graduate programs in sociology.

The meaning that I give to "policy research" is a modest extension of that proposed by Davis: policy research is that which yields findings that would persuade decision makers "to favor one course of action over another" by showing the probable differential consequences of alternative policy choices. (The last clause has been added to Davis' statement, but is probably implicit in it.) By its nature, then, social policy research pertains to the effects of possible alternative collective actions, or public policies. Such a task evidently presents a formidable methodological challenge; it requires that the causes of social events and the magnitude of their separate effects be accurately specified. Among the five papers in Section C being discussed here, only the paper by Reiss has focused primarily on methodology, and he has not focused on causal analysis. Although the need for causal inferences in policy research seems to be implicit in some of the papers, none has highlighted (1) the crucial role of causal inferences in social policy research, (2) the methodological difficulties that such inferences entail, and (3) the kind of methodological training policy researchers will need if such difficulties are not to sap the worth from policy-relevant research conclusions. Reiss has appropriately chastized the discipline for our laxity in training potential policy researchers to be sensitive to issues of reliability and validity in measurement. This, too, suggests that the methodological training of policy researchers should be especially strong. Without belaboring the point, it seems clear that, for most graduate students in sociology, current methodological training is inadequate for the demands of useful policy research.

But successful policy research requires more than methodological skill. Although many kinds of research of limited policy relevance call for causal inferences and concern for the reliability of measures, policy-relevant research calls for special kinds of causal theory and special kinds of "action theory." The emphasis must be on potentially manipulable variables, as Davis points out. Furthermore, if policy research is to be more than the funeral dirge for well-intentioned but ill-founded and ineffective social programs (too often the fate of contemporary evaluation research), the policy researcher must play a role in devising the policy alternatives to be assessed, and these policy alternatives must be founded on a solid theoretical base. The "design" of policy (in the sense emphasized by Entwisle) requires the consideration of untried policy alternatives, including alternatives imperfectly represented in existing variations in social arrangements. Such a design task also requires a strategy for translating general causal assumptions into concrete social policies and actions, as Short (who alludes to the distinction between a "theory of causation" and a "program of action"), Entwisle (who distinguishes between "analysis" and "design"), and Reiss (who draws a distinction between "theories of social control" and "theories of social intervention") have pointed out. Hence, even if policy researchers have a sweeping command of the substance of sociology, they will face "design" problems for which existing sociological theory will provide only a very incomplete guide. The "enlightenment" mode of policy relevance, to which Short gives favorable attention, seems to consist largely in attempting to bring to bear on policy, both sociological theory and findings. But someone (and who else but the policy researcher?) has to master that theoretical base, perceive its potential relevance to policy concerns, and translate it into action programs, if the potential of such "enlightenment" is to be realized. Successful policy research, then, demands genuine theoretical creativity in addition to methodological skill.

The "design" of policy is the middle of the policy-research process, not the end. The design must be implemented, and an impact study executed. This will commonly entail administering a substantial expenditure, coordinating the efforts of a sizable staff, and managing complex relations with public agencies, funding sources, and the client public. The administrative demands of this advanced phase of policy research have not been heavily emphasized in the papers being discussed here, but it would certainly be evident in a reasonably complete history of any action program such as that discussed by Short.

In sum, "the *compleat* policy researcher" must be a knowledgeable methodologist, a creative theoretician, a capable manager, and a skilled politician. This is not the job description for a graduate student who is never quite able to understand what internal validity is all about, whose conception of theory is limited to a terminological maze that makes no claims about how things "work," and whose administrative skills are taxed by managing to get a dissertation typed and turned in on time. The policy-researcher role demands one who is steeped in relevant substantive ideas and whose creative facilities have been thoroughly exercised, one who can translate abstract ideas into feasible policies and programs and who can lay out evaluative studies that will hold up under penetrating critiques and hostile attacks, and one who can interact in the nonacademic community in a way that commands respect.

If one grants my basic premise—that worthwhile social policy research imposes more demanding requirements than those commonly met in most other kinds of sociological research—what can we conclude? My own conclusion is that some relatively small proportion (perhaps 10% or 20%) of the students who earn graduate degrees in sociology have the potential skills and aptitudes to become successful policy researchers, and that their graduate training does little either to attract this select few to policy research as a specialty or to enhance their potential for doing it well. One might even question whether university graduate programs in sociology—with their built-in impediments to change, their scholarly focus that is sometimes translated into disdain for direct policy relevance, and their sometimes shocking tolerance for mediocre performance—provide a promising training ground for such a demanding specialty. At best, most current graduate programs in sociology seem to be capable of providing the basic training for policy researchers. Although I am skeptical of DeFleur's proposal for a quick "retreading" of Ph.D.s for policy research because it would probably attract the academic failures and would be in danger of simply adding a quick policy gloss to an inadequate training base, the idea of post-doctoral training for a select few in special centers devoted to social policy research is worth very serious consideration.

But before we become fixated on a particular policy for training policy researchers, perhaps we should devote some hard effort to the design, implementation, and evaluation of alternative programs for training capable, imaginative, and effective policy researchers. In the attempt we would at least learn to appreciate more fully the perplexing problems of designing and assessing policy in an area in which we presumably have a considerable fund of expertise. We might even devise something that works.

TROY DUSTER
University of California, Berkeley

There are policy implications to all social research. I want to avoid any mere terminological argument with those at the conference who would argue otherwise; therefore I will be precise, if arbitrary, in my usage of these terms.

When Davis says that he finds a remarkable absence of policy implications in sociological research reporting, I take that to mean that *he rarely finds explicit and specific guidelines to policy-makers* in these reports. If that is what is intended, we could all probably reach quick consensus if not complete agreement. But to argue that there are no implications is to say that there are no *implicit* and general policy positions that can be ferreted from such research.[1] I want to argue that there are always such implications, that such implications are lodged firmly in the very structure of the formulation of the social research problem. The attempt to explain an event or a circumstance is an implicit charter to act. If you explain the absence of rain by reference to the anger of the gods, then if you want rain, an implicit charter is to placate the gods. If you explain the absence of "Mexican-American youth in the higher levels of educational achievement in American society" by reference to parental socioeconomic status, parental encouragement, college plans, peer encouragement, ethnic composition of school, and IQ, then, indeed, if you are a policy-maker who wants this situation changed (how badly?), you might well throw your hands up in the air and conclude that sociologists lust after the nonmanipulable variables and go back to shuffling paper and acquiescing to the status quo. That is, the policy implications to such research stare us in the face. No "reasonable" or specific social policy will touch all those variables; therefore, policy becomes no policy. And before I am suspected of toying with words when I suggest that no policy is social policy, I need only to make the reminder that "benign neglect" was, and is, social policy in this country whose most important advocate, if not architect, is a prominent social scientist.

---

[1] Entwisle, for example, draws policy implications from Stinchcombe's research on high school failure and rebellion which Stinchcombe disregards (p. 245, this volume).

That brings me to my second point, and this time I must be even more cautious in my creation of a terminological problem. We tend to be clear about the term for research done for the purposes of social policy (Coleman 1972). The use of research by policy-makers, if not the research itself, can be seen as coming "from the top down" because the findings get used by those in policy-making positions, namely those with some power. I wish to distinguish this kind of research from that which is used by those without institutional power who want to change things, and, despite the various possible alternative meanings, I want to call this "action research" with "action implications" or, "from the bottom up." There is no good place for a House Radical in the Carmel Highlands Inn, but someone besides Martin Lipset should point out that there is a difference between these two uses (if not kinds) of research, and that difference is not being acknowledged with any degree of forthrightness, or perhaps even consciousness. Davis concludes in his paper, hedging, uncertain, and unconvinced, but "suspecting" that if sociology is to play a truly applied role in this country ". . . it will be through the unglamorous route of providing the top-level decision makers with fast, reliable, isolated pieces of information about our large, heterogeneous, and changing society . . . [p. 241, this volume]." In the aftermath of the Watergate revelations, of Halderman and Ehrlichmann, ITT, the wheat deals, etc., etc., it may appear to be a particularly cruel kick with benefit of hindsight to put two and two together. But the unscrupulous and vicious use of power to retain power can be no surprise to any serious analyst of politics. Give the top-level policy-makers what they want? It was Lipset who asked, "What kinds of prostitutes are here?" That's slander on prostitutes, who often use judgment to refuse some would-be clients. Given our own studies of the rigidification of bureaucracies in contemporary society, sociologists might more profitably ferret out the "action" implications rather than the policy implications of our research. To use the study that Davis cited as an illustration, one inclined to "policy" might well read the implication of benign neglect into the TenHouten research, but one inclined to "action" might easily extract the implication of the need for thorough and fundamental change.[2] Such ferreting might get a prominent soci-

---

[2] I should emphasize the feature of "implicitness" in the word implication again, for articles and research reports are rarely, if ever, expository; never cook-book recipes for social change. But implications there are, perhaps as abundant as the imagination of the reader, whether policy or "action" oriented. Here I would certainly agree with Davis that there are no explicit guidelines in this article, neither for policy nor for action.

ologist or two on the Enemies List of the White House, though I doubt if any established figure in this business of inquiring into social structure in the United States could have made it.

REFERENCE

Coleman, J. S.
  1972 *Policy research in the social sciences.* Morristown, New Jersey: General Learning Press.

DAVID R. HEISE
University of North Carolina, Chapel Hill

Perhaps science discovers eternal principles, but from the standpoint of human experience, it is more as if science generates new principles recreating the world. Some features of the new worlds are beneficial; others are superficially beneficial, and others—e.g., the generation of ever more devastating weaponry—have no survival value for the species at all. It would be convenient if the human value of an idea and its repercussions always matched its academic value, but at this point in human history it is obvious that this is not the case. An idea can meet scientific and intellectual criteria of goodness and yet be malevolent in some of its applications.

With redundancy of thinking in manifold centers around the world, the growth of knowledge and science is now, if not before, an uncontrolled force in human life. Individual thinkers cannot unilaterally stop an idea from developing, even if they clearly see undesirable ramifications, because sometime or somewhere else another thinker will receive social support and be willing to complete the thought. Like the evolution of viruses, the process cannot really be stopped. Perhaps this is just as well, since control might endanger positive as well as negative developments. But lack of control means that negative products of ideas can be dealt with only after they have been formed.

Sociology was identified by Comte as the science dealing with human values, and in sociology ethics, values, and morality are not peripheral concerns but are central topics of inquiry. The founders saw these concerns as involving more than passive curiosity about social and cultural relativism, and an activist orientation is required even more today. When moral problems abound in civilizations, and particularly when some implementations of ideas and technologies threaten the species itself, the discipline has a larger responsibility—to try, at least, to give human beings control over the societal and cultural repercussions of ideas. In this sense, those who work in the profession have a humanitarian responsibility as compelling as a physician's, and similar in the sense that the central task of this discipline is to identify and to control malignant sociocultural emergences.

Yet the discipline has no special criteria of health by which to identify pathology, and only a short supply of knowledge and technology for interdicting destructive processes. The attitude of some sociologists—perhaps especially those with humanitarian commitment—is to get on with it anyway: move close to the positions of power where sociological knowledge and intuitions may be called upon for widespread application, even exaggerating the discipline's capabilities, if necessary, to get there. One problem with this is that it may lead to disillusionment with the discipline when it fails in its early promises. But what is far more important is that this approach is intrinsically backward, adding sociology to the set of uncontrollable intellectual growths with partially pathogenic impact, making sociology part of the problem rather than an ingredient of a cure. Without criteria defining what is socially beneficial, sociological studies may respond principally to the paymasters who will not always be acting in the broadest public interests. To move into applied fields without constraints is no more sensible than it would be for physicians to open their pharmaceutical chests and make their skills responsive to patients' whims. (A cynic may say that the sociological medicine chest can hardly pose a danger since it is empty. But if it is empty, it will not always be; were it empty now, it would be hypocritical to offer it for application; and even were it to continue to be empty, sociologists still would be quoted with some effect as legitimating or debunking specific programs.)

As the need and the pressure for applied sociology become greater, one of the most urgent issues before the discipline is the definition of a set of standards defining social malevolence so that the impacts of applied ideas, and sociological ideas in particular, can be evaluated. Even criteria that are only roughly accurate and narrow to the discipline would be of value in preventing usurpation of the discipline by political interests, and in beginning to provide a more complete service of evaluating new societal developments in terms of their full range of consequences, thereby providing a basis for controlling the morbid. But how can such criteria be defined? Centuries of philosophizing have accentuated how difficult it is to define "the good," and today practitioners of sociology cover such a wide ideological range that one wonders whether they can agree on any core set of values.

If no consensus is possible, then the discipline is destined to contribute to, and aggravate, social and cultural pathologies. For this reason sociology must provide its practitioners with a code of ethics defining standards for their professional dealings with government and other interests. On the other hand, it cannot hurt if this preparation is guided by the goal of defining criteria for assessing the human value of scientific applications in general. The process of constructing a set of ethical standards is difficult—even painful (I think of the recent experience of the American Psychological Association)—but it is a necessary task for applied disciplines.

The Carmel Conference was oriented largely toward determining the salability of sociological theories and research. Developing a code of ethical standards must be the preeminent task for sociologists interested in applications, and salability is an irrelevant, perhaps even interfering, consideration (our government has bought even botulin germs). It is for this reason that I have not participated in the salability exercise.

LAURA NADER

University of California, Berkeley

The papers in Section C discuss sociological research on areas deemed "problematic" in our society: educational achievement, drugs, adolescent crises, self-reported delinquency and law enforcement, and juvenile delinquency. The work surveyed deals solely with American society, reflects traditional methodological interests of sociologists, and is concerned with narrowly defined domains. The problems are not considered in cross-cultural context, nor are they seen as part of the wider American political scene. There is more acceptance than question as to whether the area being researched really *is* a social problem, or, if it is, whether in any list of priorities these problems are the most important social problems for sociologists to investigate. With the exception of Short's essay, there is little self-consciousness on the part of those writing these case-excursions as to the way in which sociologists are being used and the roles that sociologists play as handmaidens to people in positions of greater power. The general tone of the papers is self-effacing and pessimistic.

I would like to discuss the papers in the context of what social scientists study, the methods we use, and the conditions necessary for impact, and then relate my observations to questions of social research as it affects policy and graduate training.

In Davis's essay the article on "low level of educational achievement among Mexican-American youth in American society," which he reviewed, did not include an analysis of what happens to high level educational achievement in the same group, nor did it consider a comparison of educational achievement among Mexicans in Mexican society and Mexican-American youth in the United States to find out whether internal colonialism and selective migration were important dimensions. It was a tight study, a controlled domain. Nevertheless, explaining variance without considering the position of Chicanos in the wider society is anathema.

Similarly, DeFleur discusses a paper which again attempts to explain variance. The question, "Why do some slum siblings become drug addicts and others not?" leads us to see the necessity of detecting potential deviants early. While DeFleur points out that there is little research on the drug problem by mainstream sociologists, I would predict that among the 50 articles on the subject between 1967–1971, few dealt with drug companies and drug advertisements (a long-range approach to the drug addiction problem), or with the drug addiction problem among doctors. The social problem has been defined for us as criminal rather than medical, as DeFleur notes, and consequently slum, rather than industry, is the object of concern.

Entwisle comments on research on identity crises, and in particular on the thesis that rebellion and alienation in high school result from an absence of articulation between schools and occupational structures. She goes on to suggest that such articulation is unlikely to occur. She further notes that the high school research does not outline changes necessary in other institutions in order to "make high schools work." A time perspective is lacking in almost all of the work reported in this section. The shift over the past century from a nation of self-employed to a nation of employees is a major change in American society. We have also moved from a period of growth and affluence to a period bordering on scarcity. Entwisle points out that we have traveled from a time when high school diplomas were scarce and valued to a time when such diplomas do not mean much in prestige or occupational preparation. While not all sociological work need be historical, I think it particularly important to consider the time dimension if and when we attempt to document trends.

Reiss's paper notes that the poor are disproportionately victimized by crime, and by inference he raises the question as to why sociologists have not studied the ghettos as "lawless" in the sense, "without law." Courts are not geared to the complaints of the poor, nor are they geared for cheap and quick resolution of conflict—crucial features for the poor. The fact that social scientists focus on the less powerful people has meant that our study of crime is characterized by a classic mind-set. If we were principally studying the most powerful strata of urban society, our study of the poor might be in terms of those relationships that affect the lives of the poor, as for example the banks and insurance industries that mark out areas of the city to which they will not sell insurance or extend credit. We would study the landlords that "pay off" or "influence" enforcement or municipal officials so that building codes are not enforced. Slums are technically illegal; if building codes and other municipal laws were enforced, slums would not be slums, or they might be called by another name which would indicate that they were results of white-collar crime. We might test the hypothesis: if business crime is successful, it will produce street crime. With this perspective, our analysis of gang delinquency might be correspondingly affected. And in developing theories about criminal and delinquent behavior, we might ask: Is it sufficient to understand delinquency as products of the value systems of that subculture alone? Packer (1968) argues that if the criminal sanction is to work, it must be used parsimoniously. Again it appears that the sociologist is receiving the problem for analysis, rather than actively pursuing questions that relate to priorities in dealing with delinquent behavior. It is also interesting that Reiss deals more with how the subject is studied rather than exploring why the subject is being studied. It is the fascination with method in the social sciences that is central to the image we have of ourselves as scientists; what we study is not top priority except for purposes of funding. We have methods courses in our university programs; we do not teach courses that discuss priorities for sociological study. One could argue that our infatuation with method determines that much of what we study is not amenable to policy impact.

The last paper in this section by Short surveys a half of a century of sociological effort to understand and cope with crime and delinquency policy. While Sutherland wrote about white-collar crime, few followed in his footsteps. Most of the work dealing with crime and delinquency still revolves around one particular income group: the poor. In fact, as Short points out, the setting up of the Uniform Crime Index has almost insured that this would be so. Accordingly, the major delinquency prevention program that he describes was carried out in New York City's Lower Eastside as a theoretical test of delinquency cause. The fascinating story Short tells is somewhat reminiscent of crash attempts to improve driver habits. In the area of car safety, it was a breakthrough to realize that although accidents are difficult to prevent, injuries are not, and that it would make for more successful safety programs to concentrate on redesigning the automobile. The Koreans believe that the best way to prevent crime is to have good government; or, in the case of New York's Lower Eastside, the best way to prevent lawlessness may be to have law. The Lower Eastside is not easily characterized as a place where courts are set up to hear and resolve problems of the poor, not is it characterized by a police whose primary purpose is to prevent victimization of the poor. Short's review, in brief, indicates a mind-set as deep as that among Detroit auto producers. Social science training which teaches us to relate *down* rather than *up* (Nader 1972) insures that we get involved in "driver education" only, and to the exclusion of questions of macrostructure and power. Our domain is narrowly defined, perhaps in order to be methodologically more manageable. There is little cross-class comparison to test theories such as the relationship between delinquency and opportunity, although the Watergate hearings have shown that opportunity is a relative concept at best. There is a focus on institutions and organizations rather than networks; Mitford (1973) describes the use of prisoners for testing drugs for drug companies—an area apparently rarely explored by social scientists who study prisons as organizations.

One could argue for methodological eclecticism after reading these papers. Survey research, for example, is anathema to anthropologists as anything but research starters. The surveys reported by Reiss—self-reported surveys measuring prevalence of offenders in a population—are intriguing as starters, not conclusions, from which social science policy recommendations would emanate. The people who do this research have found a vertical distribution of offending populations which analyses of police statistics would not have revealed. So the surveys are useful; they make us take a second look at traditional sociological studies of crime and delinquency, but we could not base policy on such research.

Social scientists today are either indifferent or pessimistic as regards their impact on policy-makers. We worry about not knowing enough to recommend anything, or we believe that recommendations without social scientists in power positions are useless. First, we should realize that social scientists have made an impact, both negative and positive. During World War II anthropologists worked in Washington successfully: their goals toward the war effort and the government's goals were one. Anthropologists helped plan the entrance into Japan. In Scandinavia there is also a good working relationship between sociologists and government. So there are precedents. For those who believe that social science does not know enough, take note that Madison Avenue has built a billion dollar industry on social science findings. Then there are the negative cases alluded to in Short's paper: the impact of the development of the Uniform Crime Reporting System. The availability of law is lessened if we use police for trapping drunks, prostitutes, and homosexuals; when the courts are clogged, they will not be available to citizens with everyday problems. There are economic consequences—$12,000 a year on a child in a California detention home with close to 70% recidivism rate is not a good use of taxpayers' funds. There are political consequences of stigmatizing a specific class—the low-income peoples—of having a monoply on crime. And the mental health consequences stare us in the face at every turn. We are having impact. Spradley's study *You owe yourself a drunk* (1970) stimulated a drastic change in the handling of drunks in that city; it also cost the city of Seattle $500,000 a year to replace the drunks as trusties in the jail.

I would argue (1) that the most knowledgeable' (and knowledgeable here refers to people with data and experience) should take an active part in defining and adumbrating social problems in a complex society, and (2) that a healthy mix of trained people in government is what we need, and not a monopoly by any one professional group such as lawyers and economists. The Norwegians have come to the realization over the past 100 years. As they have moved toward decision making based on evidence and experience, the number of lawyers in their legislature has decreased, and the group is more heterogeneous. We have to realize that the United States is still in an era when most decisions are political decisions made in total ignorance of evidential or experiential thinking. Social scientists do not have political power in this country; they do not understand power, and they do not, for the most part, study power. Perhaps it is for this reason that we do not understand the power of knowledge.

The choice in graduate school training is not between the "enlightenment" approach and the "engineering" approach; it is a combination of both. First I recommend that we pay more attention to undergraduates; how we train them may be very important to creating an enlightened constituency. For the most part we have not developed a policy about undergraduate training except, of course, that it should be better. I recently visited an anthropology department that had a policy; they were going to train competent ethnographers: people who knew how to describe in context some aspect of the human experience. The people they train learn how to do something well; they identify with the aims of this skill—to understand the human experience; it is applicable to any walk of life they embark upon. They are not training preprofessionals.

If there is to be a change in the graduate programs, we need to change the status of research that may be useful. We might start by clarifying what I think is a muddled dichotomy between applied and basic research: "When you do genetics on drosophilae, it is basic science; when you do genetics on corn, it is applied." This is another one of those mind-sets. It is important that high- and low-risk endeavours be tolerated in science, and that we not restrict research to only those problem areas that are seen as important today. Moreover, it is necessary to destroy the notion that the more esoteric, the more scientific. We need to instill our students with the idea that some things are more important to study than others, and that it is possible, as Spradley has shown, to make a scientific contribution and at the same time to be a citizen. We must also realize that some important subjects are long-term projects. Because of the short research time involved in the Ph.D. programs, we often discourage students from tackling studies that might take about 10 years to research well. I have a student who as an undergraduate became interested in studying a major industry. He carried this study into graduate school. It will take him about 10 years to complete the work. It took Sutherland about the same amount of time to research White Collar Crime. We need to change the time perspective on research in our training programs.

Finally we have to get organizations and people in this country used to being studied, and by the participant/observer method. This means that we will have to work to understand why people are resistant to being studied, and to find out if they resent some methods more than others, and if they are defensive and why. With answers to all these we hope to change the climate about the scientific study of contemporary peoples.

REFERENCES

Mitford, J.
  1973 Kind and unusual punishment. New York: Alfred A. Knopf.

Nader, L.
   1972   Up the anthropologist—perspectives gained from studying up. In *Reinventing anthropology*, edited by D. Hymes. New York: Pantheon.
Packer, H. L.
   1968   *The limits of the criminal sanction*. Stanford, California: Standford Univ. Press.
Spradley, J. P.
   1970   *You owe yourself a drunk: An ethnography of urban nomads*. Boston, Massachusetts: Little-Brown.

ALBERT PEPITONE

The University of Pennsylvania

An implicit prescriptive assumption of the Carmel Conference was that the social sciences should produce more information that can be of direct use in policy-making with respect to the great social problems of the day, and that graduate training in the social sciences should become, both in substance and method, more relevant to the formation and evaluation of policy.

The pervasive push, inside and outside the federal government, toward policy research and training stems from the fact that, because of the shrinkage of jobs for which we have traditionally trained graduate students, both in academic teaching and research, an overproduction of Ph.D.s has created a glut. To continue the traditional kind of training at the same rate no longer makes sense.

Correlated with the pressure for policy research is a decline in the support of basic social science. Thus, in discussions of federal policy, one often hears the argument that tax monies should be used only for social science that can help with the massive problems of crime, drugs, poverty, etc. More extreme views—that social science should be dropped altogether for being irrelevant, too expensive, or antihuman—are not uncommon.

The growth of an antisocial science bias in government circles where social science policy is made is not only the consequence of the economic squeeze; but also the result of two sociopolitical attacks from opposite sides of the ideological spectrum: the production-minded, profits–loss orientation of political conservatives, especially within the administration; and the anti-intellectual, political action "nowists" of the radical left. For the former group, fundamental research in the social sciences is, at best, a waste of time and money; at worst, part of a vast "radic–lib" conspiracy designed to weaken America's "moral fabric." From the radical perspective, basic social science research is not only an irrelevant and elite activity but a corrupt practice. Those who carry it out have been co-opted by the mandarins whose business it is to oppress the powerless.

In view of the economic and sociopolitical difficulties facing social science at the present time, it is unfortunate that the Carmel Conference was structured as a "test" to see what social science has to offer policy in various social problem areas. Of course, it was, and is, a foregone conclusion that basic theory and research (even social problem-oriented studies in sociology) can make little direct and immediate contribution to policy programs. Social science aims to develop general statements about human conduct and society. The particular research setting is typically only a convenient source of data for supporting statements of cross-situational significance. Policy programs, on the other hand, are designed for problems whose definition is typically context-bound. Effective policy research must deal with relatively concrete variables which operate under particular contextual conditions. Except for research methodology that can be applied to the evaluation of a wide variety of policy programs, the contributions of social science data to policy-making can only be long term and indirect. Occasionally, the interpretation of basic research findings by social scientists may play a role in social policy. Thus, the 1953 Supreme Court decision outlawing racial segregation was partially based on the input of social scientists concerning the negative effects of "separate but equal" educational experiences on personality development. Even when basic research as such has implications for public policy, the policy-makers are not usually standing by ready to convert the findings into concrete programs. The evidence on the harmful effects of TV violence, for example, seems to have made no impact whatsoever, not so much because the evidence, so far, is weak, but because elimination of violence from the media threatens profits and because public policy-makers, such as those at the Federal Communications Commission, are ideologically allied with the television industry. This example reminds us that the role of social science in social policy depends as much on political and economic factors, and on the sophistication of policy-makers, as on the existence of potentially useful theoretical principles and research data.

The need for information relevant to social change has helped develop the genre of "social problem" research. Sadly, it has been the experience of many, and certainly the literature will show, that all too frequently social problem research not only fails to be of significant help to policy-making, but because of its restricted focus in terms of the sample and setting, fails to supply general statements about society and human conduct. It is often neither fish nor fowl as far as its contributions are concerned.

Findings of sweep and depth can only be formulated when research covers a broad sample of cultural and subcultural settings, and, in some cases a comparative sampling of biological species. In other words, to become more "basic," social science must adopt a comparative perspective. I cannot think of any social problem to which this recommendation does not apply.

On the other hand, sound and effective social policy in any of the social problem areas can develop only from information about the effects of concrete procedures administered in concrete settings under certain conditions at given times. Thus, whether we are dealing with the problem of drugs and alcohol or crime and delinquency, or aging, etc., the principal questions are: What might work with this or that group of people to ameliorate the problem? How can we implement a program built around such and such ameliorative variables? How can the program be evaluated against relative and absolute criteria? To get answers for these questions involves not only policy research and insight on what the ameliorative variables are likely to be, but also ethical analysis to detemine whether the program conflicts, or is congruent with important social values. Also required for these questions is political strategy to deal with (1) justified or unjustified resistances of the public, government officials, and (2) those who are going to be directly affected by the ameliorative program.

Let me proceed from these general introductory points to some observations about social science, policy, and graduate training that derive from the reports of the Carmel Conference. Each of the five papers on which I was assigned to comment is a concise report on a published research paper which to some degree is addressed to one of the major social problems in contemporary American society. It may be said straightway that the panelists found little that could be useful for policy programs. Perhaps we can find an explanation for this outcome by briefly examining these reports.

Lois DeFleur reports that she did not find a paper in the prime research and theory literature of sociology concerned with the serious problem of drug addiction. She also judges that the work published in the less prestigious applied social science literature, explicitly focused on drugs, is more or less policy-barren. The selected research paper, which evidences this conclusion, describes an investigation of drug-addicted and nonaddicted siblings. The researchers found that the former had a longer history of occupational and educational problems than the latter. Apparently, early on, the addict enters the "illegitimate opportunity structure," while his or her nonaddicted sibling takes the legitimate route.

This is a good example of social-problem oriented research from which we can gain little fundamental knowledge. Typically, the demonstration of differences begs the question of "Why?" And when a "why" is suggested (for instance, early drug-taking is the means of immediate status-gratification, which creates a self-reinforcing system of illusions about status that interferes with real status achievement), the suggestion is unconfirmable by this type of research design.

The limitation of such research for policy programs is also evident. Even if the demonstration of differences between groups did allow inferences about causation, policy programs still could not easily be generated. But, one may ask, what about implications for change that can be drawn from a proposition about causation. For if the craving for status is a cause of drug addiction, then the provision of status gratification—theoretically to get youth into the legitimate opportunity structure—should bring about a reduction of addiction. While such a suggestion is logically clear, it lacks specification as to the kind of status gratification that will be necessary and sufficient, and as to the means by which it is to be provided.

Speaking of causes and cures of addiction both at the theoretical and policy levels, I do not see how any one social science can provide answers. For instance, to answer the question of why one sibling becomes an addict while the other does not requires more than a sociological analysis. We need to know the group dynamics of the family and to grasp the peer group influence process. To get down to individual cases, psychological analysis in depth is necessary. And, when we deal with the mysteries of addiction, pharmacology has to be brought in.

As Short reminds us, sociologists have been working in the area of crime and delinquency for decades and have produced a striking volume and diversity of theoretical statements. Yet the contribution to successful ameliorative programs is not impressive. Short's case history of Mobilization for Youth keenly illustrates the point that even when programs are explicity designed by a sociological theory, they run aground or at best accomplish minimum reform.

According to what has been called "opportunity" theory, crime and delinquency are the consequences of the absence or inaccessibility of legitimate opportunities to conform to widely accepted cultural values and to pursue conventional goals of success. The reduction of crime and delinquency requires that conventional opportunities for value-conformity and success be expanded. Why did not these theoretical ideas about causation and reform work?

Part of the answer is that practitioners, the people who were supposed to implement the theoretically guided programs, had ideas of their own. These were not theories about crime and delinquency; they were ideologies of what has to be done to change political systems. Activists' ideas about social reform typically involve gains and losses in political power and often the particular methods with which this can be done. Opportunity or any other similar sociological theory does not print out a manual setting forth the steps needed to change things.

There is another difficulty in trying to implement theoretically-based policies which may be quite independent of the problems of political ideology and the activists. Pragmatically, to implement a social policy in a concrete social system requires at least the passive approval of certain people in that system. The democratic ethic—with which funding agencies, community leaders, and sociologists largely identify—encourages, if not demands, wide participation in the action research process, especially by the people who are to be affected by it. From the sociologist's standpoint, this participation expresses not only a belief in democracy but also a judgment that the policy will be more readily accepted if it is not imposed from above or from without. Of course, this assumption is not necessarily a correct one and certainly not correct under all circumstances. And we now know that conflicts often arise among the participating groups and individuals, with results that are sometimes disastrous for the theoretically-derived policy. Thus, an important policy question for ameliorative programs in all social problem areas is how much participation should be permitted in the execution of the program by those to whom it is relevant.

But even if these difficulties of implementing policy did not arise, would opportunity theory be helpful in practice? In my opinion, no. The theory lacks operational specification. Indeed, the theory has never been tested. To test a theory, there needs to be specifiable referents—"reduction sentences," we used to call them—on the empirical plane. "Opportunity" theory is a relatively vague perspective rather than an empirically testable theory. Thus, it is not clear what are "legitimate" and "illegitimate" opportunities and what are not.

Albert Reiss convincingly exposes the serious limitations of self-report surveys of delinquent behavior. Over-all, they have contributed little either to policy programs or to a basic understanding of the phenomenon. On the contrary, these self-surveys have provided data which give an erroneous picture of the incidence of delinquency in sex, class, and race categories. Moreover, these data reinforce ideological positions which exaggerate the causal role of the law enforcement process in delinquency and underestimate its role in reducing the rate.

As Reiss points out, insufficient attention has been given to the reliability and validity of instruments and to the criterial question of what conduct constitutes delinquency.

Although graduate education in theories and basic research findings in the social sciences are of limited value in policy-making, training in methodology is not only useful but indispensable. In this connection, there is no quarrel with Reiss's argument that training in survey methods should be more thorough and deep, with attention to problems of reliability and validity of survey instruments. We would add that graduate training for policy research should include a multi-method curriculum. The methods studied should include those drawn from a broad spectrum of disciplines: scaling, content analysis, use of cross-cultural files, and archival data, computer programming, interaction observation systems, questionnaire construction, etc.

Doris Entwisle's trenchant analysis of Stinchcombe's *Rebellion in a High School* again shows that a diagnosis of the cause of a social phenomenon does not necessarily help in designing ameliorative policy programs. It is easy to see why.

Stinchcombe argues with evidence that it is the high school/vocational world "disarticulation" that is the cause of alienation and rebelliousness, rather than the family or community. The high school curriculum is without relevance to the working world into which blue-collar youths expect to enter.

One may entertain reservations about the completeness of Stinchcombe's diagnosis or even its precision. Indeed, other alternative hypotheses come to mind: high schools are paying less and less attention to individual students and do not come close to satisfying the emotional needs of adolescents—needs for closeness and warmth, etc. Or, it is not the content of the curriculum and its relationship to the vocational world that cause the alienation, but the teacher's failure to make the curriculum interesting and worth knowing, and the community's failure to endorse the value of the curriculum. This view does not deny that some parts of the curriculum are so difficult as to preclude interest.

But what to make of *any* such theory of alienation and rebellion for the making of policy? Entwisle finds no policy implications. There are no specific options as to how schools can be changed to reduce disarticulation.

Policy starts with a correct diagnosis of a problem that requires amelioration. But broad policy implications—such as increasing vocational training in high schools, encouraging (and financing) afternoon, on-the-job training for high school seniors—involve value assessment, political negotiation, and, of course, money. The setting in which to fashion policy programs in secondary education out of these ingredients is the school, the school district, the state, or the federal department of education, rather than the university.

Davis examines a research paper which addresses itself to the problem of the determinants of low aspiration. He, too, finds absolutely no policy implications in the study.

Davis makes the important and often unrecognized point that sociological investigators have a penchant for nonmanipulable variables and that these usually cannot lead to policy programs. The call for studying manipulable variables would seem to suggest that field and laboratory experiments can provide solid grounds for policy development. There is in fact a large experimental literature on the social psychology of aspiration. If the authors had crossed a disciplinary boundary and looked into this literature, they might have developed a more detailed accounting for the correlations between the several nonmanipulable variables and college aspiration. On the other hand, some of the correlational findings are amenable to experimentation. For example, the finding that Mexican-Americans show higher college aspiration when they are in the majority suggests an important research question that can be answered precisely by controlled experimentation. All of which recommends that we do more boundary crossing, or rather boundary-erasing, for the benefit of both policy and basic research.

HANAN C. SELVIN

State University of New York at Stony Brook

Like the conference as a whole, the five papers in Section C (this volume) have taught me much; yet, again, like the conference as a whole, they leave me with a curiously empty feeling. Concepts, findings, and problems seem to float in the air, perhaps because the basic terms of "policy" and "research" are undefined.

In saying this I am not asking for a set of textbook definitions, but rather for conceptual schemes in which to locate these two important terms. I cannot hope to present such schemes, or even one of them, in the short space allotted me here; instead, I will take the first steps and hope that others will follow me in these important directions.

POLICY RESEARCH

This appears to be research intended to uncover, explore, or test ideas for ameliorating some social problem. Examples abound. De-Fleur suggests research on alternative ratifications for slum youth so that they will not take up drugs; Short considers the informal social organization within which delinquency thrives; and Entwisle focuses on the ways in which schools encourage adolescents to conform or to deviate. Each of these papers looks at a single link in a causal structure that accounts for some form of delinquency, a link in which the independent variable is susceptible to deliberate manipulation by government or social agencies. In this view the causal structure is at the center of policy research; and empirically tested causal theory (or even hypotheses) provides the theoretical structure of policy research.

Policy research, then, is not divorced from empirical research of the kind with which sociologists are familiar; rather, it extends that research by selecting causal relations in which the values of the independent variables are manipulable.

MOBILIZING SOCIOLOGISTS FOR POLICY RESEARCH

The problem of motivating and organizing sociologists, be they grey beards or neophytes, to engage in policy-relevant research is surprisingly similar, as Robert Merton surely must have taught us in his classic paper on *Anomie*, to the problem of why people behave contrary to social norms. The problem again is to find the sources, causes, contexts, or concomitance of such mobilization, and to test these new causal hypotheses in relevant situations—in other words, to treat this question as a problem for sociological theory and research. In this view it avails little to bemoan the emphasis placed on publication. And there is surely a lesson here from recent work in the sociology of science. As Stephen and Jonathan Cole (1971) have shown, prestige in the natural sciences tends to go with the quality of published research, and prestige and high quality research are concentrated in a small number of departments in each field.

I believe it is illusory to suggest, as DeFleur and Entwisle have done, that simple changes in the training of sociologists or in the behavior of funding agencies would increase the number of sociologists who seek to engage in policy research. Of course there are those who have come to be known as the "cream-skimmers," those who rush to be first in a new area of scientific or policy research, but this conference is not concerned with these few "big time operators." Just as most theoretically oriented research is done in the high-prestige departments that turn out significant numbers of Ph.D.s, so I predict that most policy research will be done by faculty members and students in these departments. Where an exceptional effort is made to organize a project, task force, or research agency independent of these departments, it will probably be staffed by people temporarily lured away by money, prestige, a sense of public service, or a desire to get away from the old place for a year or two. As just one example, note the academic sources of the staff that produced *The American Soldier* (Stouffer et al., 1949): they were the leading universities of that era.

Another way of stating this last point is that most research will continue to be done in formally organized research centers but the relatively skimpy knowledge we now have of what makes these centers "tick" ought to be expanded. Veterans of such organizations as Michigan's Survey Research Center, Columbia's Bureau of Applied Social Research, and Chicago's National Opinion Research Center can all point to "Golden Ages" in each center, times when fruitful new ideas came so fast that one could hardly keep up with them. Many of these ideas were clearly relevant to important questions of policy, yet there is little codified knowledge of how these golden ages came about.

The importance of organizational factors in producing and maintaining a stimulating research climate appears in the rise during the past two decades of research institutes, e.g., the set up of "think tanks," and other organized research groups that are not part of traditional universities. As a kind of ultimate sanctification, one problem-oriented agency of the federal government has even established its own internal think tank in which salaried members of the staff are free to work on whatever interests them.

I should like to close by calling attention to a long-neglected essay of Robert K. Merton ([1945] 1968), entitled "The Role of the Intellectual in Public Bureaucracy," in which these and related problems are handled with characteristic Mertonian power. This nearly 30-year-old essay needs precious little reworking to bring it entirely up to date.

Indeed, had the organizers thought of it, it would have served well as a theoretical beginning for this conference.

REFERENCES

Cole, J. and S. Cole
  1971 Measuring the quality of sociological research: Problems in the use of the science citation index. *The American Sociologist* **6** (Feb.): 23–29.
Merton, Robert K.
  1945 Role of the intellectual in public bureaucracy, *Social Forces* **23,** 405–415. (Reprinted in 1968 in R. K. Merton, *Social theory and social structure.* New York: Free Press.)
Stouffer, S. A.
  1949 The American soldier. In *Studies in social psychology in World War II,* edited by Samuel A. Stouffer *et al.* Vols. 1 and 2. Princeton, New Jersey: Princeton Univ. Press.

PART II

GRADUATE TRAINING
AND FEDERAL FUNDING

Report on a Survey of Graduate Training

RICHARD J. HILL

University of Oregon

This article summarizes selected findings of a study of graduate-level research training provided by departments of sociology in the United States from 1969 to 1971. It draws from two previous reports (Hill 1971a, 1971b), which contain a general discussion of the research design, sampling procedures, methods of data collection and some detailed analysis.

This report is based upon three types of data. Questionnaires were mailed to selected graduate students and faculty in 84 Ph.D.-granting departments. Usable returns were received from 1209 graduate students (representing a return rate of 67.5%) and 222 faculty (a return rate of 70.5%). Data were also collected by interviewing selected graduate students and faculty in 16 departments.[1] Finally, program descriptions, course syllabi, and reading lists were examined in an effort to determine patterns of requirements and sequences of research experience.

[1] In three pretest departments, interviews were conducted with 10 faculty and 12 graduate students. In the 13 "test" departments, 97 faculty and 115 graduate students were interviewed.

The analysis of these data has revealed much that now seems obvious and expected—some things that are puzzling, a few problem areas, and considerable opportunity for speculation. To begin with the obvious, the content of departmental, graduate-level research training corresponds in both matters of general strategies and technical details to the expectations and competencies of departmental faculty. The research skills developed by graduate students during the period investigated reflected the procedures employed by faculty in the conduct of their own research.

What about differences between departmental programs? Certain departments had developed distinctive programs of research training. Illustrative examples include the first-year experience provided at the University of Michigan in connection with the Detroit Area Study, the intensive mini-semester research projects at Johns Hopkins, and the highly integrated course sequence in data analysis at the University of North Carolina (Blalock 1969). Despite considerable variation in format, the general finding was one of over-all similarity among departments in terms of the objectives and contents of the curricula designed to develop research competence.

During the period of this investigation, there was a high degree of professional interest and a plethora of articles devoted to the relative prestige of departments of sociology. An attempt was made to utilize departmental prestige as an independent variable to explain differences in the research training provided for graduate students. When such measures as the American Council of Education rankings (Cartter 1966; Roose and Andersen 1970) were employed to categorize departments by level of prestige, over-all similarity of curriculum objectives and content continued to be the most impressive finding.

At a more detailed level, some differences by departmental prestige were found. For example, graduate students in the most prestigious departments were more likely than those in departments of less prestige to have performed a path analysis, to have used Markov processes, and to have had some acquaintance with smallest space analysis. By contrast, little or no differences between departments of various prestige levels were found with respect to more general topics such as experimental design, regression analysis, various sampling strategies, and interviewing methods.

The finding of a high degree of similarity across departments in the methodological preparation of graduate students is neither surprising nor new. The same finding was reported by Selvin (1963) a decade ago. The interviews with faculty suggest the dynamics that are involved in creating this condition. This appears to be a direct consequence of disciplinary diffusion strongly augmented by patterns of faculty mobility and recruitment.

The variations that existed between programs at the level of specific techniques and strategies reflected two differences that were found between departments. With respect to methodologically oriented courses in the graduate curriculum. Selvin reported considerable inter-departmental variation in the courses offered at the advanced level. That variation has persisted. Of more importance, in my opinion, were differences in the strategies employed by faculty in the conduct of their own research. It should be a surprise to no one that students at the University of Michigan during the 1969–1971 era were more likely to be familiar with path analysis than were students at most other universities.

The variability in advanced courses and the differences in the methodological proclivities of individual faculty result in another type of variation in the research skills mastered by graduate students. Especially in larger departments, we found little that resembled a "standard product" among the graduate students we interviewed. This suggests that the department may not have been the appropriate unit for our analysis—a problem to which we will return.

In the attempt to evaluate the effectiveness of research training and to pursue some type of "value added" analysis, we sought data on the quality of student "inputs." The effort proved to be relatively fruitless. We found little agreement among departments with respect to the data collected on application forms and assembled in admission records. Further, departmental records are surprisingly incomplete, differ by type of student, and change over short periods of time. Because of the lack of comparable data available from the various departments, and because of the grossness of the missing data problem, value-added analysis was not pursued.

The data gathered from departments did reveal distinct recruitment patterns which are related to the departmental prestige variable. In terms of source of undergraduate degree, high-prestige departments served a subset of graduate students who differed from those admitted by departments of lower prestige: graduate students in the most prestigious departments are much more likely to have been recruited from other high-prestige departments than were those recruited by departments with less lofty reputations.

Regardless of departmental prestige, faculty productivity, departmental size, or perceived quality of the resident graduate student body, many faculty expressed considerable dissatisfaction with the state of research training, not only in their own departments but in the discipline as a whole. While this was particularly characteristic of younger faculty, expressions of concern and frustration were not uncommon in the interviews with senior faculty members.

In every department visited, serious curriculum evaluation and alteration were seen as a high-priority necessity by at least some of the faculty directly and intensively involved in graduate-level research training. Nevertheless, embarking on this course was often viewed with reluctance. Most agree that curriculum evaluation and change involve a high-risk and painful process. As one department chairman remarked, "It's like pulling teeth, and you end up with dentures that don't work too well."

Perhaps one key to the difficulty is the existence of incompatible positions among staff members with respect to curriculum content, development and improvement. We were told repeatedly that graduate curricula should provide the "fundamental" methodological and theoretical orientations needed by all sociologists. On this there seemed to be agreement until we inquired into the meaning of "fundamental." The problem is well illustrated by the divergence of opinion with respect to theoretical training. In one of the departments visited, considerable emphasis was given to the mastery of nineteenth-century scholars. By contrast, in a department of approximately equal size, a graduate student said, "Here we are concerned with instant theory. Studying dead Germans doesn't pay off." Nor were such differences only interdepartmental; within departments, sharp disagreements existed with respect to a variety of methodological issues ranging from the general importance of statistical training to the relative utility of factor analysis.[2]

Perhaps it is this lack of disciplinary agreement that has led some research program directors to stress the need for highly specialized programs. For example, one program director insisted that students in his program specialize early. His claim was that creative work in his area demanded highly specialized skills, and that his students were wasting their time in the general methods courses provided by the department. His position was that none of the basic research competencies needed by those working in his area were provided by the regularly offered graduate courses within his department. He was

---

[2] Lack of agreement on the nature of the sociological enterprise is a condition of long standing. There have been a number of examinations of this lack of consensus. Among the best of these discussions are the papers contained in the monograph edited by Bierstedt (1969).

convinced that students in his program needed at *least* 1 year of calculus, at *least* one course in linear algebra, and at *least* one advanced course in econometrics.

Although the position of this director was not shared by many,[3] it is illustrative of a more widespread tendency to emphasize specialized training. Demographers and experimental social psychologists meant very different things when they reported upon what they viewed as "fundamental" research training. Both, in turn, differed from those investigating large-scale organizational phenomena. Again, the finding is not surprising. The relationship between substantive concerns and methodological appropriateness has been recognized repeatedly. What seems more difficult to understand is the continuation of departmental efforts to provide basic and extensive research training for students regardless of their substantive concerns.

Notwithstanding that some departments continued to pursue efforts to develop a single, integrated curriculum devoted to research methods, the trend toward diversification was clearly evident. In one of the departments visited, five almost totally autonomous paths to the Ph.D. were available to students. These paths were developed on the basis of the particular, substantive concerns of groups of departmental faculty, and the students in the various paths were exposed to very different methods and types of research experience.

If the discussion remained at a relatively abstract level, there appeared to be some emerging consensus about one basic issue. There was considerable support for the integration of theory, method and substance in all graduate-level courses and seminars. There were programs which were attempting to accomplish such integration within certain substantive areas. There did exist some resistance to such development, and that reluctance came primarily from what may seem to be a peculiar source. It was the substantive specialists who were most likely to have objections to such curriculum modifications, including some who felt that they were not competent to teach those methods which they agreed were becoming most appropriate for research in their own areas.

---

[3] Most of the program directors, including all demographers and experimental social psychologists, did advocate greater preparation in mathematics than was characteristic of the graduate students from whom questionnaires were received. The position taken by the majority of these program directors can be summarized by a statement written 10 years ago: "A prerequisite of high proficiency in formal methods of research and analysis of data is more competence in mathematics than most students of sociology possess when they enter graduate schools [Sibley 1963:35]."

There is, then, concern over the graduate curriculum. There is disagreement with respect to what that curriculum should contain, how courses should be taught, and how training experiences should be sequenced. There also is a paradox contained within this general concern. Almost all of the faculty and most of the more advanced graduate students interviewed agreed that effective research training could not be provided simply by altering departmental course structures and content.

There was near consensus with respect to the belief that one can not learn how to do research in some formal abstract way. According to our colleagues, one learns to do research—any kind of research—by doing it. If this belief is true, and if research competence is the objective, then much of the effort devoted to curriculum modification and development is probably wasted, unless the result is to increase the student's involvement in the actual research process.

The vast majority of the faculty interviewed were strong advocates of some form of apprenticeship model for research training. Some expressed concern over what they saw as the invidious status implications of a master–apprentice relationship, a concern shared by many graduate students.[4] Nevertheless, no other training model emerged as a seriously competing alternative. The strong advocacy of the apprenticeship transcended all differences in methodological orientation, theoretical commitment, substantive concern, departmental prestige, academic rank, and departmental size.

Large and high prestige departments were more likely to have had the intellectual and financial resources required to provide apparently effective apprenticeships in a variety of areas. In smaller departments, a prerequisite for most effective research training programs seemed to be the existence of three or four vigorous faculty with shared interests in a set of related problems. In the largest departments, such "critical masses" were taken more or less for granted as a natural fact of department life, while in the smaller departments, effective research training programs appear to have emerged only after a conscious con-

---

[4] Especially among younger faculty, there were some who employed a model of "cooperating equals" in their relations with graduate students. Even the most egalitarian admitted that the model introduced serious difficulties when there were great differences between student and faculty members in experience and level of skill mastery. With respect to the problem of role and status differentiation, those committed to the apprenticeship model frequently mentioned that in the successful application of the model, the apprentice progressively approached the status of colleague.

centration of resources was devoted to the recruitment of faculty with compatible, if not congruent, research interests.[5]

Even where a critical mass of faculty existed, where research support was at least adequate, and where the apprenticeship model was adopted, training programs had failed. Thus, even in large, high-prestige departments, there were programs operating under conditions that many would envy but nonetheless were defined as failures by both the faculty and the students involved.

Some training programs listed by departments were clearly moribund, including those which had experienced earlier periods of vitality. Such programs seemed particularly susceptible to two types of threat. The first was change in the level of support and the alteration of priorities of funding agencies. This type of difficulty seems to be more acute at present than it was from 1969 to 1971. However, even in the earlier period many faculty and students were concerned over trends in funding patterns, and many expressed a feeling of powerlessness with respect to the continuation of their programs.

Faculty mobility is the second serious threat to existing training programs. Some programs have attempted to insure against such disruption by staffing in depth; however, in training programs involving several faculty, role differentiation does occur. Thus, the insurance provided by involving several faculty in a given program is, at best, limited coverage.

In the previous pages, much of our attention has been devoted to the department. These departments constituted the sampling unit for this investigation, and now I am convinced that this early design decision was an error. If the desire is to describe effective research training, the department simply is not the appropriate unit of analysis. I now recognize what perhaps I should have known from the beginning

---

[5] We use the concept "effective training program" throughout this chapter. A program was *judged* to be effective if (1) students expressed satisfaction with the training they received, (2) the faculty involved expressed satisfaction with student progress, (3) other departmental faculty referred to the program as effective, (4) the program director reported having little or no trouble placing the graduates of the program, and (5) the director reported regular success in receiving financial support for the program. A special class of such programs—"most effective"—were those which were consistently referred to by faculty in other universities as models for research training. Only seven such programs were identified; five of them in departments visited during the research.

The concept "effective training program," as used in this chapter, is fundamentally subjective, and the identification of a particular program as "effective" is, in the final analysis, based on my judgment.

of the investigation. Departmental units—at least those which were studied intensively—are administrative inventions and conveniences; they are not integrated scholarly or research enterprises. Rather than extending the research effort in an attempt to cover entire departments, we should have sampled research and training programs and focused our attention much more intensively on such units.

During the period of investigation. many departments were in a state of crisis and turmoil. One of our respondents, a department chairman, told us, "Mao Tse Tung has forwarded the very good concept of the permanent revolution. The nearest thing to it in contemporary America is the graduate department." Given such conditions, it should come as no surprise that we had difficulty in finding clear and detailed patterns characterizing groups of departments or even single departments.

Despite the turmoil, we also found what we judged to be effective research training occurring within departmental subunits. It was the smaller, more specialized program, not the department as an entity, that provided the most effective mechanism for advanced research training.

What can be said about the characteristics of effective programs? (1) As mentioned earlier, the existence of a critical mass of faculty addressing common problems increases the probability of effectiveness. Programs essentially involving only one faculty member are fragile, high-risk ventures.[6] (2) Students in effective programs seem to have a stronger identity with the program than with the department as a whole. Especially in larger departments, this resulted in programs which have what one of our respondents described as an "insular character."[7] Here it seems important to note that the particular character or personal style of the director was less crucial than many faculty may assume. One program referred to as a model by persons in several departments was directed by a person described by the students working in that program as being arrogant, authoritarian, and

---

[6] We did encounter some effective programs which were essentially "one-person shows." In such instances, the director was invariably a person of high energy who had developed excellent communications with funding agencies.

[7] A number of observers have commented upon the tendency for departments, especially large ones, to fragment. Some (cf. Borgatta 1969) view the development of such subdepartmental units with concern. That such developments have a high probability of occurring in large departments seems beyond debate. The relative balance of the costs and benefits associated with "compartmentalization," we believe, remains problematic. On the basis of our data, we cannot agree with Borgatta's characterization of such subunits as liabilities.

demanding. Despite such castigations, those students, without exception, felt that they were receiving the best training available in the United States; they identified themselves strongly with the program and defended the director's approach. Another director was seen as a brilliant but other-worldly character who had to be protected by his students against the normal contingencies of everyday life. The personal character of the director, then, seems to account for very little of the variance in perceived program effectiveness.

Related to the identification of the graduate student with the specific program was the allocation of physical space. On one of the campuses visited, the department's largest and best financed research program was housed in a building separated from the departmental offices by several miles. Students in the training program reported that "I never go over to the department" ; "Everything I need to do my work is right here" ; and "I really don't know anybody who isn't in this program." Thus, the physical separation led to social and intellectual separation, and reinforced the student's identification with the program as something distinct from the department. We obtained evidence of this phenomenon in 10 of the 16 departments visited.

Faculty behavior also reinforced and probably accentuated such intradepartmental divisions. The faculty who were heavily involved in large research and training programs frequently commented to the effect that this involvement forced them to concentrate their concern on the students who were in their programs. Students *not* in such programs tended to perceive this behavior differently; they tended to define many program directors as being "overcommitted," "not interested in the department," "unavailable" and, at least on occasion, as "narrow specialists."

The strong identity of students with a particular program and the physical separation of program activities from those of the department can foster a type of "elitism" among both the faculty and students involved in the programs. In interviews with students in highly effective programs, comments of the following kind occurred with impressive frequency: "Of course X has the power to select only the best graduate students for our program." "The students in this program know they are good." "Somehow we seem to take on more significant problems than other people." "We are productive. We have to be to stay in the program." Such expressions may strike many as being contradictory to the anti-elitist attitudes expressed by numerous sociologists. I do not wish to engage in a debate on such matters, but at least during the period of 1969 to 1971, students in successful programs reported candidly that they "knew they were good," felt that they were receiving excellent training, and were optimistic about their future careers.

The feelings and identifications just described are associated with students' perceptions of the faculty involved with the programs. While personal styles of the faculty can apparently vary from the martinet to the detached dreamer who cannot remember where he parked his car, the faculty must be viewed by the students as being productive of what the group defines as significant work. In those programs which we judged to be most successful, the students defined the total work of the program as intellectually important. It must be stressed that this is a perception of the totality rather than the work that the student happens to be doing at a specific time. Students did define some of their assigned tasks as trivial or mundane, but they expressed satisfaction with their involvement when they viewed the total enterprise as important and saw the relationship of their tasks to the total effort.

The work in which students engage obviously is crucial. Faculty and students repeatedly advocated the rotation of students through every phase of research from problem formulation to publication. The limited opportunity to provide students with assignments matching their individual stages of development, prior experiences, and current interests was a frequently expressed concern of program directors. Of the 97 faculty interviewed,[8] 42 had direct responsibility for research training programs. Of these 42, only 3 felt that they had sufficient opportunities available to make totally appropriate assignments for all of their students. All 3 of these faculty were involved in multiproject programs directed toward a clearly delimited set of interrelated problems.

To summarize, certain conditions appear to increase the likelihood of effective research training. The existence of a critical mass of faculty who have related research concerns and who are not intellectually or geographically peripatetic is of great importance. A director (or small set of faculty) viewed as being engaged in significant work, even if not "well-liked," is apparently a prerequisite. The students' identification with a program which they define as doing important work seems essential. Other variables, such as the opportunity to assign students to a wide variety of tasks, probably enhance the chances of effective training. The relationship between effective research training and a department's curriculum remains problematic, and the nature and magnitude of that relationship deserve the most serious

---

[8] This omits the 10 faculty in pretest departments who were not uniformly questioned about opportunities for student assignments.

scrutiny. What occurs in the classroom may be essential to certain objectives of graduate education, but it may be of very marginal utility for the process of developing creative researchers.

REFERENCES

Bierstedt, R. (Editor)
  1969   A design for sociology: Scope, objectives, and methods. Monograph 9. Philadelphia, Pennsylvania: The American Academy of Political and Social Science.
Blalock, H. M., Jr.
  1969   On graduate methodology training, *The American Sociologist* **4**(1), 5–6.
Borgatta, E. F.
  1969   Some notes on graduate education, with special reference to sociology, *The American Sociologist* **4**(1), 6–12.
Cartter, A. M.
  1966   *An assessment of quality in graduate education.* Washington, D.C.: American Council on Education.
Hill, R. J.
  1971a   Graduate research training in sociology: A preliminary report. (A mimeographed paper.)
  1971b   Graduate research training in sociology: Some faculty views. Presented at the annual meetings of the American Sociological Association, Denver, Colorado.
Roose, K. D. and C. J. Andersen
  1970   *A rating of graduate programs.* Washington, D.C.: American Council on Education.
Selvin, H. C.
  1963   The teaching of sociological methodology in the United States of America, *International Social Science Journal* **15**(4), 2–20.
Sibley, E.
  1963   *The education of sociologists in the United States.* New York: The Russell Sage Foundation.

Remarks on the Changing Relationship between Government Support and Graduate Training

HOWARD E. FREEMAN

Brandeis University

EDGAR F. BORGATTA

Queens College

NATHANIEL H. SIEGEL

Queens College

This article has gone through several major rewritings in the short period of its development, largely because of the changing situation in regard to federal support of training programs—from being threatened to their demise. Many of the comments that were relevant while there was a potential for revitalizing an interest in the support of the programs are simply not relevant at this point, and so this version of the paper focuses on two things. (1) There is a brief overview of the history of the National Institute of Mental Health (NIMH) programs relevant to sociology, possibly too brief, but hopefully enough of a skeleton to indicate that the development and the demise of the training programs bear some relationship to the mandate that created them. Some perspective on the good things to which we have become accustomed and which are no longer available may be useful in considering the current situation for graduate training. (2) Many are speculating on the futures of graduate training, and we add a few considerations that may be relevant in anticipating what will happen.

THE NIMH SOCIAL SCIENCE TRAINING PROGRAM

The NIMH Social Science Training Program began in 1958–1959 as an experimental pilot program supported, somewhat surreptitiously, by psychiatric training funds. A rationale existed for the idea that it was possible to deal with mental and some physical disorders through the social sciences, and to some this idea became extremely appealing. The first programs funded had a decided medical or social psychiatric perspective. In general, the funds for the programs were spent in ways consistent with their budget categories. University deans and presidents were polite and gracious to NIMH officials who visited their campuses and, most importantly, peer review committees testified to the worth of the programs, to the high caliber of faculty and students involved, to the importance of the support for both the health areas and the social sciences. Then, members of the review committees went home to write applications for their own institutions. In the good old days, nothing seemed to have been more important to the "Washington official" than having a steady flow of requests that would support a claim for the great need and demand for the program.

In 1960 a separate social science training program was started in NIMH. Early in the development of the program a policy was formulated to have a program with a broad scope. In its experimental and fledgling years, the program was relatively narrow and instrumentally oriented—support was directed at training efforts with presumed immediate and clear pay-off for "mental health." At least, this is the way the applications were written, and the way site visitors and study sections structured their reviews. The strategy to broaden the program was based on the view that it was impossible to know what aspects of social science (sociology) would prove valuable to the general mental health effort. *Quality training* was what was needed, and the by-products of the process would feed into manpower and research of the mental health effort. Programs that looked at deviant behavior, social disorganization, social organization, the family, aging, and so forth, were all regarded as reasonable content areas for support, and the scope of relevance became virtually all inclusive.

Of key importance was the growth of sociology during the 1960s. Some deans and department chairmen were hiring young faculty almost in the same way the coaches cultivate and recruit early for, hopefully, a winning athletic team. It was the time when everyone saw an unlimited need for well-trained and technically sophisticated sociologists and other social scientists.

For much of the decade, turning out a large number of well-trained sociologists and "up-grading" social science training were part of the interpretation of the mandate for the NIMH Social Science Training Program. Indeed, for those of us who judged and received training grant support, the latter rationale was often regarded as the primary one. Even within NIMH, although there were differences of opinion and pleas for relevance from politicians, policy-makers, and administrators, a constant emphasis was to maintain the broad character of the program. While the shortage of persons for mental health and health–science-related activities was the *raison d'être* for the program, general manpower needs in sociology of both a qualitative and quantitative sort were of importance for the internal leadership of the program. Certainly the views of the advisors were directed at the "big picture," and, given the shortages that existed even at major universities with highly qualified young faculty, it was easy to take the stand that virtually all of sociology had relevance to the mandate of NIMH, and that manpower for the health-related sciences could become available only when the existing general manpower shortage was relieved. Those were the days when Congress on occasion actually appropriated more money to health agencies than the agencies asked for, and it was generally an expansive period for the social and psychological sciences.

From the point of view of the agency, "success" was judged to a large extent on the actual and potential improvement in quality of training and the increased number of Ph.D.s, although, of course, each training grant had to make a concession to "mental health" relevance. But, the concession was often treated as *pro forma,* a rationalization rather than a justification on the part of the applicant programs. From the point of view of applicants, it was probably seen as a nuisance to make such claims and, indeed, some awkwardness occasionally resulted when departments found it below their dignity to even provide a modest *pro forma* rationale. NIMH policy was quite flexible. Suppose a department did not wish to increase its graduate-student size, how could it then justify its training program? Eligibility could be readily established: if the proposed program increased the amount of attention given to students by having more staff; if its stipends aided recruitment of better students; if its funds shortened the time required to complete Ph.D. training; or if it provided for more interdisciplinary training, and in other ways improved "quality." Also, one or more joint faculty appointments with departments of psychiatry, or the use of mental hospitals as field training sites, or some other related but more distant mental health training opportunity was appreciated but not necessary.

In practice, certainly, many grants did in one way or another touch base with the mental health field. Faculty members in some cases actually were interested in the mental health and medical care fields, and some departments regarded the moral obligation to conform to the formal mandate of the program as a real one. Often, departments blatantly use their grants as unfettered institutional support. It is fair to say that NIMH and its consultants did not always protest too much; in part they were responsive to the shortage and quality issues, and in part they did not wish to be viewed as bureaucrats who did not trust professors and departments to do their own things in their own ways. On the contrary, many study sections and site visitors "bet on winners" and felt that "good people train other good people," and speculated that one could not know from what specialty a good student, in health-career terms, might eventually turn up.

Without doubt, the peer-review system associated with NIMH and other committees was instructive to the committee members, and some of us learned many things, including the fact that we will never be loved again by some of our colleagues. However, the review system and the site visits tended to be instructive for departments and universities as well. Competing for money (even though relatively plentiful was never in surplus) always raised questions about why some grants were made and others were not. Committee opinions were not made in a vacuum, and such decisions as not to recommend a grant at a prestigious institution—because the proposal was not thought out or because the site visitors found that people at the institution really had no concept of a program—were still hard to make at times. (Some people were getting degrees in some places in spite of the faculty.) Site visitors who did much traveling and comparative observation might find that their opinions and those of the "Cartter Report" could conflict seriously, but the pressures of prestige were often strong. More difficult still were decisions not to renew existing programs—decisions that had to be made in a competitive situations. Some reasonable questions have arisen about the quality and quantity of Ph.D. production of some of the programs, and at points there was evidence that neither had increased, and that in fact in some cases no program had materialized corresponding to a proposal.

What were the results of the decade? When a survey was conducted several years ago, *one in three graduate students in full-time study was an NIMH trainee;* a large number of recent Ph.D.s either were supported directly by the program or had key professors and resources that came from it; medical sociology is a major specialty for sociologists now, and their research results are read by health professionals and published to a considerable extent in professional journals in the mental health field. Furthermore, social scientists hold not only research positions in state and federal health agencies but administrative and policy-making ones as well. It appears something was purchased with the NIMH training grants.

THE CURRENT SITUATION

It has been suggested that there are now too many Ph.D.s on the market. It is a matter of reality that we have gone from debating whether ceilings should be placed on the size of universities to the problem of how to handle excess tenure commitments made in times of expansion. We cannot reject the current and projected demographic picture—the baby boom was taught by the products of a small depression cohort, and now the baby-boom cohort does not have a super baby boom to educate in turn. Analysts of supply and demand, in rather wide-read publications, have provided at least some evidence that the situation is not simply a short-term phenomenon.

The decade that saw the rise of the social science training program was one with a double shortage. There were few Ph.D.s being produced and these persons were not always well trained. At the same time there was rapid growth of university enrollments. Under these circumstances neither NIMH nor graduate departments had to confront some of the hard questions. If a person really is not going to make a research contribution (to the mental health and medical fields even in the broadest sense), and if the person does not meet moderate standards of competence, should he be permitted to complete doctoral training? Should a department that has marginal students receive federal support for them? These questions could be avoided or glibly answered when there is a severe shortage of personnel (and the graduate students who are potential personnel) in universities, or a need for persons in governmental groups and in applied research roles, and when there was uncertainty as to whether the same criteria of competence hold for the health field as for others.

The issues, when stated with regard to graduate training in general, have to do with the objectives of educational programs. The notion that a surplus of Ph.D.s exists suggests that there is an agreed upon norm of what is enough. Some appear to feel that the production of Ph.D.s should be held to a level that only the best are admitted, and the standards are raised so high that few can meet them, so that jobs will be plentiful in major institutions for Ph.D. holders. Some do not feel that the receipt of a Ph.D. should be tied closely to occupational resource allocation and that not all Ph.D.s should expect automatically to get a slot in a college or university. Rather, the educational value should emphasize that all can have an opportunity for as much education as is possible, regardless of whether or not it is used. Some argue that a "surplus" will result in Ph.D.s taking new roles, in government, in business, in high schools, and elementary education, and so on. These views have their proponents and antagonists, and arguments are phrased in quite different ways, evoking many values. Some see tightening entry requirements for graduate training as an elitist trend. Some argue the pleasure of teaching only superior students. Some argue that the Ph.D. degree will lose its status if the market is not kept tight, just as the B.A. degree pretty well has.

In general, whether rightly or wrongly, few cutbacks in the size of Ph.D. programs, have been made, although it is clear that faculty/student ratios, ceilings, standards of training, and other concepts have been activated to control individual situations. It is a reasonable prediction, however, that there will continue to be more doctorates awarded each year. In fact, many more institutions today offer the doctorate in sociology than 10 years ago and they are unlikely, differentially, to cut back. One hears of cutbacks affecting whole graduate school enrollments, but no-growth ceilings appear to be somewhat more commonplace. Some institutions tend to attract students who, for economic reasons or because of local and regional preferences, ordinarily would not go to the more established (major) centers. Some of these institutions will prosper from an economic standpoint because they turn out students to meet local demands (junior college faculty, for example) and because they exist in institutions that receive support to provide rather specialized graduate education.

Since graduate education is not centrally controlled, if there is a surplus of Ph.D.s in sociology *it probably will not result in a reduction of graduate students in those schools least equipped to give the doc-*

torate. There may be some reduction in the other two groups of programs that predominate in the field—the large public universities of good or excellent quality and the "elite" private universities. The former, however, still need their teaching assistants and their state-supported research. Therefore, although there may be some cutback, serious reductions are unlikely. Because of their appeal, the "elite" private universities will not lose too many students, and most never had very large enrollments anyway. Everyone still wants to be a "Harvard man" (correction: "Harvard person"), and both the existing university support and the creativity of students to make their own ways will keep these graduate training programs going.

In brief, what we argue is that cutbacks, and, indeed, the demise of the social science training support by NIMH and similar agencies, will not really have severe effects on the number of Ph.D.s completed.

What are some of the factors we may expect to see operating in the immediate future, now that the training grants are becoming a thing of the past? First, let us note that the concern with training grants is local in time. When this paper was first initiated, consideration of the consequences for graduate training was a burning issue, particularly if arguments could be mustered that might divert the federal government from what seemed to be an inevitable course. Somehow, almost as though there was an instant rewriting of history, the issue is no longer as important as before, because maintaining the availability of training grants is simply not in the realm of reality. Possibly we should reflect on the way we present ourselves to the public on such issues. The focus of this paper is now more on policy research and the challenge to graduate training in sociology than on the potential creation of arguments for continuing federal support of training grants.

The demise of training grants is not an isolated event. Other very relevant things are happening simultaneously. Money has become tight for research. Institutions are talking about cutbacks with a potential reduction of some aspects of their operations and, correspondingly, cutbacks in faculty, etc. The economic picture more generally is not in a "predictable and extended period of rapid expansion." The draft is no longer a factor in decisions to stay in school. And obviously many things are not as they were.

What may be expected then? If pressure for enrollment in graduate education continues, this will have several effects. In major centers this will force selection procedures to become even more difficult, and either self-selection will become more realistic or higher proportions of students applying will be rejected. From the point of view of education generally, this will of course raise issues of who should be educated and why, unless alternate options for education expand. We have noted already that marginal institutions and those that have not previously been in the business of graduate education in a big way will experience growth. They have often been ill-equipped to carry on such graduate training, but now it may come as a consequence of the "push." We know of some institutions where a few years ago applicants frequently did not have "B" averages, and now they are commonly experiencing applications from persons with grade-point averages in the 3.6 range. What will happen in these circumstances is open for speculation, but some may reflect on the experience of evaluating undergraduate institutions. It seems to indicate that the quality of students they graduate is roughly the same as when these students are admitted.

Additionally, comments have been made about how with the absence of support and the shrinking market for Ph.D.s in sociology students will turn to other areas with greater potential pay-off. But those great competing opportunities do not seem to exist. The professional schools quickly felt the pressure of applications, and they are not expanding by leaps and bounds; the demand for Ph.D.s in other areas seems to be governed by similar circumstances. Similarly, teaching in elementary and high schools, and opportunities in business, industry, and government are not so attractive that they necessarily make going to graduate school for a Ph.D. look ridiculous. So, while it may seem like a somewhat harsh view of the prospects for the products of the baby boom, there are a lot of people there, and they have to do something. It is unlikely that the "push" for at least the legitimization of status, the Ph.D., is going to go out of style.

In this context, however, it is appropriate to emphasize that the removal of support cannot help but have some material consequences. Some concentrated and focused resources on graduate education will simply not be there; professors kept free from teaching obligations to concentrate on a selected few graduate students may be less common. The purposive investment in specialists for such graduate training may similarly become less frequent. To the extent that resources and facilities govern the quality of education, there will be some problems, paritcularly if sources of support for such facilities in the universities do not materialize in other ways. However, realistically, we must ask what these resources are. For example, how many places are there, really, that do not have some computer? How many places do not have books and journals that may be used as ancillary faculty?

What is needed is in some degree determined by what one is accustomed to or, possibly better, would like to be accustomed to.

We would argue that a dominant value is that people should be able to get as much education as they want or are able to absorb; moreover, the market for the educated person should not determine the availability of education. To indicate how strong this value can be, it is useful to note that in New York City today, for example, 92% of students who graduate from high school with grade-point averages of 85 or better are going on to full-time college after graduation, and *50% of those with grade-point averages of 75 or less are also going on to college.* This must represent something like saturation, and it is not unreasonable to expect that the trend will be for more saturation at higher levels. Possibly another way of saying this is that when Ph.D.s are in surplus, as some have suggested, the demand for graduate education will go down. Some others, including myself, feel that exactly the opposite may be the case. *The moment Ph.D.s are in surplus, having one becomes even more necessary.*

The most general expectation we have with regard to graduate education is that it will become more commonplace.

Research Training from the Perspective of Government Funding [1]

KENNETH G. LUTTERMAN

Division of Manpower and Training, NIMH

When this meeting was envisaged over 2 years ago, we were aware that there would be important training issues that would need to be discussed and communicated, but at that time we did not know what problems would be facing us in 1973. However, the rumbling over supply and demand relationships, questions of relevance, and the phasing out of student training grant support by the Office of Education, by NASA and NSF and other agencies were on the horizon. Some of these issues are still with us, and others have become more salient and pressing.

HISTORY OF THE SOCIAL SCIENCES RESEARCH TRAINING PROGRAM

It is appropriate on this occasion that we take a brief look backward at the history of the Social Sciences Research Training program before

[1] The statements and opinions expressed throughout are those of the individual author and do not necessarily reflect the policy or position of the Health Services and Mental Health Administration.

we look at the current situation and at some of the problems and challenges ahead. NIMH began in 1946 with the passage of the National Mental Health Act. During the first decade, training support was limited to the clinical fields of psychiatry, clinical psychology, psychiatric social work, and psychiatric nursing. However, beginning in 1957, the training program was broadened to include support for research training. The first research training grants in the Social Sciences went to the University of North Carolina and Yale University to develop a greater number of investigators in medical sociology who would be capable of developing basic and clinical research which might lead to the more effective treament of mental illness and to a better understanding of the underlying factors in mental health. While initially the program focused in circumscribed aspects of the sociology of medicine and social psychology, it soon became clear that this limited support of social sciences was inadequate. It also became evident that it was very difficult to predict what kind of training would make for the development of a good medical sociologist or a researcher who could contribute the most to a social problem area.

The problems of the control and prevention of mental illness and the promotion of mental health were also being defined in increasingly broad social contexts. In the model of positive mental health, behavior was to be understood in the sense of productivity and creativity in addition to the variables which influence conformity and adjustment to existing norms. There was little question about the critical need to increase the quality and the number of well trained investigators to do the kinds of research that the changing conceptions of mental illness and mental health required. Reports made to the National Academy of Sciences and to distinguished congressional committees indicated that it was probably the shortage of adequately trained research manpower that placed the greatest limits on the parameters of research activities.

The rapid growth of the social sciences following World War II also added to the information explosion that was taking place in mental health services. It became apparent from the work of Hollingshead and Redlich and others that much greater knowledge of the social determinants of mental illness and of the behavioral science context underlying deviant behavior was required for both effective treatment and prevention. The thrust toward community mental health and group therapy in the 1960s further emphasized the need for a better understanding of the social factors for prevention and treatment.

Two basic ideas were built into the social sciences training program very early. (1) The NIMH Social Sciences program should support only the very best of sociological, anthropological, or other social science training. (2) The program should have some particular relationship to mental health (not only mental illness) that could be demonstrated. The over-all goal of NIMH support was to improve the quality of research training as well as increase the number of doctorates of particular kinds.

The Social Science Research Training Committee has played an important and somewhat atypical role in the development of the NIMH Social Sciences Training Program. The committee has consistently held an attitude of "convince me that this is worth support." As a consequence, the committee came to enjoy a reputation of strictness and fairness. Particularly in the early 1960s, a significantly larger number of programs could have been supported if standards had been lowered. The Social Sciences Training Committee rejected almost as many applications as it approved. The aim of the program was its high quality of excellence, not its size. Rather than disperse support broadly, the goal was to promote competition and to bring in new areas that had relationships to mental health.

The base of support was broadened in the 1960s with the development of new programs in such areas as urban studies, the economics of human resources, history and social science, and interdisciplinary research. The necessity of broadening and strengthening methodological training in the social sciences was recognized and vigorously pursued. One of the overriding concerns across the entire history of the social sciences training programs has been to improve the quality of methodological and theoretical training.

In the late 1960s an effort was made to increase the research involvement of trainess in all of our programs, because it was found that good research training was possible only when students were systematically and thoroughly exposed to ongoing research as a participant rather than merely as critics of the research of others. This effort was facilitated by providing a 12-month stipend support for the students and by building funds for research costs and research supervision into the training grants.

CURRENT PROGRAMS

The Social Science program which began in 1957 as a partnership between NIMH and two universities, with 14 trainees, currently supports 77 programs and provides stipends for about 560 trainees. The total Social Sciences training budget in this area for 1972 is a little over $5 million (Table 1).[2] While the period of most rapid growth was in the early years of the program, substantial increases in funds occurred in 1969 with the support of 12-month stipends. The problem areas, disciplinary and interdisciplinary programs currently receiving support, are shown in Table 2.

During the history of the Social Sciences program, there has been a substantial turnover of specific training grants. Of the 72 grants active in 1967, only 40, or 55%, are continuing to receive funds. Since 1967, 37 new programs have begun. This turnover has made the programs more responsible and has added a competitiveness which is not found in other areas of NIMH training. New programs have focused on improved training in methodology and on providing training in cross-cultural comparative research. Comparative research training has in-

TABLE 1 NIMH Social Sciences Research Training Program

Fiscal Year	No. of Grants	No. of Stipends	Total Funds Available [a]
1957	2	14	$ 84,916
1958	2	14	84,941
1959	3	27	146,865
1960	7	35	314,128
1961	13	70	420,665
1962	22	130	801,448
1963	39	226	1,332,704
1964	54	333	2,084,763
1965	62	403	2,796,515
1966	67	488	3,329,412
1967	72	575	3,891,063
1968	69	605	4,048,071
1969	77	626	4,818,518
1970	76	595	4,664,400
1971	79	586	4,892,941
1972	77	570	5,211,684
1973	77	567	5,129,208

[a] Includes unexpended balances from prior budget periods.

[2] In President Nixon's revised budget message of January 29, 1973 the phase-out of all research training programs, except for those concerned with drugs and alcohol, was announced. No new trainees can be appointed but extant trainees are to be supported to the normal completion of their training with proportionately reducing amounts for teaching costs as they complete their training. Total funds available will decline from the current (FY '73) of $5,129,208 to (FY '74) $3,969,843; (FY '75) $2,699,942; (FY '76) $1,045,390; to zero in FY '77, as the current cohort completes its training.

A postdoctoral fellowship program was announced by Secretary Weinberger in July of this year as a partial replacement for training grant support.

TABLE 2 Problem or Disciplinary Area of Social Sciences Research Training in 1972–1973

		Number of Grants
Economics of Human Resources		2
Anthropology of Cultural Change		12
Political Science—		
Alienation, Urban Conflict		3
Sociology		43
(Subfields)		
Socialization	2	
Ethnic and Minority Problems	2	
Urban Problems	1	
Family Problems	4	
Complex Organization	4	
Social Change	4	
Education Problems	1	
Comparative Social Change	4	
Deviant Behavior	5	
Methods of Research	4	
Evaluation Research	2	
Demographic Research	2	
Medical Sociology	6	
Social Psychology	2	
Interdisciplinary		17
Evaluation and Policy Research	2	
Economics—Political Science—Psychology		
Public Affairs—Sociology—Political Science—		
Economics—Psychology—Public Health		
Organizational Behavior	1	
Sociology—Education—Business Administration—		
Psychology		
Urban Problems	3	
Sociology—Political Science—Economics		
Political Science—Urban and Regional Planning		
Psychology—Sociology—Economics		
Social Psychology	4	
Psychology—Sociology		
Anthropology—Psychology—Sociology		
Sociology—Psychology—Anthropology—Ethnology		
Sociology—Psychology—Political Science		
Law and Social Science	2	
Sociology—Law		
Anthropology—Sociology—Political Science—		
Criminology—Law		
Social Psychiatry	3	
Psychiatry—Sociology		
Psychology and Political Science	1	
History and Social Science	1	

volved students receiving supervised training both in the United States and abroad in 4 sociology programs and in 11 anthropology programs. Other areas of special concern have been minority problems, child socialization, the family, and evaluation research.

NEW PROGRAMS INITIATED IN THE LAST TWO YEARS

In addition to 11 programs which were renewed for a period of 3 to 5 years, 9 new programs were funded in 1971–1972. These included disciplinary programs to train students in political science to do research on problems of conflict resolution and civic responsibility at the University of Rochester; a program at Harvard University trains students to do comparative studies of social change; a new program at the University of California focuses on problems of ethnic communities and seeks to improve the research training of minority group students. An interdisciplinary program at Florida State University trains students (including minority students) from economics, sociology, and political science to do research on minority group problems. Another interdisciplinary program was funded to train students from psychology, anthropology, sociology, and ethnology to study problems in social psychology and social control at The University of Pennsylvania. At Johns Hopkins, a new program in social psychology trains students to do research on problems of later childhood and adolescence. At the University of California, San Diego, a program in anthropology, which focuses on psychological anthropology with special attention to the problems of children and cultural factors in conflict, was initiated. Finally, a new interdisciplinary program in law and society at the University of California was funded to train law students to do social science research, and students of anthropology, sociology, criminology, and political science to do research on problems in law. The Social Sciences Section also supported a conference grant which brought together training program directors in sociology for 3 days to discuss ways of improving research training relevant to mental health.

During 1972-1973 eight programs were renewed for another 3- to 5-year period and nine new programs were begun. Three of the new programs focus on the problems of families and children; the ones at the University of New Hampshire and Washington State University are primarily sociological in orientation, while at Columbia University it is mainly anthropological. Two programs which focus on improving research competence in the areas of evaluation research and public policy began at the University of California (Berkeley) and the University of Minnesota. The latter involves an interdisciplinary program including trainees from public affairs, economics, political science, and sociology. Two programs which focus on improving the research training of psychiatrists started at Brandeis University and Duke University. These programs will attempt to meet the need for improving the research competence of a small number of psychiatrists and other service personnel so that they can more effectively draw upon the knowledge and findings of the social sciences to improve the practice of psychiatry and other service professions. A multidisciplinary program at Stanford University focuses on organizational behavior problems and trains students from the social sciences, business, and education at the pre- and postdoctoral levels. An interdisciplinary program at Yale University focuses on research training in the area of deviant behavior, social control, and law, with pre- and post-doctoral trainees from law and sociology. The Social Sciences also funded a conference on manpower needs and social science training, which will focus on manpower planning for the future and more effective training of researchers for nonacademic employment.

Among NIMH's continuing conerns is the need for improving the training of minority students and thereby enhancing the ability of universities to do research on problems of minority concern. One of the goals is that 25% of all trainees in the existing programs come from minority groups, but we also hope to begin additional training programs which focus on problems of particular concern to Puerto Ricans, Chicanos, and blacks. We hope to develop needed additional programs focusing on early childhood, deviant and antisocial behavior, community organization, family disorganization, and minority problems. We also need to develop additional programs of research training in the social sciences for professional mental health personnel. The history of past efforts in this area has not been bright but the challenge to solve this problem remains.

NIMH's training grants have been of sigular importance in improving the quality of research training—particularly its methodological and statistical aspects. In fact, the NIMH and NIH training grants have been tthe only federal programs designed to improve the quality of graduate education.[3] In recent years we have expanded the support of

---

[3] This is worthy of study. With the possible exception of the small number of NSF science development grants, which were made just as this NSF program was being phased out, why has support for improving the quality of graduate education come only from NIMH–NIH?

joint faculty-student research because we see empirical research involvement as essential for good research training. According to the report of trainees who are involved in ongoing research, theory, statistics, and methods take on a whole new dimension. Theory is no longer abstract irrelevancy; statistics and methods are no longer necessary evils to be hurdled; rather, courses in both theory and methods become essential ingredients for learning to do research. This trend towards a closer integration of training and research is likely to continue.

Among the problem areas for research training which are of special concern to NIMH are the following:

1. Child mental health, early socialization and development
2. Aging and problems of the aged
3. Minorites and related problems
4. Racism, intergroup tension and its related problems
5. Community mental health, urban problems
6. Antisocial behavior
7. Evaluation research
8. Alcoholism
9. Narcotics and other kinds of drug abuse
10. Crime and delinquency
11. The problems of adolescence
12. Aggressive behavior
13. Family conflict
14. Alienation and other forms of withdrawal
15. Motivation for work
16. Social responsibility
17. The cycle of poverty
18. The organization and delivery of services
19. Bureaucratic responsiveness
20. Organizational change and organizational effectiveness

We continue to need research of the kind that problem-focused disciplinary and interdisciplinary integrated programs can produce. While the integration of research and training will be more expensive and will mean that fewer students can be trained, they will be better trained to do research inside or outside of academia. Among the major problems to be addressed is how can we most effectively train researchers to do research in nonacademic settings on problems of great national import? The partnership of universities and NIMH has greatly improved the quality of graduate education and given us the research manpower needed to tackle our massive problems. NIMH'S investment in research training has resulted in a higher quality of research application which comes to the Division of Extramural Research Programs and in better research itself. But what is the future of research training?

THE FUTURE?

Two major factors appear to me to influence the immediate future. One of these is the changing national philosophy with respect to the support of education and research, and more specifically, with respect to the support of graduate students. This administration has made it clear that it believes that the federal government should withdraw from the support of manpower development except in highly specialized circumstances. Consequently, we have seen the phasing out or drastic reduction of graduate-student support from the Office of Education, NSF, and from NASA. Because we are a part of the NIMH and the health bag generally, we have thus far been sheltered from those cuts. We have experienced a stabilization of funding rather than a dramatic cutback; however, this year we are anticipating an actual reduction in funds.[4] In the past 4 years, even though we have not had increased budgets, the quality of applications coming in from the social sciences and the quality of the review process were high, and, as a consequence, grants from the Social Sciences Section have grown from a little over $3 million to over $5 million. However, I see no way for that pattern to continue. The basic philosophy of the administration is that those who will receive the benefits of education in terms of higher earnings and other benefits should pay for the cost of this education. Obviously, since students who receive graduate education receive substantially higher incomes than the population in general, they should be able in some way, perhaps through loans, to pay for their own education or work for their earnings.

The second factor is one of demography. This challenge comes from the fact that over 85% of sociologists have in the immediate past found employment within academia. The simple demographic facts are that the births which have already taken place mean that universities are not likely to grow to any substantial degree during the next decade. For the past 20 years, universities and colleges have expanded at an unprecented rate because of the higher birth rates following

---

[4] See footnote 2.

World War II and the higher proportion of high school graduates going on to college. In the last several years, enrollments in sociology in particular have boomed, but significant increases in faculty have lagged because of the general fiscal crunch universities have experienced and because departments have been deluded by academic deans and their own myopia from claiming their fair share of teaching positions. But booming student enrollments have also deluded us from the demographic data which indicate that 2 years from now we will have a gross oversupply of sociologists for an academic market which has stopped growing. While we read *Chains of Opportunity* (White 1970), we do not apply it to ourselves. Even though demography belongs to the field of sociology, we have denied the reality of the data. We function as individual scholars or individual departments, and to cut back student enrollment would mean depriving ourselves of students and research assistants. Only when the problems of unemployment are upon us much more urgently than at present will we respond, as our unemployed Ph.D.s have already responded. The National Academy of Sciences is only now beginning to plan a study of nonacademic employment of social scientists. Traditionally over 85% of our Ph.D.s have gone into academia. But if McGinnis' (McGinnis and Solomon 1973) data and projections are correct, and I believe them to be very conservative, we will be training at least seven Ph.D.s for every graduate position in academia by 1980. According to McGinnis, "If a balance is to be reestablished between supply and demand by 1980, Ph.D. production in social science must decline by 1976 to a steady state level of about 900 a year, *or just under 20% of the 1970 volume* [McGinnis and Solomon 1973:60].[5] We must ask ourselves: What are the implications for graduate research training?

IMPLICATIONS

We live in a "post-industrial age," and the major problems we face are not technological problems but human problems—the problems of

[5] In 1965 there were approximately 1240 Ph.D. positions for sociologists in graduate faculties, including 295 newly available positions. The 240 Ph.D.s who entered the labor market that year were insufficient to fill these positions. Clearly, 1965 was a seller's market year for new Ph.D.s in sociology. By 1970, the number of graduate positions had increased to 2580, including 255 newly available positions. However, the 470 new Ph.D.s who went on the market that year represented 1.85 times the number of graduate faculty positions available. By 1975 the ratio of new Ph.D.s in the labor force to number of graduate faculty positions available was projected to increase to 3.5. By 1980 the ratio was projected to be 7.2 new Ph.D.s per each graduate faculty position available (McGinnis and Solomon 1973:60).

social science. But thus far the contribution sociologists have made to our major social problems—racism, poverty, housing, mental illness, health care, unemployment, alcoholism, crime, antisocial behavior, narcotics, and drug abuse—have fallen far short of what they could be. Thus far, sociologists have contributed very little in the way of useful theories for understanding our major social problems or of tested knowledge which could be utilized in ameliorating them. Why is this the case?

Although sociologists claim to be students of social organization, in reality most sociologists are social psychologists. This is not surprising. It is very difficult for sociologists to study society at the level of society. It is equally difficult to study organizations at the level of organizations. It is much easier to study individual responses to organizations or to study the impact of organizations on individuals. I regard the latter kinds of studies to be social psychological studies rather than truly sociological ones. The study of societies or organizations is difficult because it requires a mobilization of data and manpower which is inappropriate and typically beyond the scope of sociologists as they are presently organized.

But if we want to understand the sociology of knowledge, the sociology of sociology, we must see the discipline for what it is. At the present time, sociology is almost entirely a teaching discipline. Most sociologists spend the vast bulk of their time teaching rather than doing research. They get paid for teaching or for writing textbooks. Over 88% of all sociologists are employed in institutions for higher learning. When they do research, and many do not, it is typically on the individual scholar basis as a part-time researcher. If sociology is "to come of age," it will require the mobilization of effort on a much larger scale. The problems of our societies are immense; the mobilization of our resources to understand them is at the handicraft stage.

As sociologists, we must ask: What are the consequences of the way in which sociology is organized today for the development of sociological theory and methodology? Since we know something about ethnocentrism and participant observation, we have a small inkling of the dangers involved in theorizing and observing from the outside in contrast to doing so from within.

Some may think that it is simply a matter of money. I think not. It is true that sociology and the other social sciences are so poorly organized that no one knows either the amounts or sources of funds available for research, to say nothing of what the effects of these sources of funding may have on the kind of research that is done. All of these issues remain to be explored. One might think that the source of funding would be of central importance to a scientific discipline but, in fact, it does not appear to be a central concern at all. I suspect the reason is that the discipline is still overwhelmingly concerned with teaching rather than with research. Today research lives off crumbs from the table, but since we have moved in two decades from no funds for research to receiving crumbs, this is an enormous improvement. But again, the main problem is not one of money, it is one of social organization.

In the past several years, funding that social scientists could have applied for has gone up substantially at NSF and at NIMH. At NSF, the Division of Social Systems and Human Resources of RANN has expanded from $7 million last year to $11.4 million this year and is likely to go up to $14 million next year. However, to date, only three applications from sociologists have been funded. While several others are pending, the significant fact is that is has been extremely difficult for sociologists to respond because of their present forms of organization or lack of organization. Sociologists in academia lack the type of organization that is necessary for submitting large proposals.

At NIMH, large sums of money are going unspent for both research and training relevant to drug abuse and alcoholism. It is not because sociologists could not contribute to our understanding of these problems, but there are organizational and social psychological problems preventing or impeding sociologists from submitting viable applications. In the case of RANN, NSF requires applications which are likely to produce results which will be of some interest or utility to someone. In the case of NIMH, I suspect that one reason is the ethnocentrism of sociologists. Although NIMH has provided more research and training money to sociologists than any other part of the federal government, when asked if they were doing any research or teaching concerning mental health, over 95% of the sociologists responded negatively. What that says to me is that sociologists carry with them a nineteenth-century conception of mental health being mental illness, that fundamentally they reject the pioneering work of Stanton and Schwartz, of Goffman, of Hollingshead, and others who have pointed out the relevance of the social system to mental health and mental illness. It says that sociologists can be just as provincial as anyone else.

All this may change, however, because of decisions being made by those providing funds. For example, the Office of Education has moved from a grant program of supporting research to a contract system in which it (The Office of Education) specifies what it wants research on. This form of research support is much more suitable for nonacademic social scientists than for those in academia. For the Office of Education it provides research on problems they perceive as having direct relevance to their mission. The changes which have occurred at the Office of Education and similar changes involving the abolition of the peer review system at the Social and Rehabilitation Service took place with very little protest from social scientists. Why? Perhaps because sociologists tend to be located and concerned with the more provincial interests of teaching rather than research or research support. Among the most urgent needs at the present time are people who are able to do competent evaluation research. Most or many of the people doing evaluation research come from law or economics—law bacause of its conceptual and data training, economics for its theoretical and econometrics training. But sociologists could make very significant contributions to evaluation research if they were trained to do this kind of research. There are also unmet needs in the area of medical education and health services organization for sociologists for research and teaching. But so far we have done a poor job of training people for these areas. Similarly, the areas of law and the legal professions have been largely neglected. In spite of fantastic rates and amounts of funding in the areas of law and justice, there has been only a very small increase in research funding or the employment of research sociologists. While cities deteriorate, research creeps along at one urban institute, and a bit at Rand. Nevertheless, virtually no graduate departments are yet explicitly training students to work outside of academia.

What is required is not more money per se but the organization of centers and institutions which can enable us to utilize the manpower which will be available to tackle pressing national problems we face. These problems must be tackled on a scale very much larger than has been done in the past or is presently being done! Thus far the amount of dollars and the number of man-years spent on research to understand these problems are trivial. This is at least in part because we lack effective social organization to utilize the resources we have to tackle these problems. I think the money and research manpower will be there. Will we have the inventiveness to create the research institutions we so urgently need to effectively utilize this research manpower to understand the massive problems which beset us, or, alternatively, will sociologists be locked into undergraduate teaching or be unemployed?

REFERENCES

McGinnis, R. and L. Solomon
  1973 Employment prospects for Ph.D. sociologists during the seventies, *American
         Sociologist* **8**, 60.
White, H. C.
  1970 *Chains of opportunity: System models of mobility in organizations.* Cam-
         bridge, Massachusetts: Harvard Univ. Press.

Putting Sociologists to Work [1]

NELSON N. FOOTE

Hunter College, CUNY

Academic employment depends on student enrollment. The bull market in higher education in America that ran for nearly 40 years, from the mid-1930s to the present, has passed its crest. In fact, it appears from a recent release [2] by the Bureau of Labor Statistics that, while college enrollments did not drop absolutely until just this year, they began to recede, relatively, 4 years ago. The proportion of high school graduates who entered college reached 51% in 1968, then began to fall; by September of 1972 it had dropped to 49% among white students. What this proportion will prove to be next month, this audience must await with trepidation.

The decline in enrollment hit the private colleges first, suggesting that inflation was a factor in limiting opportunity. When it began to hit the public colleges as well, observers turned to other explanations, such as elimination of the draft. Another suggestion was that declining enrollments reflect the baby boom of the early 1950s. The crest of the baby boom was not reached until 1955, however, exactly 18 years ago —and 18 is the normal age for entering college. So from here on, to

[1] Presented to session on "Labor Market for Sociologists," Annual Meeting, American Sociological Association, New York City, August 29, 1973.

[2] Special Labor Force Report 155, "The High School Class of 1972."

whatever other factors have been depressing college enrollment rates, the demographic factor must now be added; whereas until now it has been pushing rates upward, it will henceforth push them downward.

Sociology, like psychology, enjoyed a peculiar Indian summer boom in enrollment, during the late 1960s, sociology classes grew faster than college enrollment generally. But now even that special advantage appears to have been lost, and sociology faces the same problem as other disciplines in the humanities, natural sciences, and social sciences: loss of customers. Hence the suspicion may take root that the customers are less enamored of the product than hitherto.

No doubt wishful thinking will persist; unemployed recent and not-so-recent Ph.D.s will cling to the hope that an upturn will somehow occur, and the old seller's market for teachers will return. During that 40-year bull market, some people have entered graduate school, received their Ph.D.s, been employed, promoted, and retired, without even experiencing a year in which the number of academic jobs opening for sociologists was not running ahead of the production of doctorates. It is not surprising, therefore, that the expectation of continuous growth of vocational opportunity in college teaching had become ingrained in academic thinking as virtually a permanent feature of the landscape. Yet anyone professionally concerned with forecasting knows how tricky it is to rely on projections of past trends. Sociologists have less reason for surprise that the curve has turned than their colleagues in other disciplines, just as they have less reason to attribute to themselves freedom from vocational concerns and resulting bias.

There is an old joke about the person who believes that everybody else speaks with an accent except himself. One of the conceits of academics is that everybody else is preoccupied with his vocation, hence cannot view the world with the detached objectivity of those who are free of vocational bias. The sociologist, however, should be the first to surrender this virginal innocence and recognize that the characteristic outlook of the academic is just as much a vocational bias as that of anyone else—doctor, lawyer, merchant, or chief. Take this gathering itself as evidence: it was scheduled by the American Sociological Association Committee on Employment precisely because the production of doctorates in sociology has at long last outrun the multiplication of jobs in college teaching.

This paper was specifically commissioned to "suggest some changes in the training of sociologists designed to increase sociological opportunities." By sociological opportunities was meant opportunities for employment of sociologists, but could logically have meant opportunities for the employment of sociology. Since it happens that either one leads to the other, this ambiguity presents no problem, because the paper deals with both possibilities.

Another way of stating our purpose is to answer the question, "How does training for nonacademic positions differ from training for academic positions?" It might seem superfluous to attempt to add to the answers already given this same question at a conference convoked by the American Sociological Association, with sponsorship by the National Institute of Mental Health, only last December. It might seem superfluous, that is, until one examines some of the views to which conferees apparently gave their approval. Consider, for example, Costner's (1973) summary of points agreed upon by the members of one informal discussion group:

> 1. . . . there may be a market for academic sociologists outside of departments of sociology, e.g., in schools of education, social work, public affairs, etc. . . .
>
> 2. The non-academic market for sociologists is not known in great detail, but the members . . . anticipated that such a demand was likely to take the form of positions for staff assistants to legislative committees . . . in administrative departments . . . in assorted non-governmental association seeking social change and social reform, and in organizations doing contract evaluation research. . . . A study of "drop-outs" from Ph.D. programs in sociology might be informative in identifying the nature of some of these potential opportunities. . . .
>
> 3. The general kinds of skills that non-academic sociologists will probably need will be those that enable them to be effective research consumers, knowledgeable research "commissioners," or efficient research producers. . . .
>
> 4. This discussion group emphasized that the provision of training for non-academic sociologists must not be allowed to dilute the training standards for the discipline generally. The feature of training for non-academic sociologists that was given greatest attention was the provision of "internships" through which trainees would become familiar with the kind of role they would be expected to fill after their training period was completed. . . .
>
> 5. In a post-session . . . there was a brief discussion of the potential training of "para-professionals" in sociology, e.g., specialists in computer science whose training is geared especially to social research needs, specialists in social science writing for reporting research to policy-making audiences, and social research technicians who would function in non-academic settings much like graduate research assistants function on research projects in academic settings. . . .

This statement may be primarily significant in showing that academic sociologists (no conferees were nonacademics) are poorly qualified to speak for the nonacademic world. To the degree that anyone reads the above summary, without recognizing its implicit self-caricature, it measures his own entrapment in their hermetic provincialism.

We could ask if academic teachers of sociology are really sociologists if they never practice as sociologists. To defer controversy, however, we shall assume that some sociologists are now ready to contemplate nonacademic employment as sociologists and sketch a quite different answer to the original question.

RESEARCH METHODS

Far from presenting temptations to "dilute" academic training for sociological research, preparation for the role of nonacademic sociologist would take for granted all usable benefits that conventional research training has to offer, and then add to it a number of important respects. Let us contemplate a sociologist who is to be employed by a nonacademic institution, and whose work is presumed to be to sociologize about that institution. The activities in which sociologists have hitherto been employed within nonacademic institutions have been primarily in research, and research will figure heavily in their activity in the future—with some important qualifications. For the moment, however, let us focus on just those types and methods of research which are relevant and important to these institutions.

Mastering the Existing Literature

Many nonacademic researchers are not scholars; some are little more than technicians. This is especially true in commerical research companies, where much of the research they conduct is purchased by nonacademic institutions. Their business still consists mainly of fairly small, one-shot, cross-sectional surveys, projects unconnected with earlier or later studies. Because they are continually seeking business, the commercial firms—and many nonprofit agencies which operate on a bureau basis, handling whatever comes to their doors—are biased quite strongly in favor of obtaining work, of doing research in the sense of gathering and processing data and writing reports thereon. With few honarable exceptions, they are not, nor do they take pains to become, acquainted with the prior literature on a problem presented to them for study. While they may exhibit some cumulative development of technique, among commerical companies mastery of an area of knowdedge is rare. Yet from the point of view of the client of the research company, this bias in favor of collecting and analyzing new data often fails to serve his interests. At best, it causes unnecessary duplication and waste—"reinventing the wheel." At worst, it causes the buyer of such services, if he obtains therefrom his image of the applied sociologist, to conceive the latter as a functional illiterate, ignorant of what has gone before, or of how the new knowledge which may be gathered is to be employed. We wish, therefore, to dissociate sharply our concept of the applied sociologist from the mere research technician and data processor—even though an applied sociologist may well spend some portion of his early career mastering the technology of data gathering and data processing. Training for research must go far beyond this necessary element. First and foremost is to learn what is already known about the subject of interest. It would seem redundant to repeat an axiom so obvious were it not so continually violated.

As a general rule, it should be assumed that the bulk of existing knowledge about any nonacademic institution has *not* been assembled by sociologists and is not ensconced within sociological journals and monographs. The bibliography of academic industrial sociology, for example, is essentially quite sparse, whereas the extant bibliography about the organization, operation, history, theory, criticism, and comparative study of industry is enormous. We have often seen academic monographs on industry which seem to be informed by nothing but the extant academic writings and which appear obvious of even such highly accessible sources as the *FORTUNE 500 Survey* or the *Survey of Current Business,* not to mention the infinite variety of trade journals. Some of the best sociology is being published almost daily in the *Wall Street Journal.* The same general rule applies to medicine, law, the media, the arts, and the military.

It has been our experience that, within nonacademic institutions, the majority of officials do no more systematic reading about what is happening in their field than do the outside research technicians they may employ to study their problems. Hence when someone comes along with a substantial stock of existing knowledge, he possesses numerous advantages and can make numerous contributions. These may consist of being able to provide needed knowledge at once, without having to undertake a new study, or of being able to relay experience of knowledge gained by others, so as to obviate the cost and pain of learning the hard way of trial and error.

Digesting the available literature, both academic and nonacademic, is only one means of acquiring existing knowledge about an institution or a situation. Equally important are the following: (1) to acquire what is not in print, which may be a great deal, and (2) to do field work—to observe and make direct inquiry among informants. Sociologists could well emulate those journalists and lawyers who often display skills in swiftly grasping such knowledge. Indeed, the statement from the Carmel Conference that some "para-professionals" might be trained as "specialists in social science writing for reporting research to policy-making audiences" is as obtuse as it is condescending.

Academic training sometimes fosters a snobbish attitude toward simple, descriptive knowledge in favor of abstract theory. Yet one of the first canons of science is that theory has to be based on induction from observation and description. Much of what is called the sociology of complex organizations has little basis in empirical observation; even when it appears to be derived from research, it is often research concerned with aspects too abstruse to be of practical concern or applicability. The best management consultants and the best organization theorists should be almost indistinguishable. Yet at present it is as if they inhabit two different worlds, or at least speak two different languages. And organization theory is only one example of the present gulf.

Problem Formulation

Writing a thesis proposal, if an academic sociologist got his advanced degree in a department which required one, is often the only practice he has had in problem formulation. Those who seek grants for post-doctoral sponsored research may add to this initial experience. But most proposals for academic research are unrelated to the operation of any institutions or groups, save the perpetuation of academic sociology itself. When sociologists commence to be employed by nonacademic institutions, the writing of proposals, and the review of proposals written by others, become more frequent, and involve a quite different array of considerations from thesis proposals or applications for grants for academic research.

One does not start, for example, by assuming that he is going to do a piece of research because he is required to publish or because he is moved by some spontaneous personal interest in an area of knowledge or by the example of others, as in fashion. Instead, he is moved by his duty to determine what the institution needs to know that is not already known. It may be that no research is needed, because sufficient usable knowledge already exists and can be brought to bear, or because the decision which would be benefited by added knowledge has to be made before new knowledge could be obtained, or because the benefit to be derived from a fresh study would be worth less than its cost, or because in the course of trying to state the problem of the institution from a sociological perspective it gets reformulated in a way that makes decision or action possible, without any need for further knowledge. The outsider who must perpetually sell his services as a researcher usually is not in a position to assist in such reformulations.

On the other hand, the inside person may be in too subordinate a position to resist the will of his employer to define his problem in some unrealistic way. Hence the role of consultant on problem formulation may be difficult or hazardous to perform. Nonetheless, it seems possible both to learn a good deal more about the process then is currently taught in graduate schools and then to teach it to others in graduate schools or elsewhere. It should be possible to accumulate examples from a variety of settings of the actual proposals and related internal memoranda, which have preceded actual studies made within nonacademic institutions, and to compare these proposals with the final products which eventuated. A program for training nonacademic sociologists would enrich academic sociology by applying comparative methods to information of this kind obtained from a variety of sources. Such comparative study of proposals would also perform a function for nonacademic sociologists, ensconced within particular institutions, which they do not—and probably cannot—perform for themselves, with the possible exception of a few business schools which offer advanced training in marketing research and already utilize case materials from business sources.

Forecasting

Frequently sought from applied sociologists by the institutions which employ them is a variety of forecasts on which planning can be used. Considering the ubiquity of this demand, it is strange that normal methodological training in sociology departments devotes so little attention to forecasting. The discipline that pays it the most attention is economics. The approach to forecasting in economics, however, is usually narrow, tends to rely on data obtained ready-made from government and trade association sources, and is often full of flaws, and limits its treatment of such data to regression methods, elaborate though these have become. Yet because economists have accepted forecasting as an art to master, they are being employed more and more in forecasting in noneconomic fields. The preference of academic sociologists for what is daintily distinguished as "prediction" thus deprives them of many nonacademic job opportunities in "forecasting," where they could in fact make quite superior contributions through their sophistication in the creation of data, their catholicity toward qualitative methods, and their potential competence in synthesizing economic, sociological, political, and psychological factors in anticipating future behavior.

Continuous Information System

In all the fields of application, there has been a strong trend in the past 10 or 15 years to move away from little, one-shot studies and toward the creation of continuous information systems, which track established measures of institutional performance and the recognized environmental factors affecting them, year after year.

The accumulation of statistical experience is obviously essential to improvements in forecasting and planning. What is not so obvious is that the creation of continuous information systems opens the door to a special kind of research that has so far been much slower to appear. The usual forecaster's idea of improvement in his art is to improve his marksmanship, by finding ways to manipulate his data so that his forecast numbers will come closer to actual numbers. This narrowly technical objective and its accompanying framework of assumptions largely overlook the benefits to be derived from research on the real sources of error in forecasts and in plans based on them. (The process of translating forecasts into plans is itself worthy of much sociological scrutiny.)

In the work we have done ourselves, we have classified the sources of error into those having to do with unexpected *environmental* factors—*mishaps*—and those having to do with unexpected *internal* factors—*mistakes*. These in turn are usefully sorted into what might be called positive and negative factors. Even a hasty glance at what is meant by positive and negative factors in the deviations between expected and actual factors discloses a considerable vista for future work by applied sociologists, who get into positions where they can go beyond mere forecasting to research on forecasting.

By positive environmental factors accounting for discrepancies between actual and planned outcomes in the performance of an institution, we mean those conditions which are found to account for the institution performing better than expected during a specified time period; the negative environmental factors, of course, account for the institution doing less well than expected. By commencing to explore this vista, not only can forecasting escape from degenerating into a boring technical exercise, but it can be the channel for continuous learning about the conditions of the success or failure of the program of the institution. It would be hard to find a topic for research of more intrinsic practical interest to the personnel of an institution. And when generalized from enough instances, such findings become of theoretical interest as well, because they often contradict premises which go unchallenged by academic research. Indeed the surprises come characteristically in two steps: the discovery that some previous assumption no longer holds true, and the finding of some new assertion with more warrant and utility. Of most profound significance is the realization that *sociological generalizations do not cumulate; they obsolesce.*

It becomes evident rather soon in this continual process of renovation that findings which contradict previously accepted premises of operation still evoke ambivalent or hostile responses because they threaten someone's status or ego. One index of how fair the ethos of social science has fallen short of permeating popular thinking is the resistance that still arises to the objective examination of mishaps and mistakes. Even when a positive factor accounting for beyond expected success is identified, instead of its being recognized as an opportunity or resource to be exploited more deliberately in planning future operations, this finding sometimes is concealed so that personal credit for superior performance can be appropriated by some higher official of the institution. The ancient habit of thinking in terms of credit and blame, of friends and enemies, instead of in scientific terms about the factors which condition outcomes, is of course fortified by the pervasive tendency to shift responsibility upward in a bureaucratic hierarchy. Nonetheless it remains possible to find a few officials who will welcome and use such findings rationally, and who will furnish the base from which the claim of such findings on the attention of all concerned can be steadily propagated. There are not as many hardheaded people in business as reputed, but there is a higher proportion than in more sheltered situations.

The reception accorded findings pertaining to positive and negative internal factors seems no less ambivalent than that accorded external factors. On the one hand, internal factors are presumably more within the control of the institution than external factors; on the other hand, discoveries of unexpected talents or strengths within may or may not be greeted with joy by those who had previously failed to perceive them. And of course discoveries of unexpected weaknesses and shortcomings bring forth all the temptations toward condemnation and punishment that remain traditional in the culture. In recent years some academic sociologists have studied the dissemination of the findings of natural science and technology. It is about time for perhaps equal attention to be given to what becomes of findings about the real sources of error in social forecasts and plans—social research on social research, as it were.

Measurement

Conventional academic training in methods and statistics has been relatively deficient in attention to measurement, index construction, and the quantification of hitherto vague variables. There seems to be more interest in manipulating data than in creating superior data, despite the claim that academia is more hospitable to basic work. The one important exception to this statement is in attitude measurement, but here credit—or blame—has to be shared with the psychologists; moreover, despite several decades of attitude measurement, we have seen no comparable development of measurement of intentions and expectations, which are more nearly sociological concepts, and more relevant to the application of sociology in practice.

The most gratifying, recent development in this respect has been the rise of interest in social indicators. To a large extent, this interest was evoked by analogy to the Council of Economic Advisers to the President, and it contemplates national measures as broadly aggregated as the Gross National Product, hence not directed to measuring the performance of institutions or the behavior of their clients. Nonetheless, it has helped to create a favorable climate for the latter, as now illustrated by the emerging idea of a social audit for corporations.

Evaluation

It is readily supposed from merely projecting recent experience that the principal nonacademic source of employment for sociologists will be in doing evaluation studies, primarily for federal agencies. The recent abundance of such studies reflects the recent abundance, especially under President Johnson, of federal programs and subprograms, allegedly experimental in nature, which have seemed to require evaluation in order to determine if they should be continued, expanded, contracted, or terminated. These evaluation studies have usually been *ad hoc,* and have been conducted by outside research firms on a contract basis. Albert Biderman and Laure Sharp have recently published such a thorough and thoughtful analysis of what they termed *The Competitive Evaluation Research Industry* that we shall not attempt to summarize it, but we strongly urge every reader of this paper to read it. In view of the serious flaws in the output of that industry, I am far from sure that sociologists should deplore the fact that most of these studies are being done by nonsociologists such as systems analysts, operations researchers, engineers, computerologists, and other technicians, even though at many points they do employ social science and social scientists. Instead of merely complaining that the work has gone heavily to others, it seems far more constructive to raise some fundamental questions about the whole concept of *ad hoc* contract evaluation studies:

(a) Can *post-factum* evaluation ever be valid? Or should not any program, of which evaluation is anticipated, from the beginning build the quantitative goals of the program into its measures of performance?

(b) Can outside evaluators, far from enjoying advantages of disinterested objectivity, avoid being construed as either critics or supporters of the current administration of the program, providing ammunition either for its opponents or its protagonists? Only if the measures to be applied are adopted and accepted from the start, before actual results can be fully foreseen, can personnel of the program be properly expected to accept findings which demonstrate shortcomings in performance, or guide their programs in a way to achieve the results measured.

(c) Too many researchers are inclined to emphasize the injustice of hindsight evaluation of performance, instead of considering how to construct quantitative goals at the beginning of programs. On the other hand, because of their *ad hoc,* one-shot character, most of these studies do not in turn produce measures of performance to be built into the next cycle of agency operations. Instead of *ad hoc*—really *post hoc*—evaluation studies by outsiders who have no opportunity to acquire deep understanding of the agency, the direction in which sociologists should move is toward employment in producing evaluation and feedback on an annual basis, like a companion piece to current annual reports. There thus evolves a perspective of continuous evaluation, *pre factum* rather than *post factum,* and systematic learning from experience, as already outlined.

By way of transition, we might propose that the ideal role of the sociologist in this process of continuous evaluation, feedback, and development of new goals and measures is neither inside in the sense of in a line position, nor outside, as in a contract agency. Rather, it is to one side—that is, being privy over time to what happens both inside among agency personnel and outside among agency clientele—but in a position to speak with authority and independence to both. The captive inside researcher is usually not in such a position, nor is the outsider who must continually solicit new business. It seems possible to devise such a position structurally for the applied sociologist, just as it has been possible to devise authoritative independent statuses for third parties in industrial relations—umpires, mediators, arbitrators, fact-finders and the like. This prospect stimulates much curiosity, not to mention many questions about implementation, which cannot be satisfied here.

THE SOCIOLOGICAL PERSPECTIVE

Getting into a "semi-detached" structural position offers the best foreseeable opportunity to exercise and propagate the sociological perspective. During intimate conversations I have had over the past 30 years with others who have been employed like myself in a variety of positions as applied sociologists, nearly all who have reflected on their experience have told me that their most valuable contribution to the institutions employing them was not to relay existing knowledge or to do research or to present the findings of their research, but to present the sociological perspective.

What is that? And is it not rather inconsistent to proffer the sociological perspective as the principal benefit to be obtained from the application of sociology when application is almost inevitably interdisciplinary?

The actual behavior of people in institutions cannot be tidily sorted into economic, political, sociological, anthropological, or psychological kinds. Moreover, in these ventures in which interdisciplinary teams are self-consciously assembled in order to study problems of institutions, and take pains to manifest the contributions of their several disciplines, the results obtained are usually quite modest. Results are more prolific and valuable when the employed social scientists, while solving a specific problem, focus their attention conscientiously upon the nature of the identified problem and borrow from any of the academic disciplines whatever is appropriate and useful.

The resolution of the apparent inconsistency does not lie in claiming that sociology possesses some exotic special knowledge absent in the other disciplines. Instead, we would claim as sociological an emphasis on awareness of the social context of all behavior and on understanding this social context as consisting of a dense, highly organized and differentiated web of mutual expectations which powerfully condition all concrete phenomena of behavior. It could be argued, of course, that there is similarly an economic or political or cultural or psychological context for all concrete behavioral phenomena, and we would not object. The important point is the emphasis on context. Economists have lately commenced to pay great attention to what they call externalities affecting the phenomena they pick out for study; we would consider this interest in externalities as sociological. Although they still tend to maintain a distinction between the organism and the environment which is nonsociological, psychologists have for a generation been showing mounting interest in social influences on perception, motivation, and development of personality. Comparative studies since World War II have impressed political scientists and historians with how pervasively the functioning of any particular form of government is altered by being thrust into a different social or cultural setting. In applied ventures of multitudinous kinds, whether sponsored by government, business, or nonprofit organizations, the policies or practices recommended out of context by either home office or academic specialists have repeatedly had to be corrected by people out in the field, who know that nothing works unless it honors the requirements of the social context. The main difference between the ordinary, practical person in the field, who is sensitive and responsive to the social situation in which he works, and the applied sociologist, who presumes to contribute to his enlightenment, is, to repeat, not primarily in the latter's relaying some bits of specialized lore peculiar to his discipline but in his being able to recognize those specialized bits—regardless of source—which fit the situation, and, of course, in having a wide body of knowledge from which to select them. The same enhanced awareness of the social context permits the applied social scientist to recognize when bits from other disciplinary sources are relevant, or, if unobtainable, to describe what new knowledge is needed. We hope these comments resolve the interdisciplinary paradox. They do not, however, take us far in identifying what is meant by the sociological perspective.

Let us start with a classic illustration. Many managers of commercial firms operate under the assumption that salespeople, being in direct contact with customers, are reliable sources of information regarding customer attitudes. The most familiar fruit of this assumption is to accept at face value the conviction of most salespeople that price is a dominant consideration in purchasing decisions, because that in fact is what customers stress in talking with salesmen prior to making purchasing decisions, and because so many purchasing decisions are quite plainly precipitated by the prices quoted. From a sociological perspective, however, it is quite obvious that at a given moment most people are not engaged in purchasing at all. Furthermore, very little observation is required to realize that many of the people actually engaged in purchasing a given product do not talk with salesmen. Through their own past experience, conversations with previous buyers, advertising, shopping, and other sources, they have acquired all the necessary information to make their decisions; they merely ask for what they want, pay for it, and depart. Among the kinds of information they need to know in order to decide beforehand what they want, price may have been of much, little, or no importance. When the moment comes to pay for their purchases, they will, to be sure, learn what the price is. Hence, price has a salience in conversations between customers and salesmen far out of proportion to the weight of other factors. Salespeople are often quite unappreciative of other factors, indeed sometimes astonishingly oblivious of them.

Now this sketchy analysis of salespeople's bias toward price could be devised through applying the sociological perspective without need for any research to find out. On the other hand, most empirically minded sociologists would want to check the evidence before confidently proclaiming that salespeople over-estimate the importance of price in customer thinking—especially, if called upon to advise, let us say, on how much price should be emphasized in advertising certain products to certain kinds of customers as against other factors in purchasing. Nonetheless, this example should suffice to make clear several other benefits to be derived from applying the sociological perspective. A corollary of major importance is that if a researcher were to take at face value a sales manager's notion of what kind of information he most needs to know, he might miss looking into far more fruitful areas for new knowledge. Another corollary is that the major contribution of application may not be new knowledge in the absolute sense of discovering information never before suspected by anyone, but instead may consist of challenging existing knowledge that is untrue, even though institutional practice may have been based on it for years.

Skepticism is one of the never-failing resources of the scientific sociologist. While it often replaces old fallacies with existing knowledge, it may also open the door to new knowledge. Genuine need for new social knowledge rarely becomes apparent until a skeptic challenges the assumptions on which an insittution is currently operating, yet the stock of prejudices by which the world lives is theoretically in continual need of renovation.

There is no part of the context of any institution of more importance to its internal personnel than its external clientele, and in particular the satisfaction of its clientele with the operation of the institution. In respect to those matters about its operation with which they are dissatisfied, most momentous is to ascertain in what directions clients aspire toward changes. All the social sciences, however different the language in which they garb their notions about them, are interested in motivation and valuation. But perhaps sociology exhibits at least some special expertise in gathering primary data about which way clients want the institutions that serve them to go. We wish, however, to focus next not on methodology but on theory, from the standpoint of clients and clienteles.

The actor of human behavior, in virtually everything that he does, is the client of an institution. Economics may be said to deal with economic institutions, and political science with government; but notwithstanding this loose association, it is apparent that all social sciences pertain to all institutions, and the study of each, certainly for practical purposes, benefits from applying all of them. How much more is it true, therefore, that in trying to deal with interrelations among institutions, any disciplinary provincialism seems arbitrarily crippling. The emphasis upon the satisfactions and aspirations of the clients of institutions forces our attention upon how the client is continuously engaged every day in the course of fashioning his style of life, in putting together all the institutions and in reconciling their interrelations as they affect him. His style of life is the composite of all the dealings he has with all the institutions which serve him in his personal community, however amorphous its geographical boundaries. The fullest expression of applied sociology thus comes to be the enlargement and enrichment of the consciousness of the consumer of all his interactions with his community, to make him an ever more sophisticated critic and creator of that community, through his participation in its development.

Let us contrast this vision of applied sociology with the academic and managerial approaches which have preceded it. Academic sociology by definition and history has been construed as a segmental, abstract discipline, its output being designed primarily for an audience of other academic sociologists. Managerial sociology by history and definition has usually been the body of assumptions on which a practice that is instrumental to the operation of some particular institution is premised; its audience has usually been the top management of the personnel of that institution only. Notwithstanding its strong tendency to be interdisciplinary, managerial sociology has therefore also been segmental, confined to solving the problems of managing that one institution only and to the interests of only its personnel—or only a part of its personnel. Not until sociology is finally mobilized to contribute to the enlightenment of clienteles—and the clientele of any one institution in a community is made up of essentially the same people as constitute the clienteles of all of its other institutions—does it cease to be segmental and become comprehensive in its orientation, in what deserves to be called professional sociology—because it follows the injunction of all professions to serve their clients, takes them as its primary audience and the enlightenment of their daily living as its task.

It could be argued that in becoming analysts of the intentions and aspirations of the clienteles of institutions, professional sociologists will proliferate into many more specialties than at present. This challenge makes it worthwhile to repeat that the persons constituting a clientele for one institution are virtually the same as those making up the clientele for the next institution; as long as they occupy the same community, they are essentially the same people. And by analyzing client satisfaction with any one institution in the context of relations with all the other institutions, the familiar faults of suboptimization, of taking the part for the whole, and of provincialism and craft bias are avoided. But by assuming the perspective of the client, who is concerned with synthesizing his relations with all the institutions which constitute his social environment, paradoxically the applied sociologist multiplies the number of his own potential clients to include ultimately all of mankind. Just in illuminating the interrelations of production and comsumption, through helping individuals to reconcile their roles as employees and customers—an area of problems as yet hardly explored in academic sociology—the potential demand for the services of sociologists who can genuinely shed useful light seems enormous.

Employment for applied sociologists is not already neatly packaged and labeled, as it is for economic forecasters or survey analysts or clinical psychologists. A long and complex process of realizing the potential just described lies ahead. But the very nature of the general opportunity seems to outrun the potential for many of the more specialized disciplines. Applied sociologists could imaginably become as common as lawyers.

CONCLUSIONS ON TRAINING

The kinds of supplements to existing graduate training called for by the foregoing perspective have already been sketched. We would therefore conclude with only a final paradox, namely: to insist that one of the most grievous shortcomings of present-day training for academic sociology—its lack of explicit preparation of students for the practice of teaching itself—be repaired in order to prepare people for nonacademic sociology. I can think of no way to illustrate this need more dramatically than to call attention to the care that is exercised in nonacademic presentations.

The normal medium within nonacademic institutions for conveying the findings of research, selections and syntheses of existing knowledge, and sociological analyses of current situations is not publication in learned journals. The most important medium, if not the most frequently used, is the oral presentation, usually accompanied with a variety of visual aids. The most frequently used is no doubt the written memorandum or simple conversation, but these too differ characteristically from academic memos and discussions. Since the formal oral presentation comprises all those features which distinguish normal nonacademic communication of sociological content from normal academic communication, let us briefly list their salient differences:

1. The presentation, unlike a journal article, is obviously addressed to a specific and often very small audience of nonsociologists, sometimes a single person.
2. The presentation is oriented to and tailored for this audience. It takes account of a previously agreed upon purpose for the information or analysis which is to be presented; it also takes account of the previous knowledge already possessed by this audience, without taking too much for granted nor engaging in redundancy; and it usually takes account of some impending decision to be made by this audience, to which the presentation is presumed to contribute.
3. It takes place within conscious constraints or resources of time, money, personnel, and other competing claims on attention.
4. It usually assumes that other sources of information, analysis, and advice are available to this audience, against which or whom its content will be compared and tested.
5. Because the content is presumed to contribute to some impending decision by this audience, it anticipates that some real consequences will follow from utilization of this content in later ac-

tion; hence, it often attempts to estimate the character, extent, probability, and cost of those consequences. Thus it can be seen that the normal nonacademic presentation differs as much in content as in form. Form is properly based on content, but both depend on being directed to an audience of clients, not of colleagues. That is the heart of the whole matter.   ·

Indeed, if we were to sum up all that we have said to this moment, it would be to say that the salvation of sociology lies in shifting its attention from colleagues to clients. That is not to become less professional, but at last to become professional. By concluding with a call to orient training to the intelligible, purposeful presentation of sociology to nonsociologists, we are nt redirecting sociologists back to academic sociology, but are redirecting them at last to sociology.

For such a redirection to be implemented, however, the profession must confront itself with the dilemma exposed at the Carmel Conference: Are academic sociologists equipped to train nonacademic sociologists? Who is to teach the teachers? How eager are the latter to learn? Or will the learning or relearning be easiest as always for those who have the least to unlearn?

REFERENCE

Costner, H.
   1973   *Footnotes* (Feb.). Washington, D.C.: American Sociological Association.

Epilogue

N. J. DEMERATH, III

University of Massachusetts

Any conference is vulnerable to the cliche that "when all is said and done, more will be said than done," but perhaps this conference more than most. Certainly there was a great deal said, and quite apart from the formal presentations. In fact, one of the objectives of this "epilogue" is to report on the discussions and debate which occurred in the chinks and on the margins of the program. There was no risk of reaching a total consensus. As it happened, the setting was ironically appropriate, for the weather was every bit as varied as the climate of opinion, and Carmel may still hold sociology responsible for the first recorded snowfall in the town's otherwise temperate history.

The ratio of talk to action was increased by the nature of the issues involved. It would be difficult enough to solve independently the challenges of improving graduate training and responding to social policy, but how much more difficult to seek simultaneous solutions. The two issues are not ordinarily treated together and John Clark noted bemusedly:

> It reminds me of what might happen if two very good professional football and baseball teams were placed in a stadium to provide a high quality combined performance. . . . No one doubts the importance of policy research, but it is hardly the dominant concern of graduate training. Likewise, no one would doubt the serious concern for graduate training, but we not very likely agree that policy research shows us the way out of this deep-and-dark jungle.

339

Of course, neither of these concerns was new to the conference itself. For generations, graduate students have cut their teeth on the problems of improving their education, and faculty who have long since lost their teeth continue to gum the issues like an academic cud. The question of sociology and social policy is also far older than some would have us believe. Works such as Ogburn's (1933) *Recent Social Trends* and Lynd's (1948) *Knowledge for What?* were benchmarks for previous ears and remain significant for our own. More recent volumes such as Gouldner and Miller's (1965) *Applied Sociology* and Lazarsfeld, Sewell, and Wilensky's (1967) *The Uses of Sociology* have continued the tradition of periodic assessment. In addition, there has emerged a considerable hortatory literature urging the discipline on and seeking to steer its course. Certainly the Brim (1969) and "BASS" (Smelser et al. 1970) reports gave policy pertinence a strong emphasis. Debate on how best to realize this pertinence has produced a variety of statements and examples from such noted scholars as Sheldon and Moore (1968), Duncan (1969), Coleman (1971) and Janowitz (1972). The work of Duncan, Sheldon, and many others in the new and burgeoning area of social indicators has helped to bridge the gap between basic and policy research, as has the work of Campbell (1969), Rossi and Williams (1972), and others on social experimentation and evaluation.

All of this activity has conferred considerable legitmacy upon the realm of social policy. But its relative priority remains precarious. This was especially evident at the conference where natural differences of opinion were accentuated in the early stages by a mood of urgency compounded by uncertainty. The participants squirmed under the threatened cutback in graduate-student support and funding for basic research (a threat which has subsequently become a reality). The prospect of rapidly shifting at least part of the field's emphasis into policy research and training was hardly calcuated to appeal to faculty members representing bastions of traditional scholarship. When such changes appeared to be originating from outside the discipline, specifically from a federal administration professing suspiciously new policies with respect to science and higher education in general, the anxieties were exacerbated. As Robert Hall put it in an extensive post conference analysis:

> The reaction of the participants in the early stages of the conference to this ambiguous but threatening situation was a kind of elementary collective behavior. . . . Rumors were flying as people tried to clarify what the conference was all about. . . . Lacking an authoritative statement, participants began improvising plausible stories about the "real" meaning of the conference and trying (some-

times in a rather hostile, aggressive tone) to get the "real" purpose stated openly. Thus, there seemed to be established, early in the conference, a tone that inhibited detached, deliberative analysis of training issues, and encouraged hostile expression against the administration responsible for cutting training grants and against any sociologist so spineless or stupid (so the beliefs seem to be) as to yield to governmental pressures. . . . One of the important values in contemporary sociology is a rather chaotic pluralism. There seemed to be a powerful fear that some single style of sociology was going to be imposed on sociologists, and hence the conference became preeminently defensive—partly a defense of chaos, and partly a defense of particular styles of sociology practiced by those present. It was difficult to tell which was feared more—the Washington threat, or the well-meaning efforts of sociologists who respond to the Washington threat in some unified way.

But Robert Winch's comment indicates debate even among those seeking to account for it:

If we had had a clear conception of why we were there, we might have that single theme out in the course of a day and bored each other for the balance of the period. As it was, we were constantly rediscovering interactions among the several themes, and this made for a most interesting interchange.

By the second day, many of these earlier sparks had flown and the conference settled down to generate both light and heat with respect to the primary issues. What is policy research and what are the problems and obstacles which it entails? If there is any agreement at all that it represents a valid objective for the dscipline, what kinds of changes in graduate training and professional practice are recommended if we are to pursue it more successfully?

THE WHAT AND WHY OF POLICY RESEARCH IN SOCIOLOGY

It is always disconcerting to be asked to change without a clear definition of what the change might entail. The phrase "social policy" alone is pregnant with meanings, some of them deformed. The term "policy research" has almost as many connotations as there were conference guests. Other catch-words such as "applied sociology" and "social engineering" only add to the confusion, especially when they are counterposed by "basic" research and "pure" science as keenly felt but vaguely defined *summa boni*. Consider the range of positions which were articulated in the informal discourse.

Charles Bidwell reasoned that "since sociology is an applied discipline, when conducted well and centered on sociologically important problems, sociological research is by its nature policy-centered." Kurt Back tended to agree but with a variation on the theme:

> Science itself has a social value. . . . I feel that we are not doing our part if we accept completely the pressure for some immediate solution to current problems without looking at the wider perspective. . . . The function of the academy in society is exactly the preservation and enhancement of these (intellectual) values, and we should talk about a way in which that can be preserved while we deal with practical problems.

But if Bidwell and Back tend to minimize the distinction between pure and applied research, Robert Winch underscores it and prefers "to have some institutionalized way of distinguishing sociologists as pure scientists from people who are engaged in policy, in tasks of social amelioration, and so on." On the other hand, Winch also recalls William Ogburn's admonitions against bucking a social trend, and "given the tenor of the times, of funding sources, of the administration, the economy, the polity, etc., it seems advisable to initiate programs that will be both in the letter and spirit of the emphasis on policy."

In all of this, Bidwell, Back, and Winch tend to side with Jim Short in opting for an "enlightenment" rather than an "engineering" mode for sociology according to the recent distinction made by Janowitz (1972). That is, sociology is far better off confining itself to the making of knowledge rather than the making of policy. To the extent that this is more likely to reinforce canons of rigor wihin the discipline, Elton Jackson, Bernard P. Cohn, and Herbert Costner all concurred. Costner explicity juxtaposed three particular modes and preferred the "theory comes first" posture to either a "muckraking conception of policy-relevant research" or the "evaluation research position." However, Costner also remarked that the conference provided further support for his "conviction that if you scratch a sociologist you find beneath the surface a genuine concern for the human condition—although you may have to scratch some sociologists deeper than others to see evidence of humane concern."

One hesitates to label these positions as traditional, especially since they stress a level of scholarly rigor that has rarely been the norm for sociology. Certainly there was consensus on the point that there is no substitute for rigor and that good research is as much a boon to both the discipline and the society as sloppiness can be a bane to both. On the other hand, there were others who argued that rigor for rigor's sake can produce a kind of "rigor-mortis." Many chided the discipline for its inadequate response to questions of policy. And to mix the biological metaphors, Bruce Biddel used the titilating phrase, "reproduction without sex," to describe the current status of our graduate training and scholarly productivity.

But, of course, sex comes in a variety of forms and the issue remains as to the particular type of contribution which sociologists might make to the wider societal orgy. Some, like Robert Alford, feel that we are at our best in assessing general policy postulates and alternatives rather than focusing on specific policy programs. Because we are frequently at our worst when relying on quantitative data concerning limited variables and formal properties of particular concepts, we should emphasize qualitative perspectives which include a theoretical sensitivity to overriding societal patterns.

Samuel Preston did not eschew the development of such perspectives, but he felt that this can often be better served by the kind of formal, even mathematical, modeling and quantitative techniques that have proved so useful in demography.

James Davis argued from still a third vantage-point. Thus, many socioligists tend to shy away from the possibility of uncovering ideologically repugnant findings. Moreover, they are often unwilling to perform the very limited functions for which they are appropriate, preferring to wait instead for the grand societal license and laurels which may never come. Very few sociologists respond to specific needs for information or to the government's requests for proposals as listed in the Commerce and Business Daily:

> We are getting lost in the shuffle and losing out to the Schlockmeister Research and Development Companies which are rushing in to fill the void and getting fat while remaining sloppy.

In the view of Davis and others, many sociologists would do well to settle for providing rigorously determined facts as opposed to broader and ideologically informed perspectives. It is precisely the former which are in greatest demand in the policy process.

But even if one could agree on the most desirable style of sociological contribution, there remains considerable doubt as to whether the potential benefits from such policy involvement outweigh the potential risks entailed in immersion. Burkart Holzner is almost certainly right that "we sociologists know rather little about the way in which policies are shaped and the many direct and indirect ways in which sociological findings can influence it." He points out that the recent spate of evaluation studies poses a kind of "crisis of Negative findings" as one after another turns up results which cast doubt on highly publicized policy innovations. While some of these negative results may be traceable more to our own methodological problems and measurement errors, the fact remains that we need to understand the context in which these results are interpreted. Holzner recommends more specific case studies in the area.

As this suggests, many participants had considerable apprehnesion about the potential pitfalls and "pratfalls" which may be involved. According to Albert Reiss, "We tend to be afraid of assuming control and avoid 'dangerous knowledge' because of intellectual self-doubt." While this insecurity sometimes takes the form of a snobbish aloofness, the insecurity itself is not totally unrealistic. As one of the conference's "outsiders," economist John Brandl, puts it: "We know a lot less today than we thought we knew 10 years ago." In one sense, this implies that we have learned a great deal. In another respect, it recommends the sort of caution expressed by Robert Winch:

> I agree with Brandl and others who emphasized that we have relatively little knowledge that is directly usable in forming a policy. Accordingly, I am sorry to see us risk putting ourselves in the exposed positions where the sparseness of our talent may lead to disastrous results.

Howard Schuman noted the very real danger that sociologists will move too quickly and too simplistically from very limited findings to very expansive policy applications.

Doris Entwisle elaborated the concern further. Pointing out that it is one thing to teach sociologists sound research methodology but quite another thing to teach them the art of policy design and invention, she indicates that our training may be out of step with our aspirations. In suggesting that "policy-related research differs primarily from 'pure' research in that consequences other than 'truth' become relevant," Entwisle fused a number of conference concerns. S. M. Lipset was not alone in articulating apprehension concerning the potential prostitution of scholarship in the employ of policy agencies. Robert Straus concurred in pointing out the danger. Joan Aldous asked whether we should be involved in policy formulation at all if this means entering the political arena as partisans and sacrificing our objectivity and intellectual expertise in the process. Charles Bidwell pointed out an implicit threat to the academic freedom and moral autonomy of sociology and sociologists that may exist short of explicit or self-conscious compromise.

Justification for a New Emphasis on Social Policy

As important as the aforementioned concerns were, they seemed insufficient to dash an emerging consensus that a somewhat bolder move out of the cloister was desirable. True, the more cautious preferred the mode of "enlightenment" to that of "engineering," and many would opt for "policy research" rather than "applied research," defining the former as concerned with the background knowledge, premises, and evaluated experiences and experiments from which policy decisions arise, while the latter is concerned with the implementation or application of decisions once made. But even the least ambitious tack here would challenge the discipline to change its present course. Although my own bias as "rapporteur" may be suspect, I discerned three types of justification for such a change.

First, there was sentiment that sociology has a social if not a moral obligation to muster whatever expertise it may have in response to societal problems. We can afford no delusions of grandeur or visions of dispensing quick panaceas. But we must realize that decisions will be made anyway, and, in our absence, they will probably be made by persons even less knowledgeable. It would be comfortable to remain on the sidelines until that utopian day when we have all of the intellectual tools in hand to do this job well. But it may be that we can learn only by doing, and there is now increasing pressure to do precisely this in the form of statutes requiring social scientific expertise as, e.g., in environmental protection studies.

A *second* justifcation for policy involvement is more intellectual. To the extent that the discipline runs the risk of sterility in its platonic state, exposure to the abrasions of reality may be intellectually fruitful. Like John Dewey, we might regard social policy as the test of sound theory, with bad policy reflecting bad theory. In the same vein, we may wish to stress the value of feedback loops which would reintegrate the results of policy work into the discipline's continually changing paradigms. It is in this sense, perhaps, that biology has benefitted from medicine and physics from engineering. In fact, one might argue that the most intellectually advanced social sciences are precisely those that have been grappling with policy issues over the longest period of time, e.g. economics and demography.

Third, if moral and intellectual reasons for policy research seem uncompelling, a final justification may prove the most persuasive since it concerns the bread and butter issues of the academic marketplace. As was pointed out particularly in the papers by Borgatta, Freeman,

Siegel, Lutterman, and Foote, the threatened surfeit of Ph.D.s is now very real even in sociology. Part of the problem, however, is that almost 90% of our Ph.D.s are employed in higher education. Clearly the pressure would be reduced with the development of further non-academic employment markets and career patterns. But even those who remain within the universities will feel increased pressures for policy pertinence as a condition of continued research funding in the style to which we have become accustomed. It now appears to be hubris alone which leads us to expect continued financial largesse in support of traditional scholarship alone. While basic research will always be important, it will be increasingly difficult to justify without at least some coordinating mechanisms to insure broad application in the realms of policy deliberations and social intervention.

So much, then, for a recapitulation of the discussion surrounding the first of the two issues which confronted the conference. The challenge of social policy will no doubt continue to provoke divergent opinions and assessments. But, since the challenge shows no prospect of disappearing, it is worth considering the second issue of the conference; namely, what changes might be contemplated so as to respond to it more effectively?

POSSIBLE CHANGES IN GRADUATE TRAINING AND PROFESSIONAL PRACTICE

Changing any scholarly discipline may be every bit as difficult as changing the society at large. Certainly, the same kinds of interests and inertia exist in both. Changing a discipline requires no less attention to basic values and norms, traditional patterns of status and reward, organizational structures for task performance, and problems of socialization and self-identify. All of this is pretentious preamble to an important conference discussion centered on two major areas which are crucial to any change which sociology itself undergoes. The first concerns graduate training; the second concerns professional career options and contingencies. Let us take them in that order.

Patterns of Graduate Training

As if to underline the elemental virtues of a solid base of theory and methods in any graduate program, Karl Schuessler suggested a mental experiment that would substitute an applied DSS (Doctor of Social

Science) for the traditional and philosphically-oriented Ph.D. This would signal our abandonment of the intellectual "frills and niceties" and our resolve to move into the applied realm with a vengeance. Of course, the idea had all of the charm of a proposal to dispense with salaries in favor of altruism. The conference was unyielding on the point that basic training, like basic research, should, if anything, be made more rigorous and with more requirements in the future. Indeed, many schools have recently reintroduced curriculum requirements that were relaxed during the stormy years of the late 1960s. But if the conference was united in its allegiance to basic training at the core of doctoral study, spirited differences returned where further aspects of graduate training were involved.

Some, like Richard Simpson, were suspicious of any specific training program which might become the national norm:

> There is no proven "one best way" to educate policy analysts, evaluation researchers, or any other kind of social scientists. . . . A broadly educated sociologist can readily adapt his skills to a variety of problems but a narrow specialist in some policy or social problem area may be unable to transfer his skills to any other area. . . . Hence, let a hundred flowers bloom. Encourage a variety of types of programs turn out a variety of types of sociologists.

At one level, Simpson may appear to be endorsing the status quo. But on another level, he is suggesting that we might well begin to cultivate more of the hundred flowers he has endorsed, and with more than the kind of fertilizer that was in abundance at the conference itself. Indeed, Burkart Holzner implies that we might encourage our students to pick a wider assortment for their own bouquets.

> As far as graduate education in sociology is concerned, it may well have to become more technical *and* broader so that future sociologists are not only capable of technically proficient performance in the processing of information, but are also sensitive to the broad political and historical context of their work. . . . This could well lead to the unpopular conclusion that doctoral study in sociology should take more rather than less time.

The latter suggestion may not prove quite as unpopular in light of the changing job market for new Ph.D.s. Since we are no longer faced with a shortage of new sociologists, we may well want to encourage people to take longer in their training not only to increase their knowledge but to slow up the market mechanisms.

Turning to specific changes in graduate curricula, a number of participants suggested adding the area of "Social Policy" to the standard list of options that many departments offer as specialties for Ph.D. examinations. Moreover, there was no dearth of suggested new courses and course sequences which would alert the student to both the possibilities and problematics of policy work. For example, John Kasarda proposed a two-course sequence dealing with the interactions between theory, methods, and social policy. The first course would provide an overview of past efforts in the area, and the second would be a practicum allowing individual students to focus on particular problems. Many others proposed similar kinds of course experiences pertaining to social policy. Thus, Joan Aldous was concerned that training should involve some systematic attention to values and value premises which lie behind policy alternatives. Howard Freeman underscored the need to incorporate recent work on program evaluation and experimentation into the graduate curriculum.

As noted earlier, however, Doris Entwisle emphasized that it is one thing to teach pertinent sociological methods but quite another to teach the arts of policy design, invention, and choice among alternative programs. Evaluating a program after the fact may be well within the current sociological province, but devising innovative programs is something we neither train nor reward our students for at the moment. In this light, Samuel Preston suggests that graduate training should involve students in the process of preparing at least hypothetical research proposals suitable for submission to governmental line agencies concerning particular policy problems. As Preston implies, we all too frequently overlook some of the most common forms of scholarly output in devising student assignments. Research proposals, consulting evaluations, and workshop memoranda are frequently both more common and more important than the few scholarly articles which the typical sociologist may produce over a career.

In all of this, there was concern that the interdisciplinary nature of social policy work should be emphasized more in our graduate training. Thus, Kasarda proposed that related departments on a given campus offer "interdisciplinary workshops" in particular policy areas. It was pointed out that more and more universities have devised interdepartmental programs in social policy. Also, an increasing number of universities are playing host to interdisciplinary research institutes with policy portfolios. It may well be that some of these institutes have had a greater informal input into the training of graduate students than the traditional departments within the conventional academic structure. Certainly such research operations help to instill students with a working knowledge and respect for the range of methodological techniques that are necessary if we are to provide relevance on a rigorous basis. As Albert Reiss noted, "The terms validity and reliabil-

ity must be made more than mere definitions for purposes of exams."
And as Robert Straus put it:

> We must not only train students to continue to ask with Sumner, "What of
> it?" We must also give them better training in techniques of generating socially
> significant data. These include not only the standard "building blocks of survey
> research" which many students know only second hand and all too glibly. They
> also include longitudinal research.

All of the aforementioned involve amendments and augmentations
in the on-campus training of graduate students. But there was considerable sentiment in favor of off-campus experiences as well. Insofar as
social policy is played out in nonacademic contexts, there was wide
support for a variety of programs that would provide students with far
more knowledge than they have now concerning these arenas. The
chief rubric here is that of the "internship," and internships of various
sorts were recommended. These included stints in off-campus policy
research institutes as recommended by Kasarda; Babchuk's emphasis
on service in the diverse institutional settings subject to change (for
example, mental hospitals, social work centers, job retraining programs, etc.); and experiences in governmental agencies responsible for
sifting through the policy alternatives on the basis of research evidence. The latter might occur at local, state, or federal levels. Indeed,
it already has occurred in some instances, as pointed out by Kent
Miller with respect to the program at Florida State:

> Our doctoral students begin with research field placements in state and com-
> munity agencies in their second year of graduate work, frequently completing
> the masters and doctoral research on data drawn from these agencies. Thus
> there is a built-in probability that policy implications will be drawn. The process
> not only provides helpful information for the agency, but heightens the interest
> and commitment of the student to research careers. Financial support has been
> forthcoming from most of the agencies involved. This has had the effect of
> freeing fellowship and more traditional student support for those who are pursu-
> ing more theoretical or basic careers in sociology. I view the tightening of the
> academic market as a plus in the sense that sociology has much to offer in
> other settings. Thus far we have had no difficulty in placing Ph.D.s in full-time
> research positions with state departments of mental health, regional PHS offices,
> local community mental health centers, mental health research institutes, etc.
> This has been done without turning them into clinical sociologists. . . . The
> hand-wringing seems inappropriate to me.

Miller's remarks concerning the distinction between students who
are interested in policy work and those who are "pursuing more theo-

retical or basic careers in sociology" raise a final set of issues which was important to the discussion. Insofar as the distinction is allowed to persist as invidious, it will obviously frustrate efforts to change not only the training practices but the career patterns of sociologists. Many new graduate students come to the field with a policy interest and no real intention of future academic employment, only to learn informally that academia is all. As many participants noted, graduate training in sociology has long operated on the assumption that every graduate student is a potential basic researcher of international repute. Alas, this has always been unrealistic and appears to be growing more so in light of the increasingly divergent mix of graduate students and graduate departments. As several participants pointed out, if sociology is to flourish according to the model of other disciplines, it requires a division of labor, and must train research consumers as assiduously as it trains its research producers. One put it this way:

> Perhaps we should recognize what we have tried to avert our eyes from for so long; namely, that most of our products will never be scholars in the strict sense, and many turn out to occupy roles for which they were never adequately trained in the first place. At the level of the B.A., the M.A., and even the Ph.D., it may make sense to self-consciously train some of our students as sound social policy bureaucrats. These are the people who are going to shape most of the decisions which affect us. Why not train them and reward them so as to maximize their talent and their effectiveness?

It is worth noting that persons subscribing to this view also subscribe to the importance of sound basic training in theory and methods as part of a core curriculum. The question was not one of substitution but rather one of supplementation with meaningful options.

Changes in Professional Practice and Career Patterning

Much of the foregoing emphasis on graduate training appears to have taken its cue from sentiments like the following from Lois De-Fleur: "Since most of the participants in the Carmel Conference are fat and happy, there are probably few prospects for specific action at the moment from these individuals. If we are to move ahead, perhaps we need to locate some young professionals who have some real concern in the area of social policy and let them forge ahead with whatever action they can get initiated." Certainly it is difficult to expect the establishment in any discipline to preside over radical changes within it. On the other hand, it is perhaps no less important for establishment types to take the lead if changes are to come at all quickly or effectively. As George Bohrnstedt put it, "We simply can't expect our students to provide the impetus and example for all of these changes. They require role-models. We must do policy research and we must get into policy settings to a much greater extent than is now the case."

It is in this spirit that a number of participants extended the concept of the internship to apply to more than simply graduate students. Thus, Laura Nader proposed a program of five post-doctoral Washington fellowships each year to go to the best new Ph.D.s in sociology, psychology, and anthropology. Others talked of internships that would go to establsihed professionals even beyond the immediate post-doctoral phase. This would not only help to provide the kind of role-models which Bohrnstedt and others underscored, it would also provide a cadre of experienced policy participants and a form of participant observation in the policy process.

All of this is part of changing a system of norms and rewards that many view as so purely academic as to stifle legitimate nonacademic pursuits. Holzner and Biddle elaborated both the importance and the difficulty of change in this regard. It is not enough to alter the allocation of kudos. There is also need for other mechanisms which would facilitate greater flexibility in employment and experience. Thus, Lois DeFleur concluded her paper on drug research by calling for a crash program in continuing education in response to national policy emergencies. On the assumption that it simply takes too long to train new cohorts of graduate students in particular policy areas and the further assumption that there are a great many professionals who would seize the opportunity to supplement and redirect their skills so that they can do more exciting work, DeFleur proposes that extensive retraining become a major additional responsibility of graduate departments around the country. It should also become a high priority of funding agencies concerned with policy-research manpower.

This, however, raises yet another issue concerning career lines within the discipline. To what extent is it desirable to delineate wholly separate career tracks along the great divide of academic vs. nonacademic? Some felt that this is not only realistic but desirable; others replied that it is neither. Certainly there is some danger of producing a false dichotomy and estranging two camps which should work together rather than apart. While there will inevitably be some persons for whom one track alone is appropriate, there should be many others whose careers might involve an interweaving between the two modes. This is now common among economists. While their primary appointments are still preponderantly in academic settings, they frequently take leaves of up to 2 years for nonacademic work which is more explicitly oriented to policy problems. This in itself would go far toward creating the desired role models. Surely it is not necessary for academics to abandon tenure for the vicissitudes of the governmental market place. It is proposed instead that many shuttle back and forth between a variety of roles, lending their eminence as well as their expertise to nonacademic pursuits in the process.

And yet there were other sorts of changes called for in the discipline, changes that reach beyond career-patterns into basic intellectual proclivities. For example, several participants chided sociologists for the kinds of variables to which they are sensitive in their research. James Davis describes sociologists as having a "genuine lust" for nonmanipulative variables that cannot be germane in the policy process because they cannot be readily affected by policy decisions. Peter Rossi makes a similar point in noting that sociologists have very little aptitude or inclination for translating their research results into policy terms. Charles Bowerman laments that even if we were so inclined, we would have great difficulty gaining knowledge of anyone's research results but our own, given the piecemeal and chaotic state of a research literature that cries out for more cumulative summaries in specific areas.

There are theoretical problems as well. Several participants, including Robert Alford, Kurt Back, Howard Schuman, and James Short decried the tendency to mechanically apply theories to policy problems without careful examination of their empirical basis and the ideological biases which lurk behind every axiom. Albert Reiss points out that many sociologists apply the first thoery at hand or the one they feel most comfortable with, even when the theory turns out to be inappropriate for the particular policy problem at issue. Finally, anthropologist Laura Nader suggested that social scientists suffer from a general problem of "analyzing *down* rather than up" in search of society's problems. Thus, we tend to look first at the nature of lower classes rather than the pathologies of elites. To the extent that this has become part of our intellectual heritage, it can be debilitating for both basic and applied pursuits.

In order both to highlight particular problems involved in policy research and create a set of rewards appropriate to solving them, many people proposed changes in the journals of the discipline as one kind of response. Joan Aldous suggested explicit revisions of the American Sociological Association's (ASA's) editorial policies so as to give a higher priority to careful policy research. William Liu, Walter Gove, and Peter Rossi all suggested that the ASA create a wholly new but uncompromisingly "hard-nosed" journal devoted explicitly to rigorous research within the policy arena. This would partly answer the complaints of many that there is no way of publishing policy work in such a way as to gain conventional academic credit. It would also provide some degree of intellectual monitoring for work which is now sub rosa and inaccessible to the discipline's processes of quality control.

In addition to new journals, it was suggested that we need new organizational efforts on behalf of increased policy work. Joan Aldous called for a new division of the American Sociological Association concerned with "policy development." Robert Hall recommended large-scale multiuniversity structures to aid and foment policy responsiveness through mutual planning and collaboration. He called specifically for a Consortium for Applied Social Science or CASS (a cynical wag suggested a substitute title of Group for Applied Social Science —GASS). Hall pointed to several models for such an operation, including the Interuniversity Consortium for Political Research, the Brookhaven National Laboratory, and the National Center for Atmospheric Research, all of which are operated by nonprofit corporations representing as many as twenty universities banded together. Such a consortium would have four major functions in providing for (1) an organized response to national problems; (2) a mechanism for placing our Ph.D.s in positions outside of universities; (3) a way of using the projected surplus of sociological talent; and (4) an organizational center for assessing the effectiveness of graduate training.

Discussion concerning the Hall proposal was characteristically divergent. On the one hand, Howard Freeman found that sociologists frequently talk about organizational innovations outside of the conventional departmental structure when they want to avoid making the really important changes required within the departments themselves. On the other hand, Richard Scott felt that something along the lines of Hall's proposal was called for, though he was not sure that the consortium concept was apt and felt it premature to specify precise structures. In this spirit, Scott recommended that the ASA commission a number of papers by selected sociologists proposing new organizational forms in the area. He was particularly sensitive to the need to create new employment structures for policy-sensitive sociologists outside of the academy:

> It seems to me to be irresponsible to consider the structure of new training programs without taking into account the types of careers and, more importantly, the types of settings in which such "new sociologists" are to be em-

ployed. Training for "what" includes in my mind not only training for what
kinds of research but also for what kinds of careers in what kinds of employment settings.

Scott's concerns resonated widely. Indeed, several pointed to a
problem which is common to all academic disciplines but especially
acute for sociology; namely, the wide gulf between the academy and
the world at large. Peter Rossi borrowed a phrase from James Coleman in referring to a set of "missing institutions" which are needed to
fill the gap. While the field of economics has benefited enormously
from organizations such as the Brookings Institution, the Urban Institute, and even the Council of Economic Advisors within the federal
government itself (Lyons 1969), we have no functioning equivalents.
Some encouragement may be drawn from recent activities on the part
of the Russell Sage Foundation and the Social Science Research Council, as well as continuing Senate hearings concerning an additional
Council of *Social* Advisors. But here as elsewhere, there is a considerable difference between first steps and final strides, let alone between
talk and action.

POSTSCRIPT

Remembrances of conferences tend to pass through several phases.
Gradually the locale and the interpersonal interaction recede in favor
of the basic issues probed. Specific differences of opinion tend to
give way to more general consensus. And with the help of volumes
such as this, a conference may be transformed from an "event," or an
"encounter" of the past, to an agenda for the future.

There is no doubt that such an agenda did emege, but there remains considerable uncertainty as to how it might be implemented.
Of course, one answer is to hold more such conferences so that, like
the storied Italian tenor, the participants could keep singing until they
got it "right." But in the final analysis, conferences are a poor substitute for action, and the problems at issue require action at many different levels. Thus, insofar as changes are recommended in the patterns of student support and research funding, these require new
priorities among those who control both the public and the private
purse strings. Certainly action is needed to prod the nonacademic employment market for sociologists, whether in industry, labor, voluntary
associations, or the various levels of federal, state, and local government. Responsive changes are also possible on the part of our own
American Sociological Association, where suggestions include the

sponsorship of new journals, new intership programs, possible new curriculum guides, and certainly new attempts to recognize sociologists working outside of higher education. Some of the important and most difficult changes must occur at the departmental level where the resistance may be more predictable than the rewards. It is not inertia alone which will discourage new course sequences or the adoption of social policy fields as respectable Ph.D. specialties. Considerable spade work is needed to develop a viable program which may either supplement or substitute for more traditional course work and requirements. Certainly greater interdisciplinary training will require a carrot as well as a stick. And we all can imagine the problems of translating a faculty member's policy accomplishments into terms on which the typical academic is evaluated and rewarded.

In the final analysis, of course, the ultimate prodding can come only from individual sociologists. Joan Aldous raised perhaps the most disturbing question of all in asking simply, "Is anyone listening?" With the thought that people are more likely to listen when they know who is talking, I have not kept the names of the participants anonymous.

It is true that this conference, like all such gatherings, was frustrating. On the other hand, frustration was appropriate as an indication that our age of complacency may be past. Perhaps the most fitting exchange of all occurred on the last day when one commentator remarked that we all resembled the fabled blind men of India trying to describe an elephant by touching his trunk, his feet, and his girth respectively. A voice from the back of the room was heard to mutter, "But some of us were on the ball."

REFERENCES

Brim, O. G., Jr.
    1969 *Knowledge into action.* Washington, D.C.: National Science Foundation.
Campbell, D. T.
    1969 Reforms as experiments, *American Psychologist* **24,** 409–428.
Coleman, J.
    1971 *Resources for social change.* New York: Wiley.
Duncan, D.
    1969 Social forecasting: The state of the art, *Public Interest* **17,** 88–119.
Gouldner, A. W. and S. M. Miller (Editors)
    1965 *Applied sociology: Opportunities and problems.* New York: Free Press.
Janowitz, M.
    1972 Professionalization of sociology, *American Journal of Sociology* **78,** 105–135.
Lazarsfeld, P. F., W. H. Sewell, and H. L. Wilensky (Editors)
    1967 *The uses of sociology.* New York: Basic Books.

Lynd, R. S.
  1948   *Knowledge for what?* Princeton, New Jersey: Princeton Univ. Press.
Lyons, G. M.
  1969   *The uneasy partnership: Social science and the federal government in the 20th century.* New York: Russell Sage Foundation.
Ogburn, W. F. (Editor)
  1933   *Recent social trends in the United States.* New York: McGraw Hill.
Rossi, P. H. and W. Williams (Editors)
  1972   *Evaluating social programs.* New York: Seminar Press.
Sheldon, E. B. and W. Moore (Editors)
  1968   *Indicators of social change.* New York: Russell Sage Foundation.
Smelser, N. et al. (Editors)
  1970   *The behavioral and social sciences: Outlook and needs.* ["BASS"] Washington, D.C.: National Academy of Sciences.

Appendix

CARMEL CONFERENCE PARTICIPANTS

Joan Aldous (Minnesota)
Robert Alford (Wisconsin— Madison)
Nicholas Babchuk (Nebraska— Lincoln)
Kurt Back (Duke)
Wendell Bell (Yale)
Bruce Biddle (Missouri— Columbia)
Charles Bidwell (Chicago)
George Bohrnstedt (Minnesota)
Edgar Borgatta (CUNY—Queens)
Charles Bowerman (Washington State)
John Brandl (Minnesota)
Harry Cain (NIMH)
John Clark (Minnesota)
Bernard Cohen (Stanford)
Herbert Costner (Washington)
James Davis (Chicago)
Lois DeFleur (Washington State)
N. J. Demerath, III (Massachusetts—Amherst)
Troy Duster (California— Berkeley)
Franklin Edwards (Howard)
Leona Egas (NIMH)
Joseph Edler (Wisconsin— Madison)
Doris Entwisle (Johns Hopkins)
Howard Freeman (Brandeis)
Walter Gove (Vanderbilt)
Robert Hall (Illinois—Chicago Circle)
David Heise (North Carolina— Chapel Hill)

Richard Hill (Oregon)
August Hollingshead (Yale)
Burkart Holzner (Pittsburgh)
Elton Jackson (Indiana)
Maurice Jackson (ASA)
John Kasarda (Chicago)
Lorraine Klerman (Brandeis)
Otto Larsen (ASA)
Seymour Lipset (Harvard)
William Liu (Notre Dame)
Kenneth Lutterman (NIMH)
John Macisco (Fordham)
Robert McGinnis (Cornell)
David Mechanic (Wisconsin— Madison)
Kent Miller (Florida State)
Alice Myers (ASA)
Laura Nader (California— Berkeley)
Albert Pepitone (Pennsylvania)
Samuel Preston (Washington)
Albert Reiss (Yale)
Peter Rossi (Massachusetts)
Karl Schuessler (Indiana)
Howard Schuman (Michigan)
Richard Scott (Stanford)
Hanan Selvin (SUNY—Stony Brook)
James Short (Washington State)
Nathaniel Siegel (CUNY— Graduate Center)
Paul Siegel (Michigan)
Richard Simpson (North Carolina—Chapel Hill)
Murray Straus (New Hampshire)
Robert Straus (Kentucky)

Sheldon Stryker (Indiana)
Marvin Sussman (Case Western
    Reserve)
Guy Swanson (California—
    Berkeley)
Ruth Useem (Michigan State)
Maurice Van Arsdol (Southern
    California)

Frederick Waisanen (Michigan
    State)
James Wiggins (North Carolina—
    Chapel Hill)
Robert Wilson (North Carolina—
    Chapel Hill)
Robert Winch (Northwestern)
Marguerite Young (NIMH)

CARMEL CONFERENCE PROGRAM

December 6–9, 1972

New Directions in Graduate Training:
Policy Implications of Sociological Research

Wednesday, December 6

5:00 P.M.   Conference convenes: Social Hour
7:00 P.M.   Dinner Meeting: Otto Larsen, Presiding
            Remarks: Kenneth Lutterman, NIMH
                      Harry Cain, NIMH

            "Government Support of Graduate Training"
                      Howard Freeman, Edgar Borgatta, and
                      Nathaniel Siegel

Thursday, December 7

                        First Seminar
9:30 A.M.–12:00 P.M.
            Sheldon Stryker, Presiding

Topic	*Author*	*Discussants*
"Poverty"	Peter Rossi	John Brandl
"Race"	Howard Schuman	Maurice Jackson
"Urban Affairs"	John Kasarda	Franklin Edwards
		Paul Siegel

Second Seminar

2:00 P.M.–4:30 P.M.

Guy E. Swanson, Presiding

Topic	Author	Discussants
"Alcoholism"	Robert Straus	Murray Straus
"Mental Health"	Kurt Back	Walter Gove
"Medical Care"	David Mechanic	August Hollingshead
		Robert Wilson

Third Seminar

8:00 P.M.

Herbert Costner, Presiding

Topic	Author	Discussants
"Drug Use"	Lois DeFleur	Troy Duster
"Delinquency	James Short, Jr.	Hanan Selvin
Control"	Doris Entwisle	Albert Pepitone
"Adolescent Crisis"		David Heise

Friday, December 8

Fourth Seminar

9:30 A.M.–12:00 P.M.

Wendell Bell, Presiding

Topic	Author	Discussants
"Public Schools"	James Davis	Charles Bidwell
"Law Enforcement"	Albert Reiss, Jr.	Laura Nader
"Community	Robert Alford	Elton Jackson
Planning"		Robert McGinnis

Fifth Seminar

2:00 P.M.–4:30 P.M.

Robert Winch, Presiding

Topic	Author	Discussants
"Family"	Joan Aldous	Charles Bowerman
"Aging"	Nicholas Babchuk	Joseph Elder
"Population	Samuel Preston	William Liu
Dynamics"		Marvin Sussman

8:00 P.M.

Panel Discussion: Changing Pattern of Graduate Training

Kenneth Lutterman, Presiding

Louis A. Wienckowski, NIMH

Richard Hill, Graduate Training Study
Francis N. Waldrup, NIMH

Saturday, December 9

9:30 A.M.–12:00 P.M.

General Session: Conference Conclusions
and Recommendations

Panel: Nicholas J. Demerath, III
George Bohrnstedt
Karl Schuessler
James F. Short, Jr.

Name Index

Numbers in italics refer to the pages on which complete references are listed.

361